# The GIANT Encyclopedia of Monthly Activities

### Edited by Kathy Charner, Maureen Murphy, and Charlie Clark

# The GIANT Encyclopedia of Monthly Activities

## For Children 3 to 6

*Written by Teachers for Teachers*

*Edited by Kathy Charner, Maureen Murphy, and Charlie Clark*

*Illustrations by Kathi Whelan Dery*

gryphon house
Beltsville, Maryland

© 2006 Gryphon House
Published by Gryphon House, Inc.
10726 Tucker Street, Beltsville, MD 20705
800.638.0928; 301.595.9500; 301.595.0051 (fax)

Visit us on the web at www.gryphonhouse.com

Illustrations: Kathi Whelan Dery

Library of Congress Cataloging-in-Publication Data
The giant encyclopedia of monthly activities / edited by Kathy Charner,
Maureen Murphy, and Charlie Clark.
    p. cm.
 ISBN-13: 978-0-87659-012-6
 ISBN-10: 0-87659-012-1
 1. Early childhood education--Activity programs. 2. School year. I.
Charner, Kathy. II. Murphy, Maureen. III. Clark, Charlie, 1977-
  LB1139.35.A37G533 2006
  372.21--dc22
                                                          2005034134

**Bulk purchase** Gryphon House books are available for special premiums and sales promotions as
well as for fund-raising use. Special editions or book excerpts also can be created
to specification. For details, contact the Director of Marketing at Gryphon House.

**Disclaimer** Gryphon House, Inc. and the authors cannot be held responsible for damage,
mishap, or injury incurred during the use of or because of activities in this book.
Appropriate and reasonable caution and adult supervision of children involved in
activities and corresponding to the age and capability of each child involved, is
recommended at all times. Do not leave children unattended at any time.
Observe safety and caution at all times.

Gryphon House is a member of the Green Press Initiative, a nonprofit program
dedicated to supporting publishers in their efforts to reduce their use of fiber
sourced forests. For further information visit www.greenpressinitiative.org

## September

# April

TABLE OF CONTENTS

*It's almost the end of January. The children are growing tired of the classroom environment and are weary with being cooped up indoors due to bad weather. You and your co-teacher are slightly frazzled and are wondering what you are going to do to keep the children happy and occupied while still teaching them important skills. You dive into your new* **GIANT Encyclopedia of Monthly Activities** *book and suddenly your problems are solved. You discover, for example, that January 28th is National Kazoo Day! A quick trip to the local toy or dollar store yields an inexpensive kazoo for each child. The interesting activities in the book provide hours of fun and learning—children can make different sounds with their kazoos, play songs, have a parade, and even make their own kazoos. Say goodbye to the post-holiday doldrums and hello to your new kazoo band!*

When thinking about curriculum planning, teachers often choose a theme related to a certain month or season. A heavy snowfall in January might inspire activities about snow and cold weather while October might have a fall theme. Teachers, directors, childcare providers, and other early childhood professionals have come together to build this resource of developmentally appropriate activities that allow you to take those themes, build on them, and expand them across the curriculum.

Young children learn best when presented with hands-on activities, the freedom to make choices, and many opportunities for seeing, touching, tasting, learning, and self-expression. To construct knowledge, children need to manipulate their environment actively. Inside this book you will find a wealth of activities that provide children with opportunities to control and act upon their environment, and that stimulate the children's senses and curiosity. These teacher-designed and classroom-tested activities integrate the children's needs, interests, and abilities and focus on the whole child; including activities that promote cognitive, social, emotional, and physical development. The fresh and innovative ideas found within will help you provide an interesting, challenging, and engaging environment that will encourage the children to learn to think, reason, and become decision makers and problem solvers.

The activities in this book are organized in a way that is most helpful to early childhood teachers. The book is divided into 13 chapters, one for each month of the year, as well as a "13th month," which is filled with activities that can be done anytime. Each section contains activities designed specifically for holidays and special days in that month, such as National Safety Month and Be Kind to Animals Week, and the season. In addition, some sections have activities related to a specific event, such as the start of a new school year.

Following is a small sample of some of the special days and themes mentioned:

| | |
|---|---|
| **January** | Martin Luther King Day |
| | National Hugging Day |
| **February** | Black History Month |
| | Clifford the Big Red Dog's Birthday |
| | President's Day |
| **March** | National Kite Month |
| | St. Patrick's Day |
| **April** | National Umbrella Month |
| | Earth Day |
| **May** | National Egg Month |
| | Cinco de Mayo |
| | Mother Goose Day |
| **June** | National Safety Month |
| | Father's Day |
| **July** | Summer |
| | Independence Day |
| **August** | Moon Festival |
| **September** | Labor Day |
| | Back to School |
| | Johnny Appleseed's Birthday |
| **October** | End of Daylight Savings |
| | Fire Safety/Prevention Week |
| | Fall |
| **November** | American Indian Heritage Month |
| | Election Day |
| | Children's Book Week |
| **December** | Christmas |
| | Hanukkah |
| | Kwanzaa |

Each activity is designed in an easy-to-follow format and contains some or all of the following elements:

**Materials**  The materials needed are clearly listed. With this list as your guide you can gather what you will need to complete the activity successfully without wondering if you have forgotten anything. Remember to contact local sources for free or at-cost items. Local businesses are usually willing to donate items, and parents of the children in your care might just be looking for an excuse to clean out the attic or the junk closet.

**What to do**  Children learn by doing and by thinking about what they are doing. Play is a child's work! The step-by-step instructions in this section serve as a guide that will make it simple for you to present the activity in a way that engages the minds (and hands) of curious young children and allows for easier comprehension of the idea presented.

**More to do**  This section offers suggestions on expanding the activity across the curriculum. The activities in this section allow you to take your holiday or special day celebration into the different interest areas in your room. This ensures that you are covering important developmental areas such as math, science, language, and gross and fine motor skills.

**Related books**  Why use valuable planning time researching library websites or perusing the stacks? Books that are specifically related to the holiday or special celebration are already listed in this section.

**Related songs and poems**  Most of the songs and poems in this section were written or adapted by teachers. They provide another resource for building important language and movement skills.

Using *The GIANT Encyclopedia of Monthly Activities* will help you to enrich, organize, and structure the children's environment, providing them with many opportunities to make choices among a wide variety of activities that stimulate their natural curiosity, along with providing a balance of unstructured and structured time, and the space and materials needed to promote child-centered, self-initiated play.

Before selecting one of the great activities in this book, keep in mind the children's interests and developmental levels. Regularly record observations of the children at play; note their interests and listen carefully when they talk to each other. Children's conversations provide valuable clues and this information is vital to activity selection. Activities based on the children's interests provide intrinsic motivation for exploration and learning. These meaningful experiences are more easily comprehended and remembered.

There are many methods for planning curriculum other than using monthly activities. You may prefer not to use any monthly activities during parts of the year. If this is your choice, you can still use this book as an educational resource, as you integrate ideas and experiences from the variety of activities included.

Remember these tips when choosing activities from this book. First, keep in mind the cultural and ethnic make-up of the children in your class. Second, don't attempt to celebrate every special day or holiday included in this book. Activities based on holiday celebrations should not be the main focus of your curriculum.

*Before introducing any activity, find out how the families in your class celebrate cultural and religious events. Select activities that respect their wishes and needs. This is especially true in December but also applies throughout the year.*

We, the teachers and early care professionals who wrote these activities, and the editors at Gryphon House hope you find this book to be a valuable guide in planning curriculum for young children. The ideas and activities included will help you construct a fun and educational learning environment that will the children begging to come back for more. Have fun!

# September

# Color Walk

ART

**Materials**    small pieces of construction paper in a variety of colors
paint, markers, or crayons
paper

**What to do**    1. To help familiarize children with their new surroundings, go for a color walk around the school.
2. Give each child a different piece of colored construction paper.
3. Take the children for a walk around the building and have them match their construction paper color to like-colored objects in the building.
4. After returning from the color walk, talk about the children's findings.
5. Encourage them to take a piece of paper and paint or color the things they saw.

**Related books**    *Colors Everywhere* by Tana Hoban
*Is It Red? Is It Yellow? Is it Blue?* by Tana Hoban
*Little Blue and Little Yellow* by Leo Lionni
*Mouse Paint* by Ellen Stoll Walsh
*Of Colors and Things* by Tana Hoban
*Red, Blue, Yellow Shoe* by Tana Hoban

 *Kaethe Lewandowski, Centreville, VA*

# Fall Placemats

ART

**Materials**    autumn leaves in several colors and shapes
construction paper
glue
crayons or markers
laminate

**What to do**    1. Go outside with the children and collect autumn leaves. Talk about why leaves change colors in the fall. Identify some of the leaves the children collect.
2. Encourage the children to arrange their leaves on a piece of construction paper and glue in place.

3. Invite the children to decorate their papers with crayons or markers.
4. Help each child put her leaf-covered paper into a laminator. Supervise closely, or do this step by yourself.
5. Let children use their placemats at snack time.

LAMINATED PLACEMAT

LEAF

**More to do**   **More Art:** Invite the children to trace leftover leaves on construction paper and cut them out.

**Related books**   *Autumn: An Alphabet Acrostic* by Steven Schnur
*Fall Leaves Fall* by Zoe Hall
*It's Fall* by Linda Glaser
*Red Leaf, Yellow Leaf* by Lois Ehlert
*Why Do Leaves Change Color?* by Betsy Maestro

⭐ *Katelyn Thomas, Port Deposit, MD*

# Standing Autumn Tree Decoration

ART

**Materials**   tissue paper (red, brown, orange, yellow, green)
small branch with small twigs (one per child)
snack-size applesauce or pudding containers (clean and empty)
white glue
paper cutter
green tempera paint
brush

**What to do**   1. Find a branch about ¼" thick and 1' tall for each child.
2. Have the children tear small pieces of tissue paper in a variety of autumn colors to use as leaves.

3. Invert the applesauce containers and cut an "X" in the center of each. Give one to each child. If necessary, use playdough or clay for stability.
4. Mix white glue with green tempera paint. Have the children paint their containers. Let dry.
5. Trim each branch into the shape of a tree.
6. Help the children push the cut branch into the "X" on the inverted containers, making sure it will stand upright.
7. Have children put dots of white glue all over the branch twigs. The children put the torn tissue paper on the dots of glue to make leaves.

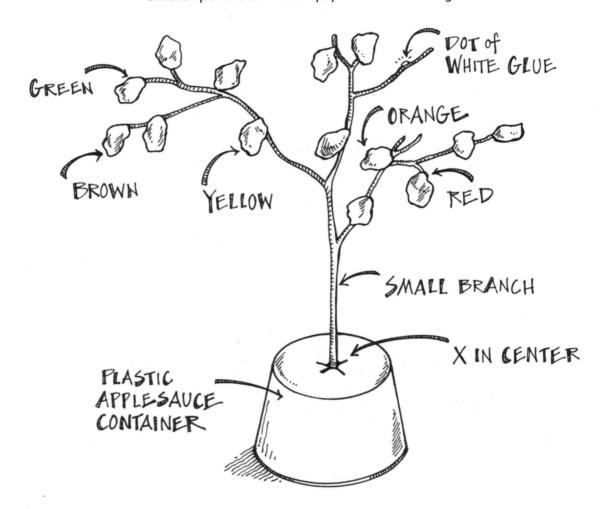

GREEN

DOT OF WHITE GLUE

ORANGE

BROWN

YELLOW

RED

SMALL BRANCH

X IN CENTER

PLASTIC APPLESAUCE CONTAINER

**MORE TO DO**

**Math:** Show leaves in a variety of shapes (maple, oak, elm, plum, and so on). Invite the children to match leaves by shape.

**More Math:** Cut out felt leaves in a variety colors. Use them for simple addition or subtraction problems for the children to solve.

⭐ *Mary Brehm, Aurora, OH*

# Good Morning

FINGERPLAYS, SONGS, & POEMS

**Materials**   none

**What to do**   1. When the children arrive, chant the following call-and-response rhyme:

Teacher: *Good morning, good morning, and how are you?*
Children: *I'm fine, I'm fine, and I hope you are, too!*

2. Greet the children in different ways, for example, sing "good morning" in different languages, use sign language in place of words, or use body language to greet each other (shake hands or wave).

 *Kaethe Lewandowski, Centreville, VA*

# Shout and Whisper

FINGERPLAYS, SONGS, & POEMS

**Materials**   none

**What to do**   1. This call-and-response song helps children learn each other's names.
2. Sing the following song to the tune of "Pick an Apple Off My Tree," making the necessary gestures when prompted.

Teacher: *Shout it.*
Children shout: *1, 2, 3!*
Teacher: *Whisper it.*
Children whisper: *1, 2, 3.*

Teacher: *Shout it.*
Children shout: *I like you!*
Teacher: *Whisper it.*
Children whisper: *I like you.*

*Shout and whisper,*
*That's what we do,*
*Shout and whisper,*
*I like you.*

*Shout and whisper,*
*That's our game.*
*Shout and whisper,*

Teacher: *Shout your name!* (point to a child in the group, child shouts first name)
Teacher: *Whisper it.*
Child whispers name.

3. Repeat this last verse over and over again until each child has shouted and whispered his or her name.

⭐ *Andrea Hungerford, Plymouth, CT*

# Friends Everywhere

FINGERPLAYS, SONGS, & POEMS

**Materials**     none

**What to do**
1. Whenever you need to count the children in your care, involve the children by singing the following song.

**Friend Everywhere** (Tune: "Row, Row, Row Your Boat")
*Friends, friends everywhere*
*As far as I can see.*
*We'll know how many friends we have*
*If you'll count with me.*

2. Encourage the children to count together as you point to each child.

**More to do**    Use the above song in other centers by changing a few of the words. For example, in the block center, recite the following rhyme. Have the children count with you as you pick up blocks to put them away.

*Blocks, blocks everywhere,*
*As far as I can see.*
*We'll know how many blocks we have*
*If you'll count with me.*

**Math:** Make graphs to show the characteristics of the children in your class. Graph by gender, hair color, eye color, color of shirts, and so on.

**Related books**    *Anno's Counting House* by Mitsumasa Anno
*Count!* by Denise Fleming
*Knots on a Counting Rope* by Bill Martin, Jr.
*Let's Count* by Tana Hoban
*Numbers* by John J. Reiss
*One Gorilla: A Counting Book* by Atsuko Morozumi
*This Old Man* by Jon Z. Haber
*What Comes in 2's, 3's, and 4's?* by Suzanne Aker

⭐ *Virginia Jean Herrod, Columbia, SC*

# What's the Weather Like Today?

FINGERPLAYS, SONGS, & POEMS

**Materials**     none

**What to do**    1. Recite the following rhyme with the children:

*What's the weather?*
*What's the weather?*
*What's the weather like today?*
*Tell us, _____ (say a child's name)*
*What's the weather like today?*
*Is it sunny?*
*Is it cloudy?*
*Is it sun and clouds today?*
*Is it rainy?*
*Is it snowy?*
*Is it windy out today?*

2. After reciting the rhyme, pick a child (or ask the leader of the day or "weather watcher" helper) to look outside and tell the class what the weather is like outside.

**More to do**    **Group or Circle Time**: The classroom "weather watcher" or leader can put a daily weather symbol on a weather calendar or chart.

★ *Andrea Hungerford, Plymouth, CT*

# AUTUMN LEAVES ARE FALLING DOWN

### FINGERPLAYS, SONGS, & POEMS

**MATERIALS**  none

**WHAT TO DO**  Sing the following song to the tune of "London Bridge":

*Autumn leaves are falling down,*
*Falling down, falling down.*
*Autumn leaves are falling down,*
*Falling down.*

*Autumn leaves are falling down,*
*Red and yellow, orange and brown.*
*Autumn leaves are falling down*
*All over our town.*

**MORE TO DO**  **Art:** Make leaf rubbings.

⭐ *Kathy Kalmar, Macomb, MI*

# FALLING LEAVES

### FINGERPLAYS, SONGS, & POEMS

**MATERIALS**  none

**WHAT TO DO**  1. Take the children into a large, open area (indoors or outdoors).
2. Encourage the children to pretend they are trees. Say the following rhyme with them.

*A seed is dropped on the ground.*
*The seed begins to grow.*
*It grows very slowly and becomes a tree.*
*Leaves grow on the tree.*
*The tree grows flowers.*
*The flowers turn into apples.*
*The apples fall to the ground and people pick them.*
*The leaves turn into fall colors and drop to the ground.*

3. If desired, play soft music as the children sway like branches in wind.

⭐ *Barbara Saul, Eureka, CA*

# Leaves Fingerplay

### FINGERPLAYS, SONGS, & POEMS

**Materials**       none

**What to do**      Say the following rhyme, making the appropriate corresponding gestures.

*Leaves are green,* (nod yes)
*Nuts are brown,* (nod yes)
*In a tree they are found.* (nod yes)
*They are so high,* (raise hands up)
*They touch the sky.* (nod yes)
*Wait for the brisk cool weather* (nod yes)
*When they'll fall down altogether.* (make falling motion with fingers)

**More to do**      **Art:** Make a leaf collage with the autumn leaves.

 *Kathy Kalmar, Macomb, MI*

# Out in the Rain

### FINGERPLAYS, SONGS, & POEMS

**Materials**       none

**What to do**      1. Read the following action rhyme and model the motions for the children.

*Pit-pat, pit-pat, goes the rain* (make small, quick clapping sounds)
*As it hits the windowpane.*
*The gusty wind spins up and down,* (spin around)
*Blowing dry leaves all around.*
*With my umbrella open wide* (mimic opening umbrella)
*I hold on tight and go outside.* (step forward to go "outside")

2. Repeat the action rhyme as desired so the children can do the motions again.

**Related books**   *A Letter to Amy* by Ezra Jack Keats
*Rain Romp* by Jane Kurtz
*Sunshine and Storm* by Elisabeth Jones

 *Theresa Callahan, Easton, MD*

# The Squirrel Finds an Acorn

FINGERPLAYS, SONGS, & POEMS

**Materials**  none

**What to do**  Sing the following song to the tune of "The Farmer in the Dell":

*The squirrel finds an acorn,
The squirrel finds an acorn,
Hi-ho the derry-o,
The squirrel finds an acorn.*

*The squirrel digs a hole…
The squirrel buries the acorn…
The acorn grows and grows…
An oak tree grows there now…
The oak tree grows leaves…
The oak tree grows acorns…
The leaves fall down…
The acorns fall down too…*

*Then the squirrel comes around,
The squirrel comes around,
Wait a minute.
The whole thing starts all over!*

**More to do**  Cut out felt pieces of the elements of the song—squirrel, acorn, oak tree, and so on. Use the felt pieces and a flannel board to re-tell the song.
**Music:** Sing the "Farmer in the Dell." Chart the similarities and differences between the two songs.

*Kathy Kalmar, Macomb, MI*

# Daily Routine Lotto

GAMES

**Materials**  9 pictures or drawings of daily routines
construction paper
glue
contact paper or laminate

**What to do**
1. Divide the paper into squares (three rows up and across) and put a picture in each square (in random order).
2. Cover the paper with contact paper or laminate.
3. Make a variety of boards for the children.
4. To play the game, call out a daily routine (brushing teeth, lunch, and so on). If the child has that routine on her board, she marks the square. You can play this game like Bingo or have them cover the whole board.
5. If you use contact paper, the child can put an "x" on the square using a water-soluble marker. It will wash off with a damp paper towel.
6. Children can play the game without adult help if you make two sets of drawings. One set can be used as cards and turned over one at a time.

★ *Phyllis Esch, Export, PA*

# "Good Morning" Name Game

GAMES

**Materials**  chair
blindfold (optional)

**What to do**
1. Have the children sit in a circle. Select a child to sit with her eyes closed or blindfolded in a chair facing away from the group.
2. Choose another child to walk over quietly behind the blindfolded child and say, "Good morning, (child's name)." This child should disguise the sound of his voice.
3. The child then sits back down.
4. The blindfolded child removes the blindfold and guesses who spoke.

⭐ *Andrea Hungerford, Plymouth, CT*

# School Feely Bag

GAMES

**Materials**  variety of small classroom items (see activity)
large bag

**What to do**
1. Place a variety of classroom items in a large bag (such as a crayon, book, puzzle piece, plastic spoon, pencil, paper, small block, plastic hammer, paintbrush, and plastic cup).
2. Review with the children the various classroom centers, using a visual prompt for each center (for example, a paintbrush for the art center).
3. Ask the children to reach inside the feely bag one at a time and touch an item.
4. Encourage each child to guess what the item is and say what center it belongs in.
5. Have the child pull the item from the bag and place it in the appropriate center.

**Related books**  *Froggy Goes to School* by Jonathan London
*If You Take a Mouse to School* by Laura Numeroff
*School Days* by B.G. Hennessy
*Timothy Goes to School* by Rosemary Wells

⭐ *Kaethe Lewandowski, Centreville, VA*

# WHAT'S MISSING?

GAMES

**Materials**  classroom objects that children can put away

**What to do**
1. Place three to five classroom objects in the middle of the circle.
2. Point to and name each of the objects.
3. Ask the children to put their hands over their eyes.
4. Remove one of the objects and hold it behind your back.
5. Encourage the children to name the object that is missing, giving hints as needed for them to be successful.
6. Ask a child to put the object in its designated place within the classroom.

**More to do**  **Morning Greeting:** At the beginning of the day, have the children stand in a circle and name those children who are not there that day.

 *Barb Lindsey, Madison City, IA*

# WHO WILL BE A FRIEND OF MINE?

GAMES

**Materials**  red construction paper
scissors
laminate or clear contact paper

**What to do**
1. This is a great activity to begin the year, and it allows everyone to have a turn being picked as a friend.
2. Cut out an apple shape from construction paper. Laminate for durability.
3. Have the children sit in a circle on the floor. Select one child to walk around the outside of the circle, holding the apple shape.
4. Ask the children to sing the following song to the tune of "Mary Had a Little Lamb":

*Who will be a friend of mine,*
*Friend of mine, friend of mine?*
*Who will be a friend of mine?*
*Number one, number two, number three.*
*It must be you!*

5. The child circling the group stops and gives the apple to someone else.
6. The new child walks around the group and chooses the next person to receive the apple. Make sure everyone gets picked.

**MORE TO DO**     Use different laminated cutouts corresponding to other months, such as a snowflake for January, a heart shape for February, a clover for March, and so on.

⭐ *Susan Myhre, Bremerton, WA*

# Matching Friends

GAMES

**MATERIALS**     photos of each child in class (double prints)
clear contact paper

**WHAT TO DO**
1. Cover each photo with clear contact paper. If desired, back photos with construction paper before covering with contact paper.
2. Use the photos for a memory game. Turn the photos face down and encourage the children to take turns turning them over to find a match.
3. This is great for matching skills as well as learning about their classmates.

**MORE TO DO**     **Group or Circle Time:** This is a great way for children to learn each other's names. Cover a coffee can with red contact paper. Put one photo of each child inside. Sing, "I'm glad I have a little red can to put (child's name) in; I'd take her out and kiss, kiss, kiss and put her back again." Children love this activity and will soon learn everyone's name.
**Home-School Connection:** Extend this idea to include photos of parents.

⭐ *Phyllis Esch, Export, PA*

# Squirrels in Trees

GAMES

**MATERIALS**     large open area, inside or out

**WHAT TO DO**
1. Put the children into groups of three and have two of the children hold hands around the third child. These two children represent the trees. The third child in the group is the squirrel.

2. When you say, "Change trees," the "trees" lift their hands, still holding each other, so that the "squirrels" can run to other trees.
3. Repeat five times.
4. Change the positions so that each squirrel has become a tree and one tree has become the squirrel.
5. Change again so that every child has the opportunity to be a squirrel.

★ *Barbara Saul, Eureka, CA*

# Just Me and My Mom/Dad on the First Day of School
## GENERAL TIPS

**Materials**    camera
film

**What to do**    1. On the first day of school, take a picture of each child with his or her parent(s).
2. Put this photo in the child's end-of-the-year book. Parents will appreciate the fact that they were included in the memories.

★ *Wanda Guidroz, Santa Fe, TX*

# Reassurance Chain
## GENERAL TIPS

**Materials**    chart paper
markers
pre-gummed paper chain strips, or 2" x 6" strips of colored paper and tape

**What to do**    1. Starting school or starting a new year in a different class can be a scary experience for a young child. A large part of this is fear of the unknown. This activity is a way to help children adapt to the classroom routine.
2. Make an attractive chart, assigning colors to different activities. For example, green=outdoor play; red=music and movement; blue=circle time; yellow=snack; orange=art; purple=storytime; white=rest time. Make sure to include lots of fun pictures on the chart to make everything look exciting.

3. When the children arrive in the morning, explain exactly what they will be doing that day using the color chart. Tell them that the chart will help remind them what happens next.

4. Help each child make a paper chain showing all the day's activities. For example, if the first activity is circle time, followed by outdoor play, then the first two links would be blue (circle time), then green (outdoor play), and so on. To avoid confusion about which end is the last link, designate gold or silver as the color for pick-up time.

5. After every activity, the child can cut or tear off one link from the chain. This gives the children a visual image of how much time is left and exactly what will be happening throughout the day. Soon the children will be able to cope without the chain.

ART →
STORY TIME →
SILVER LINK →
NAPTIME →

**MORE TO DO**    Whenever a new child joins the class, ask another (enthusiastic) child to be the new child's partner for the first week, and tell him about each activity as it happens.

**RELATED book**    *Starting School* by Janet and Alan Ahlberg

★ *Anne Adeney, Plymouth, United Kingdom*

# TOUR of School

GENERAL TIPS

**MATERIALS**    camera
clipboard
large pieces of paper
markers

**WHAT TO DO**    1. To acquaint the children with their new surroundings, walk around the school or center with them.

2. Take photos of the main office, library, cafeteria, principal's (or director's) office, clinic/nurse's office, gym, computer lab, music room, and so on.

3. Write down the name of each location and directions explaining how you got to each.

4. Using large paper, create a map with the photographs to identify each location.

 *Kaethe Lewandowski, Centreville, VA*

# The Communication Station
### GENERAL TIPS

**Materials**    cardboard shoe organizer

**What to do**
1. Label each section of a cardboard shoe organizer with a child's name.
2. Tell the children that these are their "mailboxes" or a "classroom communication station."
3. If they want to write a letter or draw a picture for a friend, they can fold it and place it in their friend's mailbox.

**Related song**    **Check Your Mail** (tune: "The Alphabet Song")
*Don't forget to check your mail.*
*There might be something there for you.*
*Big or small, you never know.*
*Full or empty, it's hard to tell.*
*Don't forget to check your mail.*
*Look inside and see what's there.*

 *Susan Myhre, Bremerton, WA*

# Smock Storage
### GENERAL TIPS

**Materials**    clothespins
paint smocks

**What to do**
1. Have a designated place in the room for children to hang paint smocks when they are finished wearing them.
2. Use pinch-type clothespins so children can practice their fine motor skills.

 *Sandie Nagel, White Lake, MI*

# Photos for Subs

GENERAL TIPS

**Materials**
camera
paper
glue
marker
manila folder

**What to do**
1. Make it easy for a substitute teacher to find his or her way around your classroom. At the beginning of the year, take photos of several areas in the classroom that require the substitute's attention.
2. Glue the photos to paper and write captions and notes of explanation underneath each picture.
3. Put the pages in a "substitute folder" and place it in an easy-to-find location.

⭐ *Jackie Wright, Enid, OK*

# Hear Ye, Hear Ye! Calling All Volunteers

GENERAL TIPS

**Materials**
paper
computer
color printer

**What to do**
1. Prepare a colorful, eye-catching flyer asking for parents to serve as classroom volunteers to share their time, talents, and treasures with the children.
2. List many categories and interesting options. For example, parents could help with easy baking projects, share hobbies or collectibles, play an instrument, demonstrate a skill such as needlepoint or crocheting, read or tell stories, give a nature talk/walk, teach a new game, show how to do woodworking, teach a foreign language lesson, and so on.
3. It is especially enjoyable to include senior citizens for a memorable intergenerational experience.

⭐ *Judy Fujawa, The Villages, FL*

# Everyone Needs a Nametag

GENERAL TIPS

**Materials**  durable nametags in different colors or cut in different shapes
marker
hole punch
string
hooks

**What to do**
1. Have each child (and adult) choose a nametag. Write each child's (and adult's) name on her nametag.
2. Punch two holes in each nametag and tie string through (to hang).
3. Hang easy-to-reach hooks in each center.
4. Walk around the room and introduce all of the classroom centers and point out where the hooks in each center are located.
5. Explain to the children that they should hang their nametags on the hooks when they play in different centers.
6. Begin free play with everyone using a nametag.
7. Model putting your own nametag on a hook as you move to different centers.

 *Ann Kelly, Johnstown, PA*

# New Ways to Greet

GENERAL TIPS

**Materials**  none

**What to do**
1. Introduce the idea of "new ways to greet" to the children.
2. Encourage the children to come up with new ways to greet one another. Provide a few examples, such as using sign language, speaking in a robot voice and moving hands mechanically, or giving high fives.
3. Once the children have chosen a few new greetings, use these greetings at arrival time each morning.

 *Freya Zellerhoff, Towson, MD*

# The Crop Is Here

GENERAL TIPS

**Materials**

poster board or bulletin board paper
markers or tempera paint
laminate (optional)
die-cut apples (one per child)
basket
tape

**What to do**

1. Draw or paint a large tree on a poster board or bulletin board. Laminate for durability, if desired. Make sure the green part of the tree is large enough to hold all the die-cut apples. Write the heading "The crop is here!"

2. Cut out enough apples so that there is one for each child. Write each child's first name on an apple and laminate for durability, if desired.

3. Place the apples in a basket and place it next to the tree along with a tape dispenser.

4. When each child arrives, she finds her apple with her name on it and places it on the tree.

5. Let one child (class leader) take attendance by counting the number of apples on the tree. Have the child (or all the children) count the number of children in the room and see if that number corresponds to the number of apples on the tree. Make sure to rotate children so each child gets a turn.

6. After a few weeks, when the children get the hang of it, they may even start reading each other's names and figuring out whose apple is not on the tree.

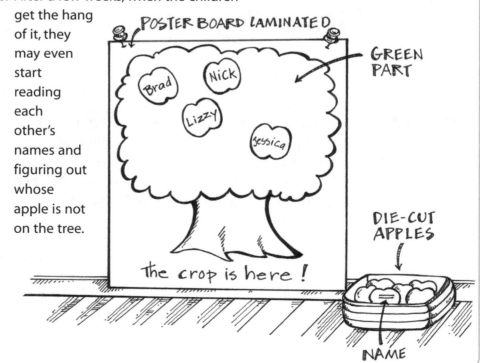

POSTER BOARD LAMINATED

GREEN PART

Brad  Nick
Lizzy
Jessica

the crop is here!

DIE-CUT APPLES

NAME

**MORE TO DO**   **Art:** Make Apple Trees. Have children paint trees at the easel. When the trees are dry, encourage them to use round sponges to make apples.

⭐ *Shelley Hoster, Norcross, GA*

# BirthdAy Balloons

GENERAL TIPS

**MaterIals**   large sheet of railroad board
black felt-tip pen
list of children's birthdays

**What to do**
1. Use the pen to draw 12 balloons on the railroad board.
2. Write the name of a month under each balloon.
3. Help the children write their names in the appropriate balloons.
4. Display the Birthday Balloon Board for references throughout the year.
5. Count how many children have birthdays in the same month, comparing and contrasting months.

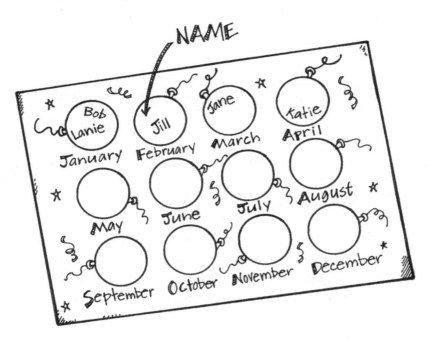

**ReLated book**   *A Busy Year* by Leo Lionni

⭐ *Barbara Saul, Eureka, CA*

# My Goal This Month

GENERAL TIPS

**Materials**    card stock paper
markers or computer and printer

**What to do**
1. Make decorative certificates with the words "My Goal This Month" at the top. In the middle of the certificate write," For the month of _____ I would like to _____."
2. At the start of each month, show the children the certificates and ask them to consider something new they would like to do before the month ends. Suggest modest goals, such as playing a game with a child they've never played with before, drawing a picture of something new, tasting a new fruit or vegetable, teaching a younger brother or sister how to do something, and so on.
3. Individually ask each child her goal, and write it on the certificate. After you have written all of the children's goals, let them share their goals with the class, if they wish.
4. As children accomplish goals, share successes with the class.

*Karyn F. Everham, Fort Myers, FL*

# Where Does It Go?

GROUP OR CIRCLE TIME

**Materials**    variety of classroom objects that can be put away by children

**What to do**
1. Gather a variety of classroom objects, such as soap, sponges, rubber bands, spoons, jump ropes, dolls, balls, and so on.
2. Present each of the objects one at a time.
3. For each of the objects, encourage the children to name it, discuss what it might be used for, and where it might be stored.
4. Ask a child to put each object in its appropriate place in the classroom.

*Barb Lindsey, Madison City, IA*

# WEATHER REPORT

## GROUP OR CIRCLE TIME

**Materials**     newspapers (weather forecast page)
toy microphone
chart paper
marker

**What to do**     1. Cut out the picture weather forecast from the newspaper each week and post it on the bulletin board. (You might want to do this activity only when the weather conditions in your area are most variable, or you might want to do this daily or weekly throughout the year.)
2. Choose a child each day or week to be the "weather reporter."
3. Give the child a toy microphone to hold (often available at dollar stores) and have her go to the window and report the weather of the day.
4. Then ask the child to look at the forecast posted and report the forecast.
5. Look at the previous day's forecast and ask the children to determine if it was correct. Talk about the following day's forecast. This also helps children understand the meaning of *yesterday, today*, and *tomorrow*.
6. Let the child use a marker to fill in a square on a classroom weather graph.
7. At the end of each month, encourage the children to count how many sunny, rainy, snowy, or cloudy days occurred that month.

 *Laura Durbrow, Lake Oswego, OR*

# Daily Calendar

## GROUP OR CIRCLE TIME

**Materials**     large sheet of white poster board
permanent markers
clear adhesive plastic
3 clear vinyl strips (2" x 12")
clear adhesive tape (package tape)
20 tagboard cards (3" x 11")
31 tagboard cards (3" x 8")
5 tagboard cards (3" x 10")

**What to do**     1. Divide the poster board into four equal sections, drawing guide lines lightly with pencil.

2. On the top line, print: "Today is…" Leave the second line blank.
3. Print "The weather is…" on the third line.
4. Cover the poster board with clear adhesive plastic for protection.
5. Make pockets with the 2" x 12" clear plastic strips, attaching them with clear plastic tape. Put one after "Today is," one at the beginning of the second line, and one centered on the bottom. These will hold the cards to complete the sentences.

CARD GOES IN HERE

2" X 12" POCKET

3" 2005 YEAR

11"

6. Use one color marker to write the days of the week on seven of the 3" x 11" cards, and use another color marker to write the twelve months of the year on the same size cards. Write 2005 on the remaining card (tape this card next to the pocket on the second line to remain until the new year).
7. Write the numerals 1-31 on the 3" x 8" cards using a third color.
8. On the 3" x 10" cards, write "sunny," "cloudy," "snowy," "rainy," and "windy" with an appropriate symbol (sun, cloud, snowflake, or raindrops).

Windy cloudy sunny snowy rainy

ALL 3" X 10" CARDS

Days of the week    Month    Number of Day

3" x 11"    3" x 11"    3" x 8"

9. Mount the calendar where it can be used during circle time. Store the cards in boxes nearby (labeled: months, days, dates, weather).
10. At the beginning of the month, present the new month. It will stay in place until the month is ended.
11. Each day a child will place the correct day and date (help her, if necessary) after the month.
12. Children will enjoy choosing the weather symbol each day.

⭐ *Mary Jo Shannon, Roanoke, VA*

# Where, Oh, Where Are Our Friends?

GROUP OR CIRCLE TIME

**Materials**
flannel-backed pictures of each child
flannel board

**What to do**
1. This is a great game for helping children learn each other's names at the beginning of the year.
2. At circle time, bring out the flannel board and pictures. Sing the following song to the tune of "Paw Paw Patch":

*Where, oh, where is our friend, _____?*
*Where, oh, where is our friend, _____?*
*Where, oh, where is our friend, _____?*
*Way down yonder in the preschool patch!*

3. Put each child's photo on the flannel board as you say her name.
4. Continue until all the children's pictures are in the "preschool patch."

**More to do**
**Games:** Make a guessing/memory game of the board. Have the children cover their eyes, then remove one child's photo from the board. Ask the children to guess whose photo has been removed.

⭐ *Ann Scalley, Orleans, MA*

# LISTEN AND DO

GROUP OR CIRCLE TIME

**MATERIALS**      large basket, box, tub, or bag
classroom items

**WHAT TO DO**
1. Place a variety of classroom items in a large basket or tub.
2. Introduce this activity at a circle time, letting the children take turns.
3. Name an item in the container. Tell the child where to put the item. ("Billy, find the red car and place it under a chair.")
4. Near the end of the activity, change the directions and have the children put the various items back into the container.
5. Let the children take turns instructing other children where to put items.

**MORE TO DO**      At the end of free play/center time, ask the children to come to the circle area and leave their toys out. Play the "Listen and Do" game by having children put the items away.

⭐ *Sandie Nagel, White Lake, MI*

# SAY "HELLO" SONG

GROUP OR CIRCLE TIME

**MATERIALS**      paper
crayons or markers

**WHAT TO DO**
1. Recite the following rhyme, inserting the children's names.

    *Say hello to _____*
    *To _____*
    *To _____*
    *Say hello to _____*
    *He/she's a friend of mine.*

2. Have the children clap to the words.
3. Continue reciting the rhyme until all the children are named.
4. Finish the rhyme with your name.
5. When finished, have the children draw pictures of a friend in the class.

**RELATED books**      *I Love You, Stinky Face* by Lisa McCourt
*Will I Have a Friend?* by Miriam Cohen

⭐ *Judy Contino, Ozone Park, NY*

# We Are All Special

GROUP OR CIRCLE TIME

**Materials**      nametags
mirrors

**What to do**

1. Write each child's name on a nametag. Make one for yourself too.
2. Put everyone's nametag on the floor in the middle of the circle.
3. Pick up a nametag and read the name.
4. Ask that child to tell the group one thing about herself. You may want to go first to model for the children what to say, or have a list of questions to help them get started. For example, "Do you have a pet?" "What is your favorite thing to eat?"
5. After a child names something about herself, have her choose the next nametag.
6. Let children use mirrors to look at their faces or eye colors.
7. Once everyone has had a turn, return the cards to the circle for another round if the children still seem interested.

**More to do**      Make lists of similarities as the children name their traits. For example, all the children with brown hair, with pets, who live with their grandparent, and so on.

**Related books**      *It's Okay to Be Different* by Todd Parr
*Mixed-Up Chameleon* by Eric Carle
*The Okay Book* by Todd Parr
*This Is My Hair* by Todd Parr

⭐ *Ann Kelly, Johnstown, PA*

# Whooo's Here Today?

GROUP OR CIRCLE TIME

**Materials**      camera
tagboard
picture of owls in a tree
laminate
scissors
basket
pocket chart

**What to do**

1. Ahead of time, take a head-and-shoulders photo of each child in the class.
2. Mount each photo on a separate piece of tagboard with the child's first name below the picture.
3. Prepare a header card for the pocket chart with the title, "Whooo's Here Today?" and a picture of owls in a tree.
4. Laminate the header card and the pictures, and cut out.
5. Display the header card in the pocket chart.
6. Place the photos in a basket nearby.
7. Have a volunteer take attendance by placing the photos of the children who are present in the pocket chart.

⭐ *Jackie Wright, Enid, OK*

# Graphing Apples

GROUP OR CIRCLE TIME

**Materials**

red, green, and yellow apples
slicing knife (adult only)
red, green, and yellow crayons
circles or apple shapes cut from white paper
chart paper for graph
tape

**What to do**

1. Prior to the lesson, draw three columns on the chart paper and label them red, green, and yellow.
2. Cut the apples into slices. Give each child a slice of each variety of apple to taste. **Safety Note:** Check for any fruit allergies before doing this activity.
3. Discuss how each apple tastes: sweet, sour, crunchy, soft, and so on.
4. Give each child a circle or apple shape and ask them to color it the color of their favorite apple.
5. Tape the apples to the graph and discuss results. Which color has the most apples? Which has the least?

**Related books**

*Apples* by Gail Gibbons
*How Do Apples Grow?* by Betsy Maestro
*Little Apple: A Book of Thanks* by Brigitte Weninger
*The Seasons of Arnold's Apple Tree* by Gail Gibbons

⭐ *Cassandra Reigel Whetstone, San Jose, CA*

# WELCOME TO OUR CLASS

## LANGUAGE AND LITERACY

**MATERIALS**
8 ½" x 11" outlines of a boy and girl
copy machine
construction paper
tempera markers (or colored markers)
scissors
glue stick
hole punch
string or yarn

**WHAT TO DO**
1. Make a copy of an outline of a boy or girl on white construction paper for each child in the class.
2. Let each child decorate her pattern using colored markers or tempera markers to match her clothing and hair style.
3. After the paint has dried, have them cut out their self-portraits and glue them to a sheet of brightly colored construction paper.
4. Label each portrait with the child's name.
5. Use a hole punch and yarn to assemble the pages together into a class book.
6. Make an appropriate cover for the book, such as "Welcome to Our Class."
7. Whenever a guest, substitute teacher, or new student comes to the classroom, let the children introduce themselves by "reading" the class book like *Brown Bear, Brown Bear, What Do You See?* by Bill Martin, Jr.

*(First child's name), (first child's name), whom do you see?*
*I see (second child's name) looking at me.*
*(Second child's name), (second child's name), whom do you see?*
*I see (third child's name) looking at me.*

8. Continue in this manner and have each child stand when you turn to his page.
9. Remove or add pages as needed as children leave or join the class throughout the year.
10. At the end of the year, take apart the book (as well as all class books done throughout the year).
11. For each child, assemble all of their pages from the various class books made throughout the year. Use the outline picture as a cover.
12. Send the finished products home for families to treasure.

 *Jackie Wright, Enid, OK*

# Alphabet Mail Call

**Materials**
mailbox
envelopes
writing paper
marker or pen

**What to do**

1. Ahead of time, write the following letter to each child. Fill in a different child's name and letter on each (filling in the child's name):

   *Dear _____,*
   *This week we are learning about the letter _____.*
   *Name three things that begin with this letter.*
   *Keep up the good work.*
   *Sincerely,*
   *Your name*

2. Put the letters into separate envelopes and write each child's name on her envelope.
3. Put all the envelopes in the mailbox.
4. Pick one child to be the mail carrier. This child takes removes one envelope from the mailbox to deliver.
5. The envelope drawn will determine the letter of the week.

**More to do**

**Art:** Have children make their own envelopes and stationery with rubber stamps and card stock paper.
**Dramatic Play:** Turn the area into a post office or a stationery store. Add materials such as fancy pens, stamps, envelopes, cards, postcards, calligraphy pens, an assortment of stationery, and so on.
**Language and Literacy:** Encourage the children to practice writing letters to friends, parents, and siblings.

⭐ *Quazonia Quarles, Newark, DE*

# Yearly Journals

**Materials**
9-pocket clear pages (used to collect baseball cards), one for each child
hole punch
double-sided tape
folders (2 pockets with 3-prongs in the middle), one for each child
card stock or index cards

**What to do**
1. Punch three holes on the left side of the clear pocket pages.
2. Using double-sided tape, tape each clear pocket page to the front of a folder, making sure that the pockets are facing out. Make one for each child.
3. Cut card stock into cards that will fit into the pockets of the pocket page.
4. Starting in September, have each child draw a picture for that month on a card and slip it into the first pocket of her folder.
5. Continue this each month, labeling each card with the month. Children can draw a picture that relates to a holiday or theme for that month, or they could draw a monthly self-portrait.
6. These are great for seeing the children's development throughout the year. Fill the journals with assessments, art work, journal pages, or pictures from the year.
7. The two pockets on the inside of the folder are handy for extra items that will not fit in the journal.
8. It's helpful to add a note on the inside cover explaining to the parents the pictures on the cover. These are great to use during conferences with parents.

★ *Gail Morris, Kemah, TX*

# MARY WORE HER RED DRESS
## LANGUAGE AND LITERACY

**Materials**
*Mary Wore Her Red Dress and Henry Wore His Green Sneakers* by Merle Peek
camera (preferably digital)
full-body photos of each child
paper
stapler or book binder

**What to do**
1. This is a great activity to do at the beginning of the school year for children to become familiar with their classmates' names.
2. Read *Mary Wore Her Red Dress and Henry Wore His Green Sneakers* to the children. When you finish reading the book, say the following sentence for each child, filling in appropriate items. "(Child's name) is wearing a (color) (piece of clothing) all day long."
3. Take a full-body photo of each child, making sure it shows the child from head to toe.
4. Glue one photo on separate pieces of paper.
5. Encourage each child to focus on one item in her picture. On each page write: "_____ is wearing a _____ _____ all day long."

6. If the child can print her name, let her do so. If not, write it for her. Help the children write the color and article of clothing.
7. Bind the pages together for a class book.
8. Let the children make a cover for the book and choose a title.
**Note:** If you do not have access to a camera, have the children draw pictures of themselves instead.

 *Sandie Nagel, White Lake, MI*

# CHICKA CHICKA BOOM BOOM
### LANGUAGE AND LITERACY

**MATERIALS**  brown and green felt
scissors
sticky-back magnetic tape
magnetic letters
magnet board
*Chicka Chicka Boom Boom* by Bill Martin, Jr.

**WHAT TO DO**  
1. Make a palm tree using green felt for leaves and brown felt for the trunk.
2. Put magnetic tape on the back of the tree and put in on a magnet board.
3. At the beginning of the year, talk about the alphabet and read *Chicka Chicka Boom Boom* to the children.
4. Use the magnetic letters and the tree on the magnet board as you read the book, and act it out if you wish. Have the children act out the story later during center time in small groups.

**MORE TO DO**  
**Art:** Have the children paint with real palm leaves instead of paintbrushes.
**Science:** Open a real coconut and let the children examine it. They may even want to try some coconut milk. **Safety Note:** Check for food allergies before letting children taste the milk.
**Sensory:** Make a letter sensory bottle. Remove the label from an empty water bottle. Add some water to the bottle. Add palm tree confetti and letter confetti (found at party stores) to the water bottle. Glue the lid on the water bottle. Encourage the children to find the letters in the story.

*Gail Morris, Kemah, Texas*

# Favorite Things

## LANGUAGE AND LITERACY

**Materials**
photos of each child
paper
stapler or hole punch and yarn
magazines
crayons
scissors
glue

**What to do**
1. At the beginning of the school year, take individual pictures of each child, or ask parents to send a picture of their children.
2. Staple together (or use a hole punch and yarn) a few pieces of paper to make a blank book. Make one for each child in the class.
3. Give each child a pre-made book. Help them create covers for their books using their individual photos and help them print their names.
4. Discuss favorite things and encourage children to fill their books with their "favorites." They may cut out pictures from magazines or draw their favorite things.
5. Encourage the children to add to these books every week or month throughout the year.

**More to do**
**Group or Circle Time:** Encourage the children to talk about their favorite things. Have a show-and-tell with favorite things.
**Snack:** Have the children make a "favorite foods" placemat for snack time by cutting out pictures of foods and pasting them to a large piece of paper. Laminate for durability. These can be wiped off after use.

 *Barb Lindsey, Madison City, IA*

# Our Apple Story Time

## MATH

**Materials**
red felt
scissors
flannel board
*Ten Red Apples* by Pat Hutchins

**What to do**
1. Ahead of time, cut out 10 apples from red felt.
2. Introduce the main character, a farmer, from the book.
3. Place the 10 red apples on the flannel board.
4. As you read the story, remove one apple from the board for each apple eaten in the book.

**Related books**
*Apples* by Gail Gibbons
*Apples, Apples, Apples* by Nancy Elizabeth Wallace
*How Do Apples Grow?* by Betsy Maestro
*Seasons of Arnold's Apple Tree* by Gail Gibbons

 Elizabeth Thomas, Hobart, IN

# "How Did You Come Here Today?" Graph

MATH

**Materials**
digital camera
scissors
magnetic tape
magazine
whiteboard pen
magnet board
yardstick

**What to do**
1. Take a close-up photo of each child.
2. After the photos are printed, cut out the children's faces from each picture and attach a piece of magnetic tape to the back.
3. Cut out pictures of a car, a bus, and a pedestrian from a magazine. Put magnetic tape on the back of each picture.
4. Divide the magnet board into three sections using the whiteboard pen and yardstick.
5. At the top of each column, write: Car, Bus, and Walk.
6. Ask the children how they got to school that morning. Have them place their pictures in the appropriate section of the graph.
7. When working with the graph, use the terms *most* and *least* and encourage the children to talk about modes of transportation.

**MORE TO DO**   Send the magnetic faces home to use as refrigerator magnets.
**Dramatic Play:** Make a bus in the dramatic play area by lining up two rows of chairs. The driver may sit in the front seat, and passengers in the back seats.

★ *Barbara Saul, Eureka, CA*

# Fall Gardening

OUTDOOR PLAY

**MATERIALS**   shovels, spades, and trowels
topsoil
fertilizer
snowdrop, daffodil, and tulip bulbs
watering cans

**WHAT TO DO**   1. Find an outdoor area to use as a garden bed. Show the children how to prepare it for planting by turning over the dirt.
2. Add topsoil and fertilizer, if needed.
3. If desired, divide the area using rocks and branches to delineate individual spaces. Help the children paint their names on a rock to place in their individual gardens.
4. Create a class garden. Show the children how to dig holes and plant bulbs.
5. If desired, ask families to donate leftover plants from their own perennial gardens.
6. Have the children water the bulbs.
7. Look for the flowers in the spring.

**RELATED BOOKS**   *Christopher's Harvest Time* by Elsa Beskow
*The Story of the Root Children* by Sibylle von Olfers

★ *Linda Atamian, Charlestown, RI*

# PRIMARY COLOR TABLE

OUTDOOR PLAY

**MATERIALS**    small table
red, yellow, or blue cloth or construction paper (enough to cover table)

**WHAT TO DO**
1. This is a nice project to do at the beginning of the year to introduce colors.
2. Select one primary color (red, yellow, or blue) to start. Cover a small table with that color cloth or paper.
3. Print the color name on a sign and place it on the table.
4. Ask the children to find objects in that color and place them on the table.
5. After one week, change the color table to another primary color.

★ *Elaine Commins, Athens, GA*

# SORTING LEAVES

SCIENCE

**MATERIALS**    plastic bag (one per child)
leaves from various trees
wax paper
iron (adult only)
large mat

**WHAT TO DO**
1. Give each child a plastic bag. Take the children on a walk through the neighborhood to gather leaves from different kinds of trees.
2. While the leaves are still fresh, place them between two sheets of wax paper and press with a warm iron (adult only).
3. Glue one leaf of each type to a large mat divided into several areas. Each leaf should have its own section of the mat.
4. Identify the species of trees to the children. Talk about the leaves and the trees they come from.

**MORE TO DO**    **Art:** Make Leaf People. Help each child tape a large leaf to a piece of drawing paper. Encourage the children to use the leaf as the body of a "leaf person," using the stem as the neck. Invite them to draw the rest of the person, or use multiple leaves to create an entire leaf family.

**Bulletin Board:** Make a large tree trunk with bare branches out of brown construction paper. Tack it to a classroom bulletin board. Invite the children to cut out autumn leaves from construction paper. Let the children tape their leaves to the branches of the tree.

 *Iris Rothstein, New Hyde Park, NY*

# Adopt a Tree or Bush
SCIENCE

**Materials**
tree or shrub near school
spool of ribbon
chart paper
markers

**What to do**
1. Identify an adoptable tree or bush within walking distance of your school. Help the children understand the meaning of the word "adopt."
2. Visit the tree in the early fall. Tie a piece of ribbon around the trunk or a substantial branch. Encourage children to remark on the tree's characteristics. "What kind of leaves does it have?" "How tall is it?"
3. Make a bark rubbing and take a leaf sample back to the classroom.
4. Back in the classroom, give the tree a name. Make a chart of what the children remember seeing. Date the chart and place it in an area where the children can refer to it.
5. Revisit the tree occasionally throughout the year. Encourage the children to note any changes in size, leaves, branches, and so on. Record observations and compare with those from the previous visit.
6. At the end of the year, talk about the differences in the tree each season.

*Margery Kranyik Fermino, Hyde Park, MA*

# Snails
SCIENCE

**Materials**
clear plastic or glass animal container with a lid
lettuce
snails
magnifying glasses
*Snail Trail* by Ruth Brown

**What to do**

1. In September, it's helpful to introduce a class pet to the children that they can handle and examine. Remind them to be careful and respectful of small animals.
2. Snails are very low maintenance. Keep one in a clear animal container and add a few lettuce leaves as needed. (Your cafeteria or local grocery store may be able to donate all you need.)
3. Encourage the children to use magnifying glasses to examine the snail.
4. Read *Snail Trail* by Ruth Brown to the children.

**More to do**

**Art:** Cut strips of brown paper about 6" to 8" long and about 1" wide. Show the children how to curl the paper around a pencil to make snails. Invite them to glue them on green or brown paper.
**Fine Motor:** Have children roll playdough into snail shapes. First have them roll out "snakes," and then coil the snakes into snails. They can also roll pipe cleaners into snails.

**Related books**

*Are You a Snail?* by Judy Allen
*How Many Snails?: A Counting Book* by Paul Giganti
*The Snail and the Whale* by Julia Donaldson

⭐ *Linda Ford, Sacramento, CA*

# Friendship Salad

SNACK AND COOKING

**Materials**

cutting boards
table or plastic knives
vegetable peelers
large bowl
individual bowls and spoons

**What to do**

1. This is a good activity to do at the beginning of the year because it provides an opportunity to talk about diversity and sharing.
2. Ask each child to bring in her favorite fruit (already washed).
3. Help the children peel fruit if needed. Cut the fruit into strips and remove the core and seeds, if necessary.
4. Let the children use plastic knives to cut fruit into bite-sized pieces.
5. Place the fruit pieces into a bowl and mix.
6. Eat for snack.
7. Talk about the diversity of flavors and colors. Compare to people. Emphasize that everyone has different likes and dislikes. Talk about how we can all share our favorite things.

**MORE TO DO**     Make large circles on the floor using yarn or tape. Encourage the children to move in and out of groups as you list favorite foods, colors, and so on. This demonstrates that we are the same in some ways and different in others.

**Math:** Make a graph showing the sizes of the children's families, colors of their houses, types of pets, and so on.

**RELATED books**     *Amigo Means Friend* by Louise Everett
*Eight Animals Bake a Cake* by Susan Middleton Elya
*Just My Friend and Me* by Mercer Mayer

⭐ *Sandra Gratias, Dublin, PA*

# CROCKPOT APPLESAUCE

SNACK AND COOKING

**MATERIALS**     1 whole, unpeeled apple
vegetable peeler
plastic knives
crockpot
3 lb. apples, peeled and sliced
½ cup brown sugar
1 teaspoon cinnamon
1 tablespoon lemon juice
½ cup water
wooden spoon
bowls or small cups
plastic spoons

**WHAT TO DO**     1. Show children a whole apple and discuss how to make applesauce.
2. Peel the apple, slice it, and put it into the crockpot.
3. Help the children peel and slice the rest of the apples (supervise closely).
4. Let them help add the apples, brown sugar, cinnamon, lemon juice, and water into the crockpot. Stir.
5. Cook on high for three hours or low for six hours. **Safety Note:** Make sure the crockpot is in an area away from the children.
6. Let applesauce cool. Serve in bowls or cups for snack.

⭐ *Cassandra Reigel Whetstone, San Jose, CA*

# We Can Share at School

SOCIAL DEVELOPMENT

**Materials**      *We Can Share at School* by Rozanne Lanczak Williams (or any favorite book about sharing)
paint
pencils and crayons
butcher paper
camera

**What to do**      1. Read *We Can Share at School*. In this book, the children work together to complete a mural of flowers, sunshine, and butterflies.
2. Invite the children to do the same thing.
3. As they work together, take pictures of the children.
4. Use the pictures to make a classroom "We Can Share at School" book.

**More to do**      **Social Development:** Encourage the children to do other cooperative projects, such as putting together large floor puzzles or making block buildings.

**Related books**      *Let's Share* by P.K. Hallinan
*Mine, Mine, Mine: A Little Help With Sharing* by Sheryl Berk

⭐ *Linda Ford, Sacramento, CA*

# Introductions

SOCIAL DEVELOPMENT

**Materials**      none

**What to do**      1. This is a great activity to do at the beginning of the year because it helps children get acquainted with each other. It also aids social development, as shy children often find it easier to talk about another child rather than themselves, and memory skills.
2. Ask the children to find a partner they don't know very well. Have them sit in a circle.
3. Tell them they have two minutes to find out the other child's name and if the child is a boy or a girl (this usually makes them laugh but sometimes younger children are surprised at what they find out).
4. Encourage the group to sit quietly while each child takes a turn to say something about her partner. ("My partner is a boy and his name is Alex.")

5. After everyone has been introduced, give the children two minutes to find out their partner's favorite toy.

6. Go around the circle again, and have each child repeat the initial information, as well as the next thing learned. ("My partner is a boy. His name is Alex and his favorite toy is his red fire truck.")

7. Continue this activity within the attention limits of your age group, asking questions such as age, favorite foods, and so on.

8. If desired, ask for volunteers to take turns standing in the middle of the circle while the other children (not the partner) say what they have learned about him.

**More to do**    **More Social Development:** Talk about friends—what they are, how to make friends, how to make up after an argument, and so on.
**Games:** Play a game that requires the cooperation of a partner.

**Related books**    *Chester's Way* by Kevin Henkes
*Frog and Toad Are Friends* by Arnold Lobel
*George and Martha* by James Marshall
*How to Be a Friend* by Laura Krasney Brown
*Two Cool Coyotes* by Jillian Lund

 *Anne Adeney, Plymouth, United Kingdom*

# Transition Songs
TRANSITIONS

**Materials**    none

**What to do**    When transitioning throughout the day, sing what you want the children to do. For example:

● At cleanup time, sing the following song to the tune of "Mary Had a Little Lamb."

*It's time to put the toys away,
Toys away, toys away.
It's time to put the toys away
And save them for another day.*

- When the children need to wash their hands, sing this song to the tune of "Here We Go 'Round the Mulberry Bush."

*This is the way we wash our hands,*
*Wash our hands, wash our hands,*
*This is the way we wash our hands*
*Before we eat our lunch.*

⭐ *Phyllis Esch, Export, PA*

# Class Video Clips

## WORKING WITH FAMILIES

**Materials**     video camera

**What to do**
1. At the beginning of the school year, show the children the video camera and how it works. Have a discussion about the kinds of activities and experiences they want to capture.
2. Explain that they will be making a classroom video to show to their families and friends during a Video Night at the school, complete with popcorn!
3. Talk about their interests, the different activity centers, outdoor play, and so on.
4. Encourage them to produce, direct, and stage the tapings.

⭐ *Judy Fujawa, The Villages, FL*

# Bring a Book

## WORKING WITH FAMILIES

**Materials**     books from home

**What to do**
1. At the beginning of the school year, send a note home suggesting that instead of sending food to school to celebrate a child's birthday, the birthday child should choose a book to donate to the class library.
2. When a child brings a donated book to class, write the child's name and date of the donation inside the book.
3. On the child's birthday, read the book to the class.

⭐ *Barbara Saul, Eureka, CA*

# Family Collage

### WORKING WITH FAMILIES

**Materials**      poster board
letter to parents

**What to do**      1. On the first day of school, send home a piece of poster board with the following note:

*Family Collage*
*We are sending home this piece of poster board for you and your child to decorate. Help your child glue on pictures of your family or magazine pictures of favorite things; decorate it with markers, paint, stickers, and glitter; write on it—anything your child would like to do. We will hang these around the room. Please make sure your child's name is somewhere on the collage.*

2. Once the collages start to come in, hang them on the walls so the pieces connect like a giant quilt. The children will likely spend long periods of time looking at them and discussing the different people they see in the collages.
3. Look at the collages with the children and ask questions. "Who has a brother named Ben?" "Who has a sister named Tess?" Make a game out of it.

⭐ *Ann Scalley, Orleans, MA*

# Take-Home Literacy Bags

### WORKING WITH FAMILIES

**Materials**      totes or containers
children's books centered around various themes
literacy items and activities to accompany the books
paper
luggage tags
permanent marker

**What to do**      1. At the beginning of the year, send home a permission slip for parents to sign notifying them that take-home literacy bags are available for check-out.
2. Ask them to return the signed slip saying that they will be responsible for the contents of the bag.
3. Place several books centered around a theme, along with an activity or literacy item in each bag. Include a letter explaining the purpose of the

bag, the theme, a list of the contents, and when it is to be returned.

4. Attach a luggage tag to the handle of each bag with theme written on one side and the due date on the other.

5. Make a chart to keep track of who has which bag.

6. Rotate the contents of the bags so that each family has an opportunity to check out each bag.

7. Following are suggested themes for literacy bags:

- ABCs
- Math
- Shapes
- Clouds
- Bugs (Ladybugs, Ants, Spiders)
- Cowboys
- Shoes
- Animals (Alligators, Mice, Dogs, Cats, Owls, Fish, Penguins, Pigs, Frogs)
- Dinosaurs
- Authors (Dr. Seuss, Jan Brett, Audrey Woods, Bill Martin, Jr.)
- Weather (Snow, Rain, Sunshine)
- Moon
- Stars
- Food (Apples, Pizza)
- Nursery Rhymes
- Sports
- Artists
- Family
- Farm
- Bedtime
- Teddy Bears
- Bees
- Friends
- Tools
- Birthdays
- Plants and Seeds
- Teeth
- Glad to Be Me
- Butterflies
- Growing
- Transportation (Trains, Trucks, Airplanes)
- Helping
- Rainbows
- Circus
- Homes
- Seasons
- Zoo

 *Jackie Wright, Enid, OK*

# Library Manners

GROUP OR CIRCLE TIME

**Materials**

*Check It Out!: The Book About Libraries* by Gail Gibbons
chart paper
marker

**What to do**

- September is National Library Card Sign-Up Month.
1. Read a book about the library, such as *Check It Out!: The Book About Libraries* by Gail Gibbons.
2. Talk to the children about the importance of good library manners.
3. Brainstorm a list of library rules that are appropriate for the public library and your classroom reading area, such as using a quiet voice, treating books with care, and returning books to their proper places.
4. If desired, write the rules on a sheet of chart paper and post the chart in the reading area.

 *Jackie Wright, Enid, OK*

# The Clothes We Wear

PROJECTS

**Materials**

*Joseph Had a Little Overcoat* by Simms Taback
copy of clothes pages for each child
drawing paper
marker
glue
1" squares of cotton batting
1" squares of fabric
thread
small shirt shapes cut from fabric
scissors

**What to do**

- September is National Sewing Month.
1. Read *Joseph Had a Little Overcoat* by Simms Taback.
2. Talk about how clothes are made.
3. Give each child a copy of the four pages in the book.
4. Divide a sheet of paper into four equal sections. Write each of the following sentences in a separate section.
   - page 1: Pick the cotton from the plant.
   - page 2: Spin the cotton into thread.

- page 3: Weave the thread into fabric.
- page 4: Sew the fabric into clothes.

5. Make a copy of this page for each child.

6. In the first section (page 1), children glue a piece of cotton batting; in the second section (page 2), they glue pieces of thread; in the third section (page 3), they glue the fabric square; and in the final section (page 4), they glue on the shirt shape.

7. When dry, cut apart the pages and staple them together with a cover to make a book.

**MORE TO DO**    **Art:** Let children make a collage using fabric, lace, ribbons, yarn, buttons, and thread.

**Fine Motor:** Put out plastic needles or bobby pins and encourage children to try sewing with yarn on a plastic canvas. (Younger children can weave pipe cleaners through plastic canvas.)

**Sensory:** Make a texture book using silk, leather, flannel, and burlap.

**RELATED SONG**    Sing the following song to the tune of "London Bridge."

*Pick the cotton from the plant,*
*From the plant, from the plant*
*Pick the cotton from the plant,*
*To make clothes.*

*Spin the cotton into thread,*
*Into thread, into thread.*
*Spin the cotton into thread*
*To make clothes.*

*Weave the fabric from the thread,*
*From the thread, from the thread.*
*Weave the cotton from the thread*
*To make clothes.*

*Sew the fabric into clothes,*
*Into clothes, into clothes.*
*Sew the fabric into clothes*
*To make clothes.*

**RELATED books**    *Animals Should Definitely Not Wear Clothing* by Judi Barrett
*The Hat* by Jan Brett
*The Principal's New Clothes* by Stephanie Calmenson

★ *Sue Fleischmann, Sussex, WI*

# Classroom Farm

PROJECTS

**Materials**
books and pictures of farms
cardboard boxes
scissors
glue and tape
miniature straw bales
oatmeal boxes
cake pans
paint and brushes
eggs and milk
mixing bowl
sponges
lightweight cardboard
cotton balls, feathers, fake fur, and so on

**What to do**
- National Farm Awareness Week is the third week of September.
  1. Few children live on farms today. Many don't realize the food they eat doesn't originate in a supermarket. Find books and pictures of farms to share with the children. Talk about farms with the children. Explain that they will be doing a few different activities related to farms.
  2. Help the children make a barn from a square cardboard box. Construct the peaked roof from cardboard cut from a similar-size box. Store tiny straw bales (available in craft stores) in the barn loft.
  3. Make a silo by gluing together two round oatmeal containers. Have the bottom of one container on top for the closed roof.
  4. Construct a smaller cardboard box hen house.
  5. Use a round, shallow cake pan for a large animal water trough, and a small lid for a water container for fowl. If you choose to have ducks, provide another cake pan for the pond where they will swim. **Note:** Don't put water in the containers when children are playing with the farm; paper-based barns and other items disintegrate quickly.
  6. Encourage the children to paint the buildings. Let dry.
  7. Provide plastic farm animals or glue coloring book or magazine cutouts to poster board and cut them out. Encourage the children to move them around.
  8. Show pictures of farms while the children pretend to milk the cows and gather the eggs.
  9. Bring in real eggs and talk about where they come from. If you have cooking facilities, make omelets with the children.
  10. Serve milk when you talk about cows. Have children beat heavy whipping cream in a mixer to make butter. (This takes time, so provide a related coloring activity for children to work on until the butter is ready.)

11. Serve bread and butter for snack. **Note:** Be aware of any egg or dairy allergies before doing these activities.

12. Help the children cut out sponge shapes of different farm animals. Show them how to dip the sponges into paint and then onto paper to make prints.

13. Cut out animal shapes from lightweight cardboard. Encourage the children to decorate the animals. For example, decorate lambs by tearing cotton balls into bits of fluff before gluing it on. Use fake fur bits or feathers to decorate other animals.

14. Let the children take home their farm animal prints and cutouts so they can explain the different farm animals to their parents and siblings.

PIG  CHICKEN  SHEEP  COW

★ *Margaret Shauers, Great Bend, KS*

# The Jobs People Do

PROJECTS

**Materials**
poster board
tape recorder (optional)
markers
graphics representing different jobs (from a computer or hand drawn)
glue
clothing props representing different jobs (lab coats, work shirts, caps, hard hats, and so on)
various props representing different jobs (stethoscope, hammer (plastic), typewriter, postal workers letter bag, and so on)
magazines
construction paper

**What to do**
* Labor Day is the first Monday in September. It is a celebration of workers, as well as the unofficial end of the summer season.
1. Ask parents what they do for a living. Make a list of their jobs.
2. Ask the children to talk about their parents' jobs. Record their responses using a tape recorder or by writing them down.
3. Compare what the children say with what the parents actually do. Talk a little about each type of job. Make sure you don't make children feel as though they have answered incorrectly. For example, if Jonnie said his Mom works in an office and you know she is a doctor, say, "Yes, Jonnie, your mom does work in an office. She works in a doctor's office. She is the doctor there. What do you think a doctor does?"
4. Continue until you have talked about everyone's job. This can be spread out over several days, depending on how many children are in your class. Make a list of the jobs on a piece of poster board.
5. Make a word/picture graph depicting the parents' jobs. At the top of the graph print: "The Jobs People Do." Under the heading make two columns, one for Mom and one for Dad. Along the left side, write each child's name. Print each parent's job in the proper column. Add a small graphic that represents that job next to the printed words.
6. Add props for the different jobs represented by the parents in the dramatic play center. Encourage the children to pretend they are their parents at work.
7. Add office tools (calculator, phone, phone message pads) to the writing center.
8. Have children cut out magazine pictures of people working to make a Jobs Collage as a group project. Provide glue, scissors, and other craft materials.
9. Work with the children to create a unique and colorful jobs mural on poster board. Title it: "The Jobs People Do" and display it for all to see.

10. Wind up your celebration of the jobs people do by inviting several parents to visit the class and give a short talk about their jobs.

**More to do**    **Books**: Make a "Jobs People Do" book. Ask the children to draw pictures of their parents at work. Under each picture, print a short description (provided by the children) of the parents' jobs. Create a front and back cover and bind together by punching three holes along one edge and threading the pages together with heavy yarn.
**Field Trip:** If possible, take a field trip to one parent's workplace. Let the parent lead the children on a short and interesting tour.

**Related song**    **Moms and Dads All Have Jobs** (Tune: "The Armour Hot Dog Song")
*Great jobs!*
*They have great jobs!*
*Our moms and dads all have great jobs!*
*Doctors, lawyers, mechanics who fix things,*
*Writers, sales clerks, this is the song we sing*
*About their great jobs!*
*They have great jobs!*
*Our parents have great jobs!*
(Substitute jobs that actually represent the ones the parents have)

**Related books**    *Arthur Babysits* by Marc Brown
*Arthur's Pet Business* by Marc Brown
*Chester, the Out of Work Dog* by Marilyn Singer
*A Day's Work* by Eve Bunting
*A Good Morning's Work* by Nathan Zimelman
*Mr. Griggs' Work* by Cynthia Rylant
*My Car* by Byron Barton
*The Night Worker* by Kate Banks

 *Virginia Jean Herrod, Columbia, SC*

# FAVORITE COMMUNITY HELPER GRAPH

SOCIAL DEVELOPMENT

**Materials**    pictures of community helpers
tagboard
pocket chart
name card for each child

**What to do**
- Labor Day is the first Monday in September. Fire Prevention Week is the week in which October 9th occurs.
1. Whether you're discussing occupations around Labor Day in September or observing Fire Prevention week in October, take an opportunity to salute community helpers with this graphing activity.
2. Review the duties of different community helpers and let each child choose a picture that represents a career he or she would like to have as an adult.
3. Create a graph by placing a tagboard header card with the heading, "Which would you rather be?" in the top row of a pocket chart.
4. Place pictures of various community helpers in the pockets to form columns.
5. Have each child, in turn, place her name card under the column of her choice.
6. Discuss the results of the graph.

**Related book**    *Guess Who?* by Margaret Miller

⭐ *Jackie Wright, Enid, OK*

# Yeah! It's Grandparent's Day!

WORKING WITH FAMILIES

**Materials**
construction paper
crayons

**What to do**
- Grandparent's Day is the first Sunday after Labor Day.
1. Prior to Grandparent's Day, teach the children the following song to the tune of "You Are My Sunshine."

*You are my grandma (grandpa),*
*You are my grandma (grandpa).*
*You make me happy when skies are gray.*
*You'll never know, dear, how much I love you,*
*I'm so glad you came today!*

2. Ask the children to think of something they enjoy doing with their grandmother or grandfather (or both), and then ask them to draw a picture of this.
3. Invite grandparents to class to celebrate Grandparent's Day. Share the pictures and song.

⭐ *Karyn F. Everham, Fort Myers, FL*

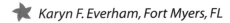

# Teddy Bear Brigade
### LANGUAGE AND LITERACY

**Materials**
computer and color printer or die-cut teddy bears
pocket chart
tagboard
colored pictures representing beginning sounds
glue stick
paper cutter
laminating machine
scissors

**What to do**
- Teddy Bear Day is September 9th.
1. Label four computer-generated or die-cut teddy bears with a different letter of your choice.
2. Use them to form four columns at the top of the pocket chart with a header card that has the title "A Teddy Bear Brigade!" and the instructions: "Place the cards under the correct teddy bears."
3. On tagboard, draw or glue pictures representing the beginning sounds of each of the four letters on the teddy bears.
4. Using a paper cutter, cut the pictures into cards of the desired size.
5. Laminate the header card and picture cards for durability, and cut out.
6. To use this center, a child identifies a picture's beginning sound and adds it to the pocket chart under the appropriate teddy bear.

**Related books**
*Corduroy* by Don Freeman
*Where's My Teddy?* by Jez Alborough

⭐ *Jackie Wright, Enid, OK*

# Teddy Bear Graph
### MATH

**Materials**
teddy bears
chalkboard
chalk

**What to do**
- Teddy Bear Day is September 9th.
1. Ask the children to bring their teddy bears to school. Make sure to have a few extra for children who might not have one or who forget to bring one.
2. Make a graph on a chalkboard with categories such as color, size, clothing, and so on.

3. Ask the children what categories their bears belong in (for example, brown, small, wearing a shirt, and so on).
4. Compare which category has the most, least, and so on.

⭐ *Kathy Kalmar, Macomb, MI*

# Elephant Headband

ART

**MATERIALS**
white tagboard
scissors
gray construction paper
white glue
stapler
black marker
25 mm wiggle eyes

**WHAT TO DO**
- September 22nd is Elephant Appreciation Day.
1. Make tagboard patterns for an elephant head, trunk, tusks, and ears (see page 70).
2. Help children trace the head, ears, and trunk on gray paper. Cut out.
3. Help children trace the inside of the ears on pink paper. Cut out.
4. Let the children glue wiggle eyes, ears, tusks, and trunk to their elephant's head.
5. When dry, make a headband the size of each child's head.
6. Help the children staple the headband to the elephant head.
7. Demonstrate how to curl up the end of the trunk.
8. Encourage the children to put on their elephant headbands and play. If desired, have the children walk like elephants with their arms hanging low.

**MORE TO DO**
**Geography:** Find Africa and India on a map or globe.
**Group or Circle Time:** Discuss the differences between African and Indian elephants. Explain that African elephants have larger ears and tusks than Indian elephants. They also have two finger-like extensions on the ends of their trunks. Indian elephants have just one finger-like extension, and more of a hump in their backs.
**Language:** Talk about elephant terminology. The mother is a "cow," the father is a "bull," and the baby is a "calf."

**RELATED BOOK** *The Saggy Baggy Elephant* by Kathryn Jackson

⭐ *Mary Brehm, Aurora, OH*

HEADBAND

– GRAY –

CUT ONE

CUT 2

–WHITE–

– GRAY –

CUT 2

– PINK –

CUT 2

HEADBAND / SIZE to CHILD'S HEAD

# Celebrate Johnny Appleseed's Birthday

FIELD TRIPS

**Materials**   none

**What to do**
- Johnny Appleseed's birthday is September 26th.
1. Talk about Johnny Appleseed. He was born on September 26th, 1774. His real name was John Chapman. He spent 49 years planting apple seeds in the wilderness. He wanted to plant apple trees all over so people wouldn't be hungry.
2. Go to a local apple orchard. In areas where no orchard exists, visit a large grocery store and discuss the wide variety of apples available.

**Related books**   *Apples* by Gail Gibbons
*The Apple Pie Tree* by Zoe Hall
*How Do Apples Grow?* by Betsy Maestro
*Johnny Appleseed* by Steven Kellogg

★ *Kristi Larson, Spirit Lake, IA*

# Johnny Appleseed Fingerplay

FINGERPLAYS, SONGS, & POEMS

**Materials**   none

**What to do**
- Johnny Appleseed's birthday is September 26th.
Sing the following song, making the appropriate corresponding gestures.

*Once Johnny had an apple seed* (make a seed with fingertips)
*He planted in the ground.* (pat floor)
*Out came the sun* (raise arms in a circle)
*And down came the rain,* (make fingers move up and down)
*Up came the apple tree,* (raise hand up from floor)
*And Johnny began again.* (make a seed again)

**More to do**   **Art:** Cut an apple in half. Dip the apple half in tempera paint using a plastic fork to hold it, and make apple prints on paper.

★ *Kathy Kalmar, Macomb, MI*

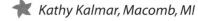

# Apple Fractions

MATH

**Materials**     three apples
one knife (adult only)

**What to do**
- Johnny Appleseed's birthday is September 26th.
1. Show the children the three apples. Encourage them to children guess what is inside before cutting. For those who guess seeds, ask them if they think there are a lot of seeds, or a few.
2. Cut the first apple in half and count the seeds.
3. Prior to cutting the second apple, ask the children if they think the number of seeds will be the same or different.
4. Cut open and count.
5. Repeat with the third apple.

**More to do**     **More Math:** Cut an apple in half. Talk about how the two parts make one apple. Repeat with thirds and fourths.

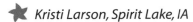 *Kristi Larson, Spirit Lake, IA*

# Are All Apples the Same?

SNACK AND COOKING

**Materials**     apples in as many different varieties and colors as possible
knife (adult only)

**What to do**
- Johnny Appleseed's birthday is on September 26th.
1. Celebrate Johnny Appeleseed's birthday by showing the children all the different kinds of apples. If you can, try to have both an extra sweet and Granny Smith apple.
2. Pass the apples around for the children to see if they feel or smell differently.
3. Cut open each apple and see if the insides are the same.
4. Cut the apples into slices and let the children experience the variety of different apple flavors.

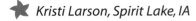 *Kristi Larson, Spirit Lake, IA*

# October

# PAPER PUMPKINS

ART

**MATERIALS**       construction paper (orange, yellow, and brown)
crayons
scissors
empty paper towel tubes
glue

**WHAT TO DO**
1. Ask the children to choose a few sheets of construction paper in fall colors, or use white paper. Encourage them to color their paper with crayons, layering different fall colors over each other for a rich, multi-layered effect. The children can use several colors per sheet, and color both sides if desired.
2. Help them cut most of their papers into long, narrow strips, making sure they leave some whole sheets for stems, leaves, and vines.
3. Cut paper towel tubes into thirds. Give one-third of a tube to each child.
4. Help them cover their tubes with their construction or colored paper. Glue the paper in place. This will be the central core of each pumpkin.
5. Show the children how to glue five or six paper strips into one end of the central core. Let each strip dry slightly before attaching more strips. Continue this process until the entire top of the core is filled evenly with paper strips. Let dry.
6. Help the children gently curl the end of each strip around and down so it can be glued into the bottom of the central core. Each strip should bow out. This creates the round pumpkin. Help the children glue each strip in place and dry slightly. Complete this step with all of the strips. Help the children add more strips to fill any spaces. Dry thoroughly.
7. Demonstrate how to cut green construction paper, crayon-colored paper, or a paper bag into the size of a large index card. Help them roll the paper into a cylinder. Insert this cylinder into the top of the central core for a stem. Help the children glue it in place.

① ⅓ of a PAPER TOWEL TUBE

③ STRIPS THAT BOW OUT

② COVERED WITH STRIPS

8. Trace paper leaves and vines on a sheet that the children colored. Help them cut out the leaves and vines and glue them to the pumpkin anywhere they desire.

**RELATED BOOKS**   *The Biggest Pumpkin Ever* by Steven Kroll
*It's Pumpkin Time!* by Zoe Hall
*Jeb Scarecrow's Pumpkin Patch* by Jana Dillon
*Pumpkin Circle: The Story of a Garden* by George Levenson
*Pumpkin Eye* by Denise Fleming
*The Wonderful Pumpkin* by Lennart Hellsing

 *Virginia Jean Herrod, Columbia, SC*

# Pumpkin Pictures

ART

**MATERIALS**   small pumpkins
paint and brushes
newsprint
bins of water
towels

**WHAT TO DO**   1. Put small pumpkins, paint, paintbrushes, and newsprint in the art center. Have small bins of water and towels available.
2. Encourage the children to cover their pumpkins with paint and make a print by wrapping newsprint around their pumpkins.
3. Help them carefully peel the newsprint off the pumpkins.
4. Have the children dunk their pumpkins in water and rub the paint off.
5. Dry the pumpkin for the next person to use.
6. If desired, let each child paint a pumpkin and bring it home.

**MORE TO DO**   **Books:** Read *It Looked Like Spilt Milk* by Charles Shaw. Ask the children if they see any images in their pumpkin prints.

**RELATED BOOKS**   *It Looked Like Spilt Milk* by Charles Shaw
*One Potato: A Counting Book of Potato Prints* by Diana Pomeroy

 *Ann Kelly, Johnstown, PA*

# Tissue Paper Pumpkins

ART

**Materials**    tagboard
scissors
orange tissue paper
orange watercolor or crayon
glue
brown crayons or tissue paper

**What to do**    1. Pre-cut pumpkin shapes from tagboard. Cut orange tissue paper into squares.
2. Encourage the children to paint or color their pumpkin shapes. Allow them to dry.
3. Have the children crumple tissue squares and glue them on their pumpkin shapes.
4. Have them color or add brown tissue to make a stem.

**More to do**    Carve a real pumpkin.
**Snack:** Serve pumpkin muffins and pumpkin seeds for snack.

**Related books**    *The Pumpkin Blanket* by Deborah Turney Zagwyn
*Pumpkin, Pumpkin* by Jeanne Titherington

⭐ *Linda Atamian, Charlestown, RI*

# Weird Pumpkin Faces

ART

**Materials**    paper
old magazines
scissors
glue sticks

**What to do**    1. Before doing this activity, cut out pumpkin shapes from paper and eyes, ears, mouths, and noses from paper or old magazines (older children can help with this step). For added fun, use facial features from animals too.
2. Encourage the children to mix up eyes and make silly faces on their pumpkin shapes.

CUTOUT PUMPKIN

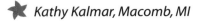

⭐ *Kathy Kalmar, Macomb, MI*

# Fall Walk

ART/SCIENCE

**Materials**
sandwich zipper-closure plastic bags
permanent marker
construction paper in fall colors

**What to do**
1. Give each child a zipper-closure plastic bag and write his name on his bag with a permanent marker.
2. Go on a nature walk to search for fall items such as leaves, acorns, small twigs, and so on.
3. After the children have filled their bags, return to the classroom.
4. Place construction paper in fall colors on the table.
5. Encourage the children to match their nature items to the same or similar color construction paper.

**Related books**   *Autumn* by Gerda Muller
*Autumn Harvest* by Alvin Tresselt
*Fall Is Here! I Love It!* by Elaine W. Good
*Red Leaf, Yellow Leaf* by Lois Elhert
*Why Do Leaves Change Color?* by Betsy Maestro

★ *Kaethe Lewandowski, Centreville, VA*

# Fall Bookmarks

ART

**Materials**     pressed leaves, ferns, and grasses
watercolor paper
scissors
watercolor paints or crayons
hole punch
thread or yarn

**What to do**    1. Collect and press small fall leaves, ferns, and grasses.
2. Cut watercolor paper into bookmark shapes and give one to each child.
3. Encourage the children to paint or color their bookmarks. Allow to dry.
4. Punch a hole at the top of each bookmark.
5. Invite children to glue arrangements of pressed plants to their bookmarks.
6. Laminate or cover with clear contact paper. Tie yarn or thread at the top.

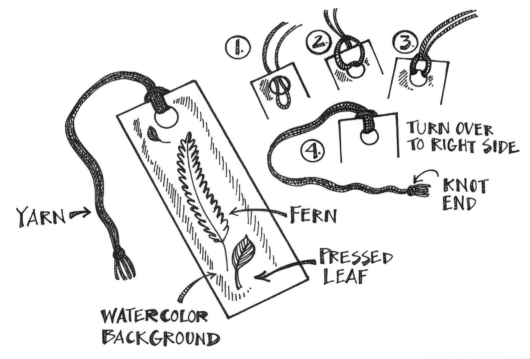

① ② ③

④ TURN OVER TO RIGHT SIDE

KNOT END

YARN →

FERN

PRESSED LEAF

WATERCOLOR BACKGROUND

**More to do**     Make smaller gift tags.

**Realted book**     *Red Leaf, Yellow Leaf* by Lois Ehlert

★ *Linda Atamian, Charlestown, RI*

# "Hand-y" Leaves

ART

**Materials**     red, yellow, and orange drawing or construction paper
crayons
small fall-colored pompoms or sequins

**What to do**     1. Help the children trace their hands on paper (hands open, but fingers together to resemble the shape of a leaf).
2. Encourage the children to color their leaves (hand outlines) with fall colors.
3. Write each child's name on his paper.
4. Let the children cut out their leaf shapes, helping them as needed.
5. The children can decorate their leaves with pompoms and sequins.
6. Put the leaves on a bulletin board.

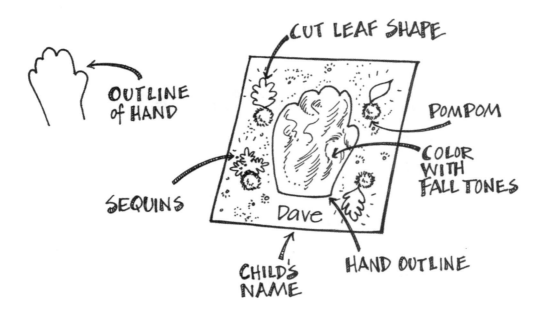

★ *Deborah Hannes Litfin, Forest Hills, NY*

# Fall Leaves

ART

**Materials**
white paper
scissors
red, orange, yellow, brown, and gold tissue paper squares
container of water
paintbrushes

**What to do**
1. Cut out a variety of leaf shapes from white paper.
2. Encourage children to place tissue squares on their paper leaves one at a time and brush with water.
3. Allow to dry.
4. Have the children remove the tissue squares. The leaves will be colored from the tissue paper dye.
5. Display the leaves in the room.

**More to do**
**Art:** Collect and press leaves for art projects.
**Math:** Have a "Biggest and Smallest Leaf" contest. Have the children collect very small and very large leaves for the contest. Back in the classroom, encourage the children to compare the sizes of leaves.
**Outdoors:** Make a pile of leaves and jump in them with the children.

**Related book**
*Red Leaf, Yellow Leaf* by Lois Ehlert

 *Linda Atamian, Charlestown, RI*

# Flashy Fall Leaves

ART

**Materials**
leaf-shaped cookie cutters
12" x 18" paper in fall colors
shallow containers
metallic paints in copper, gold, silver, and bronze
newspapers

**What to do**
1. Ahead of time, cover the tables with newspapers and pour small amounts of metallic paints into shallow containers.
2. Encourage the children to dip leaf-shaped cookie cutters into the paint, pressing on the paper without sliding them around to get a clear leaf shape.
3. Have them repeat with other leaf-shaped cookie cutters and colors of paint.

**More to do**     **More Art:** Let children use the metallic paint at the easel to create more flashy fall paintings.
**Science:** Compare leaves from different plants and trees.

**Related books**     *Red Leaf, Yellow Leaf* by Lois Ehlert
*A Tree Is Nice* by Janice May Udry
*Why Do Leaves Change Color?* by Betsy Maestro

⭐ *Susan Oldham Hill, Lakeland, FL*

# Leaf Mobile

ART

**Materials**     paper bags
colored construction paper
pencils
scissors
yarn
tree branches, about 12" long and 2" thick (one for each child)
hole punch (optional)

**What to do**     1. Take the children for a walk outdoors. Give them paper bags to collect leaves.
2. After the walk, have the children place a leaf on construction paper, trace around it with a pencil, and cut it out.
3. Encourage them to trace and cut out five or six more leaves on different colored construction paper.
4. Use a pencil or hole punch to punch a hole in the top of each paper leaf.
5. Give each child five or six pieces of yarn, each varying in length from 6" to 15" long.
6. Give each child a tree branch. Help the children tie a piece of yarn through each leaf and knot it. Have them tie the other end of the yarn to their tree branch.
7. Cut a piece of yarn about 24" long. Help the children tie it to both ends of the branch.
8. Let them hang their branches on a doorknob or suspend from the ceiling.

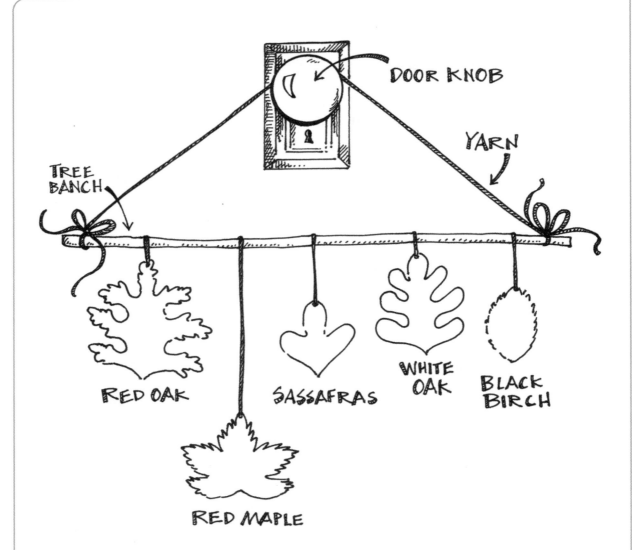

DOOR KNOB

YARN

TREE BANCH

RED OAK      SASSAFRAS      WHITE OAK      BLACK BIRCH

RED MAPLE

**More to do**  **More Art:** Have children make leaf sachets by tracing and cutting out more leaves from construction paper. Pour almond extract into a bowl. Ask the children to dip a paintbrush into the bowl and paint their leaves with the extract. They may prefer to spray their leaves with room fragrance. Invite them to bring their leaves home and place them in a drawer to make their clothes smell nice.

**Related books**  *Autumn Leaves* by Ken Robbins
*How Do You Know It's Fall?* by Allan Fowler
*Leaves* by Kristin Ward
*Red Leaf, Yellow Leaf* by Lois Ehlert
*Why Do Leaves Change Color?* by Betsy Maestro

⭐ *Randi Lynn Mrvos, Lexington, KY*

# Red Leaf, Yellow Leaf

ART

**Materials**
*Red Leaf, Yellow Leaf* by Lois Ehlert
red and yellow 9" x 12" construction paper
Styrofoam trays
X-Acto® knife (adult only)
red and yellow paint
paint smocks
paintbrushes
crayons
glue
newspapers

**What to do**
1. Read the book with the children many times to familiarize them with the story and the illustrations.
2. Ahead of time, glue the 12" side of the red sheets of construction paper to the 12" sides of the yellow sheets so that you have a 12" x 18" of paper (half red, half yellow) for each child. Also ahead of time, use an X-Acto® knife to cut out leaf shapes from the center of Styrofoam trays to create leaf stencils. Use the shapes of oak, maple, elm, and other leaves.
3. Spread newspaper on the tables and help each child put on a paint smock. Give the children the red and yellow papers, positioned so that the yellow portion is on the left.
4. Show them how to place a stencil on the yellow side and paint in the area with red paint to create a red leaf. Repeat on the other side with the yellow paint and a different leaf stencil.

**More to do**
**Field Trip:** Visit a local tree nursery, or invite a nursery employee to bring plants into the classroom.
**Language:** Discuss the illustrations from the book. Compare the collage illustrations by Lois Ehlert with the collage illustrations of Eric Carle.
**Snack:** Enjoy a snack of pumpkin seeds and sunflower seeds.

**Related books**
*A Tree Is Nice* by Janice May Udry
*Why Do Leaves Change Color?* by Betsy Maestro

*Susan Oldham Hill, Lakeland, FL*

# Gorgeous Gourds

ART

**Materials**
gourds of all shapes, colors, and sizes
paint
brushes
construction paper
scissors
glue
glitter, cotton balls, and yarn

**What to do**
1. Put all the supplies in the art area.
2. Introduce the gourds to the children at circle time. Talk about their sizes, colors, and shapes.
3. Ask the children if they think any of the gourds look like something else (such as an animal). Ask them what they could do to the gourds to transform them into something else.
4. Introduce the supplies at the art table and invite the children to decorate their own gourds during free play.
5. Have an adult near by to keep the creative juices flowing. Be sure to encourage and question, not take over the project with your influence.

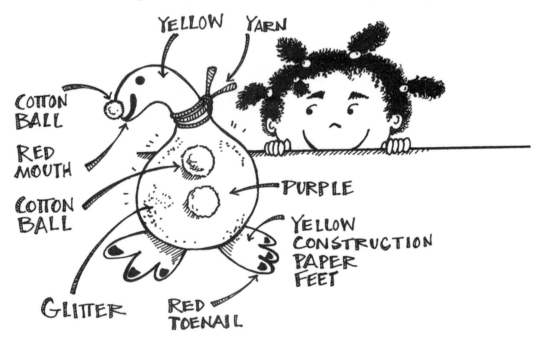

YELLOW    YARN
COTTON BALL
RED MOUTH
COTTON BALL
PURPLE
YELLOW CONSTRUCTION PAPER FEET
GLITTER    RED TOENAIL

**More to do**
Hold an art show for parents using the gorgeous gourd creations.

**Related book**
*How Are You Peeling?* by Saxton Freymann

*Ann Kelly, Johnstown, PA*

# Field Trip to the Pumpkin Patch

FIELD TRIP

**Materials**
camera
chart paper
glue

**What to do**

1. Check the area around your school to see if there is a pumpkin patch for the children to visit. Alternatives are apple orchards or sunflower gardens. In urban areas, visit a market that sells pumpkins.
2. Invite parents to come and help their children pick out pumpkins.
3. Upon arrival, gather the children and talk to them about how pumpkins grow, how long it takes to grow a pumpkin, and how pumpkin crops are irrigated and fertilized.
4. Pumpkin Patch Rule: Children can only pick pumpkins they can carry themselves.
5. Bring a camera and take a picture of each child standing next to his pumpkin. Take group shots as well.
6. Back at school, brainstorm with the entire group about what they saw, felt, and smelled at the pumpkin patch. Write down what the children say on chart paper.
7. Glue the photos of the children and their pumpkins to chart paper.
8. Take everyone's stories and bind them into a book.

**Related book**    *Apples and Pumpkins* by Anne Rockwell

 *Barbara Saul, Eureka, CA*

# Autumn Is...

FINGERPLAYS, SONGS, & POEMS

**Materials**
none

**What to do**

1. Read the following action rhyme and model the motions for the children.

    *Autumn is apples*
    *Fresh-picked from the tree.* ("pick" an apple)
    *Here's one for you,* (hold out hand to offer "apple")
    *And here's one for me.* (indicate self)

*Autumn is a pumpkin*
*With a funny face,* (make a funny face)
*And bright-colored leaves*
*Blow all over the place.* ("chase" leaves by running in a circle)

*Autumn is wind;*
*The air's getting cool.* (hug your arms)
*It's time for hot chocolate* (make an "mmmmm" sound)
*And going to school.* (go to seats and sit down)

2. Repeat the action rhyme as desired so the children can use the motions again.

**MORE TO DO**  **Language:** Make an Autumn Grab Bag by putting autumn items (real or pictures of them) in a bag. Let the children pull out items one at a time. As a group, identify and discuss the items. Item suggestions: apple, squash, small pumpkin, colorful leaf, Canadian goose, turkey, jacket, hay, Indian corn, and seasonal holiday items.

**RELATED BOOK**  *I Know It's Autumn* by Eileen Spinelli

 *Theresa Callahan, Easton, MD*

# SCARECROW, TURN AROUND

FINGERPLAYS, SONGS, & POEMS

**MATERIALS**  none

**WHAT TO DO**  Sing the following song, making the appropriate gestures.

*Scarecrow, scarecrow, turn around.* (turn around)
*Scarecrow, scarecrow, jump up and down.* (jump up and down)
*Scarecrow, scarecrow, arms up high.* (put arms straight up)
*Scarecrow, scarecrow, wink your eye.* (wink your eye)
*Scarecrow, scarecrow, bend your knees.* (bend your knees)
*Scarecrow, scarecrow, flop in the breeze.* (flop loosely)
*Scarecrow, scarecrow, climb into bed.* (climb as if into bed)
*Scarecrow, scarecrow, rest your head.* (rest head on hands)

 *Kathy Kalmar, Macomb, MI*

# I'm a Little Pumpkin

## FINGERPLAYS, SONGS, & POEMS

**Materials**      none

**What to do**     1. Sing the following song to the tune of "I'm a Little Teapot."

*I'm a little pumpkin*
*Orange and round.*
*Sometime I smile,*
*Sometime I frown.*
*When you lift my top up*
*You will see*
*All the seeds inside of me.*

2. Sing the song again, substituting "jack-o-lantern" for pumpkin.

**More to do**     **Art:** Make a collage with dried pumpkin seeds.
**Snack:** Open a pumpkin, remove the seeds, and make roasted pumpkin seeds.

⭐ *Kathy Kalmar, Macomb, MI*

# Changing Colors

## FINGERPLAYS, SONGS, & POEMS

**Materials**      none

**What to do**     Sing the following song to the tune of "London Bridge Is Falling Down":

*Leaves are changing colors now,*
*Colors now,*
*Colors now,*
*Leaves are changing colors now,*
*Red, yellow,*
*Orange and brown.*

⭐ *Kristi Larson, Spirit Lake, IA*

# Changing Leaves

FINGERPLAYS, SONGS, & POEMS

**Materials**    red, yellow, orange, and brown paper
                 scissors

**What to do**   1. Cut the paper into large leaf shapes, one for each child.
                 2. Have the children hold up their leaves when their color is sung. This should go fairly fast, like a wave at a sporting event.
                 3. Sing the following song to the tune of "The Wheels on the Bus":

*The leaves change to orange,*
*Red, yellow, and brown,*
*Red, yellow, and brown,*
*Red, yellow, and brown,*
*The leaves change to orange,*
*Red, yellow, and brown,*
*And soon will all fall down.*

4. At the end, everyone falls to the ground.

★ *Kristi Larson, Spirit Lake, IA*

# Acorn Beanbag

GAMES

**Materials**    cardboard
                 scissors
                 marker
                 brown felt
                 needle and thread
                 safety pins
                 rice or beans

**What to do**   1. Cut cardboard into an acorn shape. Trace around the acorn shape onto brown felt.
                 2. Cut out two acorn shapes for each child.
                 3. Safety pin the two pieces together temporarily. Help the children sew the two pieces together, leaving an opening on one side.
                 4. Invite the children to stuff their beanbags with rice or beans and sew shut.

5. Cut out a cardboard tree and leave an opening in the trunk. Encourage the children to toss their beanbags into the hole ("squirrel's nest").

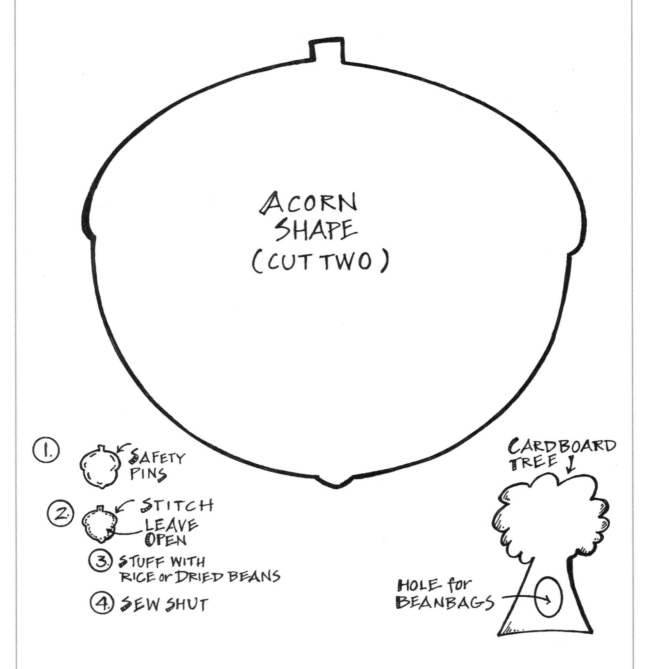

ACORN
SHAPE
(CUT TWO)

1. SAFETY PINS
2. STITCH LEAVE OPEN
3. STUFF WITH RICE or DRIED BEANS
4. SEW SHUT

CARDBOARD TREE ↓

HOLE for BEANBAGS

**More to do**    **Outdoors:** Gather real acorns and feed them to the squirrels in the winter.
**Science:** Plant a few acorns in small containers.

**Related book**    *The Oak* by Andrienne Soutter-Perrot

★ *Linda Atamian, Charlestown, RI*

# Fall Lotto Game

GAMES

**Materials**
oak tag
marker
ruler
pictures of items that represent fall
glue
contact paper or laminate

**What to do**

1. Divide a piece of oak tag into nine equal squares.
2. Glue fall-related pictures in each square of the oak tag in random order. Make a variety of these cards, making sure to glue the pictures randomly on each card.
3. Cover the oak tag with contact paper or laminate.
4. Make a duplicate set of pictures to use as game cards. Cut oak tag into equal squares and glue one picture to each card.
5. Cover with contact paper.
6. Put the cards face down and draw the top card. The children who have that item on their cards can mark it.
7. Play according to Bingo rules or have them cover the whole card.

 *Phyllis Esch, Export, PA*

# Scarecrow Says

GAMES

**Materials**
picture of a scarecrow
scarecrow costume (hat, jeans or overalls, straw or hay) (optional)

**What to do**

1. If desired, dress in scarecrow clothes. Stuff straw or hay into shirt sleeves and pant legs.
2. Show the children the picture of the scarecrow. Discuss how and why a scarecrow scares away crows.
3. Tell the children that they are going to pretend to be scarecrows. Ask them to follow your directions.
4. Play Scarecrow Says like Simon Says. For example:
   - Scarecrow says, "Wiggle your nose."
   - Scarecrow says, "Stomp your floppy feet."
   - Scarecrow says, "Wave your floppy arms."

- Scarecrow says, "Make a scary face."
- Scarecrow says, "Say, 'Shoo!'"

**MORE TO DO**    **Sensory:** Put a pile of straw or hay into a basket for sensory exploration.

**RELATED books**    *The Little Scarecrow Boy* by Margaret Wise Brown
*Scarecrow* by Cynthia Rylant
*The Scarecrow's Hat* by Ken Brown

★ *Cassandra Reigel Whetstone, San Jose, CA*

# Things That Go Together
## GROUP OR CIRCLE TIME

**MATERIALS**    pictures of items that go together
computer and printer
computer-generated pumpkin
tagboard
paper cutter
scissors
glue stick
laminate or contact paper
pocket chart

**WHAT TO DO**    1. Collect colored pictures of nouns that go together: raindrops and umbrella, witch and witch's hat, car and child safety seat, horse and saddle, stars and moon, table and chair, cup and saucer, right mitten and left mitten, money and cash register, school bus and school, paper and pencil, pumpkin and jack-o-lantern, and so on.
2. Print out the desired number of computer-generated pumpkins onto tagboard.
3. Flip the image so that the stem of the pumpkin points in opposite directions.
4. Print out the same number as before onto tagboard.
5. Cut both sets of pumpkins into cards of the desired size using a paper cutter.
6. Glue one picture from the set of go-together pictures onto the first set of pumpkins and the other picture from the set onto the second set of pumpkins. Laminate the cards for durability.

7. At circle time, pass out all the pumpkins with stems going one direction.
8. Place the pumpkins with stems going the other direction in the pocket chart, leaving room between them.
9. Encourage each child, in turn, to place his pumpkin next to the correct pumpkin to make pairs of things that go together. If a pocket chart is not available, this activity can be done on a learning mat on the floor or put in a center for table use.

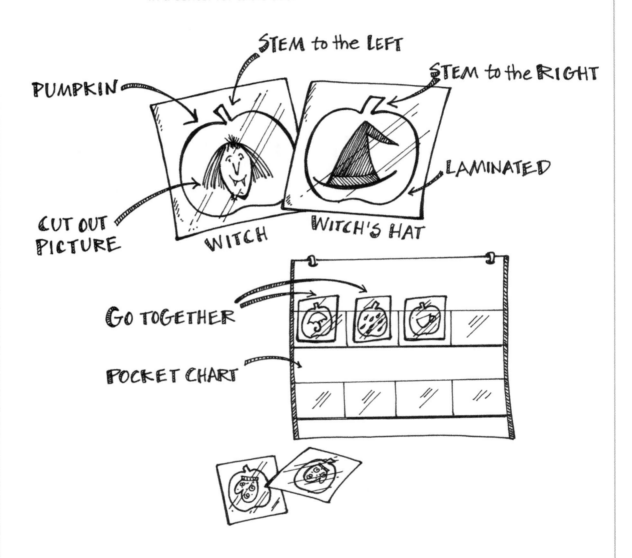

⭐ *Jackie Wright, Enid, OK*

# THE SCARECROW SEES...
# (Rebus)

LANGUAGE AND LITERACY

**MATERIALS**    picture of a scarecrow's face
marker
sentence strips
copy machine
paper cutter
crayons
construction paper
laminate
scissors
binding machine, optional

**WHAT TO DO**

1. Make a sentence strip with these words: "The scarecrow sees a _____." Use a picture of a scarecrow's face to replace the word "scarecrow."
2. Make copies of the rebus sentence and cut the sentence strips to 3 ⅛" x 11."
3. Show the children a sentence strip with the picture of a scarecrow to color.
4. Point to each word on the sentence strip as the sentence is repeated by the whole group.
5. Give each child a sentence strip and encourage him to color the scarecrow and make a drawing to complete the sentence.
6. If the child is able to label his drawing by himself, allow him to do so. If he needs assistance, record his response for him under his drawing.
7. Make covers from construction paper approximately 3 ⅛" x 11". Print the title, "The (picture of a scarecrow) Sees" on the front.
8. Laminate the covers for durability, and cut out.
9. Assemble the completed pages and bind them between the covers into a class book. Put the finished book into your reading area for all to enjoy.

**RELATED book**    *Barn Dance!* by Bill Martin, Jr.

⭐ *Jackie Wright, Enid, OK*

# Exploring Pumpkins

MATH

**MATERIALS**
large paper
large pumpkin
large knife (adult use)
pumpkin carving kit (available at most grocery stores)
two cookie sheets
salt
cooking oil

**WHAT TO DO**

1. The children will see a lot of pumpkins in the fall. Ask them what they know about pumpkins. Make a Knowledge Web to record their responses. Draw a circle in the center of a large sheet of paper. Draw a pumpkin in the circle and print the word "pumpkin" below it. Record their responses in smaller circles around the large circle. Draw lines from their response circles to the center circle to create a "web." Post the web in a prominent spot in the room.

2. Show the children a large pumpkin. Invite them to feel its surface and describe how it feels. Write down their responses. Draw a pumpkin in the middle of a piece of poster board. Print the children's descriptions around the drawing.

3. Ask them to predict how much the pumpkin weighs. Record their responses. Weigh the pumpkin and the children. Graph the results on poster board ("Do You Weigh More Or Less Than a Pumpkin?"). Write the pumpkin's weight under the label. Make two columns: More and Less. As you weigh each child, put his weight and name in the appropriate column. If your pumpkin is large enough, it may weigh more than some children in the class.

4. Ask the children to predict what is inside the pumpkin. Ask leading questions: "What do you think the pumpkin looks like inside?" "Will it be wet or dry?" Record their responses with a mini-recorder.

5. Cut off the top of the pumpkin. **Safety Note:** This should be done by an adult. Do not leave the knife where children can reach it.

6. Encourage the children to look at and touch the inside of the pumpkin. Ask them to describe how it looks, feels, and smells. Record their responses.

7. Make a graph that shows the difference between what the children thought would be inside the pumpkin and what they actually observed. Label the top of a large piece of poster board: "Exploring Pumpkins." Make three columns and one row for each child. On the top of the first column, print "This child ..." Label the second column: "thought the insides of the pumpkin would be ..." Label the third column: "and the insides were ..."

8. Print the children's names in the first column. Print something the children said BEFORE seeing the insides of the pumpkin in the second column and something the children said AFTER seeing the insides of the pumpkin in the third column.
9. Let the children use a scoop to scoop out the pumpkin's pulp.
10. As some children are scooping, have others sort the seeds from the stringy pumpkin pulp. Encourage the children to count the seeds as they sort them. Place the seeds in a bowl of water.
11. Wash the seeds to remove the pulp. In a bowl, toss the seeds with oil and salt to taste and spread them on an ungreased baking sheet. Bake the seeds at 250°, stirring occasionally, for 1 hour to 1 ½ hours or until they are golden and crisp. Let cool and enjoy this seasonal treat.
12. If you wish, use the tools contained in the pumpkin carving kit to carve a happy pumpkin face.

**More to do**   **Snack:** Make a pumpkin pie with the children using the following recipe.
Ingredients
Pie crust, bottom only
2 cups pumpkin pulp (mashed with a fork)
¾ cup apple butter or plum butter
¾ cup sugar
1 teaspoon cinnamon
½ teaspoon ginger
½ teaspoon ground nutmeg
¼ teaspoon ground allspice
3 eggs
1 cup half-&-half

Pre-heat the oven to 375°.
Mix pumpkin, apple or plum butter, and all the dry ingredients in a bowl.
Mix the eggs and half-&-half in another bowl, then add to the first.
Pour the filling into the crust. Bake for about an hour.

**Rrelated books**   *Albert's Halloween: The Case of the Stolen Pumpkins* by Leslie Tryon
*Arthur's Halloween* by Marc Brown
*Arthur's Halloween Costume* by Lillian Hoban
*By the Light of the Halloween Moon* by Caroline Stutson
*Halloween Pie* by Kevin O'Malley and Michael O'Tunnell

⭐ *Virginia Jean Herrod, Columbia, SC*

# Pumpkin Math

**Materials**
pumpkin
plastic tablecloth
scale
white board and marker
string
scissors
sharp kitchen knife (adult only)
pens

**What to do**

1. Spread a plastic tablecloth on the floor with the pumpkin in the middle, and have the children sit around it.
2. Weigh the children and tell them how much they weigh. Encourage them to estimate how much the pumpkin will weigh. Write their estimations on the white board.
3. Weigh the pumpkin and refer back to the children's weight as a comparison.
4. Cut a piece of string the height of each child. Encourage the children to put their strings around the of the pumpkin. See whose string is closest to the pumpkin's size.
5. Ask the children what is inside the pumpkin. Have them estimate how many seeds are inside. Write down the estimations.
6. Cut off the top of the pumpkin (adult only). Let volunteers reach in and bring out the seeds. Use descriptive words such as *slimy* and *soft* to describe the touch of the pumpkin's insides. **Note:** Let children know that it is okay if they do not want to reach in and touch the seeds.
7. When the seeds are out, wash them off. Spread them out to dry.
8. When the seeds are dry, count them by using small paper cups. Put ten seeds into each cup to count by tens. Refer back to the children's estimates. See who was closest.

**More to do**    **Snack:** Bake the pumpkin seeds. Add salt and eat them as a snack.

*Barbara Saul, Eureka, CA*

# Pumpkin Weigh-In

MATH

**Materials**
pumpkin-shaped objects or decorations
small, real pumpkin
balance scale
candy corn (optional)

**What to do**
1. Gather an assortment of pumpkin-shaped objects or decorations in a variety of materials, such as candle, wood, plastic, rubber, resin, cloth, and so on.
2. Introduce the balance scale. Use the real pumpkin and the pumpkin-shaped items in different combinations to balance each other. It will surprise children that a big pumpkin might weigh less than a small one. Explain that size and weight don't always agree.
3. If desired, add pieces of candy corn, one at a time, to the lighter side of the scale to create balance. Encourage children to guess how much they need to add.

**More to do**
**More Math:** Line up children by height and then by age. Is the tallest child the oldest child? Probably not. Explain why to the children.
**Language:** Expand their vocabulary. Explain that the word *biggest* is not as accurate as *oldest, tallest, heaviest*, and so on.

**Related books**
*The Biggest Pumpkin Ever* by Steven Kroll
*It's Pumpkin Time!* by Zoe Hall
*The Little Pumpkin Book* by Katharine Ross
*The Pumpkin Patch* by Elizabeth King

⭐ *Sandra Gratias, Dublin, PA*

# Pumpkin Patch

SENSORY

**Materials**
pumpkin
paint and brushes
knife (adult only)
large spoon
oven
chart paper

**What to do**

1. During a unit study on pumpkins, organize a field trip to a local pumpkin patch. Many pumpkin patches will give hay rides as a part of your visit. You may choose to collect a small amount of money from the children for the field trip so that they can pick out their own personal pumpkins to take home.

2. While at the pumpkin patch, choose a larger "class pumpkin" to bring back to your classroom. Purchase an additional pumpkin to use for seeds.

3. Let the children decorate the class pumpkin.

4. As a class, scoop out the seeds from inside the second pumpkin. Let the children take turns getting handfuls of seeds from inside the pumpkin.

5. As the children are removing the seeds, review the five senses. Ask questions. "What do you smell?" "What do the seeds look like?" "What do the seeds feel like?"

6. Rinse off the seeds.

7. If possible, roast some of the seeds in an oven. If you do not have an oven to use, bring home some of the seeds, roast them, and bring them back the next day. Have the children taste the seeds.

8. Make a prediction chart with the children:
   - The seeds taste like _____.
   - The seeds look like _____.
   - The seeds sound like _____.
   - The seeds smell like _____.
   - The seeds feel like _____.

9. Rinse the rest of the seeds (not roasted). Have the children count them and sort them according to size.

**More to do**

**Books:** Ask the children individually to tell you how they think a pumpkin pie is made. Ask them for the ingredients and the ingredient amounts. (Accept any responses. This is just for fun.) Construct their recipe guesses into a "cookbook" and let each child decorate his recipe page. Give to parents for Thanksgiving.

**Snack:** Make pumpkin pie (or another pumpkin recipe). Enjoy together as a class.

**Related books**

*Apples and Pumpkins* by Anne Rockwell
*The Biggest Pumpkin* by Steven Kroll
*Pumpkin Fair* by Eve Bunting
*Pumpkin, Pumpkin* by Jeanne Titherington

⭐ *Lori Dunlap, Amarillo, TX*

# Pumpkin Feeders

SCIENCE

**Materials**      newspaper or plastic tablecloth
small pumpkins
knife (adult only)
spoons
bowl
twine
birdseed

**What to do**
1. Cover the science table with newspaper or a plastic tablecloth.
2. Cut the pumpkins in half (adult only) and put them on the table with the spoons. Have the children scoop out the contents and separate the seeds.
3. Place the seeds in a bowl and put aside.
4. Make a hanger for the pumpkin halves using the twine.
5. Have the children fill the halves with birdseed and hang outside the classroom window or somewhere it can be seen.
6. Wash and bake the seeds for snack.

**More to do**    **Math:** Encourage the children to count the slippery seeds.

**Related book**    *Birds of North America: A Guide to Field Identification* by Chandler Robbins

 *Ann Kelly, Johnstown, PA*

# Helicopters

SCIENCE

**Materials**      variety of tree seeds that spin
thin card stock (5 ½" x 1 ¼")
paper clips

**What to do**
1. Show the children seeds from maple, oak, and sycamore trees. Drop the seeds and watch them spin like a helicopter.
2. Pre-cut a 2 ½" slit in the top center of each 5 ½" x 1 ¼" piece of card stock.
3. Give each child two card stock rectangles to make his own helicopter or gyrocopter.
4. Show the children how to fold the two cut pieces of card stock at right angles to the length, one going backwards and one going forwards (see the illustration on the next page).

5. Help them attach a paper clip pointing straight up in the center of the bottom of the card.

6. When these helicopters are dropped from a height, they will spin to the ground.

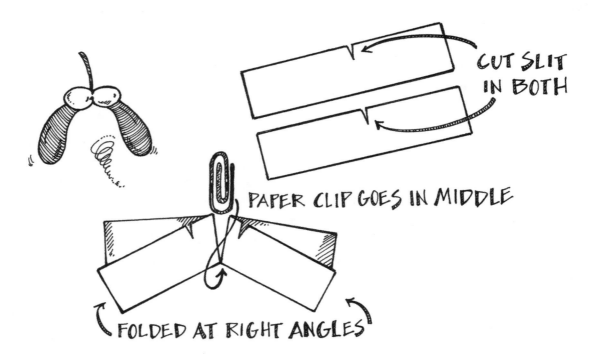

CUT SLIT IN BOTH

PAPER CLIP GOES IN MIDDLE

FOLDED AT RIGHT ANGLES

**MORE TO DO**     Use this activity as part of a nature or aircraft theme.
**More Science:** Talk about seeds and the different ways they travel from place to place and are propagated.
**Language:** Talk about different meanings of the word "spin."
**Music and Movement:** Have the children spin around to appropriate music.

**RELATED books**     *The Dandelion Seed* by Joseph P. Anthony
*Harry's Helicopter* by Joan Anderson
*Helicopter* by Chris Oxlade
*Rocket Science: 50 Flying, Floating, Flipping, Spinning Gadgets Kids Create Themselves* by Jim Wiese
*The Seed and the Giant Saguaro* by Jennifer Ward
*Tell Me, Tree: All About Trees for Kids* by Gail Gibbons
*Ten Seeds* by Ruth Brown

 *Anne Adeney, Plymouth, United Kingdom*

# NUTS!

SCIENCE

**Materials**   various nuts
nut crackers

**What to do**
1. Talk about what animals do to prepare for the winter. Explain that animals such as squirrels collect acorns in the fall to eat in the winter.
2. Check your class list for food allergies, making sure that no one is allergic to nuts before you do this activity. **Safety Note:** If any of the children is allergic to nuts, it is safest NOT to do this project. Some children can have an allergic reaction simply from inhaling the smell of nuts.
3. Have a variety of nuts for the children to crack open. Let them taste the nuts, if appropriate.
4. Tell the children that nuts grow on trees so peanuts, which grow underground, are not really nuts! Peanuts are *legumes*.

**More to do**
**Art:** Use nut shells to make a collage.
**Games:** Play "What's Missing?" Place four to eight nuts (depending on the age of the children, and the variety of nuts you have) on a tray. Use a handkerchief to cover the nuts and remove one. Ask the children to guess which nut is missing.
**Sensory:** Place nuts and nutcrackers in the sensory table for exploration.

**Related book**   *Nuts to You!* by Lois Ehlert

 *Linda Ford, Sacramento, CA*

# BE A PUMPKIN COOK

SNACK AND COOKING

**Materials**   whole pumpkin
knife (adult only)
9" x 12" baking pan
water
aluminum foil
blender or food processor
butter
ingredients for pumpkin muffins or bread
muffin tin or loaf pan
measuring cups and spoons
mixing spoon and bowl

**WHAT TO DO**

1. Wash and cut open the pumpkin. Encourage children to smell it.
2. Remove the seeds. Using your hands, remove and save the pulp.
3. Encourage the children to describe the textures of the pumpkin.
4. Cut off thin slices of pumpkin flesh and have the children taste it.
5. Place the pumpkin, cut side down, in the baking pan. Add ½ cup of water.
6. Cover with foil and bake at 350° for one hour. Let cool.
7. Remove the foil and encourage the children to observe the changes in the pumpkin. The pumpkin is darker and soft because heat changes the consistency of things.
8. Scoop out some of the soft pumpkin pulp. Puree it in a blender or food processor. Add some of the liquid from the baking pan, if needed.
9. Use the pureed pumpkin in any recipe that calls for canned pumpkin. Let the children measure, pour, and mix.
10. Eat the muffins. Compare the appearance of the batter to the finished product. Explain again how heat changes things.

**MORE TO DO**

**More Snack:** Melt butter and coat the pumpkin seeds. Bake at 250 degrees until golden brown. Salt and eat.

**Science:** Let uncooked seeds dry and then plant one of the seeds, encouraging the children to watch the growing process occur over time.

**RELATED books**

*Patty's Pumpkin Patch* by Teri Sloat
*Pumpkin, Pumpkin* by Jeanne Titherington
*Too Many Pumpkins* by Linda White

⭐ *Sandra Gratias, Dublin, PA*

# Virtual Zoo

SCIENCE

**Materials**
bulletin board
construction paper
markers
scissors
stapler
glue

**What to do**
- October is International Zoo Month.
1. Draw empty cages and paddocks on construction paper. Cut out each cage and staple in position on the bulletin board. You are creating an empty zoo.
2. Talk to the children about how they would create their very own zoo. What animals will live at the zoo? What will they eat and drink? What will the enclosures need to be furnished with?
3. Have each child pick an animal to live at their zoo. Invite them to draw their chosen animals on construction paper and cut them out.
4. Staple each animal into one of the enclosures. Make sure the animals have food and water.
5. Ask them what else a zoo would need to have, for example, an admission gate, a snack shop, souvenir store, picnic area, and a place for animal shows. Add those to the display.
6. For fun and problem-solving experience, change the display to present different problems. Perhaps an animal escapes or an animal becomes sick. Turn an animal upside down in its cage and ask the children what they should do.

EMPTY CAGE

ANIMAL FALLS ON ITS BACK

STRAW to PUT IN CAGE

ELEPHANT

PEANUTS

WATER

⭐ *Amelia Griffin, Ontario, Canada*

# MAKE A COMPUTER

ART

**MATERIALS**
aluminum foil
scissors
black paper
glue
alphabet stickers
yarn
tape

**WHAT TO DO**

- October is Computer Learning Month.
1. Cut foil into 5" x 7" pieces, one for each child. Give each child a piece of black paper.
2. Encourage the children to glue the foil onto a piece of black paper. (This will represent the computer screen.)
3. Help them stick letter stickers on the paper to represent a keyboard.
4. Cut yarn into 4" to 6" pieces. Have the children tape a piece of yarn to the back of their papers.
5. Encourage the children to cut out a "mouse" from another piece of paper and tape it to the other end of the yarn.

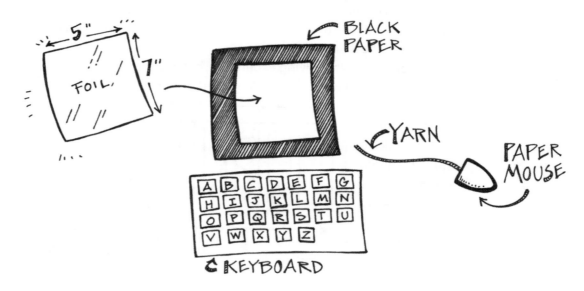

*Kristi Larson, Spirit Lake, IA*

# Boom Chicka Clock

MATH

**Materials**

paper plates
marker
paper
scissors
*Boom Chicka Rock* by John Archambault
real clock
paper fasteners
circle stickers

**What to do**

- October is National Clock Month.

1. To prepare for this activity, make paper clocks by writing clock numbers on paper plates (one for each child). Cut out the hands of a clock (minute and hour) from paper (one set for each child). Write the numbers 1 through 12 on circle stickers (one set for each child).

2. Read the story *Boom Chicka Rock* to the children. Show the children an analog clock with numbers and the hour and minute hands. Encourage them to count as you point to each number. Show the children how to tell time by the hour.

3. Invite the children to make their own clocks.

4. Help each child attach the clock hands in the middle of his paper plate clock with paper fasteners.

5. Ask the children to put a numbered circle sticker on top of the same number on the plate.

6. Encourage the children to make their number circles into mice by putting a small dot on the top of each circle (nose) and a small line (tail) at the bottom of the circle.

CIRCLE STICKER

EARS
NOSE
TAIL

BRAD

PAPER PLATE

| | |
|---|---|
| **MORE TO DO** | **Language:** Read the book again and invite the children to say "Boom Chicka Rock" along with the story.<br>**Movement:** Put the hour hand of the play clock on different numbers and invite the children to jump that many times. |
| **RELATED books** | *Hickory, Dickory Dock* by Heather Collins<br>*Hickory, Dickory Dock* by Patricia Sechi Johnson |

★ *Sue Fleischmann, Sussex, WI*

# My Dinosaur Is Big
FINGERPLAYS, SONGS, & POEMS

| | |
|---|---|
| **MATERIALS** | none |
| **WHAT TO DO** | • October is International Dinosaur Month.<br>Sing the following song to the tune of "Happy Birthday."<br><br>*My dinosaur is big, My dinosaur is green,*<br>*Isn't my dinosaur*<br>*The biggest thing you've ever seen?* |
| **MORE TO DO** | Repeat the song, substituting *Tyrannosaurus Rex, Pterodactyl,* and other dinosaur names. |

★ *Kathy Kalmar. Macomb, MI*

# Dinosaur Turn Around
FINGERPLAYS, SONGS, & POEMS

| | |
|---|---|
| **MATERIALS** | none |
| **WHAT TO DO** | • October is International Dinosaur Month.<br>Sing the following song, making the appropriate corresponding gestures.<br><br>*Dinosaur, dinosaur, turn around.* (turn around)<br>*Dinosaur, dinosaur, sit right down.* (sit down)<br>*Dinosaur, dinosaur, stand up tall.* (stand and stretch arms over head)<br>*Dinosaur, dinosaur, don't you fall!* (shake head no)<br>*Dinosaur, dinosaur, catch a fish.* (pretend to catch fish) |

*Dinosaur, dinosaur, make a wish.* (act like you're thinking)
*Dinosaur, dinosaur, climb into bed.* (climb as if into bed)
*Dinosaur, dinosaur, rest your head.* (rest head on hands)
*Dinosaur, dinosaur, turn out the light.* (flip switch)
*Dinosaur, dinosaur, say, " Good night."* (say, "good night")

⭐ *Kathy Kalmar, Macomb, MI*

# 1, 2, 3

## FINGERPLAYS, SONGS, & POEMS

**MATERIALS**   none

**WHAT TO DO**

- October is International Dinosaur Month.
1. Recite the following rhyme and make the correct corresponding gestures.

*1, 2, 3,* (raise three fingers)
*There's a stegosaurus on my knee.* (tap knee)
*Shoo it away,* (make shooing motion)
*Shoo it away,* (make shooing motion) *Away from me!* (point to self)

2. Repeat the fingerplay and substitute other dinosaurs, such as Tyrannosaurus rex or pterodactyl. Make each child's name into a dinosaur name (for example, Juan-o-saurus).

**MORE TO DO**   **Art:** Provide large grocery bags, scissors, glue, and construction paper. Encourage the children to make dinosaur costumes.

⭐ *Kathy Kalmar, Macomb, MI*

# The Dinosaurs in the Dell

## MUSIC AND MOVEMENT

**Materials**   none

**What to do**
- October is International Dinosaur Month.
1. After a few days of learning about dinosaurs, play this fun action game. Tell the children they are going to play this game like "The Farmer in the Dell" but instead of being the farmer, the wife, and so on, they will all pretend to be dinosaurs.
2. Have the children form a large circle while holding hands.
3. Choose a child to be the first dinosaur and have him stand in the middle of the circle. Ask the child to state what dinosaur he would like to be.
4. The rest of the children walk around in a circle around the child while singing (use the dinosaur name the child chooses):

*The Stegosaurus in the dell,*
*The Stegosaurus in the dell,*
*Hi-ho the derry-oh,*
*The Stegosaurus in the dell.*

5. The "Stegosaurus" chooses a friend to join him in the middle of circle while the rest sing:

*The Stegosaurus finds a friend,*
*The Stegosaurus finds a friend,*
*Hi-ho the derry-oh,*
*The Stegosaurus finds a friend.*

6. The friend states what dinosaur she would like to be. The children sing (use the dinosaur name the child chooses):

*The Brachiosaurus in the dell,*
*The Brachiosaurus in the dell,*
*Hi-ho the derry-oh,*
*The Brachiosaurus in the dell.*

7. Repeat until all the children have had a turn and you are the only one left to circle the others as everyone sings. For the last verse, sing:

*The dinosaurs in the dell,*
*The dinosaurs in the dell,*
*Hi-ho the derry-oh,*
*The dinosaurs in the dell.*

**More to do**    **Art:** Using paper plates, have the children design and make dinosaur masks they can wear while they play. Provide markers, crayons, and other art supplies for children to create cool, funny, or scary masks. Cut eye holes for the children and attach a length of narrow elastic to the masks. For those who don't like wearing a masks, create a pendant in the same manner and hang it on the child's neck with heavy yarn.

**Related books**    *Big Old Bones: A Dinosaur Tale* by Carol Carrick
*Bones, Bones, Dinosaur Bones* by Byron Barton
*Danny and the Dinosaur* by Syd Hoff
*Dinosaur!* by Peter Sis
*Dinosaur Bob* by William Joyce
*Dinosaurs, Dinosaurs* by Byron Barton
*How I Captured a Dinosaur* by Henry Schwartz
*How Do Dinosaurs Say Goodnight?* by Mark Teague
*If the Dinosaurs Came Back* by Bernard Most
*The Most Amazing Dinosaur* by James Stevenson
*Patrick's Dinosaurs* by Carol Carrick

 *Virginia Jean Herrod, Columbia, SC*

# Germ Play

DRAMATIC PLAY

**Materials**    cot
toy medical kits
mini flashlights
gauze wraps
notepads for "prescriptions"
slings
splints or large craft sticks
vinyl gloves (use non-latex only)
plastic test tubes and cups

**What to do**
- October is Child Health Month and Family Health Month.
1. Talk to the children about germs and how they make people sick. Ask if they have ever been to a doctor's office or hospital. Talk about the things they do when they are sick (go to the doctor, stay in bed, eat chicken soup, and so on).
2. Put the materials into the dramatic play center and invite the children to pretend they are doctors, nurses, other medical experts, and patients.

**More to do**
Set up an area to make get well cards using paper, markers, glue, and stickers.

★ *Kristi Larson, Spirit Lake, IA*

# Germs and Our Bodies

GROUP TIME

**Materials**
spray bottle filled with water on mist setting

**What to do**
- October is Child Health Month and Family Health Month.
1. At group or circle time, talk about how germs are spread.
2. Pretend to cough or sneeze and spray mist in that direction.
3. As the children feel the mist fall on them, explain that this is also how germs work.
4. Spray some of the water into your hand to demonstrate how coughing or sneezing into one's hand spreads germs.

★ *Kristi Larson, Spirit Lake, IA*

# SPRAY OUT THE FIRE
# PICTURES

ART

**MATERIALS**

paper
red, yellow, and orange washable markers
spray bottles filled with water

**WHAT TO DO**

- Fire Safety Week is the week in which October 9th occurs.
1. Encourage the children to color with the red, yellow, and orange markers, to represent fire.
2. Invite the children to spray their drawings with the water to practice "putting out the flames."

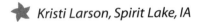 *Kristi Larson, Spirit Lake, IA*

# FIRE EXTINGUISHER
# DEMONSTRATION

FIELD TRIP

**MATERIALS**

**WHAT TO DO**

- Fire Safety Week is the week in which October 9th occurs.
Visit a fire department or invite someone from the fire department to come to your class to demonstrate putting out fires with extinguishers.

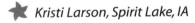 *Kristi Larson, Spirit Lake, IA*

# Stop, Drop, and Roll

FINGERPLAYS, SONGS, AND POEMS

**MATERIALS**

**WHAT TO DO**

- Fire Safety Week is the week in which October 9th occurs.
Sing the following song to the tune of "The Farmer in the Dell":

*Stop, drop, and roll,*
*Stop, drop, and roll,*
*If fire's around, get to the ground,*
*And stop, drop, and roll!*

⭐ *Kristi Larson, Spirit Lake, IA*

# If I Could Be a Firefighter
## FINGERPLAYS, SONGS, AND POEMS

**MATERIALS**    none

**WHAT TO DO**   • Fire Safety Week is the week in which October 9th occurs.
Sing the following song to the tune of "Have You Ever Seen a Lassie?"

| | |
|---|---|
| *If I could be a firefighter,* | *I'd race there with a truck,* |
| *A firefighter, a firefighter.* | *Save people who are stuck,* |
| *If I could be a firefighter* | *If I could be a firefighter,* |
| *I'd put fires out.* | *I'd put fires out!* |

⭐ *Kristi Larson, Spirit Lake, IA*

# Five Little Firefighters
## FINGERPLAYS, SONGS, AND POEMS

**MATERIALS**    none

**WHAT TO DO**   • The week in which October 9th occurs is Fire Safety week.
Do the following fingerplay with the children.

**Five Little Firefighters**
*Five little firefighters standing in a row* (hold hand up)
*1, 2, 3, 4, 5, they go.* (raise finger as you count)
*Hop on the engine with a shout,* (make fingers hop)
*Quick as a wink* (wink)
*The fire is out!* (Make a pretend hose, clap)

⭐ *Kathy Kalmar, Macomb, MI*

# Everybody Needs a Rock

ART

**Materials**

*Everybody Needs a Rock* by Byrd Baylor
variety of rocks
magnifying glasses
permanent markers
paint
small paintbrushes and Q-tips
spray shellac
white or craft glue
wiggle eyes

**What to do**

● Earth Science Week is the second week of October.
1. Read *Everybody Needs a Rock* to the children. Point out that the illustrations by Peter Parnell have a Native American influence.
2. Bring in your own rocks, or invite children to bring a rock from home. If there is an area with rocks near your school, take the children outside to collect some.
3. Examine the rocks with the children. Encourage them to use magnifying glasses. Touch them and talk about their textures. "Are they rough or smooth?"
4. If desired, put rocks in a tub of water to bring out the colors of the rocks.
5. Let each child choose a rock to decorate.
6. Ask them to find the flatter side of their rocks. The flat side will be the bottom or base of their new rock "friend." Put the child's name on this bottom area.
7. Invite the children to paint and draw on their rocks.
8. When the children are not present, take the dry, painted rocks outside. Place them on newspaper and spray with shellac. This prevents the paint from washing off or rubbing off on the children. (If you do not want to use shellac, have the children paint with acrylic craft paint rather than tempera paint. But keep in mind that this paint may stain clothing.)
9. Let the children glue on wiggle eyes. Tell them their rock friends may have more than two eyes, if they desire! The children may want to name their rocks.

**More to do**

**Books:** Have other books about rocks available for children to look at.
**Literacy:** Encourage the children to draw pictures of the rocks and dictate stories about them.

CHILD'S NAME ON BOTTOM
Pete
WIGGLE EYES
PAINTED DESIGN

★ *Sandie Nagel, White Lake, MI*

# Dirt Day

SCIENCE

**Materials**

plastic zipper-closure bags
dirt
sifters
trays
spoons
brushes
tweezers
magnifying glasses

**What to do**

- Earth Science Week is the second week of October.
1. Send a note home to parents asking that on a particular day their children bring baggies of dirt to class. Include a plastic bag for their convenience.
2. When the children have brought in their dirt, put it in a tray.
3. Encourage the children to use magnifying glasses to look at the soil more closely. Provide tweezers, brushes, sifters, and colanders for them to further explore the dirt.
4. Make a list of the objects they find in the dirt (grass clippings, moss, worms, rocks, leaves, sticks, and so on).
5. Ask them to compare the various objects found in the dirt. Explain how these objects got in the dirt.
6. Display any interesting objects found in the dirt.
7. Have each child leave with a bag of dirt to return it to the place from which it was taken.

**Related book**

*The Diggers* by Margaret Wise Brown

 *Ann Scalley, Orleans, MA*

# Rock Collecting

SCIENCE

**Materials**
paper bags
egg cartons

**What to do**
- Earth Science Week is the second week of October.
1. Plan a trip to a park for an outdoor walk during Earth Science Week.
2. Explain to the children that they will be looking for rocks.
3. Provide paper bags for collecting rocks.
4. While on the walk, talk to the children about the different sizes, textures, shapes, and colors of the rocks. Help them compare the sizes, textures, shapes, and colors of the rocks.
5. Back in the classroom, have the children sort the rocks by their sizes, textures, shapes, and colors.
6. Let the children create a rock collection by displaying the rocks in egg cartons.

**More to do**
**Art:** Invite the children to wash and dry the rocks, and then paint them with tempera paint.

**Related books**
*Everybody Needs a Rock* by Byrd Baylor
*Let's Go Rock Collecting* by Roma Gans
*Painting on Rocks for Kids* by Lin Wellford
*Rocks and Fossils* by Chris Pellant

★ *Elizabeth Thomas, Hobart, IN*

# Volcano Lava Painting

SCIENCE

**Materials**
clay or playdough
paper
lemon juice
red or orange tempera paint
baking soda
liquid dish soap
cups for mixing

**What to do**

- Earth Science Week is the second week of October.
1. Talk about volcanoes with the children. Show pictures, if available.
2. Encourage the children to form clay or playdough into a 1" tall mound.
3. Have them place their mounds onto paper.
4. Show the children how to make an indentation in the top of the clay to make a "crater."
5. Mix baking soda and tempera paint in a cup. Let the children fill their craters with this mixture.
6. In another cup, mix two parts lemon juice to one part dish soap.
7. Let the children the pour mixture into the craters and observe what happens (the baking soda mixture will run over the top of the crater).
8. Let dry.

⭐ *Kristi Larson, Spirit Lake, IA*

# Help Make a Difference

WORKING WITH FAMILIES

**Materials**
boxes
bags
items collected

**What to do**
- "Make a Difference Day" is the 4th Saturday in October.
1. Start this activity several weeks before "Make a Difference Day." Talk to the children about how they can help make a difference to other children.
2. Ask the children what they would like to do to help others in need. Some ideas could be collecting food, toothbrushes and toothpaste, out-grown clothing, or toys in good condition that are no longer played with.
3. When the children have decided what they would like to do for others, research to see which agency in town could help disperse the collected items to families in need.
4. Send a note home with the children letting parents know what the children decided to do as their project. Ask the parents to help their children collect the items and send them back to school.
5. Have the children help package the goods to take to the agency.
6. Hopefully (with your help) the agency will send a note back to the children to let them know how their items were used.

**More to do**
**Language:** Talk about other things that can be given to others, such as a smile, a thank you, and a helping hand.

**Related book**
*The Giving Tree* by Shel Silverstein

 *Monica Hay Cook, Tucson, AZ*

# Backwards Day

GROUP OR CIRCLE TIME

**Materials**
wall clock

**What to do**
- Daylight savings time ends on the last Sunday of October (starting in 2007, it will end on the first Sunday of November). October is also National Clock Month.
1. Bring a clock to circle time on the Friday before daylight savings time ends.

2. Discuss what daylight savings time is and use a wall clock to demonstrate to the children.
3. Talk about the word *backwards*. Explain what it means and ask the group to list things that can be done backwards.
4. Invite the children to do some of the things listed (such as walk, hop, pretend to drive, scoot, say the alphabet, count, and so on).

**MORE TO DO**    Celebrate by having a "Backwards Day." Do as many things as you can backwards.

**RELATED BOOKS**    *The Grouchy Ladybug* by Eric Carle
*Silly Sally* by Audrey Wood

★ *Ann Kelly, Johnstown, PA*

# CREATION STATION

ART

**MATERIALS**    crepe paper
large grocery bags and trash bags
markers and crayons
craft materials
tape
glue

**WHAT TO DO**    • Halloween is celebrated on October 31st.
1. Provide crepe paper, large paper grocery bags, trash bags, tape, crayons, markers, and a variety of craft materials.
2. Encourage the children to design their own capes and costumes.
**Safety Note:** Closely supervise this activity so children do not put plastic bags on their heads or around their necks.

**MORE TO DO**    **Math:** Graph the costumes they make.

★ *Kathy Kalmar, Macomb, MI*

# FrankenMonster

ART

**Materials**

*Frank Was a Monster Who Wanted to Dance* by Keith Graves
camera
scissors
sticky-back adhesive (Velcro)
flannel board

**What to do**

● Halloween is celebrated on October 31st.

1. Read *Frank Was a Monster Who Wanted to Dance* by Keith Graves. Ask the children if they would like to make their own FrankenMonsters.

2. Take a full-length photo of each child. Make sure you take the photos from about the same distance each time and that the child fills the whole frame from head to toes. Have each child stand with arms slightly away from the body and legs slightly apart.

3. Develop or print the photos and make three copies of each one. (8" x 10" photos are the best for this activity, but 5" x 7" will do. Anything smaller makes the resulting project too small to appreciate.)

4. Cut around the child's outline in each photo. Cut the photo apart according to body parts and label the back of each one with the child's name.

5. Sort the pieces into separate containers. You should end up with a container of heads (with hair and neck attached), trunks, left arms, right arms, left hands, right hands, left legs, right legs, and left and right feet. **Note:** For younger children, simplify this activity by dividing each photo into four parts. First cut around the child's outline; then cut each outline into four equal parts by cutting just below the neck, at the waistline, and below the hips.

6. Attach a piece of Velcro to each piece so it will stick to a flannel board.

7. Place the containers next to a flannel board and let the children experiment with the pieces. They will naturally put the pieces together to form a person. Comment on what they are doing. Ask questions. "Whose face did you use?"

8. The children will enjoy this activity just for the pure silly fun of it without realizing they are developing visual discrimination and verbal skills.

**MORE TO DO**    Follow steps 1-4 above. Let the children create their own FrankenMonsters to take home by gluing the pieces of their own bodies to construction paper.
**Music and Movement:** Play a rousing game of "Hokey Pokey"!

⭐ *Virginia Jean Herrod, Columbia, SC*

# DESCRIBE A GOBLIN

ART

**MATERIALS**    markers and crayons
paper

**WHAT TO DO**
● Halloween is celebrated on October 31st.
1. Ask the children to describe a goblin.
2. Record their answers.
3. Have them draw a goblin and share it with the other children.
4. Put all the pages together to make a classroom goblin book

⭐ *Kathy Kalmar, Macomb, MI*

# Spooky Spiders

ART

**MATERIALS**    hot glue gun (adult only)
card stock or file folders
paper
orange and black crayons
black stamp pad

**WHAT TO DO**
● Halloween is celebrated on October 31st.
1. Ahead of time, use a hot glue gun to form different shaped spider webs on card stock or file folders and allow them to harden and dry.
2. Let each child pick a web. Have them place a blank sheet of white or manila paper on top of the glue and use black and orange crayons to rub across the paper until the web appears on their paper.
3. After they are satisfied with their webs, have the children stamp their thumbs on the web using black stamp pad.

4. Encourage the children to draw legs coming from the thumb stamp, forming a spider inside a spooky web.

5. As a variation, have the children use regular glue to form their own webs. Allow a day for the glue to dry, and then proceed as above. This takes a little more time, but the children will get their own "one-of-a-kind" webs.

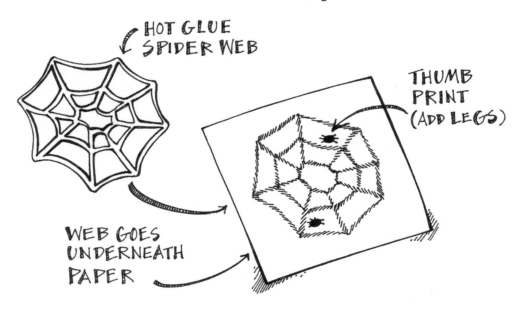

HOT GLUE SPIDER WEB

THUMB PRINT (ADD LEGS)

WEB GOES UNDERNEATH PAPER

⭐ *Wanda Guidroz, Santa Fe, TX*

# Halloween Dress Up

DRAMATIC PLAY

**Materials**     costumes and dress-ups

**What to do**
- Halloween is celebrated on October 31st.
1. Invite the children to dress up and pretend to go trick-or-treating in the classroom and to other classrooms.
2. Do this after Halloween so the children can play out their experiences.

**More to do**     **More Dramatic Play:** Have a Halloween Fashion Show. Encourage the children to take turns modeling Halloween fashions. Let children take turns describing the costumes. Use a cylinder block for a microphone.

⭐ *Kathy Kalmar, Macomb, MI*

# Five Little Spiders

FINGERPLAYS, SONGS, & POEMS

**Materials**
plastic spider rings (optional)
tissue

**What to do**

- Halloween is celebrated on October 31st.
1. If possible, purchase plastic spider rings from a party store or dollar store. If spider rings are not available, you can do this fingerplay without them. Give each child five plastic spider rings and a tissue.
2. Recite the following rhyme with the children, inviting them to act out the appropriate gestures.

*Five little spiders coming in the door,*
*One stopped to spin a web, and then there were four.* (hold up five fingers up, then four)
*Four little spiders climbing up a tree,*
*One stayed to play on a leaf, and then there were three.* (hold up three fingers)
*Three little spiders help to stir the brew,*
*One fell in then there were two.* (hold up two fingers)
*Two little spiders playing in the sun,*
*One went to look for shade, and then there was one.* (hold up one finger)
*One little spider is really quite a sight,* (put tissue over spider)
*Dressed in his costume on Halloween night.*
*Boo!*

⭐ *Kathy Kalmar, Macomb, MI*

# Jack-o-Lantern Fingerplay

FINGERPLAYS, SONGS, & POEMS

**Materials**
none

**What to do**

- Halloween is celebrated on October 31st.
Sing the following song and make the appropriate gestures.

*Here's my pumpkin* (make a circle with arms)
*Big and fat,* (make circle bigger)
*Change into a jack-o-lantern*
*Just like that!* (smile and clap)

⭐ *Kathy Kalmar, Macomb, MI*

# HERE'S A PUMPKIN FINGERPLAY

FINGERPLAYS, SONGS, & POEMS

**Materials**   none

**What to do**   • Halloween is celebrated on October 31st.
Sing the following song, using the appropriate corresponding gestures.

*Here's a pumpkin* (make a circle with arms)
*Big and fat.* (make circle bigger)
*Here's a cat* (point to a pretend cat)
*Soft and black.* (pet the cat)
*Here's an owl* (make circle around eyes)
*With great big eyes.* (point to eyes)
*Here's a witch* (make a pointed hat with arms on top of head)
*See how she flies.* (make arms zoom like a make-believe plane)

 *Kathy Kalmar, Macomb, MI*

# I'VE GOT A PUMPKIN

FINGERPLAYS, SONGS, & POEMS

**Materials**   none

**What to do**   • Halloween is celebrated on October 31st.
Sing the following song and make the appropriate corresponding gestures.

*I've got a pumpkin* (nod yes)
*With a great big grin.* (grin)
*Lift up his lid* (pretend to lift a lid)
*And put his candle in.* (pretend to put a candle in)

**More to do**   Decorate a pumpkin using markers.

 *Kathy Kalmar, Macomb, MI*

# Black Cat Turn Around

FINGERPLAYS, SONGS, & POEMS

**Materials**   none

**What to do**   • Halloween is celebrated on October 31st.
Sing the following song and make the appropriate corresponding gestures.

*Black cat, black cat, turn around.* (turn around)
*Black cat, black cat, touch the ground.* (touch the ground)
*Black cat, black cat, climb the tree.* (make climbing motions)
*Black cat, black cat, meow at me.* (meow)
*Black cat, black cat, sit up tall.* (sit up tall)
*Black cat, black cat, curl up like a ball.* (curl up like a ball)
*Black cat, black cat, that's all!*

 *Kathy Kalmar, Macomb, MI*

# Halloween Lotto

GAMES

**Materials**   paper
Halloween stickers
marker
glue
letter-size file folder
oak tag or poster board
scissors
laminating machine

**What to do**   • Halloween is celebrated October 31st.
1. Make a grid of nine equal squares (2 ½" x 2 ½"), three across and three down.
2. Put a set of Halloween stickers on the squares of the grid.
3. Open a letter-size file folder.
4. Glue the pictured grid to one side of the file folder.
5. Repeat steps one and two for the other side of the file folder.
6. Cut out nine 2 ½" x 2 ½" squares from tagboard for each player with stickers that match those on the lotto boards. These will be the cover cards.

7. Print the title of the activity on the front of the file folder. Include instructions on how to play, if desired.
8. Laminate the opened file folder and 18 cover cards, and cut out.
9. To use, invite two children to play together.
10. Each player, in turn, draws a card from the pile and places it on the matching sticker on his lotto board. If he already has that square covered, he places the card at the bottom of the pile of game cards and the next player goes.
11. The play continues until the children cover all their squares.

**Related book**    *Scary, Scary Halloween* by Eve Bunting

*Jackie Wright, Enid, OK*

# Ghost So Scary

GROUP OR CIRCLE TIME

**Materials**
sentence strips
marker
pocket chart
pointer
picture of each child in your class

**What to do**
- Halloween is celebrated on October 31st.
1. Write each of the following lines on a separate sentence strip:

*Ghost so scary,*
*Ghost so white,*
*Don't scare _____*
*On Halloween night!*

2. Insert the sentence strips into a pocket chart.
3. Teach the chant to the children. Give each child his or her photograph.
4. Have the children take turns using a pointer to direct attention to each word as the chant is read. Have the child place his picture in the pocket chart at the appropriate place.
5. Repeat until every child has had a turn putting his picture up and using the pointer.
6. Invite the children to practice reading the chant and displaying the pictures during free time.

 *Jackie Wright, Enid, OK*

# MAGIC ROCK HALLOWEEN GAME

GROUP OR CIRCLE TIME

**MATERIALS**    circle time rug

**WHAT TO DO**
- Halloween is celebrated on October 31st.
1. At circle time, have all the children sit on their knees and bend over with their chests on their thighs and faces facing the rug. (Ask them to try to look like a rock.)
2. Chant, "Magic rock, turn into...", and then call out something associated with Halloween.
3. The children (and you) "turn into" the Halloween symbol. For example:
   - Bat: stand with arms flapping
   - Cat: crawl and meow
   - Ghost: walk around making ghost sounds
   - Monster: stomp around with arms raised up high, roaring
   - Spider: crawl around on hands and feet
   - Pumpkin: spin around in seat
   - Skeleton: wiggle entire body

4. After acting out one character for a few seconds, call out, "Magic rock," and all the children return to their rock positions on the rug and wait to hear what they will "turn into" next.
5. Ask the children what they would like to turn into.

**MORE TO DO**    Play the game with a different theme, such as animals, transportation, or dinosaurs.

 *Andrea Hungerford, Plymouth, CT*

# WITCH'S STEW RECIPE

GROUP OR CIRCLE TIME

**MATERIALS**
chart paper
markers and crayons
magazines
glue
paper
pre-cut black paper pots

**What to do**
- Halloween is celebrated on October 31st.
1. Ask the children what they would put in witch's stew.
2. Record their answers on chart paper.
3. Encourage the children to draw or cut out items from magazines to put in their stew.
4. Give each child a pre-cut black paper pot to glue pictures for the stew.

⭐ *Kathy Kalmar, Macomb, MI*

# Boo Bag

GROUP OR CIRCLE TIME

**Materials**
white pillowcase
gourds
mini pumpkins
candy corn
facial tissue

**What to do**
- Halloween is celebrated on October 31st.
1. Put gourds, mini-pumpkins, candy corn, a tissue "ghost", and other Halloween items (such as a small witch) in a white pillowcase.
2. At circle time, let the children take turns removing an item from the pillowcase and talking about it.
3. Encourage children to tell a story using the items they picked out of the Boo Bag. Go around the circle and have each child add a sentence to the story.

⭐ *Kathy Kalmar, Macomb, MI*

# Goodbye, Scary Monsters!

LANGUAGE AND LITERACY

**Materials**
ten sheets of 8" x 10" poster board
markers
*Seven Scary Monsters* by Mary Beth Lundgren
laminate

**WHAT TO DO**
- Halloween is celebrated on October 31st.
1. On each sheet of poster board, write in large letters one of the following words: *eek, boom, rip, thwomp, splat, zap, yow, plop, ouch*, and *wow*. Laminate for durability.
2. Read *Seven Scary Monsters* to the children.
3. Read the story a second time, and ask the children to help tell the story by calling out the refrain and the *onomatopoetic* words on the poster boards. As you read the story, hold up each board at appropriate moments.
4. Invite the children to hold up poster boards on cue during reading.
5. Start a discussion by asking the question, "How would you get a monster out of your room?" Make sure they know monsters are make-believe.

⭐ *Karyn F. Everham, Fort Myers, FL*

# Halloween Night Predictions

LANGUAGE AND LITERACY

**Materials**
paper
marker

**WHAT TO DO**
- Halloween is celebrated on October 31st.
1. Write "On Halloween night I think I'll see_____" on the front of a piece of paper. Write "On Halloween night I saw_____" on the back of the paper. Make one for each child.
2. Before Halloween, invite the children to dictate or write what they think they will see on Halloween night. Let them draw pictures of things they might see.
3. The day after Halloween, encourage them to dictate or write what they actually saw on the back of the paper.

**MORE TO DO**
**Math:** Make a graph of things children saw on Halloween night.

 *Kathy Kalmar, Macomb, MI*

# Halloween Syllables

LANGUAGE AND LITERACY

**Materials**        orange paper
                    scissors

**What to do**
- Halloween is celebrated on October 31st.
1. Pre-cut small pumpkin shapes.
2. Give each child six pumpkin shapes.
3. Say a word. Have the children repeat the word and then place a pumpkin down for each syllable they hear. For example:
    - Pumpkin: pump/kin
    - Halloween: Hal/lo/ween
    - Ghost: ghost
    - Goblin: gob/lin
    - Witch: witch
    - Haunted: haunt/ed
    - Monster: mon/ster
    - Jack-o-lantern: jack/o/lan/tern

 *Linda Atamian, Charlestown, RI*

# Pumpkin Patch Math

MATH

**Materials**        *Jack-o-Lantern* by Charles Reasoner (optional)
                    orange paper
                    black paper
                    scissors
                    glue
                    laminate (optional)
                    magnets (optional)

**What to do**
- Halloween is celebrated on October 31st.
1. Pre-cut large pumpkin shapes from orange paper and a variety of smaller shapes (triangles, ovals, hearts, circles, and so on) from black paper.
2. Read *Jack-o-Lantern*, or any other book about pumpkins turned into jack-o-lanterns.
3. Have a class discussion about the shapes people carve into jack-o-lanterns. For example, some have triangle eyes and some have heart-shaped eyes.

4. Give each child a pumpkin shape. Encourage them to glue black shapes on their pumpkins to make jack-o-lanterns.

5. If desired, laminate and place magnets on the back of finished pumpkins for children to take home and use as a refrigerator magnet.

6. Have a discussion about graphs. Make a picture graph with categories such as triangle eyes, circle eyes, and triangle noses. Let each child place his jack-o-lantern in the correct place on the graph.

⭐ *Jill Martin and D'Arcy Simmons, Springfield, MO*

# Halloween Owls

MATH

**Materials**

pictures of owls
brown, white, and black felt
scissors
glue
plush owl dolls (optional)

**What to do**

● Halloween is celebrated on October 31st.

1. Before doing this activity, make felt owls. Cut out owl parts from brown, white, and black felt (see illustration). Glue them to a felt owl. Make a few of these.

2. Ask children to bring plush owls from home (if they have them).

3. Show the children pictures of owls.

4. Discuss how owls are nocturnal. Ask the children to name other nocturnal animals.

5. Make a felt tree and hang it on a wall or bulletin board.

6. Ask each child to put a specific number of felt owls in the tree.

**Related book**

*Over in the Meadow* by Olive A. Wadsworth

⭐ *Mary Brehm, Aurora, OH*

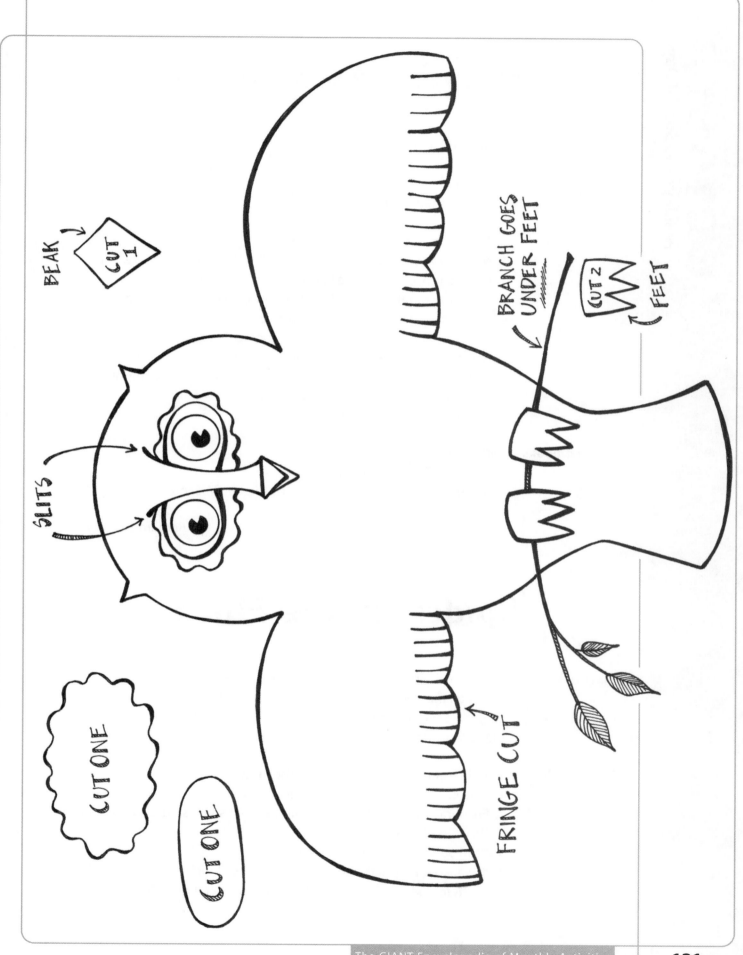

BEAK
CUT 1

SLITS

CUT ONE

CUT ONE

BRANCH GOES UNDER FEET

CUT 2
FEET

FRINGE CUT

# Pumpkin Face Graph

MATH

**Materials**
large graph paper
pens
pumpkin
sharp knife (adult only)

**What to do**
- Halloween is celebrated on October 31st.
1. Make two columns on the graph labeled "Happy" and "Scary."
2. Let each child mark under the face he wants you to carve.
3. Carve the pumpkin face according to which column has the most votes.
4. Make other Halloween graphs, such as:
   - Is your Halloween costume scary or nice?
   - Do you like to eat pumpkin pie (yes or no)?
   - What is your favorite kind of Halloween candy? (Glue the labels of candies to the top of the graph columns.)
   - Do you have a pumpkin?

**Related books**
*Clifford's Halloween* by Norman Bridwell
*It's Pumpkin Time* by Zoe Hall
*It's the Great Pumpkin, Charlie Brown* by Charles M. Schulz

 *Barbara Saul, Eureka, CA*

# Spider on the Floor

MUSIC AND MOVEMENT

**Materials**
black plastic spider rings (found at party stores)
*Spider on the Floor* by Raffi
*Singable Songs for the Very Young* by Raffi (optional)
CD or tape player

**What to do**
- Halloween is celebrated on October 31st.
1. Give each child a plastic spider ring.
2. Encourage the children to sing and act out some spider songs, such as "Itsy Bitsy Spider."
3. Read *Spider on the Floor* to the children.
4. If available, play Raffi's song "Spider on the Floor" (found on *Singable Songs for the Very Young*) and have children act it out with the spider rings.

**MORE TO DO**     **Books:** Take pictures of the children with the spider rings on different parts of their bodies. Make the photos part of a "Spider on the Floor" class book.

★ *Ann Scalley, Orleans, MA*

# PIÑATAS

PROJECTS

**MATERIALS**
large balloons (one per child)
newspaper
plain newsprint paper
glue
string
4-5 bottles of orange paint
1-2 bottles of green paint
black tissue paper
utility knife (adult only)
strawberry baskets (one per child)
masking tape
permanent marker

**WHAT TO DO**
● Halloween is celebrated on October 31st.
1. Ask a parent volunteer to blow up one balloon for each child in your class. The balloons should be approximately 4" to 6" inches in diameter.
2. Cover the tables with newspaper. This is a messy project!
3. Make papier-mâché using water and glue (two parts water to one part glue).
4. The easiest way for young children to cover their balloons is to paint a whole sheet of newspaper with the glue/water mixture, place the balloon in the middle (knotted end up), and wrap the paper around the balloon.
5. Help the children pull up the ends of the newspaper to cover the knot (stem) on their balloons (pumpkins).
6. Help them twist the ends of the newspaper to form a handle (stem) for the "pumpkin" before putting on the second layer of newspaper. Demonstrate how to wind string around the balloon with the ends coming out at the top so the piñata can be hung up, then apply another layer of newspaper.
7. Use masking tape and a marker to make a name label for each pumpkin. Attach one label to the string hanging out and one to the strawberry basket.

8. Place the pumpkin on top of the strawberry basket to dry. It will take about a week to harden.

9. The next week, repeat the process, substituting blank newsprint paper for newspaper. Have the children put two more layers of newsprint around the pumpkin (no string this time). Allow it to dry for a week.

10. The next week, have the children paint the handles green and let dry.

11. The next day, have them paint their pumpkins orange. Let dry overnight.

12. Ask a parent volunteer to make holes in the tops of the pumpkin piñatas (to put goodies inside).

13. Cut out shapes from black tissue paper. Encourage the children to glue the shapes to their pumpkin piñatas to make jack-o-lanterns.

14. At your classroom Halloween party, have the children fill their piñatas with goodies they brought for each other from home, and take them home.

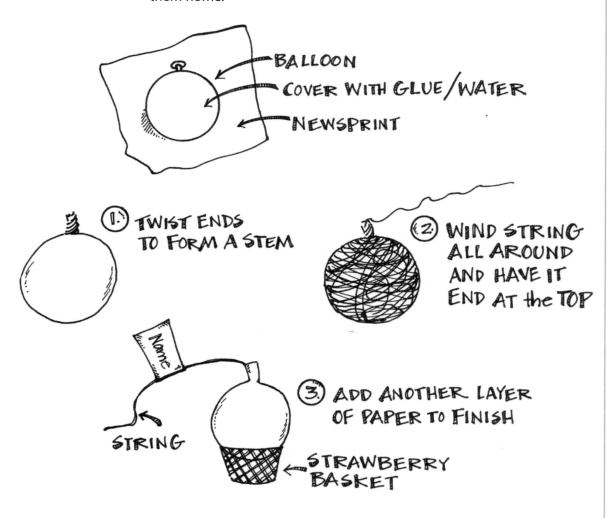

BALLOON
COVER WITH GLUE/WATER
NEWSPRINT

(1.) TWIST ENDS TO FORM A STEM

(2) WIND STRING ALL AROUND AND HAVE IT END AT the TOP

Name
STRING

(3.) ADD ANOTHER LAYER OF PAPER TO FINISH
STRAWBERRY BASKET

④ LET DRY for 1 WEEK and
ADD 2 MORE LAYERS of
BLANK NEWSPRINT

GREEN →

ORANGE →

HOLE to SLIP
GOODIES INSIDE

BLACK SHAPES

**More to do**    Bring in a "real" piñata for the children to explore.

**Related book**    *Pumpkin, Pumpkin* by Jeanne Titherington

★ *Linda Ford, Sacramento, CA*

# Witch's Brew

SNACK AND COOKING

**Materials**    grape juice
red grapes and blueberries
milk
ice
blender

**What to do**
- Halloween is celebrated on October 31st.
1. Put grape juice, grapes, blueberries, and milk into a blender.
2. Add ice and blend to make a "witch's smoothie."

★ *Kathy Kalmar, Macomb, MI*

# November

# BEAR IS SLEEPING

GAMES

**MATERIALS**
large cardboard box
small blanket

**WHAT TO DO**
1. Have the children form a circle. Put a large cardboard box in the middle of their circle.
2. Select a child to be the "bear." The bear crawls into box and covers herself with a blanket.
3. The rest of the children walk around the circle singing the following song:

*I see a big brown bear*
*With lots of thick brown hair.*
*He (she) is sleeping, sleeping in his (her) den,*
*But we will wake him (her) up again*
*If we can count to ten.*

4. The children count to ten. When they finish, the bear wakes up, stretches, and stands tall. The children continue to sing:

*Brown bear stands tall and shows his (her) paws,*
*Then crawls away on all his (her) fours.*

5. The bear crawls out of the box and joins the circle.
6. Select a new child to be the bear. Continue playing until everyone has had a turn.

**RELATED book**
*Brown Bear, Brown Bear, What Do You See?* by Bill Martin, Jr

⭐ *Ingelore Mix, Gainesville, VA*

# SLEEP TIGHT, BEARS!

SCIENCE

**MATERIALS**
refrigerator box (or other large box)
gray and brown poster paints
paintbrushes
floor pillows

**What to do**
1. Talk about animals that hibernate, which include many types of fish, amphibians, and reptiles. These creatures lower their body temperatures near freezing. Bears do not truly hibernate, since their body temperatures don't lower very much and they are easily awakened.
2. Explain to the children that bears sleep in their dens, or caves, during winter.
3. Cut a doorway into the refrigerator box. Encourage the children to paint the outside of the box to look like a bear cave.
4. Place floor pillows inside the "cave."
5. Invite the children to spend quiet time in the cave.

 *Karyn F. Everham, Fort Myers, FL*

# Amazing Corn

SNACK AND COOKING

**Materials**
strawberry corn
brown paper bags
microwave

**What to do**
1. Strawberry corn is usually sold around Thanksgiving. It is smaller than regular corn and has a deep red color.
2. Bring some strawberry corn to class. Let the children help remove the husks.
3. Help the children write their names on paper bags.
4. Place one corn cob in each bag. Close the bag and fold the end shut.
5. Place one bag in the microwave. Heat for three minutes. Do not overcook or leave unattended.
6. Remove the bag from the microwave. The popcorn should have popped on the cob, so the children can eat "popcorn on the cob."

**Related book**  *Raccoons and Ripe Corn* by Jim Aronsky

 *Ann Scalley, Orleans, MA*

# GET ME OUT

SNACK AND COOKING

**MATERIALS**

wrench
screwdriver
hammer
can opener
eggbeater
nuts with shells (peanuts, walnuts, and so on)
citrus fruits (oranges, grapefruits, tangerines)
spoon
fork

**WHAT TO DO**

1. Place the tools, kitchen objects, fruits, and nuts on the table.
2. Let each child choose a nut or fruit. **Safety Note:** Check for allergies. If any of the children are allergic to nuts, do not do this activity with real nuts (use pictures instead).
3. Ask each child which tool on the table could be used to crack open and eat the contents of the fruit or nut without damaging the insides.
4. Discuss other ways to crack open the nuts or fruit.
5. Supervise (and help) the children use different tools to open the nuts or fruits.
6. Eat the results of your work!

 *Shyamala Shanmugasundaram, Nerul, Navi Mumbai, India*

# Dream Catchers

ART

**Materials**   *Grandmother's Dreamcatcher* by Becky Ray McCain or *Isaac's Dreamcatcher* by Bonnie Farmer
glitter glue in a variety of colors or homemade colored glue
colored pencils
vinyl sheeting (available from a hardware store)
white paper (5" x 5" squares)

**What to do**
- November is American Indian Heritage Month.
1. Read *Grandmother's Dreamcatcher* or *Isaac's Dreamcatcher* to the children. Explain that a dream catcher is used to catch bad dreams and let the good dreams through. The hole in the middle of the dream catcher lets good dreams come through to the person sleeping and the web around the hole traps the bad dreams.
2. Help the children make their own dream catchers using glitter glue or homemade colored glue (add food coloring or paint to white glue).
3. Give each child a pre-cut 5" x 5" square of white paper. Encourage them to use colored pencils to sketch their dream catcher designs. Ojibwe dream catchers are modeled after a spider's web. These are easy for the children to make. Remind the children to leave the center open for the good dreams to get through to them.
4. Cover the art area with newspaper. Cut vinyl sheeting into 6" x 6" squares and give one to each child. Have them place their drawings under the vinyl sheet. Demonstrate how to trace their design's outline with black glitter glue or colored glue. Air dry overnight.
5. Encourage the children to fill in the rest of their designs with other colors of glitter glue or colored glue. Make sure they fill in the entire drawing with the glue. Air dry 24 hours.
6. Help the children carefully peel their dream catchers from the vinyl sheet and stick it to a window. If the children are going to take their dream catchers home, do not remove the vinyl sheet. Send home an instruction sheet for the parents. Emphasize that they should put the dream catchers on a low window (so children won't have to climb on furniture to see it) that is closed and locked (to reduce the chance of the children falling out the window while viewing their dream catchers).

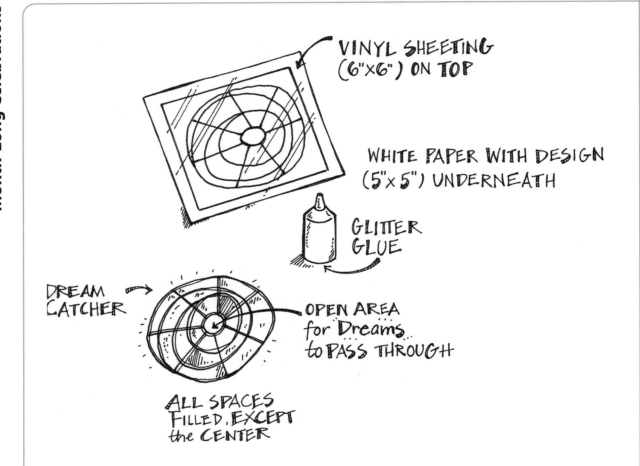

VINYL SHEETING (6"x6") ON TOP

WHITE PAPER WITH DESIGN (5"x 5") UNDERNEATH

GLITTER GLUE

DREAM CATCHER →

OPEN AREA for Dreams to PASS THROUGH

ALL SPACES FILLED, EXCEPT the CENTER

**More to do**   **Bulletin Board:** Encourage the children to tell stories about dreams they have had. Record their thoughts. Ask them to draw pictures to illustrate their dreams. Make a bulletin board about their dreams. Have the children work together to design a large dream catcher on paper. Post the drawing in the middle of a bulletin board and put the children's stories about their dreams, along with their drawings, around the dream catcher. Title it: "We Are Catching Our Dreams."

**Related books**   *Africa Dream* by Eloise Greenfield
*Beardream* by Will Hobbs
*Dream Wolf* by Paul Goble
*Dreamcatcher* by Audrey Osofsky

⭐ *Virginia Jean Herrod, Columbia, SC*

# Gathering Pouches

ART

**Materials**
paper grocery bags (one per child)
scissors
craft glue
foam meat trays
plastic forks and knives
washable paint in a variety of colors
hole punch
heavy yarn

**What to do**
- November is American Indian Heritage Month.
1. Explain to the children that the Delaware Indians of New York, New Jersey, Pennsylvania, and Delaware used pouches to gather food and other materials needed for daily life. Let the children make their own creative renditions of a gathering pouch.
2. Encourage the children to cut out a large rectangle from their paper bags. Draw the rectangle for younger children and let those who cannot cut tear their bags along a folded line. Help the children fold the narrow end up, with any printing folded inside. Leave space for a flap at the top.
3. Let the children use craft glue to seal both edges of their pouch, leaving the top open.
4. Provide plastic forks and knives and demonstrate how to carve designs into the bottom of foam trays to make printing plates. Help the children cut out the designs.
5. Spread newspaper over the work area. Pour washable paint into foam trays. Invite the children to choose their favorite color of paint and cover a design area using a paintbrush. Help them children gently press the printing plate on the paper bag to print the design. Encourage them to repeat with different designs or colors. Let dry.
6. Let the children complete the design pattern on their gathering pouches using crayons and colored pencils.
7. Help the children punch a hole in each upper corner of the pouch and thread heavy yarn through the holes to make a strap. Tape the ends together.
8. Take a nature walk and let the children fill their gathering pouches with treasures such as leaves, small stones, and flowers.

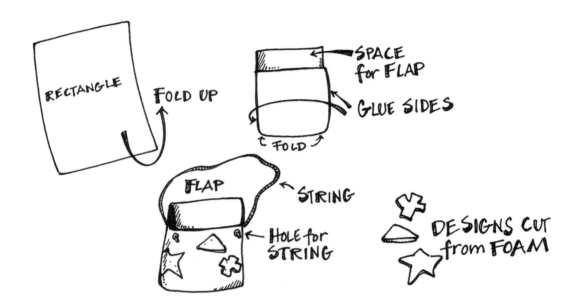

**MORE TO DO**

**More Art:** Press the flowers and leaves that the children gather. Make a simple press by layering cardboard, butcher paper, and flowers and put a heavy book on top of the stack. Use the pressed items in collages and other art projects.

**Math:** Encourage the children to sort the items in their pouches by similarities and differences.

**RELATED SONG**

**A Gathering We Will Go** by Virginia Jean Herrod
(Tune: "A-Hunting We Will Go")
*A-gathering we will go,*
*A-gathering we will go,*
*We'll find some flowers*
*With lots of petal power,*
*A-gathering we will go.*

*A-gathering we will go,*
*A-gathering we will go,*
*We'll find some stones*
*And make them our own,*
*A-gathering we will go.*

*A-gathering we will go,*
*A-gathering we will go,*
*We'll find some leaves*
*As pretty as you please,*
*A-gathering we will go.*

**Related books**    *Gathering: A Northwoods Counting Book* by Betsy Bowen
*Johnny Appleseed* by Reeve Lindbergh
*Small Wolf* by Nathaniel Benchley

★ *Virginia Jean Herrod, Columbia, SC*

# Catch It!

GAMES

**Materials**    air-dry modeling dough
yarn
glue
cardboard
scissors
various collage materials
markers, crayons, and colored pencils

**What to do**
- November is American Indian Heritage Month.
1. Before doing this activity, make a sample Flip and Catch as described on the next page.
2. Ask the children what their lives would be like without video games or TV. Make a list of their responses. Tell them that American Indian children used to make their own toys. Show them the sample Flip and Catch. Explain that different types of this cup-and-ball game are found around the world.
3. Give each child a small amount of modeling dough. Show them how to roll the dough to make a ball and form the ball around the end of a length of yarn. Let the balls dry overnight. For extra strength, glue the yarn in place with glue. Let dry.
4. Help each child trace or draw a triangle on a piece of cardboard and cut it out. Offer help as needed.
5. Cut a hole in the center of the triangle a bit larger than the ball. An adult should do this step.
6. Have the children use a variety of craft materials to decorate their triangles on both sides. Let dry.
7. Help the children punch a hole on one side of their triangles and tie the ball through the hole.
8. Now it's time to play! Demonstrate how to hold the triangle in their hands and swing the ball to catch it. It might take a while to get the hang of this game so encourage the children to keep trying.

**MORE TO DO**

**Art:** Make a multi-colored ball by mixing tempera paint into white dough or mixing two colors of dough to get a desired color. Adding torn tissue paper to air-dry modeling dough makes a beautiful marbled effect. Encourage the children to experiment with different sizes of balls, sizes of triangles, and lengths of yarn. Think about new ways to toss the ball. Make a chart of which ways work best for the children.

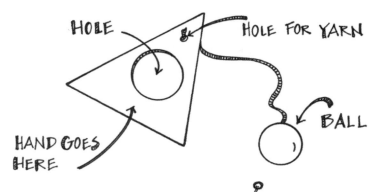

HOLE

HOLE FOR YARN

&

HAND GOES HERE

BALL

**Catch It Game Chart**

⊚ Little triangle with little ball and a LONG string

⊚ Big triangle with tiny ball and long string

⊚ 2 balls on one triangle with 2 holes

**RELATED BOOKS**

*Dream Wolf* by Paul Goble
*The Girl Who Loved Wild Horses* by Paul Goble
*Grandmother Five Baskets* by Lisa Larrabee
*Red Fox and His Canoe* by Nathaniel Benchley
*Small Wolf* by Nathaniel Benchley
*Ten Little Rabbits* by Virginia Grossman

★ *Virginia Jean Herrod, Columbia, SC*

# A Kind Deed

SOCIAL DEVELOPMENT

**Materials**  none

**What to do**
- World Kindness Week is the second week of November.
1. Tell the children that it is World Kindness Week. Talk about the importance of being kind to others and ask them for some examples.
2. Encourage the children to do kind things all week. Suggestions include:
   - Offer to play with someone who is alone on the playground.
   - Say something nice to someone.
   - Make a card and send it to someone you know.
   - Make a bead necklace or bracelet and give it to someone in your school.
   - Bring an extra snack and give it to someone in your class.
   - Help someone who has a chore.
   - Help your caregiver bake a treat for your class.
   - Set the table for dinner without being asked.
   - Tidy up your room without being told.

 *Amelia Griffin, Ontario, Canada*

# Making Wordless Books

LANGUAGE AND LITERACY

**Materials**  paper
crayons
stapler

**What to do**
- Children's Book Week is celebrated the week before Thanksgiving.
1. Tell the children it is Children's Book Week. Ask them if they would like to make their own books to celebrate the week.
2. Encourage the children to draw illustrations on paper.
3. Ask them to put their pictures in sequence to make a wordless book.
4. Invite the children to share their stories without words.
5. Another way to celebrate the week is to visit the library.

**Related books**  *Do You Want to Be My Friend?* by Eric Carle
*Pancakes for Breakfast* by Tomie DePaola
*Snowman* by Raymond Briggs
*Truck Board Book* by Donald Crews

 *Elizabeth Thomas, Hobart, IN*

# READER RECOGNITION

### SOCIAL DEVELOPMENT

**MATERIALS**
note cards
pens

**WHAT TO DO**
- National Children's Book Week is celebrated the week before Thanksgiving.
1. Encourage the children to dictate their thoughts and thanks to anyone who has come to your class to read to them.
2. Address the note cards and send the cards to the volunteer readers.

**RELATED book**
*Thank You, Clifford* by Sonila Fry

 *Ann Kelly, Johnstown, PA*

# MAKE A FAMILY TREE

### ART

**MATERIALS**
photocopies of pictures of each child
photocopies of pictures of each child's family
large piece of white paper (at least 3' x 3')
green paint
sponges
glue
markers that write on paint

**WHAT TO DO**
- National Family Week is celebrated the week of Thanksgiving.
1. Make a photocopy of the children's photos and their family photos.
2. Encourage the children to work together to sponge paint green paint all over the large paper.
3. When it dries, cut out a treetop outline and glue each child's picture to it.
4. Encourage the children to find their own pictures and write their names next to it (help them as needed).
5. Let them glue their family pictures next to their own pictures.

**MORE TO DO**
Let the children paint the treetop with their handprints instead of the sponges.

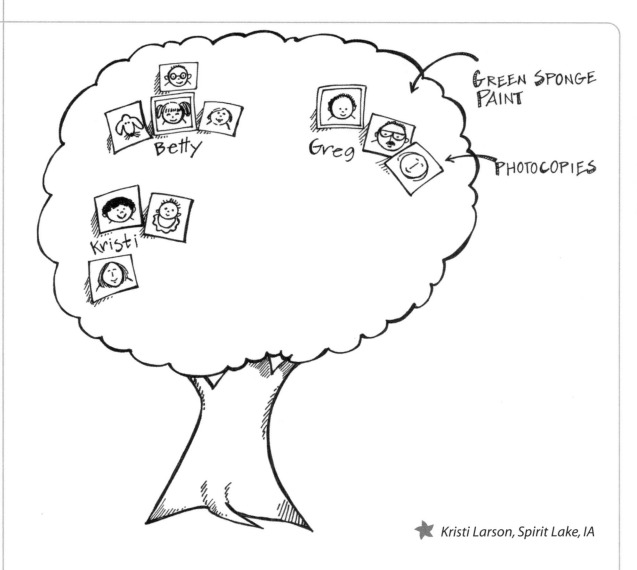

GREEN SPONGE PAINT

PHOTOCOPIES

Betty

Greg

Kristi

*Kristi Larson, Spirit Lake, IA*

# My Family

FINGERPLAYS, SONGS, & POEMS

**Materials**   none

**What to do**   • National Family Week is celebrated the week of Thanksgiving.
Sing the following song to the tune of "Twinkle, Twinkle Little Star."

*My family loves me so much,*
*They give me kisses, hugs, and such.*
*If I feel bad they're always there,*
*To cheer me up because they care!*
*My family loves me so much,*
*They give me kisses, hugs, and such.*

*Kristi Larson, Spirit Lake, IA*

# THAT'S MY NAME!

WORKING WITH FAMILIES

**MATERIALS**
5" x 7" card stock paper
markers
construction paper
glue
hole punch
heavy string or yarn

**WHAT TO DO**

● National Family Week is the week of Thanksgiving.

1. Send a letter home to each family asking the parents to give the reason they gave their child his or her name. Your letter might read like this:

*Dear Family,*
*We are currently doing a family theme in our room. We would like to make a book about how each child got his or her name. Please write a brief explanation about how your child got his or her name and return it to school by (date). The children will make self-portraits for a classroom called "That's My Name!" Each child will receive a copy of the book.*

2. Have the children draw-self portraits on 5" x 7" white card stock paper. Glue each portrait to an 8" x 11" (or larger) piece of construction paper.
3. Print the children's names under their portraits. Under each child's name/portrait, print the information from the parents. ("Frances Ellen. Frances Ellen got her name from her two great grandmothers, Grandma Frances and Granny Ellen.")
4. Create a cover for the book. You could make a collage of the children's photos or simply print each full name on the front. Also create a back cover.
5. Make a copy of each page for each child in the room.
6. Use a hole punch to punch four to six holes in each page.
7. Use heavy string or yarn to bind the pages together into a book.
8. Staple the copied pages together into individual books for each child.
9. Read your new book together and send the individual books home.

**MORE TO DO**
Broaden the theme of your book by including other facts about the child on each page. For example you could ask the children about their favorite foods, favorite colors, favorite place to go, or any other interesting subject.

**Related Song**   **This Name Is My Name** (Tune: "This Land Is Your Land")

*My name is my name,*
*Your name is your name.*
*It might be different*
*Or a little bit the same.*
*It might be a short name*
*Or a great big long name,*
*Names belong to you and me!*

*My name is Frances,*
*Your name is Harold.*
*His name is Robert,*
*And hers is Maggie.*
*Mommy's name is Lynda,*
*Daddy's name is Carlos,*
*Names belong to you and me!*
(Substitute classroom names for the names in the song)

**Related books**   *A Is for Annabelle* by Tasha Tudor
*A—My Name Is Alice* by Jane Bayer
*An Anteater Named Arthur* by Bernard Waber
*A Boy Named Giotto* by Paolo Guarnieri
*Chrysanthemum* by Kevin Henkes
*A Firefly Named Torchy* by Bernard Waber
*A Lion Named Shirley Williamson* by Bernard Waber
*The Maggie B.* by Irene Haas
*A Name on the Quilt: A Story of Remembrance* by Jeannine Atkins
*A Porcupine Named Fluffy* by Helen Lester
*Santa's Book of Names* by David McPhail
*Three Names* by Patricia MacLachlan
*Tom* by Tomie dePaola

 *Virginia Jean Herrod, Columbia, SC*

# DINOSAUR ELECTIONS

PROJECTS

**MATERIALS**
pictures of favorite dinosaurs (from computer, coloring book, or hand drawn)
white construction paper
tape
markers
three-panel display board
red, white, and blue tempera paint
United States flag
flag and star stickers
shoebox
scissors
poster board
pencil

**WHAT TO DO**
- Election Day is the second Tuesday in November.
1. Ask the children if they have heard anything about upcoming elections. Explain the election process in simple terms. For example: "Every four years, Americans must decide which person will be the leader of the country (the President of the United States). Does anyone know who the president is now?" Allow for responses, some children may know this. "Right now, people all over the country are getting ready to choose a new president. They do this by *voting*. When people vote, they go to a *polling place*. They go into a booth called a *voting booth*. In the booth, they choose the name of the person they want to lead the country by writing it down, marking a piece of paper, or pushing a button on a computer screen. The votes are all counted and the person who gets the most votes wins."
2. Continue by telling the children: "We can have our own election in the classroom. Since you are too young to vote for the president, let's vote on something fun, like our favorite dinosaurs. We can all vote, and the dinosaur that wins the election will be our classroom dinosaur for a whole month."
3. Ask the children to nominate a favorite dinosaur. Limit the nominations to three or four.
4. Find a computer graphic or picture of each nominated dinosaur. Place the pictures on a single sheet of paper and make a copy for each child.
5. Let the children help decorate a voting booth. Put the three-panel display board on a newspaper-covered surface. Have the children paint one panel red, one panel white, and one panel blue. Explain that these are the colors in the American flag. Show the children the flag and post it in a prominent place.

6. When the paint has dried, have the children decorate the display board with large star stickers. Set aside.

7. Let the children cover a shoebox with white construction paper and star and flag stickers. An adult cuts a slot in the top of the box through which the children will put their votes. Tape the top to the box.

8. Have each child trace and cut out a large circle from poster board. Help them print "I Voted!" on their circles. Put these aside for later use.

9. Cut out the letters "LET'S VOTE" from poster board. Post the letters vertically on the entrance to the room (above the door or on the side of the door frame).

10. Invite the children to make campaign posters for the nominated dinosaurs. Print out a large graphic of each dinosaur and put it at the top of a piece of poster board. Under each picture, help the children print "Vote for (Stegosaurus, T-Rex, Diplodocus, and Iguanodon)." Post these in prominent places around the room.

11. On Election Day, set up the voting booth on a table that is close to a wall (to give the children privacy when they vote).

12. Call the children, one at a time, to vote. Give the child a *ballot* (the paper with the dinosaur graphics on it). The child circles one dinosaur and then puts the ballot in the shoebox. Use looped masking tape to stick an "I VOTED" button to the children's shirts after they have voted.

13. After everyone has voted, remove the ballots from the box and have the children sort them. Count each vote with the children. Declare the dinosaur with the most votes the winner of the election!

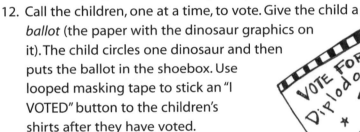

**RELATED SONG**   **A-Voting We Will Go** by Virginia Jean Herrod
(Tune: "The Farmer in the Dell")

*A-voting we will go,*
*A-voting we will go,*
*Hi-ho the derry-o,*
*A-voting we will go.*

*We'll elect a dinosaur,*
*We'll elect a dinosaur,*
*Hi-ho the derry-o,*
*We'll elect a dinosaur.*

**RELATED books**   *The Day Gogo Went to Vote* by Elinor Batezat Sisulu
*Election Day* by Margaret McNamara

⭐ *Virginia Jean Herrod, Columbia, SC*

# Exposé Election

## SOCIAL DEVELOPMENT

**MATERIALS**   three favorite classroom books
chart paper
small slip of paper for each child
masking tape

**WHAT TO do**
- Election Day is the second Tuesday in November.
1. Have a discussion about voting at circle time.
2. Explain that the children are going to vote for one of their three favorite books.
3. Make a chart with three columns, one for each book. Write numbers on the left side of the chart. Post the chart where everyone can see it.
4. Place one of the favorite books (or a representation) at the bottom of each of the three columns of the chart.
5. Give each child a slip of paper with a loop of tape on the back.
6. One by one, have them vote for their favorite book by taping their piece of paper directly above the book they like the best. Make sure they take the next available location in the column.
8. Count each column of votes and discuss which book had the most votes.
9. Read the winning book to the group.

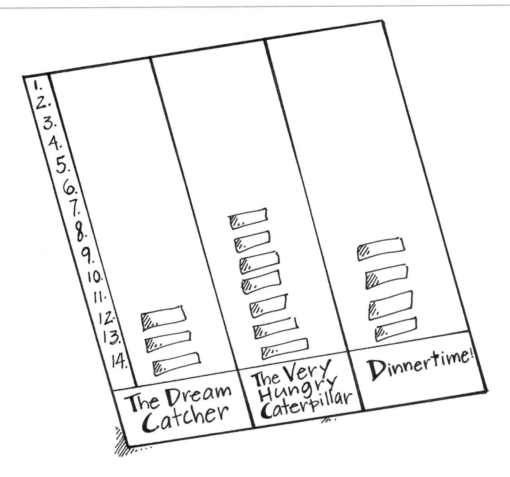

**Related book**    *Election Day* by Patricia Murphy

⭐ *Ann Kelly, Johnstown, PA*

# Veteran's Day Flag Dessert

SNACK AND COOKING

**Materials**    blue and red gelatin
whipped cream
large loaf pan or oblong plastic box
paper plates

**What to do**
- Veteran's Day is November 11th.
1. Start this dessert before Veteran's Day, so the gelatin has time to set.
2. Make red and blue gelatin with the children, using a little less water than the directions call for to make the gelatin quite firm.
3. Let the children take turns pouring a layer of gelatin into the large loaf pan, allowing it to set before adding the next color.
4. Add layers of blue and red gelatin until the pan is full.

5. When the gelatin is solid, turn the pan upside down on a plate and carefully remove it. Cut the striped gelatin into slices and put one on a paper plate for each child, to represent a flag.

6. Show children a picture of the United States flag. Invite them to squirt tiny drops of whipped cream in the top corner of their gelatin slices to represent stars.

**More to do**     Ask the children to find out if any of their family members or family friends are veterans. Have them share the information with the group.
**Books:** Read books about Betsy Ross and the flag.
**Group or Circle Time:** Talk about the significance of the colors red, white, and blue.
**Music:** Sing patriotic songs with the children.

**Related books**     *Betsy Ross* by Alexandra Wallner
*Red, White and Blue: The Story of the American Flag* by John Herman

 *Anne Adeney, Plymouth, United Kingdom*

# What Is a Cornucopia?

ART

**Materials**     pictures of cornucopias
cone-shaped paper cups and brown crayons or brown construction paper
scissors
stapler
craft glue
9" x 6" blue or green construction paper
cotton balls
seed catalogs or magazines with food pictures

**What to do**     ● Thanksgiving is celebrated on the fourth Thursday of November.

1. Show pictures of cornucopias. If possible, bring a real one to class and let the children guess what they are used for.

2. Explain to the children that a *cornucopia* is an ancient symbol for abundance. It has become a symbol for Thanksgiving, a day set aside for giving thanks for abundance.

3. Give each child a cone-shaped drinking cup. Ask them to color their cups brown. If you do not have cone-shaped cups, cut out 8" circles from brown paper and give one to each child. Help the children fold their circles into a cone shape and staple.

4. Ask the children to glue or staple their cones onto the blue or green paper.

5. Have them glue cotton balls inside their cones.

6. Encourage them to cover the cotton balls with pictures of food cut from catalogs and magazines. Let some of the pictures spill out onto the base paper.

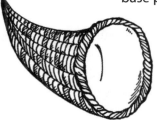

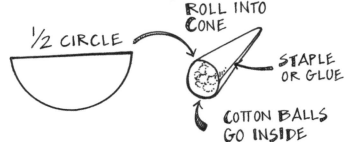

½ CIRCLE

ROLL INTO CONE

STAPLE OR GLUE

COTTON BALLS GO INSIDE

**More to do**    **Games:** Take some fruits and vegetables out of a cornucopia or basket and play a take-away memory game with the children.

MILK

YOGURT

**Related books**    *Happy Thanksgiving, Biscuit* by Alyssa Satin Capucilli
*My First Thanksgiving* by Tomie dePaola
*Thanksgiving Is for Giving Thanks* by Margaret Sutherland

PICTURES CUT FROM MAGAZINES

⭐ *Sandra Gratias, Dublin, PA*

# If You're Thankful and You Know It

FINGERPLAYS, SONGS, & POEMS

**Materials**    none

**What to do**    ● Thanksgiving is celebrated the fourth Thursday of November.
1. Sing the following song to the tune of "If You're Happy and You Know It."

*If you're thankful and you know it, clap your hands.*
*If you're thankful and you know it, clap your hands.*
*If you're thankful and you know it, then your face will surely show it.*
*If you're thankful and you know it, clap your hands.*

2. Substitute other actions your hands or face could do when thankful.

⭐ *Kathy Kalmar, Macomb, MI*

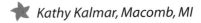

# Thanksgiving Is Here

FINGERPLAYS, SONGS, & POEMS

**Materials**    none

**What to do**
● Thanksgiving is celebrated the fourth Thursday of November.
1. Sing the following song to the tune of "Happy Birthday."

*Thanksgiving is here.*
*It comes every year*
*With turkey and dressing*
*And lots of good cheer.*

2. Ask the children to name other foods served on Thanksgiving. Sing the song again, substituting other foods.

 *Kathy Kalmar, Macomb, MI*

# Turkey and Dressing

FINGERPLAYS, SONGS, & POEMS

**Materials**    none

**What to do**
● Thanksgiving is celebrated the fourth Thursday of November.
1. Sing the following to the tune of "Three Blind Mice."

*Turkey and dressing.*
*Turkey and dressing.*
*Pumpkin pie,*
*Pumpkin pie,*
*Everybody's humming.*
*Did you ever hear such a sound in your life?*
*Yum, yum, yum.*

2. Sing "mashed potatoes and gravy" instead of "turkey and dressing."
3. Ask children what else they eat on Thanksgiving. Sing the song again using the new foods.

 *Kathy Kalmar, Macomb, MI*

# Thanksgiving or Not

GAMES

**Materials**
old magazines
scissors
felt
glue
flannel board

**What to do**
- Thanksgiving is celebrated the fourth Thursday of November.
1. Cut out pictures of a variety of foods. Include foods that are typically eaten on Thanksgiving and foods that aren't usually eaten on Thanksgiving (such as hot dogs or watermelon). Glue felt to the back of each picture.
2. Show the children the pictures of various foods.
3. Divide the flannel board into "Thanksgiving" and "non-Thanksgiving" sections.
4. Ask the children to decide which foods are eaten on Thanksgiving. Put the pictures on the appropriate side of the flannel board.

**More to do**
Do the activity using pictures of vegetables and fruits. Put fruit pictures on one side of the flannel board and vegetables on the other.

*★ Kathy Kalmar, Macomb, MI*

# Food ABC Book

LANGUAGE AND LITERACY

**Materials**
construction paper
magazines
scissors
glue

**What to do**
- Thanksgiving is celebrated the fourth Thursday of November.
1. Talk about Thanksgiving foods. Ask children what they like to eat on Thanksgiving.
2. Label each piece of paper with a letter of the alphabet. Give a page to each child.
3. Encourage the children to cut out pictures of foods that begin with the letter on their paper.
4. Share the pages and make them into an ABC Food Book.

**Related books** *Thanksgiving on Thursday* by Mary Pope Osborne
*Today Is Thanksgiving* by P.K. Hallanin

⭐ *Barbara Saul, Eureka, CA*

# Favorite Thanksgiving Food Graph

MATH

**Materials** white board or easel paper
pens

**What to do**
- Thanksgiving is celebrated the fourth Thursday of November.
1. Brainstorm with the children about Thanksgiving foods.
2. Divide the white board or easel paper into three columns. Label each column with a food.
3. Ask the children to mark the column with their favorite food.
4. Discuss the graph using mathematical terms, such as *most, least, equal, less,* and so on.
5. Make a graph of favorite Thanksgiving pies.

**More to do** **Books:** Ask the children to draw pictures of their favorite foods. An adult can label them. Children can also cut out favorite foods from magazines and glue the pictures to paper. Make a "favorite foods" class book.

**Related books** *If You Give a Moose a Muffin* by Laura Joffe Numeroff
*If You Give a Mouse a Cookie* by Laura Joffe Numeroff
*If You Give a Pig a Pancake* by Laura Joffe Numeroff

⭐ *Barbara Saul, Eureka, CA*

# What Did I Eat Today?

SCIENCE

**Materials**       food pyramid poster

**What to do**
- Thanksgiving is celebrated the fourth Thursday of November.
1. Talk about the food pyramid with the children, using the poster to illustrate.
2. Ask them what their favorite Thanksgiving foods are. Discuss which food groups the Thanksgiving foods belong in (turkey=meat and poultry).
3. Ask parents to write down the foods that their children eat for a full day. The children can illustrate the foods.
4. Read and share the results with the children. Ask the children to tell which foods belong to which sections of the food pyramid.
5. Write down the snacks or lunches that the children eat at school and put them in the correct groups.

**Related books**   *A Turkey for Thanksgiving* by Eve Bunting
*T'was the Night Before Thanksgiving* by Dave Pilkey

 *Barbara Saul, Eureka, CA*

# Giving Thanks

SOCIAL DEVELOPMENT

**Materials**       photos of children's families
large basket
real or fake fruits, vegetables, and breads
paper
stapler
glue

**What to do**
- Thanksgiving is celebrated on the fourth Thursday of November.
1. Send a note home asking parents to send in family photos, or take pictures of family members in class during drop-off and pick-up times.
2. At circle time, show the children the real or fake food. Discuss the qualities of each food.
3. Let each child place a piece of food in the basket.
4. Talk about what it means to be thankful. Focus the discussion on people that the children are thankful for and why, such as parents, siblings, relatives, friends, and so on.

5. Give each child a pre-made book (three pieces of paper stapled together). Have them glue their photos in their books and dictate why they are thankful for that particular person.
6. Send each child's book home and encourage a discussion at home about thankfulness.

MORE TO DO

**Dramatic Play:** If you use pretend foods in the basket, place them in the dramatic play center to encourage Thanksgiving role-play. Discuss and model how to show and when to tell others "thank you."

**Snack:** If you use real food in the basket, let the children help wash and prepare the foods for a "thanksgiving meal" of vegetable soup and fruit salad.

*Barb Lindsey, Madison City, IA*

# DECEMBER

Before introducing any activity, find out how the families in your class celebrate cultural and religious events. Select activities that respect their wishes and needs. This is especially true in December but also applies throughout the year.

# A Window on Winter

ART

**Materials**
construction paper
small, plastic zipper-closure bags
scissors
tape
fun foam in winter or holiday shapes (Christmas tree, snowman, and so on)
tiny polystyrene beads to represent snow

**What to do**
1. Fold a piece of construction paper in half to make a card.
2. Cut a hole in the front of the card slightly smaller than a small plastic bag.
3. Tape a zipper-closure bag inside the card, with the open edge at the top.
4. Insert a foam winter shape and some polystyrene beads into the bag. If you don't have foam shapes, use paper cutouts or old greeting cards for shapes.
5. Close the top of the bag.
6. Glue or a tape a small piece of matching construction paper to the inside of the card to completely cover the plastic bag.
7. Write an appropriate greeting inside the card.

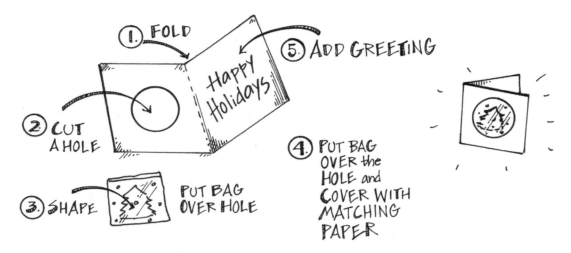

**More to do**
**Music:** Sing songs about windows, such as "Wee Willie Winkie," "Go In and Out the Window," and "How Much Is that Doggie in the Window?"

**Related books**
*Snowmen at Night* by Caralyn Buehner
*Ten Dogs in the Window* by Claire Masurel
*When Winter Comes* by Nancy Van Laan
*Window* by Jeannie Baker
*Winter: Poems, Songs, Prayers* by Wendy Mass

★ *Anne Adeney, Plymouth, United Kingdom*

# Mosaic Calendar

**Materials**

holiday or birthday wrapping paper
scissors
9" x 12" oak tag
glue
camera and film
small monthly calendar of upcoming year, one for each child
stapler
hole punch
yarn or string

**What to do**

1. This is a great activity to do in December, before the New Year arrives.
2. Encourage the children to cut different kinds of wrapping paper into small pieces.
3. Give each child a piece of oak tag. Demonstrate how to glue the paper pieces onto the oak tag in mosaic form. Make sure the entire piece of oak tag is covered.
4. Take a picture of each child. Ask them to tape their photos to the top of their decorative paper.
5. Obtain a small monthly calendar for each child. If this is not possible, make photocopies of the pages of a calendar, enough so that each child gets a full year.
6. Help the children staple their calendars underneath their mosaic pictures.
7. Punch two holes in the oak tag, one on each top corner of the paper.
8. Tie a string through the holes to make a wall hanging.
9. These make great gifts for parents.

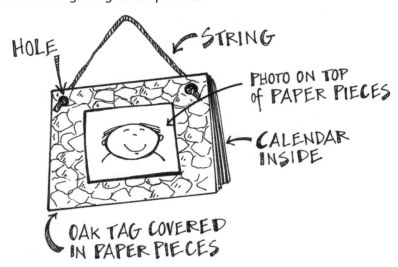

HOLE

STRING

PHOTO ON TOP
of PAPER PIECES

CALENDAR
INSIDE

OAK TAG COVERED
IN PAPER PIECES

*Andrea Hungerford, Plymouth, CT*

# Playdough Snowman Print

ART

**Materials**
chalkboard or chart paper
chalk or marker
blue paper
white, orange, black, and brown paint
playdough

**What to do**

1. Discuss the concepts of *small, medium*, and *large* with the children. Show examples, if possible, such as a small ball or block, a medium ball or block, and a large ball or block.
2. Draw an example of a snowman on a chalkboard or chart paper. Discuss the size difference of each snowball.
3. Provide blue paper, playdough, and white paint. Encourage the children to roll their playdough into three different size balls.
4. Demonstrate how to dip the playdough balls into the white paint to make a snowman print (large ball on bottom, medium ball in the middle, and small ball at the top). The children should start from the bottom of their paper and move upwards with their "snowballs."
5. Provide orange, brown, and black paint for children to add details, such as a "carrot" nose, brown "twig" arms, and a black hat and eyes.
6. If desired, provide Q-tips for children to dip into white paint and make dots to represent snow falling on the snowmen.

 *Jill Martin and D'Arcy Simmons, Springfield, MO*

# Wrap It Up

FINE MOTOR

**Materials**
miscellaneous boxes and containers to wrap
recycled or new wrapping paper (any holiday pattern)
tape
ribbons and stickers

**What to do**

1. Prior to the day of this activity, ask children and parents to save suitable boxes and wrapping paper and bring them in.
2. Tell the children that they are going to wrap their own boxes. Show one child at a time how to measure the amount of wrapping paper needed. Then, mark on the inside part of the paper where the child should cut it.
3. Help each child wrap his chosen box. Remember to let the child do as many of the steps as possible by himself.

4. Encourage the children to decorate their boxes with ribbons or colorful stickers.

5. Label the boxes for the children, if they want you to (for example, "Sam Wrapped This Box" or "From Alex to Mommy").

**MORE TO DO**    **Art:** Provide supplies for children to make their own wrapping paper.

 *Elisheva Leah Nadler, Jerusalem, Israel*

# Snowballs

GAMES

**MATERIALS**    3-4 sheets of white tissue paper for each child
2 buckets
ropes

**WHAT TO DO**    1. Place two pieces of rope on the floor about 4'-6' apart (reduce or expand the space according to the developmental level of the children).

2. Divide the children into two teams and have each team line up behind a rope. Place a bucket next to each team.

3. The child at the head of each line crunches a piece of tissue paper to make a "snowball." He then puts it into the bucket (to avoid throwing before it's time!) and runs to the back of the line.

4. This continues until all the children have made three or four "snowballs."

5. Have the children stand along the rope, facing the opposing team. The team who makes all their snowballs first gets to throw first. Have the team going second take a few paces back, so the area just behind their rope is empty.

6. Give each child on the first team three snowballs and, at a given signal, the snowball throwing begins. This can be done in turn or all at once. The object is to throw the snowball over the rope into the opposing side's space.

7. When the throwing is done, all the children count aloud to see how many snowballs have made it over the rope into the opposing team's territory.

8. Then the second team gets to throw their snowballs.

**MORE TO DO**    **Group or Circle Time:** Talk about snow and what we can do with it.
**Language:** Think of all the different words to describe snow. Find out some of the dozens of words the Inuit use for snow and share this with the children.
**Music:** Sing songs about snow and snowmen.

**Related books**  *The Big Snowball* by Wendy Cheyette Lewison
*The Biggest Snowball Ever!* by John Rogan
*The Biggest Snowball of All* by Jane Belk Moncure
*Emmett's Snowball* by Ned Mille
*Snowball* by Jennifer Armstrong
*The Snowball Fight* by Else Holmelund Minarik
*Snowballs* by Lois Ehlert

 *Anne Adeney, Plymouth, United Kingdom*

# Holiday Preparations

GROUP OR CIRCLE TIME

**Materials**  wrapping paper
tape
scissors
blocks
small Christmas tree
inexpensive plastic ornaments and decorations (made by the children)

**What to do**
1. Encourage the children to help decorate the classroom for Christmas, Hanukkah, and Kwanzaa.
2. Let the children practice wrapping blocks. Show them how to measure and cut wrapping paper and tape it around the blocks. Encourage older children to measure and weigh the different blocks. Ask them which package is bigger, smaller, wider, and so on.
3. Set up a small Christmas tree and let the children help decorate it any way they want. They can remove the ornaments and put them back on as many times as they want. Also put out a menorah and Kwanzaa decorations for children to decorate with.
4. Ask the children to talk about how their families decorate at home. If they celebrate Christmas, what do they put on their tree? If they celebrate Hanukkah, how do they decorate their homes? If they celebrate Kwanzaa, what color are the decorations? Talk about the similarities and differences between the way people decorate (whether they celebrate the same holiday or different holidays).

**Related song**  Sing the following song to the tune of "Here We Go 'Round the Mulberry Bush":

*This is the way we cut the paper,*
*Cut the paper, cut the paper,*
*This is the way we cut the paper*
*When we wrap our presents.*

*This is the way we tape the paper,*
*Tape the paper, tape the paper,*
*This is the way we tape the paper*
*When we wrap our presents.*

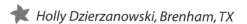 *Holly Dzierzanowski, Brenham, TX*

# Will It Snow?

## GROUP OR CIRCLE TIME

**What to do**
1. On an overcast winter day, ask the children to predict whether it will snow or not.
2. At the end of the day, graph results.

**More to do**   **Art:** Using Epsom salts, water, and black construction paper, make "frosty" pictures.

 *Kathy Kalmar, Macomb, MI*

# Family Books

## LANGUAGE AND LITERACY

**Materials**
construction paper
stapler
1-2 photos of children, with family members
crayons or markers
glue

**What to do**
1. Give each child a few pieces of construction paper. Help the children fold the paper in half and staple at the fold to make a book.
2. On the cover, write the child's and family's name, or let the child do so.
3. Encourage the children to draw pictures of their families and glue photos of family members inside the book.
4. Have the children tell you about the photos. Record that information inside the book.
5. These books make great holiday gifts, but they can be made at any time of the year.

 *Deborah Hannes Litfin, Forest Hills, NY*

# Snowflakes

MATH

**Materials**    thin white card
scissors
colored card squares, slightly bigger than snowflakes
glue

**What to do**    1. This makes a good matching, sorting, and memory game for older preschoolers. Fold a piece of paper to make two sheets. Cut out a snowflake shape, making sure to cut through both pieces of paper so you have two identical snowflakes.
2. Cut out a few more pairs of snowflakes, making each pair slightly different from the last.
3. Glue the snowflakes to colored card squares.
4. Ask the children to sort the snowflakes into exact pairs, and encourage them to talk about the parts that are similar and different.
5. Play memory games with the snowflake cards. Let the children take turns turning over two cards to try and make a pair. If the two cards do not match, turn them back over. If they do match, the child keeps them. Continue until all the cards are matched.

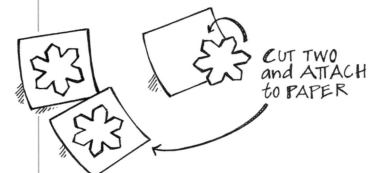

CUT TWO and ATTACH to PAPER

2 DIFFERENT DESIGNS

**More to do**    Use this activity as part of a winter or snow theme.
**Science:** Talk about how snowflakes are constructed. Show the children close-up photographs of real snowflakes.
**Math:** Play other matching games.

**Related books**    *Millions of Snowflakes* by Mary McKenna Siddals
*The Snowflake: A Water Cycle Story* by Neil Waldman
*Snowflake Bentley* by Jacqueline Briggs Martin
*The Snowflake Sisters* by J. Patrick Lewis
*The Snowflake: Winter's Secret Beauty* by Kenneth Libbrecht
*Snowflakes in Photographs* by W. A. Bentley
*Toby and the Snowflakes* by Julie Halpern

★ *Anne Adeney, Plymouth, United Kingdom*

# Jingle Bell Parachute

## MUSIC AND MOVEMENT

**MATERIALS**    large parachute
bells

**WHAT TO DO**

1. As the children hold onto the edge of a parachute, place bells in the middle of the parachute.
2. Have the children slowly raise and lower the parachute and sing "Jingle Bells" as the bells ring.

⭐ *Kaethe Lewandowski, Centreville, VA*

# Holiday Orchestra

## MUSIC AND MOVEMENT

**MATERIALS**    various sized boxes without lids
assorted rubber bands

**WHAT TO DO**

1. Wrap three to four rubber bands around each box.
2. Give a box to each child.
3. Help the children select a holiday song such as "Jingle Bells" to sing while strumming their musical box.
4. Talk about what a conductor does. Let the children take turns "conducting" the classroom orchestra.

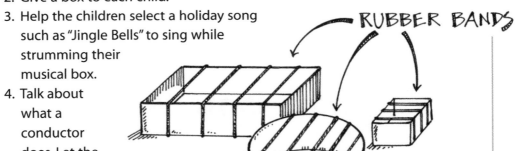

RUBBER BANDS

 *Elaine Commins, Athens, GA*

# Geo-Snow

OUTDOOR PLAY

**Materials**
several feet of string
scissors
snow

**What to do**
1. Cut string into a variety of lengths.
2. Unroll a length of string on the playground and lay it on the ground in a shape, such as a circle or an oval.
3. Demonstrate how to cover the string with snowballs, following the string pattern.
4. Lay out more patterns for the children to trace with snowballs.
5. For an added challenge, lay some of the strings in the shape of numbers and letters.
6. Encourage the children to create their own shapes with the string.

SNOWBALLS

STRING IN DIAMOND SHAPE

 *Karyn F. Everham, Fort Myers, FL*

# Snow Colors

OUTDOOR PLAY

**Materials**
water bottles with spray nozzle
food coloring
water

**What to do**
1. Add food coloring to water inside squirt bottles.
2. Bring the colored water outside and let the children spray the snow.
3. Ask the children if they think the snow is dirty (snow that hasn't been sprayed with colored water). Bring some snow inside and ask the children to predict whether or not it is clean. Let the snow melt in a clear container and check if it is clean or dirty.

 *Kathy Kalmar, Macomb, MI*

# The Mail Must Go Through

PROJECTS

**Materials**     *The Jolly Christmas Postman* by Janet and Allan Ahlberg
construction paper
markers, crayons, and colored pencils
holiday-themed stamps
washable stamp pad
standard card-sized envelopes
two first-class stamps for each child

**What to do**
1. At the beginning of December, ask parents to send in the addresses of the children's grandparents. Explain that the children will be creating their own holiday cards (Christmas, Hannukah, Kwanza, and so on) to send to their grandparents. If the children do not have living grandparents, ask for the addresses of favorite aunts or uncles.
2. Read *The Jolly Christmas Postman*. Talk about how the postman delivers holiday mail to people all over the world.
3. Ask the children if they have ever gotten any mail or sent any mail to anyone. Explain that they will be sending their own holiday mail to their grandparents, aunts, or uncles.
4. Give each child two pieces of construction paper. Show them how to fold the paper in half.
5. Offer a variety of drawing materials such as markers and colored pencils. You can also offer holiday-themed stamps and a washable stamp pad.
6. When the children are finished designing, help them print a holiday sentiment inside the card. Let them sign their own cards.
7. Give each child two envelopes. Help them print the addresses of their grandparents on each one. Let them decorate the envelope with markers or colored pencils, making sure not to obscure the addresses.
8. Help the children affix a postage stamp to each envelope.
9. When the children have completed their cards, plan a trip to the local mailbox or post office, if possible. Let the children mail their own cards.

**More to do**     **Dramatic Play:** Put mail carrier props in the dramatic play center.
**Field Trip:** Arrange a field trip to the local post office for a tour. This will help children understand how the mail they put in a mailbox gets to its intended destination. Or, invite a mail carrier to visit the classroom.
**Writing:** Add envelopes and adhesive stamps (like the kind from Easter Seals) to the writing center. Encourage the children to send mail to each other. Create a mailbox from a cardboard box or shoebox. Let the children place mail for each other or other classrooms in it. The children can take turns delivering the mail.

RELATED BOOKS  Arthur's Christmas by Marc Brown
Carl's Christmas by Alexandra Day
Dream Snow by Eric Carle
Jingle, the Christmas Clown by Tomie dePaola
Petunia's Christmas by Roger Duvoisin
Wake Up, Bear...It's Christmas by Stephen Gammell
The Wild Christmas Reindeer by Jan Brett

★ Virginia Jean Herrod, Columbia, SC

# GRAPHING THE AMARYLLIS PLANT

SCIENCE

**MATERIALS**

amaryllis bulb in a pot
tagboard
ruler and yardstick
markers

**WHAT TO DO**

1. In December, you can find amaryllis bulbs in pots for sale in most variety stores. These fast-growing bulbs grow to about two feet tall and have huge bright blooms. Because it grows so fast, the children can water it and watch it grow right away.
2. Make a green line on a graph to show the plant's height every few days.
3. When the plant begins to grow, have the children measure it with a small 6" ruler, and then move up to a 12" ruler. Finally, when the ruler is not big enough, they can use a yardstick.
4. When the blooms open, have the children measure the big blooms. (You may want to begin by asking them to predict how many blooms there will be and discover if they were correct later.)
5. Each day, choose a different child to be the "gardener," who is responsible for watering the plant and/or making the line on the graph.
6. Take photos as the plant gets bigger to show the growth.

**MORE TO DO**

**Outdoors:** Help the children plant other bulbs outside. Make labels to tag where they are and watch for them to bloom in the Spring.

**RELATED BOOKS**

The Carrot Seed by Ruth Krauss
The Reason for a Flower by Ruth Heller
The Tiny Seed by Eric Carle

★ Laura Durbrow, Lake Oswego, OR

# Welcome Winter

LANGUAGE AND LITERACY

**MATERIALS**
several large sheets of paper
index cards
markers

**WHAT TO DO**
- The first day of winter is December 21st.

1. Introduce the first day of winter (December 21st) with your favorite winter children's book (see book list below for suggestions).

2. Write the word "winter" in the center of a large sheet of paper and circle it. Ask the children to name some things that relate to winter, such as snow, cold, ice, ski, hot chocolate, mittens, boots, sled, snowman, and so on. Write their ideas on the paper outside the circle as they say them.

3. Depending on the attention span of your group, you can end the activity and post the list, end the activity and come back to it later for extension activities, or continue the activity by making a "winter word wall."

4. To continue, let each child choose a word to copy. Ask them to draw a picture of the word on an index card.

5. Write their word on the card and have them add the card in the correct location on a winter word wall. (A word wall is a bulletin board display of the alphabet that the children add words to so they can refer to them for various activities.)

**MORE TO DO**
Use the list of words to develop your next theme with the children. Vote on a category for the direction the curriculum will take. Have the children decide on how to change the room, props needed, and encourage their creativity by letting their ideas transform the room.

**Group or Circle Time:** Cut out all the winter words listed. Designate a few categories, such as "holiday," "weather," "clothes," "food," and so on. Ask the children to sort the words into the correct categories.

**RELATED books**
*Bear Snores On* by Karma Wilson
*Light of Winter: Winter Celebrations Around the World* by Heather Conrad
*White, Winter, Wonderful* by Elaine Good
*Winter* by Maria Rius

⭐ *Ann Kelly, Johnstown, PA*

# BE A DREIDEL

GAMES

**MATERIALS**  2 or 3 different types of tops or Hanukkah dreidels

**WHAT TO DO**
- Hanukkah is an eight-day celebration that is celebrated on the 25th day of the Hebrew month of Kislev, which usually occurs in December (but sometimes in November).

1. Show the children how the dreidels work and discuss the turning motion. If children are old enough, let them experiment with spinning the dreidels.

2. Encourage the children to act like spinning dreidels as you sing the traditional dreidel song:

*I have a little dreidel, I made it out of clay,*
*And when it's dry and ready, then dreidel I shall play.*
*Oh, dreidel, dreidel, dreidel, I made it out of clay.*
*And when it's dry and ready, then dreidel I shall play!*

Or try this variation:

*I have a little dreidel, I bought it in a shop,*
*I like to see it spinning around like a top.*
*Oh, dreidel, dreidel, dreidel, I bought you in a shop.*
*I like to see you spinning around until you drop!*

3. Most likely, the children will spin and drop spontaneously as the words of the song suggest! Repeats will be in demand!

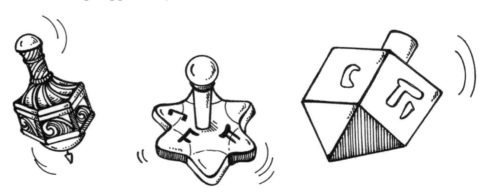

**MORE TO DO**  Ask the children to look around the classroom for other toys to spin, such as balls and hoops. See which things spin the longest.

 *Elisheva Leah Nadler, Jerusalem, Israel*

# Spin, Spin, Spin

GAMES

**Materials**

assortment of spinning tops (plastic, wooden, multi-colored, dreidels, and so on)

trays

**What to do**

- Hanukkah is an eight-day celebration that is celebrated on the 25th day of the Hebrew month of Kislev, which usually occurs in December (but sometimes in November).

1. Explain to the children that a dreidel is a well-known symbol of Hanukkah. It is a four-sided top with a Hebrew letter printed on each side.
2. Place tops on different trays and encourage the children to spin them.
3. Watch to see which top spins the longest. Ask the children why they think some tops spin longer than others.
4. For older children, try stackable tops. Challenge them to stack as many as they can while the tops are spinning.

**More to do**

**Art:** Make spin art on an old record player. Cut a hole in a paper plate and fit it on the record player. Turn on the record player, and as it spins, have the children hold markers to the plate, creating interesting designs.

⭐ *Ann Scalley, Orleans, MA*

# One-to-One Hanukkah Candle Match

MATH

**Materials**

5" x 7" cards

markers

Hanukkah candles

**What to do**

- Hanukkah is an eight-day celebration that is celebrated on the 25th day of the Hebrew month of Kislev, which usually occurs in December (but sometimes in November).

1. Beforehand, draw a menorah on eight 5" x 7" cards. Draw one Hanukkah candle on the menorah on the first card, two candles on the second card, and continue until there are eight candles on the last card.

2. Show the children individually or in small groups how to arrange the menorah cards in order from one through eight candles.

3. Provide a box of Hanukkah candles for children to place on each candle depicted in the cards to practice one-to-one correspondence.

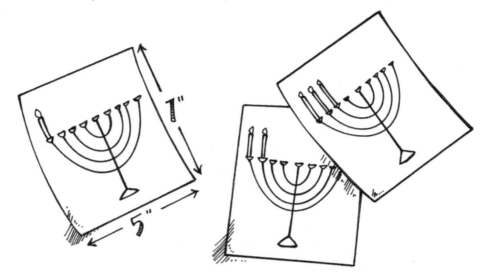

**MORE TO DO**    **Games:** Provide a real menorah. Put the menorah cards in a pile face down. The child draws a card from the pile and puts the number of candles depicted on the card into the real menorah.

 *Elisheva Leah Nadler, Jerusalem, Israel*

# Circle-Style Ornament

ART

**Materials**    3" yogurt lid with clear plastic center
cardboard or oak tag
pencil
scissors
old holiday cards
red or green construction paper
white glue
gold cord or yarn
glitter

**What to do**    • Christmas Day is December 25th.
1. Wash clear plastic yogurt lids.
2. Draw a 2 ¾" circle on cardboard or oak tag and cut it out to make a pattern.

3. Help the children do the following steps to make their own ornaments.
4. Trace the circle on a holiday card, circling the image intended for the center of the ornament.
5. Cut out the traced circle.
6. Cut out a 3 ¼" circle from red or green construction paper.
7. Glue the holiday image to the center of the colored paper circle.
8. Glue the paper to the inside of a yogurt lid, so the image shows through the plastic.
9. Glue glitter to the outside of the lid.
10. Glue gold cord or yarn to the back of the ornament to hang.

2 ¾"
(FROM CARD)

3 ¼"
TRACE and CUT
RED OR GREEN
CIRCLE

GOLD CORD

YOGURT LID

RED or GREEN PAPER

CARD IMAGE

★ *Mary Brehm, Aurora, OH*

# Candy Canes

ART

**Materials**    red and white pipe cleaners or chenille stems (five red and
five white per child)
scissors

**What to do**
- Christmas Day is December 25th.
1. Cut pipe cleaners in half. Give five red and five white pipe cleaners to each child.
2. Show the children how to wind the red pipe cleaner around the white one (or the other way around) and bend the top to make candy canes.

**More to do**    **Math:** Use some of the candy canes for counting activities. The hooked top makes them easy to hang off a cup. Write the numbers 1-5 or 1-10 on cups (one number on each cup) and have the children place the appropriate number of canes on each cup.

★ *Linda Ford, Sacramento, CA*

# Poinsettia Card

ART

**Materials**    *The Legend of the Poinsettia* by Tomie dePaola
9" x 12" white construction paper
red construction paper strips
green construction paper
scissors
finely chopped yellow pipe cleaners
craft glue
green and red markers

**What to do**
- Christmas Day is December 25th.
1. Read *The Legend of the Poinsettia* to the children.
2. Fold the white paper in half to form a card.
3. Draw a 1 ½" circle in the center of the front of each card.
4. Cut red construction paper into 3" x 9" strips and green construction paper into 3" x 3" strips. Mark each strip with 1 ½" wide triangles for the children to cut apart.
5. Give the children the red and green strips and show them how to cut them into triangles.

6. Demonstrate how to glue the red triangles with the wide ends on the line, around the circle. Slip some green triangles between or behind the red ones.
7. The children paint glue in the center of the circle and cover with yellow pipe cleaner pieces.
8. Inside the card, use markers to write a holiday message.

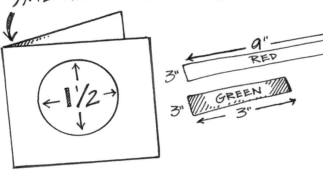

9X12 WHITE CONSTRUCTION PAPER

GREETING INSIDE

YELLOW PIPE CLEANER PIECES

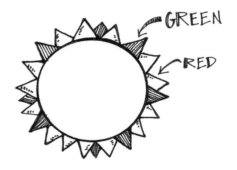

GREEN
RED

**More to do**  Make or buy a piñata for a Mexican-style Christmas party.
**Field Trip:** Visit a greenhouse or florist.
**Stories:** Talk about other traditional holiday plants, such as mistletoe, holly, and evergreen, and discuss their legends.

**Related book**  *¡Fiesta!* by Ginger Foglesong Guy

 *Sandra Gratias, Dublin, PA*

# Call Rudolph

FINGERPLAYS, SONGS, & POEMS

**What to do**

● Christmas Day is December 25th.
Sing the following song with the children to the tune of "Five Little Monkeys Jumping on the Bed."

*Eight little reindeer pulling Santa's sleigh,*
*One fell down and bumped his head.*
*The elves called Santa and Santa said,*
*"Can seven little reindeer pull my sled?"*

*Seven little reindeer pulling Santa's sleigh,*
*One fell down and bumped her head.*
*The elves called Santa and Santa said,*
*"Can six little reindeer pull my sled?"*

*Five little reindeer…*
*Four little reindeer…*
*Three little reindeer…*
*Two little reindeer…*

*One little reindeer pulling Santa's sled,*
*He fell down and bumped his head.*
*The elves called Santa and Santa said,*
*"Call Rudolph!"*

⭐ *Kathy Kalmar, Macomb, MI*

# I'm a Christmas Candle

FINGERPLAYS, SONGS, & POEMS

**What to do**

● Christmas Day is December 25th.
Sing the following song, performing appropriate gestures.

*I'm a Christmas candle* (stand; hands above head as if they were a flame)
*Growing shorter you can see.* (bend down)
*Melting all my wax* (bend some more)
*Till there's nothing left of me.* (go down to the floor)

**More to do**

Change "Christmas candle" to "spooky candle" and repeat at Halloween. Sing in a spooky voice.

⭐ *Kathy Kalmar, Macomb, MI*

# Santa, Santa

### FINGERPLAYS, SONGS, & POEMS

**Materials**   none

**What to do**   ● Christmas Day is December 25th.
Do the following fingerplay with the children.

*Santa, Santa, eyes aglow,* (make circles around eyes using hands)
*Comes down the chimney* (slide one hand down other arm)
*With a Ho! Ho! Ho!*

★ *Kathy Kalmar, Macomb, MI*

# This Is the Way We Trim Our Tree

### FINGERPLAYS, SONGS, & POEMS

**Materials**   none

**What to do**   ● Christmas Day is December 25th.
Sing the following song to the tune of "This Is the Way We Wash Our Clothes."

*This is the way we trim our tree,*
*Trim our tree,*
*Trim our tree.*
*This is the way we trim our tree*
*For Christmas Day.*

★ *Kathy Kalmar, Macomb, MI*

# MEMORY TREE GAME

GAMES

**Materials**     felt squares in five different colors (except green)
green felt large enough to cover a flannel board
flannel board

**What to do**
- Christmas is celebrated on December 25th.
1. Beforehand, cut a large tree shape from the green felt. From each of the five pieces of felt, cut out a square, circle, diamond, triangle, and star (five different colors of squares, five different colors of circles, and so on).
2. At circle time, place the tree on the flannel board.
3. Arrange the shapes on the tree in a grid pattern, colors matching vertically and shapes matching horizontally.
4. Ask the children to cover their eyes as you remove one of the shapes.
5. The children must guess the shape and color of the missing ornament.

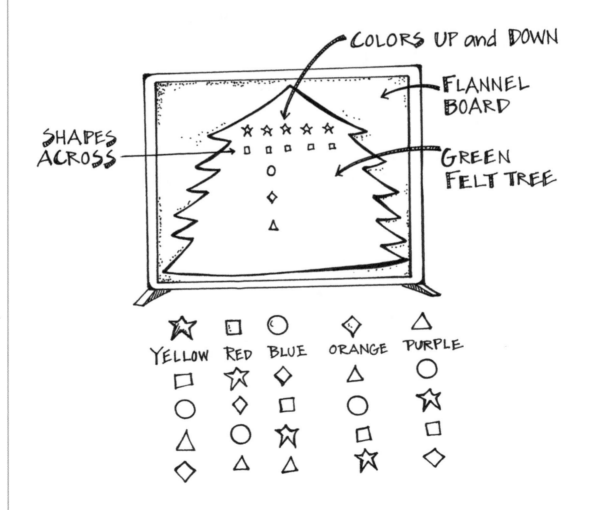

**MORE TO DO**   Use actual ornaments for a take-away game similar to the Memory Tree Game.

**More Games:** Hide ornaments around the room for an ornament hunting game.

**Math:** Provide a basket of ornaments to sort by characteristics such as color, size, material, and so on.

**RELATED BOOK**   *I Spy Christmas: A Book of Picture Riddles* by Walter Rick and Jean Marzollo

⭐ *Sandra Gratias, Dublin, PA*

# Christmas Chains

MATH

**MATERIALS**   colored paper
scissors
glue

**WHAT TO DO**
- Christmas Day is December 25th.
1. Cut colored paper into 1" x 6" rectangles (see the illustration on the next page).
2. Demonstrate how to bend a rectangle to make a circle and glue the sides together.
3. Put another rectangle through the circle, make a circle with it, and glue the sides together.
4. Encourage the children to continue in this fashion to make their own paper chains.
5. If desired, encourage the children to make patterns with the colored papers in the chains, for example, red, green, white; red, green, white; and so on.
6. Have groups of children connect their chains and measure them across the room.
7. Ask each of the groups to connect their chain to the rest of the chains to see how long the classroom chain is.
8. Use the long chain to decorate a Christmas tree or areas around the room.

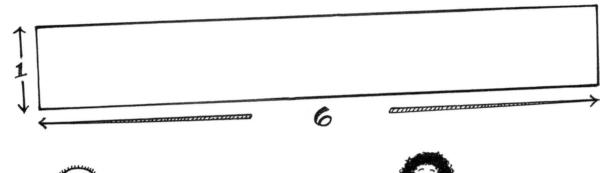

**Related books** *Angelina's Christmas* by Helen Craig
*Madeline's Christmas* by Ludwig Bemelmans

⭐ *Barbara Saul, Eureka, CA*

# Reindeer Pokey

MUSIC AND MOVEMENT

**What to do**
- Christmas Day is December 25th.
Sing the following song to the tune of "Hokey Pokey," performing the appropriate gestures with each line.

*You put your antlers in, you put your antlers out,*
*You put your antlers in, and you shake them all about.*
*You do the Reindeer Pokey and you turn yourself around,*
*That's what it's all about. (clap)*

*Additional verses:*
*You put your hooves in…*
*You put your tail in…*
*You put your red nose in…*
*You put your reindeer body in…*

**More to do**
**Art:** Make Rudolph pictures with the children. Trace the child's foot, and use that shape as Rudolph's face. Trace the child's hands to use as Rudolph's antlers. Let the child add a red nose and black eyes.

⭐ *Kathy Kalmar, Macomb, MI*

# JANUARY

# Making Snowmen

ART

**Materials**    *The Three Billy Goats Gruff* story
white and colored beeswax, plasticene, or playdough

**What to do**
1. Tell the story of the *Three Billy Goats Gruff*.
2. Talk to the children about size: *small, medium,* and *large,* or *big, bigger,* and *biggest.*
3. Invite the children to make a small ball out of white beeswax or playdough, a medium-sized ball, and finally, a large ball.
4. Talk about how to put them together to make a snowman using the size vocabulary.
5. Encourage them to use colored beeswax or playdough to add details such as a scarf and hat, eyes, nose, and buttons.

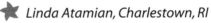 *Linda Atamian, Charlestown, RI*

# Clouds Bring Snow

ART

**Materials**    pictures of clouds
gray fingerpaint (mix white and black)
fingerpaint paper
stapler
white curling ribbon
4" white doilies
glue
white glitter

**What to do**
1. Discuss types of clouds and where snow comes from. Look at pictures of clouds.
2. Cut fingerpaint paper into cloud shapes approximately 12" x 15".
3. Encourage the children to fingerpaint on the cloud shapes with the gray paint.
4. When dry, let them staple ribbons and doilies (snowflakes) to the clouds.
5. Paint glue on the doilies and sprinkle them with glitter.
6. Hang the clouds and snowflakes from the ceiling.

**More to do**   **Math:** On a snowy day, take the children outside and measure the depth of the snow.
**Science:** Chart cloud types or cloudy vs. sunny days.
**More Science:** Pack snow in a glass and let it melt. How much water did it make?

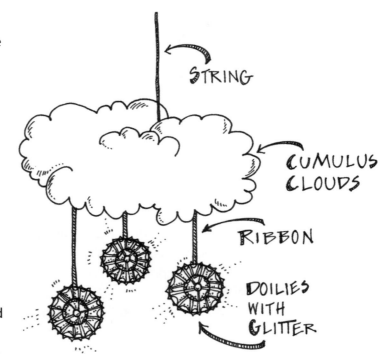

STRING

CUMULUS CLOUDS

RIBBON

DOILIES WITH GLITTER

**Related books**   *The Big Snow* by Berta and Elmer Hader
*It Looked Like Spilt Milk* by Charles G. Shaw
*Snow Is Falling* by Franklyn M. Branley

⭐ *Sandra Gratias, Dublin, PA*

# Icicles

ART

**Materials**   easel
blue paper
eyedroppers
watered-down glue
silver glitter

**What to do**
1. Attach blue paper on the easel.
2. Demonstrate how to squeeze watered-down glue into the eyedropper and then squeeze the glue mixture at the top of the blue paper.
3. Watch it dribble down the paper.
4. Let children sprinkle silver glitter on the dripped glue to create "icicles."

⭐ *Kaethe Lewandowski, Centreville, VA*

# SEAL PUP PAL

ART

**MATERIALS**
white tube socks (child size 4-6)
black fun foam
black yarn
black felt
tacky glue or fabric glue
³⁄₈" black pompoms

**WHAT TO DO**
1. For each child, cut out two foam circles for eyes, two felt circles (³⁄₄") for cheeks, and six pieces of 2" yarn for whiskers.
2. Help the children glue two foam circle eyes on their socks for eyes.
3. Help them glue three yarn "whiskers" to each felt circle. Show them how to glue the circles to the sock, yarn side down and close together, for cheeks.
4. Let children glue on a pompom nose above the cheeks.
5. When dry, use the "seals" as hand puppets.

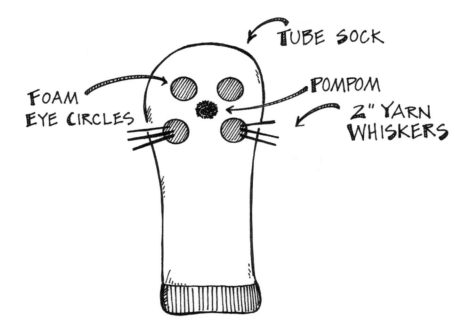

TUBE SOCK

FOAM EYE CIRCLES

POMPOM

2" YARN WHISKERS

**RELATED books**
*Animal Close-Ups: The Seal* by Joelle Soller
*Seals!* by Ellen Catala

*Sandra Gratias, Dublin, PA*

# Snip, Snip, Snow!

A R T

**Materials**     *Snip, Snip, Snow* by Nancy Poydar
              white paper
              scissors
              round plate
              paint and brushes
              glitter

**What to do**    1. Read *Snip, Snip, Snow* to the children.
              2. After finishing the story, show the children how to make snowflakes by
                 folding a piece of paper many times and cutting designs into it.
              3. Let the children decorate their snowflakes using paint and glitter.
              4. Hang the snowflakes from the ceiling.

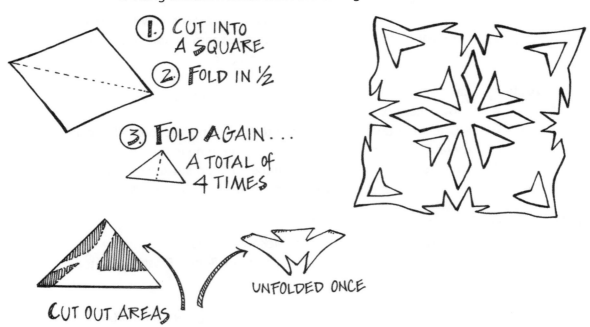

1. CUT INTO A SQUARE
2. FOLD IN ½
3. FOLD AGAIN... A TOTAL OF 4 TIMES

CUT OUT AREAS

UNFOLDED ONCE

★ *Ann Scalley, Orleans, MA*

# Snow Is Falling!

ART

**Materials**
white tempera paint
shallow paint dishes
9" x 12" dark blue construction paper
large and small, empty, plastic (not Styrofoam) thread spools with end
    labels removed
precut snowflakes or doilies
white glue
markers

**What to do**
1. Pour white paint into shallow paint dishes. Give each child a piece of dark blue paper.
2. Encourage the children to dip spools into paint and print "snowflakes" all over their blue paper.
3. If desired, children can draw a face on a precut snowflake or doily and glue it on their picture. Or, encourage them to draw, paint, or glue a snowman at the bottom of their picture.

**More to do**
**Language:** Encourage the children to dictate a story about where their snowflakes go.
**Music and Movement:** Play gentle music and encourage the children to pretend to be snowflakes floating and twirling in the sky.
**Outdoors:** On a snowy day, take the children outside to catch snowflakes on black paper and examine them with a magnifying glass.

**Related books**
*I Am Snow* by Jean Marzollo
*Millions of Snowflakes* by Mary McKenna Siddals
*Stopping by Woods on a Snowy Evening* by Robert Frost (illustrated for children)

⭐ *Sandra Gratias, Dublin, PA*

# Snowflake Prints

ART

**Materials**
white and blue tempera paint
shallow containers
newspaper
paint smocks
12" x 18" construction paper in pale blue, gray, and black
snowflake cookie cutters in various sizes and designs
glitter in silver, white, and blue

**What to do**
1. Ahead of time, pour white paint into two shallow containers. Mix a very small amount of blue into one of them to create light blue paint.
2. Cover the tables with newspaper and help the children put on paint smocks.
3. Demonstrate how to dip a cookie cutter into the paint and print several times before dipping it into the paint again. Show them how to put the cookie cutter down without sliding it to get a clear snowflake print.
4. Encourage the children to choose a piece of construction paper and use different cookie cutters and both colors of paint to make snowflake prints.
5. Shake a little glitter on the designs while the paint is still wet.

**More to do**
**Art:** Encourage the children to make snowmen out of clay or playdough.
**More Art:** Cut snowflakes from white paper to decorate the room.

**Related song**
Sing the song below to the tune of "I'm a Little Teapot" and encourage the children to twirl around like snowflakes falling.

*I'm a little snowflake, falling down*
*Joining my buddies on the ground.*
*Watch me twirling gently as I go*
*Making a blanket of soft white snow.*

**Related books**
*Curious George Goes Sledding* by Margaret Rey
*Katie and the Big Snow* by Virginia Lee Burton
*Snow Lion* by David McPhail
*The Snowy Day* by Ezra Jack Keats

 *Susan Oldham Hill, Lakeland FL*

# Sock Snowmen

ART

**Materials**
children's white socks
pillow stuffing
rubber bands
pens
buttons
white glue

**What to do**

1. Give each child one white sock.
2. Show the children how to stuff the sock with pillow stuffing.
3. Help the children put rubber bands in the middle and the top of their socks, making a snowman with two balls of "snow" (instead of three). Leave about 1"–2" above the top rubber band.
4. Let the children use pens to make faces for the snowmen.
5. Show the children how to color in the 1"–2" part of the sock above the top rubber band with a black pen and turn the hat down like a stocking hat.
6. Let the children glue buttons down the front of the bottom ball of the snowman.

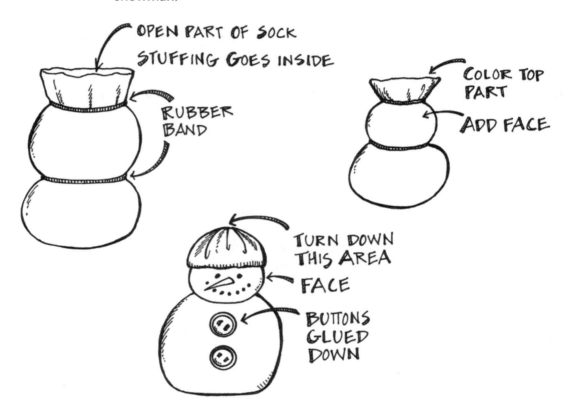

OPEN PART OF SOCK

STUFFING GOES INSIDE

RUBBER BAND

COLOR TOP PART

ADD FACE

TURN DOWN THIS AREA

FACE

BUTTONS GLUED DOWN

**Related books**   *The Jacket I Wear in the Snow* by Shirley Neitzel
*White Snow, Bright Snow* by Alvin Tresselt

⭐ *Barbara Saul, Eureka, CA*

# I'M A LITTLE SNOWMAN

## FINGERPLAYS, SONGS, & POEMS

**MATERIALS**     none

**WHAT TO DO**    Sing the following song with the children to the tune of "I'm a Little Teapot."

*I'm a little snowman*
*Short and fat.*
*Here is my broomstick*
*Here is my hat.*
*When the sun comes out*
*I melt away...*
*Down, down, down, down,*
*Oops, I'm a puddle!*

 *Sandie Nagel, White Lake, MI*

# A-Sledding We Will Go

## FINGERPLAYS, SONGS, & POEMS

**MATERIALS**     none

**WHAT TO DO**    Sing the following song to the tune of "A-Hunting We Will Go."

*A-sledding we will go,*
*A-sledding we will go,*
*We'll hold on tight*
*And sit just right,*
*And down the hill we'll go.*

 *Kathy Kalmar, Macomb, MI*

# Brrr, It's Freezing

### FINGERPLAYS, SONGS, & POEMS

**Materials**      none

**What to do**    Sing the following song to the tune of "Oh, My Darling Clementine."

*Brrr it's freezing, brrr it's freezing,*
*Brrr it's freezing outside.*
*It is winter, snow, and ice,*
*Things are frozen outside.*
*Bundle up, bundle up,*
*Bundle up to go outside,*
*Hat and coat and scarf and mittens,*
*Bundle up to go outside!*

⭐ *Kristi Larson, Spirit Lake, IA*

# This Is the Way the Snow Comes Down

### FINGERPLAYS, SONGS, & POEMS

**Materials**      none

**What to do**    Sing the following song to the tune of "This Is the Way We Wash Our Clothes."

*This is the way the snow comes down,*
*Snow comes down, snow comes down.*
*This is the way the snow comes down*
*On a cold and frosty morning.*

Additional verses:
*This is the way the sleet comes down…*
*This is the way the rain comes down…*
*This is the way the hail comes down…*
*This is the way the sun comes up…*

⭐ *Kathy Kalmar, Macomb, MI*

# Building a Snowman
## FINGERPLAYS, SONGS, & POEMS

**Materials**    none

**What to do**    1. Read the following action rhyme and model the motions for the children.

*Let's build a snowman!*
*We will make him round.* (make a circle with hands)
*We'll use lots of the soft snow*
*That's falling to the ground.* (with arms up, wiggle fingers and lower hands as a snowfall)
*First, let's roll a great big ball.* (use arms and hands to make a big circle)
*His bottom can't be little!* (shake head and wag finger "no")
*Then make a ball that's not so big*
*To put on for his middle.* (rub tummy)
*We'll make his round, snowy head*
*And put it right on top!* (pretend to put head on snowman)
*Add eyes, and nose, and a big smile,* (point to each on your own face)
*He's done! Now we can STOP!* ("freeze" in position)

2. Repeat the action rhyme as desired so the children can use the motions again.

**More to do**    **Art:** Create your own snowmen with the children. Use 8 ⅞" and 7" white plates and 12 oz. bowls to create a snowman. Using the underside of all three items, attach the smaller plate to the large one, and the bowl to the middle plate to form a snowman. Let children decorate their snowman with craft supplies such as markers, colored paper, craft sticks, and glue. Decorate the underside of a second bowl, cut two slits in the bowl's edge directly opposite each other, and add these slip-on "hats" to the snowman's head.

**Related books**    *Snowmen at Night* by Caralyn Buehner
*Stranger in the Woods* by Carl R. Sams II and Jean Stoick

⭐ *Theresa Callahan, Easton, MD*

# FUN IN THE SNOW

GROUP OR CIRCLE TIME

**MATERIALS**   newspaper, at least 20 sheets for each child
baby wipes or soap and water

**WHAT TO DO**
1. Have the children form two lines facing each other.
2. Unfold the newspaper and place a stack in front of each child.
3. Tell the children the newspaper is their pile of "snow" and they are to make snowballs out of each sheet.
4. The child crumples one sheet of newspaper into a "snowball" and throws it "snowball fight" style to the other line of children. Lots of giggles will follow.
5. As the pile of "snowballs" grows in the center of the room, invite one or two children at a time to make "snow angels" by lying down in the pile and dragging their arms and legs through the "snow." Fluff the pile as needed.
6. If the pile of "snow" is large enough, the children can "trudge" through it, "tunnel" through it, or build a fort to hide behind.
7. When finished, ask the children to flatten the sheets and stack them for recycling.

**Note:** Make sure children wash the newsprint from their hands when finished. Caution them not to put their hands in their mouths or on their faces until they have washed off any newsprint from their hands.

**MORE TO DO**   **Science:** Talk about why a flat sheet of paper doesn't fly as well as a paper snowball when thrown.

**RELATED book**   *The Snowy Day* by Ezra Jack Keats

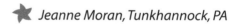 *Jeanne Moran, Tunkhannock, PA*

# INDOOR SNOW

LANGUAGE AND LITERACY

**MATERIALS**   *Snowballs* by Lois Elhert
dish tubs
sand shovels
old markers
water paints
craft sticks
buttons and scraps of material
camera
construction paper

**What to do**
1. On a snowy day, read *Snowballs* by Lois Elhert to the children.
2. If possible, let the children go outside and dig snow into dish tubs. Bring the tubs of snow back into the classroom.
3. Give each child markers, paint, craft sticks, buttons, and scraps of materials. Encourage them to explore the snow and make their own creations. Make sure they wear gloves or mittens for this activity.
4. Take photos of each child's creation.
5. Glue each photo to a piece of construction paper. Have the children dictate a few sentences about their creations and write their words under their photos.
6. Compile the photos into a classroom Snow Book.
7. Read the book to the children. Let them take turns bringing it home to read with their families.

 *Patricia Cawthorne, Lynchburg, VA*

# PENGUINS ON PARADE

LANGUAGE AND LITERACY

**Materials**
construction paper and scissors
penguin shape (to trace)
pictures of things representing each letter of the alphabet
glue stick
poster board
laminating machine
pocket chart, optional

**What to do**
1. This is a fun activity for letter sequencing. Trace penguins on paper and cut out 26 penguin shapes.
2. Write a letter of the alphabet on each penguin. Or, if children are older, cut out or draw pictures of items representing each letter of the alphabet on each penguin (apple, bat, car, dog, and so on).
3. For added strength, glue all the penguin shapes to poster board.
4. Laminate them for durability, and cut out the shapes.
5. Put the penguins in a container and place them in a center with a pocket chart.
6. The child places the penguins in alphabetical order according to the letter or sound of the picture on the front of the penguins.

**Related books**
*Cinderella Penguin, Or, the Little Glass Flipper* by Janet Perlman
*Little Penguin's Tale* by Audry Wood
*Tacky the Penguin* by Helen Lester

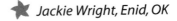 *Jackie Wright, Enid, OK*

# A SENSE OF SEASONS

## LANGUAGE AND LITERACY

**MATERIALS**
chart paper
markers
drawing paper
indoor/outdoor thermometer

**WHAT TO DO**

1. Talk about how our senses play an important role in telling us about the seasons.
2. Ask the children to talk about what they sense in winter. Answers will depend on your particular geography. For example, they might talk about the feel of ice, the smell of a log burning in a fireplace, and the sound of snow falling.
3. Encourage them to talk about how their families prepare for particular seasons. (You might want to send a letter home to parents to help children with this part.) Write their responses on chart paper.
4. Invite the children to write or draw things they enjoy about the current season.
5. On the first day of a new season, record the temperature both indoors and outdoors. Compare the differences as each season arrives.
6. If possible, take a walk outdoors during each season and ask the children to point out changes. Encourage them to use their senses.

*Margery Kranyik Fermino, Hyde Park, MA*

# UP, UP, AND AWAY!

## LANGUAGE AND LITERACY

**MATERIALS**
old magazines or markers
scissors
tagboard
glue
12" x 18" construction paper
laminating machine
pocket chart

**WHAT TO DO**

1. This is a great way for children to practice rhyming skills.
2. Draw or glue a picture of a snowman with its hat blowing away on a piece of tagboard to make a header card. Print the title "Up, Up, and Away!" and instructions ("Match the rhyming pairs on the word wall") under the picture.

3. Cut out or draw colored pictures of pairs of rhyming words, such as coat and boat, chair and bear, and so on.

4. Cut the rhyming pictures into the desired size cards.

5. If desired, make a file jacket by folding a piece of 12" x 18" construction paper to hold the activity.

6. Laminate the header card, picture cards, and file jacket for durability, and cut out.

7. Have the children sit in front of the pocket chart.

8. Give one card to each child, making sure you keep one of each rhyming pair.

9. In the top row of the chart, display the header card.

10. Place the cards you kept (one of each rhyming pair) in the pocket chart, leaving room between each picture.

11. Invite children to place their pictures in the appropriate places in the pocket chart to make rhyming pairs.

★ *Jackie Wright, Enid, OK*

# WEATHER GRAPH

MATH

**Materials**    large piece of cardboard
pen
yardstick

**What to do**    1. Use the pen and yardstick to draw six columns on the piece of cardboard.
2. Divide the columns into 2" squares.
3. Label the top of the columns: rainy, snowy, foggy, windy, sunny, and cloudy. Write the days and/or dates on the lefthand side of the graph (see sample on the next page).
4. Put the graph by the window.
5. Each day, pick a child to look out the window and color in a square(s) in the correct column. More than one square can be colored on days that have a mixture of weather.
6. Each day read the graph, counting how many days have each type of weather. Use math terms such as *more, less, higher, lowers, equal,* and so on.
7. Each month start a new graph.
8. Keep each month's graph for comparison to the others to see which months have the most rain, sun, and so on.

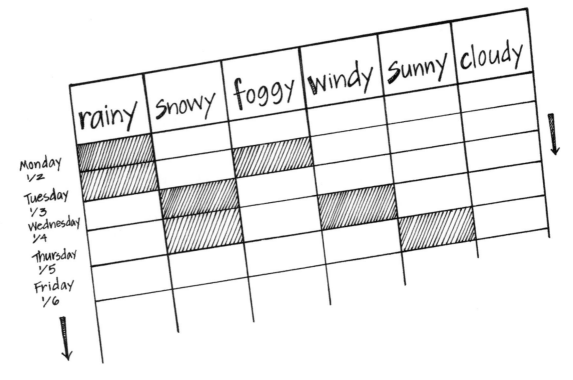

| | rainy | snowy | foggy | windy | sunny | cloudy |
|---|---|---|---|---|---|---|
| Monday 1/2 | | | | | | |
| Tuesday 1/3 | | | | | | |
| Wednesday 1/4 | | | | | | |
| Thursday 1/5 | | | | | | |
| Friday 1/6 | | | | | | |

**Related book** *Weather Words* by Gail Gibbons

⭐ *Barbara Saul, Eureka, CA*

# Mitten Activities

MATH

**Materials**
*The Mitten* by Jan Brett
various pairs of mittens
colored construction paper
scissors
hole punch
string
crayons or markers

**What to do**
1. Read *The Mitten* by Jan Brett.
2. Put out an assortment of mixed-up mittens and encourage the children to make pairs.
3. Cut out pairs of mitten shapes from colored paper.
4. Punch holes in matching paper mittens and tie a string between each pair.
5. Let the children draw animals on the mitten pairs.

⭐ *Audrey Kanoff, Allentown, PA*

# ICE SKATING

MUSIC AND MOVEMENT

**MATERIALS**     wax paper
scissors
music

**WHAT TO DO**     1. Cut two pieces of wax paper to fit the bottom of each child's shoe.
2. Play music.
3. Have the children place one piece of wax paper under each shoe and glide to the music.

**MORE TO DO**     **Field Trip:** Visit an indoor or outdoor ice skating rink.

 *Kaethe Lewandowski, Centreville, VA*

# SNOWFLAKES DANCING

MUSIC AND MOVEMENT

**MATERIALS**     recording of music that evokes images of snow (such as "Snowflakes Are Dancing" by Claude Debussy)

**WHAT TO DO**     1. Explain to the children that snow is formed when tiny water droplets in the clouds stick to salt or dust particles and freeze, forming ice crystals. These crystals stick to other crystals and form clusters, which make the larger snowflakes we can see falling from the sky. Some of the prettiest snowflakes are shaped like six-pointed stars.
2. Encourage the children to pretend to be ice crystals in the clouds.
3. Play music that evokes images of snow.
4. Ask the children to hold out their hands and spread their legs like star-shaped crystals as they dance around the room. (Model this by doing it with the children.)
5. When one child touches another, they should "stick together" (hold on to each other) until clusters of "snow crystals" are formed.
6. The dancing "snowflakes" slowly drift down towards the floor like snow falling from the sky.

**Related books**   *The First Snowfall* by Anne F. Rockwell
*Snow* by Marion Dane Bauer
*Snow Amazing: Cool Facts and Warm Tales* by Jane Drake and Ann Love
*Snowflake Bentley* by Jacqueline Briggs Martin
*Snow Is Falling* by Franklyn Mansfield Branley
*The Snow Lambs* by Debi Gliori
*Snow Music* by Lynne Rae Perkins

★ *Sarah Glassco, Alexandria, VA*

# Camping in the Cold

OUTDOOR PLAY

**Materials**   one or more pup tents
flashlights
sleeping bags
one backpack per tent
children's cooking utensils
wood scraps

**What to do**   1. Pitch the tents outside.
2. Put two flashlights, two sleeping bags, and a backpack filled with cooking utensils into each tent.
3. During recess, invite the children to pretend to camp out.
4. Build a "campfire" with wood scraps. Sit around the "fire" and sing camp songs together.
5. Do this activity in the summer, too, and compare the similarities and differences between camping when it's cold and when it's hot (see "A Sizzling Summer Camp Out" on page 443 in the July/August chapter).

★ *Karyn F. Everham, Fort Myers, FL*

# Snowball Hula

## OUTDOOR PLAY

**Materials**   several hula hoops
snow

**What to do**
1. Stand the hula hoops a couple feet apart against an outside wall of the school building.
2. Demonstrate for the children how to throw a snowball at one of the hula hoops, aiming the snowball at the inside of the hula hoop.
3. Line up the children in a row so that several can throw snowballs at the same time.
4. Vary the level of difficulty by having the children throw the snowballs from 4 feet, 8 feet, and 10 feet from the hula hoops.

*Karyn F. Everham, Fort Myers, FL*

# A Day at the Beach

PROJECTS

**Materials**
lemonade
craft sticks
ice cube trays
large piece of yellow tagboard
hole punch
string
two dishpans
play sand
small household items (measuring cups, plastic spoons, and so on)
lawn chair

**What to do**
1. Ahead of time, tell the children that they will be having a "Day at the Beach" to help them think warm thoughts! Ask them what kinds of things they do in the summer and at the beach.
2. This activity can occur over a couple of days.
3. Prepare lemon popsicles a day ahead by freezing lemonade in ice cube trays and inserting craft sticks when they are half frozen.
4. The next day, cut out a large sun from tagboard, punch a hole in the top, add string, and hang from the ceiling.
5. On the "beach day," fill dishpans with sand and small toys. Encourage children to play in the sand and pretend they are at a beach.
6. Set up a lawn chair for story time and read summertime stories.
7. Let the children wear visors or sunglasses during snack and story time.
8. Enjoy lemonade Popsicles during snack.

⭐ *Ingelore Mix, Gainesville, VA*

# Hot and Cold

SCIENCE

**Materials**
pictures of cold items and hot items
red and blue paper

**What to do**
1. Show the children the pictures of hot and cold items.
2. Ask the children to put the pictures of hot items on the red paper, and put the pictures of cold items on the blue paper.

 *Kaethe Lewandowski, Centreville, VA*

# Snow Experiment

SCIENCE

**Materials**
snow
paper cups

**What to do**
1. Gather a pile of snow.
2. Ask the children whether snow melts faster in the sun or shade.
3. Put snow in paper cups. Put some of the cups in the sun and some in the shade.
4. Observe which melts faster.
5. Measure how much water comes from melted snow.

**Related rhyme**
*I'm big and round at the bottom.* (stand and lean over to trace a big circle shape with hands)
*I'm small and round at the top.* (reach up and trace a small circle)
*And in the middle I'm medium-sized,* (draw a circle in front of you with both hands)
*And I carry a broom or a mop.* (pretend to hold a broom or mop)
*I stand up tall on each frosty day,* (stand very straight)
*But when it gets warm, I melt away.* (sink to the floor)

 *Sandra Gratias, Dublin, PA*

# Colored Ice Blocks

SCIENCE

**Materials**
variety of containers
water
food coloring

**What to do**
1. Fill the various containers with water and food coloring.
2. Leave the containers outside overnight (make sure temperature is below 32 degrees).
3. Let the children use the ice blocks as building blocks (either outside or inside at the water table). Make sure they wear mittens or gloves.
4. If using blocks inside, encourage the children to watch the colors blend as the blocks melt.

**Related book**
*Little Blue and Little Yellow* by Leo Lionni

 *Audrey Kanoff, Allentown, PA*

# ICE CUBE RACES

SCIENCE

**Materials**      boards or ramps
blocks
ice cubes
ice cube trays
food coloring

**What to do**

1. Before freezing ice cubes, add food coloring to distinguish the cubes.

2. Keep the ice cubes in the freezer or cooler until the children are ready to use them.

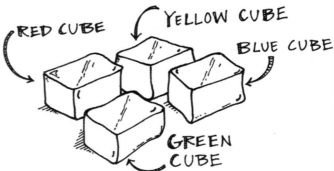

3. Help the children make ramps of various materials and heights using blocks and a variety of ramp materials, such as wood, vinyl, Formica-type surface, or plastic.

4. Let two children at a time choose an ice cube and "race" them down the ramp. Encourage them to experiment with different types of ramps and heights.

5. Afterward, discuss what they observed. On which surface did the cubes go down fastest? Slowest? What changes happened to the cubes? How did the melting affect the speed? How did the height of the ramps affect the speed?

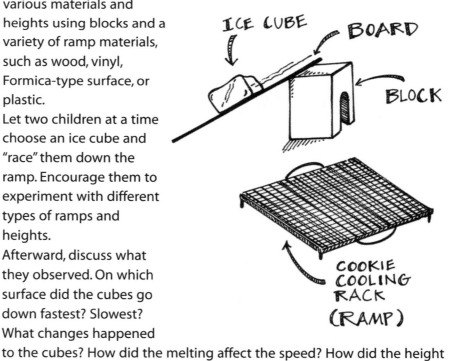

★ *Sandra Nagel, White Lake, MI*

# Make Flakes

SCIENCE

**Materials**
salt
heated water
bowl or cup (clear, heat-resistant, and non-breakable)
spoon
shallow, dark-colored dishes (white crystals show up well against a dark
    background; black plastic bowls from frozen, entrees are ideal.)
magnifiers (large, stationary magnifiers are easier for young children to use
    than hand-held magnifying glasses)
coarse salt (optional: kosher salt or sea salt crystals)

**What to do**
- Allow several days for this two-part activity. If you prepare the solutions on a Friday, by Monday crystals will be visibly forming. If the children are patient, prepare the solution on Monday or Tuesday and check each day to watch the crystals grow.
1. Make a super-saturated salt solution. In a clear cup or bowl, dissolve salt in hot water (adult only). Let the children stir and watch the salt disappear. Keep adding salt until it begins to precipitate (come out of a liquid solution into a solid form).
2. Pour the solution into one or more shallow, dark bowls. Set aside and leave undisturbed for several days.
3. As the solution cools the water cannot hold as much solute, so the salt will slowly settle out, forming crystals as it precipitates. Eventually the water will evaporate, leaving only salt or sugar behind.
4. Encourage the children to look at the crystals under magnifiers. Ask them to count their sides and compare their shapes. (Salt crystals will be squares made of interlocking triangles.) Note how the crystal plates fit together different ways. Compare them to snowflake crystals seen in pictures or during a real snowfall.

**More to do**
**Outdoors:** Go for a walk outside when fresh snow is falling. Catch snowflakes on dark clothing or a chilled piece of dark paper. Look fast—they lose their structure very quickly. Encourage the children to try to spot the seven basic kinds of snowflakes: hexagonal plates, stellar crystals, hexagonal columns, needles, asymmetrical crystals and graupels, or snow pellets (formed when tiny frozen droplets coat hexagonal plates or stellar crystals.) A simplified "field guide" to snowflakes is available at www.snowcrystals.com.

**Related book**
*The Snowflake: Winter's Secret Beauty* by Kenneth Libbrecht

 *Sarah Glassco, Alexandria, VA*

# Ice Crystals

SCIENCE

**Materials**  several containers with lids
deep buckets or plastic tubs

**What to do**

1. Make ice crystals indoors. Fill several containers with hot water. Put tight-fitting lids on the containers and place in a freezer overnight. Condensation of the hot water vapor will coat the underside of the lids. This will freeze as delicate crystals, while the water in the bowl will form a solid block of ice.
2. Carefully remove the lids and encourage the children to examine the crystals. They will melt very quickly, so it is helpful to freeze several bowls and open just one or two at a time.
3. Discuss how these crystals compare with snowflakes. (They will be mostly needle-like or feathery structures.)
4. If possible, make ice crystals outdoors. Fill deep buckets or plastic tubs with water. Place outside in subfreezing temperature.
5. When the water has partly frozen, carefully remove the thick cap of ice from the top of the container. (This may take $\frac{1}{2}$ day to 2 days, depending on outside temperature and size and shape of container.) Encourage the children to observe the ice crystals hanging from the underside of this ice block. (These will be larger than the ice crystals formed in the freezer.)

 *Sarah Glassco, Alexandria, VA*

# Snow Painting

SCIENCE

**Materials**  powdered tempera
empty salt and pepper shakers (or something similar)
paper
bowl or bucket
snow (or crushed ice)
paper or cloth towels

**What to do**

1. Put powdered tempera into the shakers.
2. Give each child a piece of paper and bowl of snow or crushed ice. (If the weather permits, let them collect their own.)
3. Let each child decide if she wants to sprinkle the paint first or put the snow on the paper first.

4. If the child chooses to add paint first, have her put snow on top of it. If she chooses to put the snow on the paper first, have her sprinkle it with tempera.
5. Place in a warm area on top of towels and watch the snow melt.
6. Observe to see if there is a different effect between the children who did paint first and those who did snow first.

⭐ *Kristi Larson, Spirit Lake, IA*

# GOING HOME FOR THE WINTER
SCIENCE

**MATERIALS**
popcorn
nuts
oranges
pinecones
peanut butter
scissors
string
birdseed

**WHAT TO DO**
1. Let the children string popcorn and oranges on a piece of string.
2. Encourage the children to coat pinecones with peanut butter, spread birdseed on the peanut butter, and tie string to the pinecones.
   **Safety Note:** Be aware of any peanut allergies or sensitivities and plan accordingly.
3. Hang the strings of food on a tree near the school or center.
4. Observe the different kinds of birds that come to feed. Make notes about them in a journal.

⭐ *Geary Smith, Mexia, TX*

# SNOW IN A BAG
SENSORY

**MATERIALS**
fresh snow
water table
meatball makers or small scoops
small baking pans
tortilla makers
small pails
extra mittens and gloves
markers

**WHAT TO DO**
1. Put fresh snow in the water table with meatball makers or small scoops, small baking pans and pails, and tortilla makers. Have children wear mittens or gloves.
2. Encourage the children to make snowballs, snow cakes, and pies.
3. As the snow begins to melt, add markers and let children color the snow.

 *Ann Scalley, Orleans, MA*

# Animals in the Snow

SENSORY

**MATERIALS**
sensory table and tubs
plastic toy figures of animals that live in the snow (polar bears, moose, wolves, seals, walrus, penguins, deer)
small plastic shovels and scoops
snow
mittens
clothespins

**WHAT TO DO**
1. Talk about animals that live in the snow. What features do the animals have that help them live in the cold?
2. Place the animal figures and small shovels and scoops in the sensory table.
3. Scoop snow from outside into tubs and add the snow into the sensory table.
4. Provide mittens for the children to wear while they play.
5. Have a designated place for children to hang the mittens when they are finished wearing them. Provide pinch-type clothespins for children to work on fine motor and self-help skills.

**MORE TO DO**
**Group or Circle Time:** Find where the animals might live and mark it on a map or globe with stickers or wipe-off markers.

**RELATED books**
*Annie and the Wild Animals* by Jan Brett
*The Mitten* by Jan Brett
*Stranger in the Woods: A Photographic Fantasy* by Carl R. Sams

⭐ *Sandie Nagel, White Lake, MI*

# All People Are Different

## FINGERPLAYS, SONGS, & POEMS

**Materials**
construction paper
markers or old magazines
scissors
felt
glue
red sticker hearts
flannel board

**What to do**
- January is It's Okay to Be Different Month.
1. Draw (or cut out from magazines) people in a variety of shapes, colors, and sizes. Back each picture with felt and place a red heart sticker on the back of each person.
2. Read the poem below and put the appropriate person on the flannel board.

   *Some people are short,* (put image of short person on board)
   *Some people are tall.* (put up tall person)
   *Some people have big feet,* (put up a clown)
   *Some people's feet are small.* (put up a baby)
   *Some people are heavy,* (put up a weight lifter)
   *Some people are light.* (put up a ballet dancer)
   *Some people's skin is brown,* (put a brown-skinned person)
   *Some people's skin is white.* (put up a white-skinned person)
   *Some people have brown eyes,* (put up a person with brown eyes)
   *Some people's eyes are blue.* (put up a person with blue eyes)
   *All people are different*
   *This is very true,*
   *But inside each person—*
   *I think this is very smart—*
   *Beats the same red human heart.*

3. Flip over all the people on the board, showing the hearts attached to the back of the images.
4. Take a poll to see what kind of differences the children have, such as eye color, hair color or texture, who has lost a tooth, and so on.
5. In the end, give a heart to each child.

 *Ingelore Mix, Gainesville, VA*

# Friends

### SOCIAL DEVELOPMENT

**Materials**     *The Color of Us* by Karen Katz

**What to do**
- January is It's Okay to Be Different Month.
1. Read the book *The Color of Us*.
2. Ask two children to stand face to face and describe the similarities and differences they see between themselves.
3. Repeat with all the children in the class.
4. Share the findings with the children.

 *Kaethe Lewandowski, Centreville, VA*

# We Wish You a Happy New Year

### FINGERPLAYS, SONGS, & POEMS

**Materials**   none

**What to do**   • January 1st is New Year's Day.
Sing the following song to the tune of "We Wish You a Merry Christmas."

*We wish you a happy new year,*
*We wish you a happy new year,*
*We wish you a happy new year*
*With lots of good cheer.*

⭐ *Kathy Kalmar, Macomb, MI*

# Ring, Ring, Ring the Bells

### FINGERPLAYS, SONGS, & POEMS

**Materials**   none

**What to do**   • January 1st is New Year's Day.
Celebrate the New Year by singing the following song to the tune of "Row, Row, Row Your Boat."

*Ring, ring, ring the bells*
*Ring them loud and clear,*
*To tell the children everywhere*
*That New Year's Day is here!*

⭐ *Kathy Kalmar, Macomb, MI*

# Calendar Numbers

MATH

**Materials**

calendar for the new year
large, old unused calendars with child-friendly pictures

**What to do**

- January 1st is New Year's Day.
1. Gather a variety of monthly calendars with child-friendly pictures. Tear out each page so that the children have an assortment to choose from.
2. Show the children an intact calendar and explain what it is used for. Point out the name of the months, the days of the week, and the dates. Explain that January is the first month of the year.
3. Let each child choose a page from the assortment of calendar pages.
4. Encourage them to practice writing the numbers in the boxes.

⭐ *Gail Morris, Kemah, TX*

# Classroom Resolution

SOCIAL DEVELOPMENT

**Materials**

dictionary
large paper, chalkboard, or dry-erase board
two large sheets of paper
marker

**What to do**

- January 1st is New Year's Day.
1. Bring a dictionary to circle time. (If this is the first time the group will be using a dictionary, introduce it to them and explain its purpose.)
2. Write the word "resolution" on a large sheet of paper, chalkboard, or dry-erase board.
3. Look up the word in the dictionary. Explain how you are locating the word and ask the children to help you sound it out.

4. Write the definition on the paper next to the word.

5. Explain that you would like the group to decide on a good resolution for the class to work on together. Explain that working on a resolution as a group will be beneficial because they can help each other to keep it.

6. Discuss any problems the group may be having (sharing, following a rule, and so on) or something they would like to do more of or get better at (read more books each day, keep the room clean, and so on).

7. Choose one of the resolutions for the group and write it on a large sheet of paper. Post it on a wall. (If there are many suggestions from the group, have a vote to choose the resolution that will be worked on.)

8. The next day at circle time, discuss the resolution.

9. Make a list of things that can be done to ensure the resolution will be kept.

10. Decide as a group how you will monitor the class' success.

11. Revisit your progress often with the group.

**More to do**    Challenge another class in the school to make and keep a resolution of their own. Track and compare each group's progress across a chosen time period.

**Related book**    *The Promise* by Larry Dane Brimner

 *Ann Kelly, Johnstown, PA*

# Birds and Beards

FINGERPLAYS, SONGS, & POEMS

**Materials**    paper plates
heavy white paper or cards
scissors
pictures of a wren, lark, owl, and hen
glue
cotton wool or yarn (optional)

**What to do**    ● National Bird Day is January 5th.

1. Teach the children Edward Lear's famous nonsense poem:

*There was an old man with a beard,*
*Who said, "It is just as I feared!*
*Two owls and a hen, four larks and a wren,*
*Have all made their nests in my beard!*

2. Cut heavy white paper or cards into a beard shape, one for each child.

3. Cut out one tiny, four small, two medium, and one large ovals for each child, making sure they will all fit onto the beard shape.

PAPER PLATE

BEARD

4. Show the children pictures of a wren, lark, owl, and hen.

5. Encourage them to draw the pictures on the appropriate oval (a wren on the tiny oval, four larks on the small ovals, two owls on the medium ovals, and a hen on the large oval).

6. Help the children glue the birds onto their beards. Let them add cotton wool or yarn for hair, if desired.

7. Fasten each child's beard securely to a paper plate.

8. Encourage the children to draw an old man's face onto the plate.

**Related books**   *Little Old Big Beard and Big Young Little Beard* by Remy Charlip
*The Runaway Beard* by David Schiller
*This Old Man* by Pam Adams
*The Old Man and the Bear* by Wolfram Hanel

⭐ *Anne Adeney, Plymouth, United Kingdom*

# Rubber Ducky Day
### PROJECTS

**Materials**   variety of rubber ducks in different styles, sizes, and colors
large tabletop basin
water source
buckets
yellow card stock paper and construction paper
yellow craft feathers
craft dough or playdough
variety of craft materials
craft glue
stuffed ducks of all sizes and colors

**What to do**

- Rubber Ducky's "birthday" is January 13th.

1. On January 13, tell the children that they are going to celebrate the birthday of a popular animal "friend." Ask them if they can guess the animal. Offer clues:
   - This animal has feathers.
   - This animal swims.
   - This animal has two webbed feet.
   - This animal has two wings.
   - This animal is yellow.
   - This animal quacks.

   Continue until the children have guessed it is a duck. Explain that it's not just any duck's birthday, but it is Rubber Ducky's birthday! Show them a yellow rubber duck and read *Rubber Duckie* by Jodie Davis.

2. Set up several centers to celebrate Rubber Ducky's birthday.

3. Place a large basin on a low table. Let the children use buckets to fill the basin about halfway with water. Put some small rubber ducks in the water for the children to explore. Encourage them to experiment with different ways to get the ducks to move (create ripples with fingers, blow on the backs of the ducks, tip the pan gently from side to side, and so on).

4. In the art center, offer playdough or craft dough and yellow craft feathers. Encourage the children to roll the dough into two balls (one slightly smaller than the other). Show them how to stack the balls together to form a duck shape. They can cover their ducks with craft feathers by inserting the pointed end of the feathers directly into the dough. Form a duck's bill by cutting two small triangles from yellow construction paper. Show them how to insert one side of the triangles into the dough on the duck's head to make a beak. Let air dry for a couple of days. Demonstrate how to create feet by cutting two heart shapes out of yellow construction paper and gluing the feet to the bottom of the dried duck.

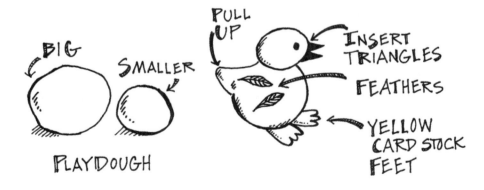

5. In the manipulatives area, place several different colors and sizes of rubber ducks in a box. Challenge the children to sort the ducks by size and color and to sequence the ducks from largest to smallest.

6. In the reading center put out books about ducks (see related books on the following page).

7. Outdoors, have feather races. Challenge the children to move from one spot to another quickly while keeping a yellow craft feather afloat in the air. The children can bat the feather with a hand, wave a hand near it to make the air move, or blow on the feather to keep it up in the air.

8. Place several different sizes and colors of feathers in the science area. Encourage the children to examine the feathers through magnifiers.

9. Add several different types of stuffed ducks to the dramatic play center. Add an empty bag of duck food and small bowls. Encourage the children to pretend to care for and feed their new pets.

**More to do**

**Art:** Let the children create funny duck shoes. Help them trace two webbed feet on heavy yellow paper. Encourage them to decorate their webbed feet as desired. Punch holes in two rows near the middle of each foot. Unlace the children's shoes and lace the webbed feet onto the tops of their shoes. Have fun waddling around to music!

**Games:** Play a fun matching game with the rubber ducks. Divide some of the large rubber ducks into pairs. On the bottom of each pair, attach a matching symbol, numeral, or alphabet letter. (Print the information on a small piece of paper, laminate, and attach to the bottom of the ducks using sticky-back looped adhesive.) Float the ducks in a small basin and let children take turns matching the symbols on the bottoms.

**Related books**

*Angus and the Ducks* by Marjorie Flack
*Duck in the Truck* by Jez Alborough
*The Duck Who Loved Puddles* by Michael J. Peliowski
*Five Little Ducks* by Raffi
*I Wish That I Had Duck Feet* by Theo LeSieg
*Make Way for Ducklings* by Robert McCloskey

*Virginia Jean Herrod, Columbia, SC*

# I Have a Dream, Too

ART

**Materials**

*A Picture Book of Martin Luther King, Jr.* by David A. Adler
*Martin's Big Words: The Life of Dr. Martin Luther King, Jr.* by Doreen Rappaport
8" x 11" white construction paper
crayons or markers
9" x 12" colored construction paper
hole punch
heavy thread

**What to do**
- Martin Luther King, Jr.'s birthday is January 15th. The holiday is celebrated on the third Monday of January.

1. Read the books *A Picture Book of Martin Luther King, Jr.* and *Martin's Big Words: The Life of Dr. Martin Luther King, Jr.* with the children. Make sure the children understand that when Dr. King was talking about his dream, he meant he wanted to see people live together in harmony.

2. Ask the children if there is something they would like all people to do. "If you could get everyone to do something important, what would you want them to do?" or "What do you think people should do so everyone can live happily together?" Avoid asking, "What is your dream?" since young children will most likely answer with a story about a dream they had at night.

3. Write down what children say or record them and transcribe their words at a later time.

4. Ask them to draw a picture on an 8" x 11" piece of white construction paper to illustrate their responses.

5. Glue the 8" x 11" illustration to a 9" x 12" piece of colored construction paper.

6. Print the children's responses below their illustrations.

7. Create a cover page for the book. (A photo or illustration of Dr. King makes a nice cover.) Print "I Have a Dream, Too!" on the cover. Use a piece of colored construction paper for the back cover.

8. Bind the pages together into book form by punching three holes in the left edge of each page and using heavy thread to sew the pages together.

9. Read the book together during story time.

10. If desired, make individual copies of the book for each child by copying each page before gluing them to the construction paper. Staple the copied pages together without the construction paper backing. Give one to each child.

**Related books**
*Just For You! Singing for Dr. King* by Angela Medearis
*Thank You, Dr. King!* by Robin Reid
*What Is Martin Luther King, Jr. Day?* by Margaret Friskey

★ *Virginia Jean Herrod, Columbia, SC*

# APPRECIATING DIFFERENCES
### FINGERPLAYS, SONGS, & POEMS

**WHAT TO DO**

- Martin Luther King, Jr. Day is celebrated on the third Monday of January. Sing the following to the tune of "Have You Ever Seen a Lassie?" for Martin Luther King Day.

*We are all different,*
*All different,*
*All different,*
*We are all different,*
*Each in our own way.*

*Whether dark skin or light,*
*We should get along not fight,*
*We are all different,*
*Each in our own way!*

 *Kristi Larson, Spirit Lake, IA*

# MARTIN LUTHER KING, JR. DAY
### SOCIAL DEVELOPMENT

**MATERIALS**

copy of Dr. Martin Luther King's "I Have a Dream" speech
paper
crayons or markers

**WHAT TO DO**

- Martin Luther King, Jr. Day is celebrated on the third Monday of January.
1. Read parts of the "I Have a Dream" speech. This is a long speech, so pull out the parts that relate to the activity. Discuss what the words mean and the overall message of the speech.
2. Do "people sorting" by grouping the children with certain characteristics, such as same hair color, eye color, shirt color, shoe type, and so on.
3. Have each child draw a picture of herself. Discuss the similarities and differences between each child.
4. Have the children dictate stories about peace and getting along with everyone. Make a class book with these stories.

 *Barbara Saul, Eureka, CA*

# Laboratory

SCIENCE

**Materials**   short-sleeved, white men's dress shirts (for lab coats)
magnifying glasses
calculators
plastic beakers and test tubes (or clear plastic measuring cups)
tweezers
tools
boxes
pipe insulation
microscope
telescope
magnets
color paddles (colored lenses one can see through)
old small appliances (with cords removed)

**What to do**
- Benjamin Franklin's birthday is January 17th and Sir Isaac Newton's birthday is January 4th. (He was born on Christmas Day, December 25th, but that was using the old calendar.)
1. Explain to the children that Benjamin Franklin and Sir Isaac Newton were great inventors, both born in January.
2. Read the children a book about these two scientists. Talk about inventors and inventions.
3. Provide the above materials for children to explore.
4. Let them take apart small appliances and encourage them to explore new objects!

⭐ *Kristi Larson, Spirit Lake, IA*

# Rolling Cans With Electricity

SCIENCE

**Materials**   balloons
empty soda can
wool item, such as a sock, scarf, or a sweater

**What to do**
- Ben Franklin's birthday is January 17th.
1. Blow up the balloons and tie a knot in them. Give one to each child.
2. Encourage the children to rub their balloons on a wool item until they hear faint crackling.
3. Place an empty soda can on its side on a flat surface.
4. Hold the balloon near, but not touching, the can. The can will begin to roll quickly toward the balloon, as if pushed by an invisible hand!

**More to do**
**Science:** Do the following activities with a charged balloon:
- Sprinkle salt in one dish and pepper in another dish. Hold the charged balloon over each one to see which jumps up and sticks to the surface of the balloon.
- Tear a tissue into small pieces and hold the charged balloon over the pieces.
- Hold the charged balloon near a running faucet. The thinner the stream of water, the better the effect.

**Related books**
*Flash, Crash, Rumble, and Roll* by Franklyn M. Branley
*Switch On, Switch Off* by Melvin Berger
*Where Does Electricity Come From?* by C. Vance Cast

 *A.M. Adams, Marysville, OH*

# Pooh Party

PROJECTS

**Materials**
*Winnie the Pooh* by A.A. Milne
air dry modeling dough in yellow, white, and brown
at least two small, plastic honey pots or plastic honey bottles (with a regular top, not the spout type)
construction paper in white, yellow, and red
glue
liquid laundry starch
yellow food coloring or yellow tempera paint
bowl

**What to do**
- January 18th is the birthday of A.A. Milne, the author of "Winnie the Pooh".
1. A few days before January 18th, begin to read "Winnie the Pooh" to the children. This chapter book might take several days to finish.

2. Explain that you have planned a "Winnie the Pooh Day" to help celebrate the birthday of A.A. Milne, the author who wrote the story you have been reading.

3. Ask everyone to wear a red shirt on January 18, as Pooh wears a red shirt.

4. Begin the day on January 18 by doing Pooh's stoutness exercises together. These can be any simple exercise such as touching toes and reaching to the sky, bending side to side, or running in place.

5. When you go outside, have "Honey Relay Races." Line up the children in two rows. Give the first child in each row a small plastic honey pot or honey bottle. Have the children race to a designated spot and turn around and race back. The children then hand off the pot to the next children in line. Continue until all have had a turn.

6. During center time, let the children use yellow, white, and brown air-dry modeling dough to make a beehive and some bees.

7. During group time, play "Pooh, Pooh, Where's Your Honey Pot?" (played the same as Doggy, Doggy, Where's Your Bone?) and "Pooh in the Dell" (see original songs on the next page).

8. Make some "honey dough." Mix equal parts white school glue and liquid laundry starch. Color it yellow with food coloring or liquid tempera paint. Mix thoroughly until the mixture forms a slightly sticky ball. Add more starch if it is too sticky. Store in an air-tight container.

9. Wind up your birthday celebration by making some birthday cards for A.A. Milne. Use red, white, and yellow construction paper to create the cards. Display them on a board titled "Happy Birthday, A.A. Milne."

10. Some interesting Pooh facts:
   - Christopher Robin was modeled and named after Alan (A.A.) Milne's own son.
   - The real Winnie the Pooh was an orphaned American black bear. She was named Winnie after Winnipeg, Canada. Winnie ended up in England when she traveled there as the mascot of the 2nd Canadian Infantry Brigade. Her caretaker, Lt. Harry Colebourn, thought it was too risky to take Winnie into action and asked the zoo to care for her until his return. The war lasted longer than Colebourn thought it would and Winnie ended up living out her days at the zoo.
   - The real Christopher Robin met Winnie at the London Zoological Gardens in 1925.

**MORE TO DO**   **Science and Nature:** Read stories about real bears and compare them to Pooh. How are they different? How are they the same? Make a graph that shows the differences. For example, Pooh lives in a home-like setting with furniture, bears live in the woods or in caves; Pooh's favorite food is honey, bears like honey but also like other foods such as berries and insects; Pooh has friends from other species of animals, bears in the wild don't get along with other animals.

**Related songs**    **Here's a Little Beehive** (Tune: "I'm a Little Teapot")

*Here's a little beehive* (cup hands together)
*Buzz, buzz, buzz.* (put cupped hands to ear)
*Pooh really loves it,* (hug self)
*Yes, he does.* (nod head vigorously)
*He'd do anything to get that honey* (shake finger in air)
*Sometimes that bear is really funny!* (cover mouth with hand and laugh)

**Pooh in the Dell** (Tune: "The Farmer in the Dell")

*Pooh in the dell,*
*Pooh in the dell,*
*Hi-ho, the derry-o*
*Pooh in the dell.*

*Pooh finds Piglet,*
*Pooh finds Piglet,*
*Hi-ho, the derry-o*
*Pooh finds Piglet.*

*Piglet finds Rabbit…*
*Rabbit finds Eeyore…*
*Eeyore finds Kanga and Roo…*
*Kanga and Roo find Tigger…*
*Tigger finds Owl…*
*Owl stands alone…*

**Related books**    *The Complete Tales of Winnie-the-Pooh* by A.A. Milne
*Disney's Winnie the Pooh: Colors* by Andrea Doering
*My First Winnie-the-Pooh* by A.A. Milne
*Pooh* by A.A. Milne
*Pooh's Five Little Honey Pots* by A.A. Milne
*Winnie the Pooh* by A.A. Milne
*Winnie the Pooh's Storybook Set* by A.A. Milne
*Winnie the Pooh: The Four Seasons* by A.A. Milne

 *Virginia Jean Herrod, Columbia, SC*

# Little Mister and Miss Hugs-a-Lot

ART

**Materials**
various colors of construction paper
scissors
markers
cardstock paper
yarn in yellow, brown, red, and black
craft glue
craft materials (wiggle eyes, tissue paper squares, aluminum foil,
    patterned papers)
self-adhesive Velcro

**What to do**
- January 21st is National Hugging Day.
  1. A week or so before January 21st, tell the children about National Hugging Day. Explain that it is a day to celebrate how fun it can be to give and receive a hug.
  2. Have each child choose a piece of skin-tone colored paper that they think matches their own skin. Help them trace both hands on the paper and cut them out. Put them aside for later use.
  3. Ask the children to draw themselves on a large piece of cardstock paper. Encourage them to glue on yarn "hair" and other craft materials for eyes, clothes, and so on. When done, help each child cut around her head and body of the drawing but cut off the arms and legs. (You will attach these in the next step.)
  4. Cut four strips of skin-tone paper to match the tones the children chose for their hands. Attach one strip to each side of the child's drawing for arms and two to the bottom of the drawing for legs.
  5. Provide patterned paper cut into shoe shapes for the children to attach to the bottoms of the legs.
  6. Help the children attach their paper hands to the ends of the arms on their drawings. Let everything dry.
  7. Help the children cut out a red or pink heart. Use edging scissors for a nice effect. Help them print "I love you" on their hearts.
  8. Let the children glue their hearts to the middle of their drawings (near where a real heart is located).
  9. Help the children attach a small Velcro dot to the hands, with the loop side on one hand and fuzzy side on the other.
  10. Fold the hands around the heart and attach them together using the Velcro.
  11. On National Hugging Day, the children can give their hugging doll to someone they love.

**MORE TO DO**

Create a poem about hugging or use the song below to print on the heart or on tags that are attached to the dolls.

**Hugging** (Tune: "Twinkle, Twinkle, Little Star")
*Hugging is something I like to do,*
*I'll hug all the animals in the zoo.*
*I'll hug my dog and I'll hug my cat*
*I'll hug a frog, what do you think about that!?*
*Hugging is something I like to do,*
*Now here's a big hug just for you!*

**RELATED books**

*How About a Hug?* by Nancy Carlson
*Hug Me* by Patti Stren

★ *Virginia Jean Herrod, Columbia, SC*

# CHINESE NEW YEAR

ART

**MATERIALS**

giant rubber ball
petroleum jelly (such as Vaseline)
newspaper
glue
brightly colored paint
paintbrushes
long piece of colorful fabric at least 10 yards long (different pieces of scrap
    fabric can be sewn together to make a long piece)
decorations such as sequins, tassels, pompoms, or buttons
stapler or tape
paper
crayons or colored pencils
Chinese music or cymbals

**WHAT TO DO**

● The Chinese New Year is a 15-day celebration, starting with the second
  new moon after the winter solstice and ending with the full moon. It can
  start any time between January 21st and February 19th, depending on
  the lunar calendar.

1. Cover half of the ball with Vaseline.
2. Glue strips of newspaper over the Vaseline. Build up the papier-mâché
   (glue and paper strips) to make a giant dragon head, including large
   eyes, high cheeks, and a big mouth.
3. When the papier-mâché dragon head is dry, slip it off the ball and paint it
   in bright colors and patterns.

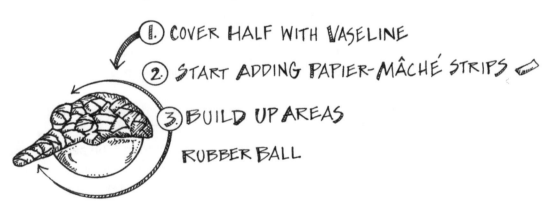

1. COVER HALF WITH VASELINE
2. START ADDING PAPIER-MÂCHÉ STRIPS
3. BUILD UP AREAS
   RUBBER BALL

4. Decorate the head and the long piece of fabric with sequins, pompoms,
   or buttons.
5. Attach the long piece of fabric to the dragon head with the stapler or
   tape.
6. Choose a few volunteers to dance around inside the Chinese Dragon.

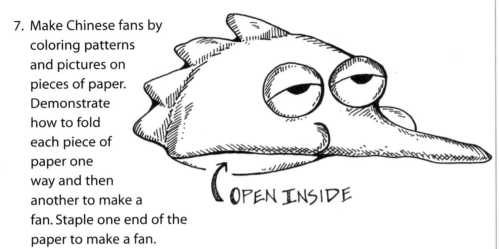

7. Make Chinese fans by coloring patterns and pictures on pieces of paper. Demonstrate how to fold each piece of paper one way and then another to make a fan. Staple one end of the paper to make a fan.

8. Play Chinese music while the "dragon" dances and the children wave their fans. Have a child clash the cymbals occasionally.

★ *Amelia Griffin, Ontario, Canada*

# Dragon's Tail

GAMES

**Materials**     none

**What to do**
- Play this game for Chinese New year. Explain the role dragons play in Chinese festivals. The Chinese New Year is celebrated on the second new moon after the winter solstice and ends 15 days later on the full moon. It can start any time between January 21st and February 19th, depending on the lunar calendar.

1. Form children into groups of 7 to 10, putting similar size children together so that smaller children are not overwhelmed by bigger children in the group. This is not a team game, so even one group of a few children is enough to play.

2. Have the groups stand in a line, holding firmly onto the waist of the child in front of them.

3. Tell the children that each of their lines is a "dragon." The person at the beginning of each line is the dragon's head, the middle ones are the body, and the end ones are the tail. If available, let the dragon heads wear dragon masks.

4. Explain that the object of the game is for each dragon's "head" to chase its own "tail" and try to catch it. The job of the body and tail is to protect themselves from the dragon's head, while staying joined together.

5. On a given signal (clap or whistle), the dragon heads start to chase their tails. The children must try and keep out of the head's way—the more children there are in the dragon, the harder this is.

6. If the body of the dragon becomes disconnected (if one or more children let go of the person ahead of them), those children or anyone else who notices must shout, "Dragon, stop!" and the dragon's head must freeze until the whole body is connected to him again. Then the dragon's body or tail can shout, "Dragon, go!" and the chasing may begin again.

7. If the tail is caught, then the last child in the line becomes the head.

8. Play until everyone in each dragon has had a turn being the dragon's head.

**More to do**      **Music and Movement:** As the children play the game, play undulating music and point out how the dragon's body moves and flows. Use different numbers of children to make the dragon and ask whether a small or large number looks better.

**Related books**    *Dragon Dance a Chinese New Year: A Chinese New Year Lift-the-Flap Book* by Joan Holub
 *The Knight and the Dragon* by Tomi DePaola
 *Moonbeams, Dumplings & Dragon Boats: A Treasury of Chinese Holiday Tales, Activities & Recipes* by Nina Simonds
 *Paper Bag Princess* by Robert Munsch
 *The Tale of Custard the Dragon* by Ogden Nash

 *Anne Adeney, Plymouth, United Kingdom*

# Do the Dragon Dance
MUSIC AND MOVEMENT

**Materials**      2' x 2' piece of tagboard
 marker
 scissors
 hole punch
 string
 rhythm instruments (bought or homemade)

**What to do**    • Chinese New Year is celebrated on the second new moon after the winter solstice. It ends 15 days later with the full moon.

1. Draw a dragon head on a 2' x 2' piece of tagboard. Cut it out, punch a hole in the upper left and right corners of the head, and tie a piece of string through the holes so it can be worn like a sign. Or, use a dragon puppet or dragon doll.

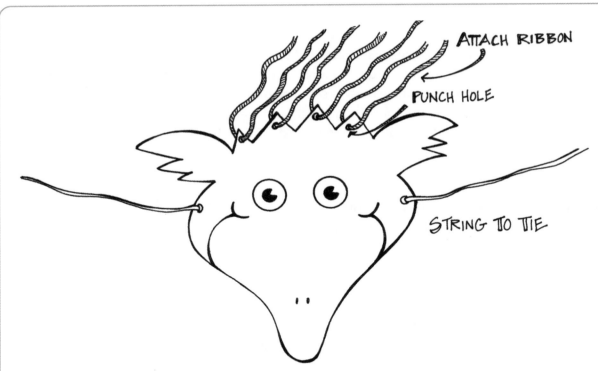

ATTACH RIBBON

PUNCH HOLE

STRING TO TIE

2. Read one of the books on the Chinese New Year (see related books below) to the children.
3. Explain that half of the children are going to line up and be the "dragon."
4. Have the child at the front of the line wear the dragon head or carry the dragon doll. The other children line up behind the leader and place their hands on the child in front of them.
5. Do a quick practice of snaking around the room together.
6. Give the other half of the children rhythm instruments. Encourage them to keep a steady booming beat while the dragon dances. It is best if they are off to one side in the "musicians' area." An adult should lead the children by playing a drum to help keep the musicians in beat.
7. If time permits, let the children take turns being the "dragon's head."
8. Have the dancers and the musicians trade places for a new experience.

**More to do**      **Art:** Reproduce a 6" dragon shape on card stock. (You should be able to put two or three shapes to a page.) You can also use an Ellison machine and a dragon die. Cut out one shape for each child. Let the children color the dragons. Show them how to tape the top of a craft stick to the back of the dragon to make a dragon stick puppet.

**Related books**    *Chinese New Year* by Tricia Brown
*Dragon Dance: A Chinese New Year Lift-the-Flap Book* by Joan Holub
*Dragon Parade: A Chinese New Year Story* by Steven Chin
*Lion Dancer: Ernie Wan's Chinese New Year* by Kate Waters
*My First Chinese New Year* by Karen Katz
*The Runaway Rice Cake* by Ying Chang Compestine

 *Christina R. Chilcote, New Freedom, PA*

# CHINESE NEW YEAR

PROJECTS

**MATERIALS**
black construction paper
several colors of glitter glue
tape
scissors
white paper precut in 2" x 4" strips (at least 5 for each child)
markers, colored pencils, and crayons
stamps
stickers
red envelopes
party supplies (paper plates, plastic ware, plastic cups, and napkins)

**WHAT TO DO**

- Chinese New Year is the longest and most important festival in Taiwan. Customs include paying off debts, purchasing new clothes, thoroughly cleaning the house, enjoying delicious family feasts, and giving friends and relatives "hong bao" (red envelopes) containing "lucky money." Firecrackers explode throughout the night on New Year's Eve and sporadically on the following days. The Chinese New Year is a 15-day celebration, starting with the second new moon after the winter solstice and ending with the full moon. It can start any time between January 21st and February 19th, depending on the lunar calendar.

1. *Read Happy New Year* by Yen Liang to the children. Talk about how people in Taiwan celebrate the beginning of the New Year.
2. Have your own celebration with the children using the following ideas.
3. Make firecracker pictures.
   - Give each child a sheet of black construction paper. Encourage them to make pictures of exploding rockets using brightly colored glitter glue.
   - Find a computer graphic of a single firecracker rocket or draw one. Place the picture in the middle of a bulletin board. Post the fireworks pictures around the firecracker under a heading that reads "Happy Chinese New Year!"
4. Make lucky money.
   - Give each child several 2" x 4" strips of paper. Ask them to design their own "lucky money" to give to others. Provide markers, colored pencils, crayons, stamps, and stickers.
   - Give each child three or four red envelopes to hold their money. Encourage them to choose family members or friends to whom they would like to give their lucky money. Help them put the money in the envelopes and print the recipient's name on the front. Remind them to save some lucky money for themselves.

5. Have a family feast.
- Pick a day for your celebration and send out invitations made by the children. Explain in the invitation that you would like each family to bring in a special family dish to share with the children and other families.
- Let the children decorate the room for the party. Make Chinese lanterns by folding regular construction paper in half and making several equally spaced cuts almost all the way through the paper. Unfold the paper and tape it together at the top and bottom to form a lantern shape. Make several to hang around the room.
- As the parents arrive for the party, greet them by saying "Ake Mashite Omedetou Gozaimasu!" (Happy New Year, everyone!). Place the family dishes on a self-serve buffet and invite everyone to dig in. This is a good way for the parents to get to know each other and to see how their children play together.

**MORE TO DO**     If you have Chinese children in your class, invite their family members to come in and teach the children two or three simple Chinese words or phrases such as "hello."

**RELATED SONGS**     **Lucky Money** (Tune: "I'm a Little Teapot")
*Here is some money and it's lucky* (hold cupped hands up in front of body)
*Only good things can happen to me.* (hug self and rock side to side)
*I'll put it in an envelope and give it to you* (fold one hand and tuck two fingers of the other hand in the fold)
*Now you can be very lucky too.* (point index finger and shake it up and down)

**LUCKY** (Tune: "BINGO")
*I have some money here with me*
*And it is very lucky*
*L-U-C-K-Y, L-U-C-K-Y, L-U-C-K-Y*
*And it is very lucky.*

*I have some money here with me*
*And it is very lucky*
*(clap)-U-C-K-Y, (clap)-U-C-K-Y, (clap)-U-C-K-Y*
*And it is very lucky.*

*…(clap)-(clap)-C-K-Y, (clap)-(clap)-C-K-Y, (clap)-(clap)-C-K-Y…*
*…(clap)-(clap)-(clap)-K-Y, (clap)-(clap)-(clap)-K-Y, ((clap)-(clap)-(clap)-K-Y…*
*…(clap)-(clap)-(clap)-(clap)-Y…*
*…(clap)-(clap)-(clap)-(clap)-(clap)…*

**RELATED books**     *Chinatown* by William Low
*In the Snow* by Huy Voun Lee

 *Virginia Jean Herrod, Columbia, SC*

# Celebrate Mozart's Birthday

MUSIC AND MOVEMENT

**Materials**
picture book about Mozart
CD or tape player
CD or audiocassette of lively Mozart music

**What to do**
- Mozart's birthday is January 27th.
1. Read a picture book about Mozart to the children.
2. Play a lively piece of Mozart, using your arms and body to sway to the music.
3. Encourage the children to stand and sway to the music.
4. Discuss what the different sounds in the song remind them of (bird, wind, horse, and so on).
5. Encourage the children to dance the way the music makes them feel.

**More to do**
**Art:** Give the children paper and crayons (or fingerpaint, tempera paint, or colored chalk). Discuss how different sounds can be represented in different ways (for example, soft sounds might be little lines, loud sounds might be big thick lines, and swooping sounds might be drawn as circles). Ask them to "paint the music," encouraging them to draw the music the way it makes them feel.

**Related books**
*The Cat Who Loved Mozart* by Patricia Austin
*Young Mozart* by Rachel Isadora

**Related CDs**
*The Mozart Effect—Music for Babies, Volume 1: From Playtime to Sleepytime*
*The Mozart Effect—Music for Children, Volume 1: Tune Up your Mind*
*The Mozart Effect—Music for Children, Volume 2: Relax, Daydream and Draw*

 *Christina R. Chilcote, New Freedom, PA*

# KAZOODLE!

MUSIC AND MOVEMENT

**MATERIALS**
one kazoo for each child and teacher
permanent marker

**WHAT TO DO**

• January 28th is National Kazoo Day.

1. On January 28th, explain to the children that it is National Kazoo Day. Show the children a kazoo. Play a tune on it that the children will be sure to recognize. When you finish playing, hold up the kazoo and shout, "Kazoodle!"

2. Explain to the children that humming any song into a kazoo will make it work. Demonstrate this technique as you play another familiar tune. Remember to shout, "Kazoodle!" when you finish playing.

3. Give each child a kazoo. Use a permanent marker to label the kazoos with each child's name. Emphasize that they should not play each other's kazoos.

4. Encourage the children to play their kazoos. Start by playing a simple song such as "Twinkle, Twinkle, Little Star." Offer help as needed. Again, shout, "Kazoodle!" together when finished playing.

5. Play a few familiar songs as the children get used to using the kazoos. Remember to shout, "Kazoodle!" after each song.

6. Have a kazoo parade! Lead the children around the room as you play a rousing tune. Extend the parade to the rest of the center (with permission). March around from room to room playing lively tunes for the other children. Encourage the children from other rooms to shout, "Kazoodle!" with you after each song.

7. Take your kazoo parade outdoors to the playground! Outside the children can really put their lungs into their songs. See who can play their kazoo the loudest. **Safety Note:** Make sure you collect the kazoos before the children begin to play on the outdoor equipment in order to avoid accidental injury. Running with a kazoo in the mouth can be dangerous.

**MORE TO DO**

**Art:** Make fun headbands for the "band" to wear. Cut strips of construction paper to fit the children's heads. Let them decorate their headbands. Print a fun name for each child on the headbands. For example, Deirdre becomes "KaDeirdreZoodle" and Tanisha turns into "KaTanishaZoodle." Have the children wear their headbands during their parade.

**More Art:** Let the children make their own kazoos by covering one end of a paper towel tube with a piece of wax paper and holding it in place with a rubber band. Decorate with markers and stickers. They can hum into the open end to produce a sound.

**Music and Movement:** Challenge the children to make different sounds with their kazoos. Who can kazoo the softest or loudest? Who can kazoo high? Low? Can everyone kazoo fast? Or slow? Move your bodies to follow the music!

⭐ *Virginia Jean Herrod, Columbia, SC*

# Chinese Tangram Puzzle
GAMES

**Materials**
paper
crayons
white poster board
crayons
glue

**What to do**
- January 29th is National Puzzle Day.
1. Before the activity, draw a tangram pattern with seven shapes (five triangles, one square, and one rhomboid) on a piece of paper. Make a copy for each child.
2. Give each child a square piece of poster board and a tangram pattern.
3. Encourage the children to color each shape with a different color.
4. Ask them to glue the tangram pattern to the poster board and cut out each shape.
5. Have the children put the tangram puzzle together.

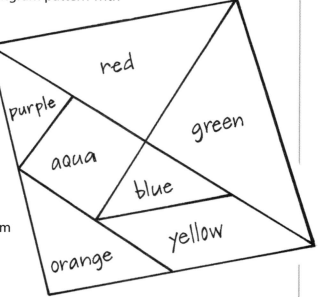

**Related books**
*Grandfather's Tang Story* by Ann Tompert
*Greedy Triangle* by Marilyn Burns
*Round Is a Mooncake: A Book of Shapes* by Roseanne Thong
*Three Pigs, One Wolf and Seven Magic Shapes* by Grace MacCarone
*Wing on a Flea* by Ed Emberley

⭐ *Elizabeth Thomas, Hobart, IN*

# February

# Bundle Up!

**Materials**

tagboard
old magazines and workbooks or markers
scissors
glue stick
paper cutter
pocket chart
12" x 18" construction paper
laminating machine
pocket chart

**What to do**

1. Draw sets of mittens on tagboard.
2. Cut out rhyming pictures (cat and bat, frog and dog) and glue them to the left and right hand of each pair of mittens (or draw rhyming pictures on the mittens).
3. Using a paper cutter, cut the mitten cards to the desired size.
4. If desired, make a header card to go in the top row of the pocket chart. Draw a picture of a snowman wearing mittens, the title of the activity, and instructions to:"Pair the mittens with matching rhyming words."
5. If desired, make a file jacket from 12" x 18" construction paper to hold the activity.
6. Laminate the header card, mitten cards, and file jacket for durability, and cut out.
7. Give each child a right mitten.
8. Hold up a left mitten and ask the children to identify the picture on it.
9. Put it in a pocket chart, leaving room for its mate to be placed next to it.
10. Ask the children to look at their mittens and if they have a picture of a rhyming word, come forward and place it next to its mate on the pocket chart.
11. Continue in this manner with each set of mittens.
12. When you have run out of mittens, display the completed pocket chart in a center for children to revisit during free time.

*Jackie Wright, Enid, OK*

# Bucket O' Snowballs

MATH

**Materials**
large bucket or other large waterproof container
smaller bucket
snow

**What to do**
1. Make a snowball and put it into the large bucket. Then ask the children to guess how many snowballs it would take to fill the bucket.
2. Together, add snowballs to the bucket, one at a time, counting out loud as each is put in.
3. Repeat with the smaller bucket.
4. Ask the children why one bucket holds more snowballs than the other. Discuss their responses.
5. As a variation, fill a bucket with very large snowballs, then very small ones. Ask the children to explain why the count is much higher with the small snowballs.

 *Karyn F. Everham, Fort Myers, FL*

# Playful Penguins

MATH

**Materials**
pocket chart
tagboard
pictures of penguins from magazines or websites
marker
12" x 18" construction paper
color scanner
glue stick
laminating machine
scissors

**What to do**
1. Make a tagboard header card to fit in the top row of a pocket chart with the title at the top and instructions to: "Solve the problem on each penguin and place it under the correct answer."
2. Draw a picture of a penguin on the left side of the chart with the numeral 9 and a penguin on the right side with the numeral 10 to form two columns.
3. Make a set of cards on tagboard using pictures of penguins. Leave space on their stomachs to put math problems.

4. Write equations on half of the cards that total nine, and on the rest of the cards write equations that total ten.

5. If desired, make a file jacket from 12" x 18" construction paper to hold the activity.

6. If possible, use a color scanner to make a reduced-size printout of the completed activity showing the penguins under the correct answer.

7. Glue the color printout to the back of the file jacket.

8. Laminate the header card, penguin cards, and file jacket for durability, and cut out.

9. Hold up a penguin card. Ask a volunteer to look at the equation and tell you the answer.

10. Place the penguin under the correct answer in the pocket chart.

11. Continue until all the penguins are in place.

12. Place the activity in a center to provide more fun and number review. The children can look at the back of the file jacket to check their work. (This picture reference helps ensure that all cards are accounted for when you put them away at the end of the month.)

**RELATED book**  *Plenty of Penguins* by Sonia W. Black

*Jackie Wright, Enid, OK*

# SPECIAL SNOWMEN

OUTDOOR PLAY

**MATERIALS**  gelatin molds
small and large ice cream scoops
plastic knives
spoons and forks
cooking utensils

**WHAT TO dO**
1. On a snowy day, bring all of the materials outside.
2. Help the children build a few snowmen and encourage them to make them special by using the materials from the list.
3. Take pictures and use them to develop stories about the snowmen.

**RELATED books**  *All You Need for a Snowman* by Alice Schertle
*Bookshelf: Biggest, Best Snowman* by Margery Cuyler
*A Snowman Named Just Bob* by Mark Moulton
*Snowmen at Night* by Caralyn Buehner

*Ann Kelly, Johnstown, PA*

# Muk

SOCIAL DEVELOPMENT

**Materials**  none

**What to do**
- This comes from an Inuit game and can be used as an ice-breaker, as well as to help teach self-control.
1. The children form a seated circle, with one child standing in the middle.
2. The child in the middle points silently to another child, who has to stand up and repeat the Inuit word "muk" three times without smiling or laughing.
3. If that child smiles or laughs, he changes places with the one in the middle.
4. If he succeeds in not laughing, the child in the middle remains standing.
5. Continue playing, making sure everyone has a turn, until the last child is standing. Then everyone together should unite to try and get her to smile.

**More to do**  Use this game as part of an Inuit, Arctic, snow, emotions, or international games theme.
**Social Development:** Show the children photographs of people showing different emotions (smiling, frowning, and so on) and encourage them to identify the emotions accurately. Talk about emotions, what they are, and why we have them.

**Related books**  *Don't Laugh, Joe!* by Keiko Kasza
*One Smile* by Cindy McKinley
*Smile a Lot!* by Nancy L. Carlson
*Smile, Lily!* by Candace Fleming

 *Anne Adeney, Plymouth, United Kingdom*

# Road Rally

DRAMATIC PLAY

**Materials**  colored electrical tape
tabletop
small cars
paper
crayons

**What to do**

1. This activity provides children with motor skill practice (lots of arm, hand and body movement) and dramatic play. Make "roads" on a tabletop with the tape.
2. Encourage the children to race the cars along the roads.
3. Invite the children to draw flags, start and finish lines, special stops, and road hurdles on paper and tape to the table.
4. Talk to the children about the Daytona 500 (which takes place in February) and the Indianapolis 500.

*Sandie Nagel, White Lake, MI*

# A Smile Today

ART

**Materials**
toothbrushes
toothpaste
mirror
yellow construction paper
scissors
markers
tape

**What to do**
- February is National Children's Dental Health Month.
1. Have the children brush their teeth using their own toothbrushes and toothpaste.
2. Let them take turns looking in the mirror. Encourage them to "smile" and see how clean their teeth look.
3. Have the children draw large circles on yellow construction paper. Then ask them to draw eyes, a nose, and a big smiling mouth with teeth on their circles.
4. Help the children cut out their smiling face circles.
5. Send the children's smiling faces home to be hung in their bathrooms as a reminder to brush their teeth every day.

**More to do**
**Dramatic Play:** Put clean toothbrushes and toothpaste in the housekeeping area for children to use with the dolls.

**Related books**
*Brush Your Teeth, Please* by Leslie McGuire
*Does a Lion Brush?* by Fred Ehrlich

⭐ *Monica Hay Cook, Tucson, AZ*

# HAVE YOU GROWN OR LOST A TOOTH?

CIRCLE TIME

**MATERIALS**    large piece of white tagboard
pen

**WHAT TO DO**
- February is National Dental Health Month.
1. Draw a large tooth, about 3" tall, and cut it out.
2. Use this tooth as a pattern to trace onto the tagboard 12 times.
3. Under each tooth write the name of a month.
4. Every time a child grows or loses a tooth, write the child's name on the correct month's tooth.

⭐ *Barbara Saul, Eureka, CA*

# TEETH CHART—Good or Bad

CIRCLE TIME

**MATERIALS**    large piece of paper
pen
old magazines
scissors
glue

**WHAT TO DO**
- February is National Dental Health Month.
1. Talk with the children about which foods are good for your teeth and which are not.
2. Draw a vertical line on a large piece of paper, making two columns.
3. Write "good" at the top of one column and "not good" at the top of the other.
4. Provide a variety of old magazines and ask the children to cut out foods that are either good or bad for their teeth.
5. After each child has cut out a few foods, let them put the pictures in the proper columns.

**MORE TO DO**    **Health:** Show the children a picture of the food pyramid and discuss it.

⭐ *Barbara Saul, Eureka, CA*

# Field Trip to the Dentist's Office

FIELD TRIPS

**Materials**     none

**What to do**
- February is National Dental Health Month.
1. Ask a pediatric dentist to give the children a tour of his or her office, or have a dentist visit the class.
2. Have the dentist explain the tools he or she uses and demonstrate what happens during a visit to the dentist's office.
3. The dentist can explain why children's teeth fall out and are replaced with permanent teeth.
4. Talk about foods that are good for teeth.

**Related books**     *Arthur's Tooth* by Marc Brown
                          *Franklin and the Tooth Fairy* by Paulette Bourgeois

 *Barbara Saul, Eureka, CA*

# The Wiggle Tooth Poem

FINGERPLAYS, SONGS, & POEMS

**Materials**     none

**What to do**
- February is National Dental Health Month.
1. Talk with the children about losing teeth.
2. Recite the following poem with the children:

*I wiggle and I wiggle and I wiggle about.*
*Why, oh, why won't my tooth fall out?*
*I wiggle and I wiggle and I wiggle some more.*
*My tooth comes out and falls on the floor!*

3. Let the children stand up and wiggle as the poem is recited.

 *Barbara Saul, Eureka, CA*

# HAVE YOU EVER LOST A TOOTH?

MATH

**MATERIALS**

tagboard
pocket chart
markers
name card for each child

**WHAT TO DO**

1. This is a fun graphing activity to do during February, which is National Children's Dental Health Month.
2. Prepare a header card for the pocket chart with the question, "Have you ever lost a tooth?" Add a picture of a tooth under the question and put "Yes" on one side and "No" on the other to form two columns.
3. Discuss the possibilities on the graph and encourage children to talk about their experiences.
4. Have each child place his name card in the appropriate column below the header card on the pocket chart.
5. Encourage the children to count the total in each column and discuss the graph's results.

**RELATED books**

*Little Rabbit's Loose Tooth* by Lucy Bate
*The Tooth Fairy* by Kirsten Hall

 *Jackie Wright, Enid, OK*

# COUNT YOUR TEETH

MATH

**MATERIALS**

dry-erase board
dry-erase marker

**WHAT TO DO**

● February is National Dental Health Month.
1. Ask the children to wash their hands.
2. Demonstrate how to count your teeth.
3. On the dry-erase board, chart the number of teeth each child has.
4. Ask the children the following questions:
   ● Why do you have different numbers of teeth?
   ● Which is the number of teeth that most of the children have?
   ● Which is the number of teeth that fewest of the children have?

 *Barbara Saul, Eureka, CA*

# Food Fair

SNACK AND COOKING

**Materials**
small carrot sticks
celery with cream cheese
variety of fruit cut into children's portions
trail mix
raisins
milk

**What to do**
- February is National Dental Health Month.
1. Ask parents to bring in various healthy foods (see list above).
2. Place the food on a large table.
3. Explain to the children that this is a food fair, and that all of the food is good for their teeth.
4. Encourage the children to sample the food.
**Note:** If any of the children have food sensitivities or allergies, do not include those foods in the tasting.

*Barbara Saul, Eureka, CA*

# Celebrate African American Writers and Musicians

WORKING WITH FAMILIES

**Materials**    none

**What to do**
- February is Black History Month.
1. Prior to Black History Month, ask parents to sign up to do one of two things:
   - Share with the children favorite music written and/or performed by an African American.
   - Read a picture book written by an African American, or read a picture book in which the central characters are African American.
2. Begin each day of Black History Month with music chosen by parents. Ask parents to talk with the children about why they like the musician, and if possible, share a little biographical information about the musician, particularly information about the musician's childhood.
3. End each day of Black History Month with a story read by a parent.

Related website www.scils.rutgers.edu/~kvander/ ("Vandergrift's Children's Literature Page" has an excellent bibliography of African American picture books.)

 *Karyn F. Everham, Fort Myers, FL*

# Make a Mini-Cherry Pie

SNACK AND COOKING

**Materials**
cupcake cups (aluminum foil variety preferred)
vanilla wafers
instant vanilla pudding
milk (for pudding)
cherry pie filling
old-fashioned hand rotary beaters
several tablespoons
plastic sandwich bags

**What to do**
- February is National Cherry Pie Month.
1. Make vanilla instant pudding according to package directions. (One package should be enough for a small class, two packages for a larger class.)
2. Let the children help mix the milk and pudding with the hand rotary beaters (not electric).
3. Give each child a cupcake cup (aluminum foil, if possible). Each child places a vanilla wafer at the bottom of his cupcake paper.
4. Let each child put about 2 tablespoons of pudding on top of the cookie and 1-2 tablespoons of cherry pie filling on top of the pudding.
5. If possible, chill the desserts in a refrigerator for at least ½ hour.
6. Eat at snack time or put them in plastic bags for children to take home.

**More to do**
Discuss the story of the young George Washington chopping down his father's cherry tree.

**Related book**
*Cherry Pies and Lullabies* by Lynn Reiser

 *Christina R. Chilcote, Freedom, PA*

# Healthy Hearts Journals

SCIENCE

**Materials**
large sheet of paper
marker
gross motor equipment
children's music CDs
exercise videos
journals (1 per child)

**What to do**
- February is National Heart Month.
  1. At circle time, ask the question of the day: "What does it mean to be healthy?"
  2. Let each child answer the question.
  3. Write the responses on a large sheet of paper and post in the room.
  4. Use the responses relating to physical activities to extend the conversation.
  5. Talk about what the children can do at school to be physically active and have healthy hearts. Make a plan to track each child's physical activities in individual "Healthy Heart Journals."
  6. Introduce a variety of gross motor equipment for the children to choose.
  7. Change the equipment weekly or before children get bored. Provide music and exercise videos.
  8. Have the children log each day's accomplishments in their journals each time they exercise.
  9. Use some of the journals every day as a recall activity. Ask the group who would like to share their activities for the day.
  10. Support the children's efforts with encouragement and praise.

**More to do**
**Dramatic Play:** Transform the dramatic play area into a doctor's office. Encourage children to go there after exercising and have a "doctor" listen to their hearts, weigh them, measure them, and so on.
**Home-School Connection:** Send the journals home for families to write activities accomplished at home.

**Related books**
*Hear Your Heart* by Paul Showers
*Thump Thump: Learning About Your Heart* by Pamela Nettleton

⭐ *Ann Kelly, Johnstown, PA*

# Mailboxes

SOCIAL DEVELOPMENT

**Materials**
shoeboxes
items to decorate boxes (glue, feathers, stickers, sequins,
  colored tissue paper)
old deck of playing cards
paper/stationery
markers
pencils
envelopes
stamps

**What to do**
- February is International Friendship Month.
1. Talk about the importance of friendship and how people write letters and send cards to their friends to keep in touch.
2. Let the children pick boxes and decorate them as mailboxes.
3. Attach a card with each child's name to the side of his box.
4. Have each child pick out a playing card with a number on it. This will be each child's box number.
5. Set up the mailboxes on shelves and open up a writing center so the children can write to one another. Ask parents to donate materials for the writing center.
6. Make sure the children address their letters to one another appropriately.
7. Encourage the children to deliver their letters to the appropriate boxes. If desired, make a mailbag, and let a different child be the postal carrier each day.
8. The children can play post office as a dramatic play activity.

**More to do**
**Field Trip:** Go on a field trip to a real post office.

 *Ann Scalley, Orleans, MA*

# 100 Thumbprints

ART

**Materials**     disposable plastic plates
10 different colors of tempera paint
paper
scissors
glue
print of "Sunday Afternoon" by Georges Seurat (optional)

**What to do**
- Do this activity to celebrate the 100th Day of School.
1. Give each child a plastic plate. Show the children how to make 10 rows of 10 thumbprints in each color of paint (10 green, 10 blue, and so on).
2. Use the prints to count by tens to 100.
3. After the thumbprints are dry, let the children cut around the prints and glue them to paper.

**More to do**     **Art:** If available, show the children Georges Seurat's *pointillism* paintings, explaining how the small dots accumulate into a whole image. Encourage the children to experiment with using thumbprints like Seurat's dots.

**Related books**     *Have You Seen My Ducklings?* by Nancy Tafuri
*Snowy, Flowy, Blowy* by Nancy Tafuri

 *Barbara Saul, Eureka, CA*

# 100 Steps

MATH

**Materials**     none

**What to do**
1. In the outside play area, have everyone hold hands and walk forward 100 steps. Talk about why some children went farther than others, even though everyone took 100 steps.
2. Count to 100 with movement, changing the actions every time you reach ten. For example, clap hands (1-10); stomp feet (10-20); clap over head (20-30); move arms like wings (30-40); hop (40-50); touch head (50-60); stand up, sit down (60-70); tap knees (70-80); march (80-90); and jump up and down (90-100).

**Related books**     *Cat Up a Tree* by Ann Hassett
*Drummer Hoff* by Barbara Emberley

 *Barbara Saul, Eureka, CA*

# 100th Day of School

WORKING WITH FAMILIES

**Materials**      100 objects from each child's home

**What to do**
1. Write a note asking the children and their parents to count 100 things to send to school. Invite the parents to bring the collections and stay and share. If the collections are small, such as pennies, tape them to a piece of tagboard.
2. Put all of the collections out, and encourage the children to touch and explore them.
3. Ask which collections are the smallest and largest. Discuss why the collections are all different sizes when they all have the same number of objects.
4. Encourage the children to count the objects by 1s and then by 10s.
5. Add the total of all the items by counting by 100s.

**Related books**   *Each Orange Has Eight Slices* by Paul Giganti, Jr.
*How Many Snails?* by Paul Giganti, Jr.

 *Barbara Saul, Eureka, CA*

# Groundhog Pop-Up Puppet

ART

**Materials**      *It's Groundhog Day* by Steven Kroll
brown felt
scissors
flower-patterned small, paper cups
fabric glue
permanent markers

**What to do**
● Groundhog Day is celebrated on February 2nd.
1. Prior to the activity, cut two simple finger puppet shapes from brown felt for each child. Cut a finger-sized hole in the bottom of a paper cup for each child.
2. Read *It's Groundhog Day* by Steven Kroll. Talk about how the groundhog pops up from his underground home. Ask the children if they would like to make their own groundhog puppet.
3. Give each child one of their two brown felt finger puppet shapes. Let them use markers to create facial features and other designs on the puppet.
4. Give the children the other half of their puppet. Help them use fabric glue to glue the two pieces together. Remind them to leave room for their finger to fit in the puppet. Let dry.

5. Give each child a flower-patterned paper cup. If you don't have flower-patterned cups, provide flower stickers and white cups for children to decorate. Show them how to make their groundhog finger puppet hide "under the ground" (inside the upside down cup) and then pop up through the hole.

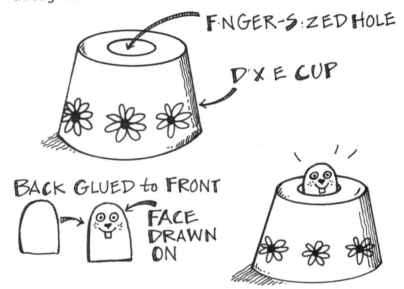

6. Say the following fun Groundhog Day rhyme:

*Little groundhog in the ground*
*Away from sights, away from sounds,* (hide puppet under cup)
*You gnaw out tunnels down beneath*
*With your great big groundhog teeth.*
*Then one wintry February Day*
*You pop up* (pop puppet up through hole in cup)
*To chase the winter away.*

**MORE TO DO**  **Math:** Discuss which animals live under the ground and which animals live above ground. Create a simple graph by dividing a piece of poster board in half with a marker. Label the bottom half "underground" and the top half "above ground." Have the children sort familiar animal pictures on the graph according to where they live.

**RELATED books**  *Geoffrey Groundhog Predicts the Weather* by Bruce Koscielniak
*Go to Sleep, Groundhog!* by Judy Cox
*Gretchen Groundhog, It's Your Day!* by Abby Levine
*The Groundhog Day Book of Facts and Fun* by Wendie Old, et al
*Groundhogs: Woodchucks, Marmots, and Whistle Pigs* by Adele D. Richardson
*Groundhog Willie's Shadow* by Barbara Birenbaum
*How Groundhog's Garden Grew* by Lynne Cherry
*It's Groundhog Day* by Steven Kroll

 *Virginia Jean Herrod, Columbia, SC*

# SEEING SHADOWS

ART

**Materials**
assorted classroom objects
black construction paper
pencil
scissors
long roll of white paper
glue
bag or container

**What to do**
- Groundhog Day is February 2nd.
1. To prepare, trace assorted classroom objects on black paper and cut them out. Glue them randomly to white paper.
2. At circle time, place all the traced objects into a container or bag. Have each child draw one out of the bag and match it to the shape outline on the white paper.
3. During center time, place the container of objects and the white paper of object outlines on the table or rug for children to match the objects independently.

BALL

BLOCK

TRIANGLE

PLASTIC
LETTER

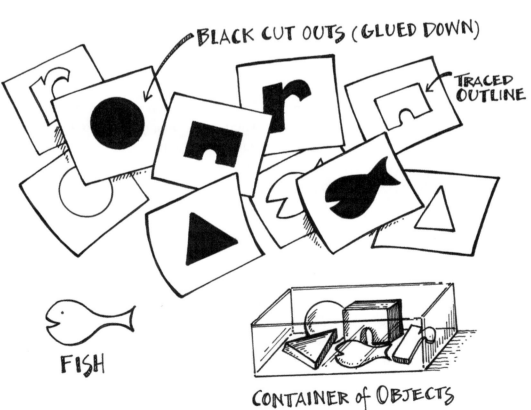

BLACK CUT OUTS (GLUED DOWN)

TRACED OUTLINE

FISH

CONTAINER of OBJECTS

**MORE TO DO**   **Games:** Play shadow tag.
**Literacy:** Make a groundhog puppet and look for stories in the news about Groundhog Day (February 2nd).
**Science:** Do shadow experiments with objects and flashlights. Move the light over an object to show how the angle of the light or the distance changes the size of a shadow.

**RELATED BOOKS**   *Go to Sleep, Groundhog!* by Judy Cox
*I Love My Shadow* by Hans Wilhelm
*The Shape of Me and Other Stuff* by Dr. Seuss
*What Makes a Shadow* by Clyde Robert Bulla

★ *Sandra Gratias, Dublin, PA*

# HERE'S A LITTLE GROUNDHOG
FINGERPLAYS, SONGS, & POEMS

**MATERIALS**   none

**WHAT TO DO**   • Groundhog Day is February 2nd.
Sing the following song, and have the children perform the appropriate gestures when prompted.

*Here's a little groundhog, furry and brown,* (raise thumb extend from fist)
*He's coming up to look around.* (pop thumb up)
*If he's sees his shadow* (raise hand to eyes)
*Down he'll go,* (pull thumb in)
*Then six more weeks of winter—oh, no!* (raise six fingers, look upset)

**MORE TO DO**   **Art:** Glue a paper groundhog on a Popsicle stick. Push the stick through the bottom of a Styrofoam cup. Then turn it right side up and raise and lower the groundhog stick as you repeat the words of the song.

★ *Kathy Kalmar, Macomb, MI*

# This Little Groundhog

FINGERPLAYS, SONGS, & POEMS

**Materials**    none

**What to do**    1. Do the following fingerplay with the children.

*This little groundhog* (make a fist)
*Met a pollywog,* (wiggle index finger)
*This little groundhog* (make a fist)
*Found his lunch* (nod yes)
*Nibble, nibble, and crunch!* (clap)

2. Let the children take turns being the groundhog and pollywog and act out the fingerplay.

★ *Kathy Kalmar, Macomb, MI*

# Will the Groundhog See His Shadow?

GROUP OR CIRCLE TIME

**Materials**    tagboard
markers
laminating machine
scissors
pocket chart

**What to do**    • Groundhog Day is February 2nd.
1. Make a header card using tagboard for the top row of a pocket chart with the question, "Will the groundhog see his shadow?" Add a picture of a groundhog.
2. On the left side of the card print, "Yes" and on the right side print, "No" to make a column for each answer choice underneath the question.
3. Laminate the header card for durability, and trim the excess away.
4. Place the header card in the top row of a pocket chart and read it to the children prior to February 2nd.

5. Make a name card for each child using tagboard. Ask them to place their name cards in the column that represents their prediction.
6. Count the responses and compare the results.
7. Follow up the activity on Groundhog Day to see if the class prediction was correct.

 *Jackie Wright, Enid, OK*

# Seeing Shadows

LANGUAGE AND LITERACY

**Materials**  *Groundhog Day* by Michelle Aki Becker

**What to do**  ● Groundhog Day is February 2nd.
1. Read the book *Groundhog Day* aloud.
2. Take the children outside to see if they can see their own shadows.
3. Later, predict what the groundhog will see.

 *Barbara Saul, Eureka, CA*

# Shadow Catchers

OUTDOOR PLAY

**Materials**  none

**What to do**  ● Groundhog Day is February 2nd.
1. Find a sunny spot outdoors.
2. Pair the children.
3. Have one child try to step on the other's shadow. When both have done so, switch partners and continue in this manner.

 *Barbara Saul, Eureka, CA*

# Stretching Shadows

OUTDOORS

**Materials**      none

**What to do**
- Groundhog Day is February 2nd.
1. Take the children outside on a sunny day and have them look at their shadows. Ask them to make their shadows tall, short, long, little, high, low, in a straight line, and so on.
2. Have them choose a partner. Show the pairs how to put themselves next to each other to form shadow letters with their bodies.

**Related book**    *Bear's Shadow* by Frank Asch

 *Barbara Saul, Eureka, CA*

# Me and My Shadow

OUTDOORS

**Materials**      sidewalk chalk

**What to do**
- Groundhog Day is February 2nd.
1. Take the children outdoors on a sunny day. Have them pick partners.
2. Have one child in each pair stand while the other child traces the standing child's shadow.
3. Let the children try to guess which shadow belongs to each child.
4. Using the same method, have the children lie down and trace one another's outlines.

**Related books**    *Bear's Shadow* by Frank Asch
*The Big Snow* by Berta and Elmer Hader

*Barbara Saul, Eureka, CA*

# We Make Shadows

SCIENCE

**Materials**
bright light source (film projector or strong flashlight)
light colored background for the light to shine upon
white newsprint paper
black and colored construction paper
easel
scissors
glue

**What to do**
● Groundhog Day is February 2nd.
1. The morning of Groundhog Day (February 2nd), find out whether the groundhog saw his shadow.
2. Explain to the children that shadows are visible on sunny days, and occur when something gets in the way of the sun or any major source of light.
3. Explain that shadows can be made indoors by putting something in front of bright light.
4. Let the children experiment with going in front of the beam of light. Encourage them to make any movements they please. Note that when the children are not in the light, their shadows disappear.
5. Attach newsprint to an easel and position the easel in front of a light source. Let the children take turns creating a silhouette by sitting between the easel and the light source. Ask the child to sit as quietly and still as possible as you trace his outline onto the newsprint.
6. Help the child cut out the shadow and trace it onto black construction paper. Cut out the black silhouette and have the child glue it onto a piece of colored construction paper.

BLACK SILHOUETTE

**MORE TO DO** Explain the word "silhouette" and share examples of silhouettes with the children, such as Abraham Lincoln on the penny or George Washington on the quarter. Both presidents' birthdays are in February. Note how you can tell who they are just by their silhouettes.

**RELATED BOOK** *Peter Pan* by J.M. Barrie

★ *Iris Rothstein, New Hyde Park, NY*

# CRAYON RESIST HEARTS

ART

**MATERIALS** 9" x 12" black construction paper
crayons in white, pink, red, purple, and blue
7" x 7" heart patterns (optional)
paintbrushes
thinned white paint
newspapers to cover the work surface

**WHAT TO DO**
- Valentine's Day is February 14th.
1. Ahead of time, test the thinned white paint to make sure it will bead up on crayon markings.
2. Demonstrate the process to the children, showing them how to press down with the crayons heavily. Show them how light crayon markings do not show up when painted.
3. Give each child a piece of black paper. Ask them to draw a large heart shape, or provide heart patterns for them to trace.
4. Invite them to color in their hearts using random splotches of different colors of crayons. Explain that it is not necessary to fill in every part of the heart, but it is important to color heavily.
5. Cover the work space with newspapers. Show the children how to move the paintbrush from left to right in one stroke across the paper, repeating until the paper is covered with the thin white paint. Explain that it is important to avoid painting over areas painted once so the paint will not cover up the crayon designs.
6. Allow to dry.

★ *Susan Oldham Hill, Lakeland, FL*

# Heart Art

ART

**Materials**
construction paper in pink, red, purple, and blue
scissors
marbles
shallow containers
paint in white, pink, blue, purple, and red
sturdy metal 8" or 9" pie tins
damp paper towels
spoons (optional)

**What to do**
- Valentine's Day is February 14th.
1. Cut pink, red, purple, and blue construction paper into 8" heart shapes.
2. Ask the children to put their heart shapes into the pie tins. Let them choose the color of paint they want to start with.
3. Have them drop a marble into the paint. Then, with a spoon or their fingers, they pick up the marble and drop it onto the heart shape in the pie tin. Show the children how to tilt the pie tin to roll the marble around, making colorful tracks.
4. When the marble has run out of paint, invite the children to choose another color and repeat the marble-painting process.

**More to do**
**Blocks:** Provide marbles in the block area for children to move through chutes and down ramps.
**Games:** Play a variation of "Who's Got the Button?" using a marble.
**Math:** Put a different amount of marbles in a jar each day and have children guess the amount.

**Related books**
*Arthur's Valentine* by Marc Brown
*Valentine's Day* by Gail Gibbons

⭐ *Susan Oldham Hill, Lakeland, FL*

# Love Quilt

ART

**Materials**   8" x 8" construction paper squares in various colors
9" x 9" red and white construction paper squares
glue
crayons and markers

**What to do**
- Valentine's Day is February 14th.
1. Discuss people we love in our families. Ask the children to choose one person they love to make a drawing for a bulletin board quilt.
2. Give each child 8" square of paper to draw the face of a person he loves.
3. Glue the completed drawings on the 9" squares and arrange them on the bulletin board in a quilt pattern.
4. If desired, glue them on bulletin board paper to make a wall hanging for the classroom or hallway.

POSTER BOARD

8 INCH SQUARES

LOVE QUILT

**More to do**   **Gross Motor:** Count the sides of a square with the children, and then choose four children to lie down and make a square on the rug.
**Literacy:** Make a list of other words that begin with the letter Q: quiet, quarter, queen, quart, and so on.
**Snack:** Serve square crackers for a treat.

**Related books**   *Arthur's Valentine* by Marc Brown
*Quilt* by Tomie dePaola

⭐ *Susan Oldham Hill, Lakeland, FL*

# A Precious Valentine's Gift

ART

**Materials**
camera and film
red poster board
scissors
tape

**What to do**
- National Child Passenger Safety Week is held every year the week of Valentine's Day.
1. Celebrate National Child Passenger Safety Week by inviting parents to come to your school for instruction on the proper use of infant and child car seats. Contact your local fire or police station for personnel to present instruction.
2. Ask parents to put children into their car seats and photograph the children buckled in.
3. Cut poster board into the shape of a heart. Tape the photos onto it, and display at children's eye level.

**More to do**
Direct parents to the National Highway Traffic Safety Administration website for more information on highway safety.

 *Karyn F. Everham, Fort Myers, FL*

# Queen of Hearts Paper Bag Puppet

ART

**Materials**
oak tag
pencil
gold wrapping paper
construction paper in various colors
scissors
pink or red paper bags
white glue
red and white design wallpaper
crayons
red marker

**WHAT TO DO**
• Valentine's Day is February 14th.

1. Use oak tag to make patterns for a crown, arm, sleeve, shoe, heart, and face.
2. Cut out a crown from gold wrapping paper, and a heart, face, and two arms from pink construction paper.
3. Glue the face on the bottom flap of a paper bag.
4. Glue arms inside the sides of a paper bag.
5. Cut four ½" strips of black construction paper for hair, curling it around a pencil at the end.
6. Glue each side of the face under the gold crown.
7. Glue gold scraps of paper under the chin area of heart to make a collar.
8. Using a crayon, draw small heart-shaped eyes, a nose, and a mouth on the face. Make the nose an upside-down heart shape.
9. Cut out shoes from black construction paper and glue under the bottom of the paper bag.
10. Decorate the queen's dress with stickers, wallpaper hearts, lace doilies, and red markers.
12. Use the puppet to recite the "Queen of Hearts" nursery rhyme.

EYE

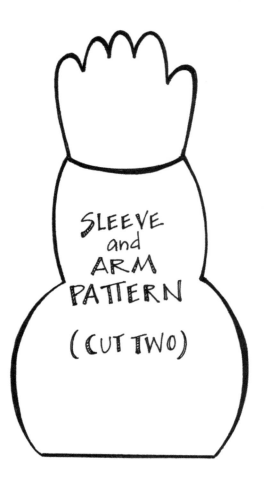

SLEEVE and ARM PATTERN (CUT TWO)

SHOE PATTERN (CUT TWO)

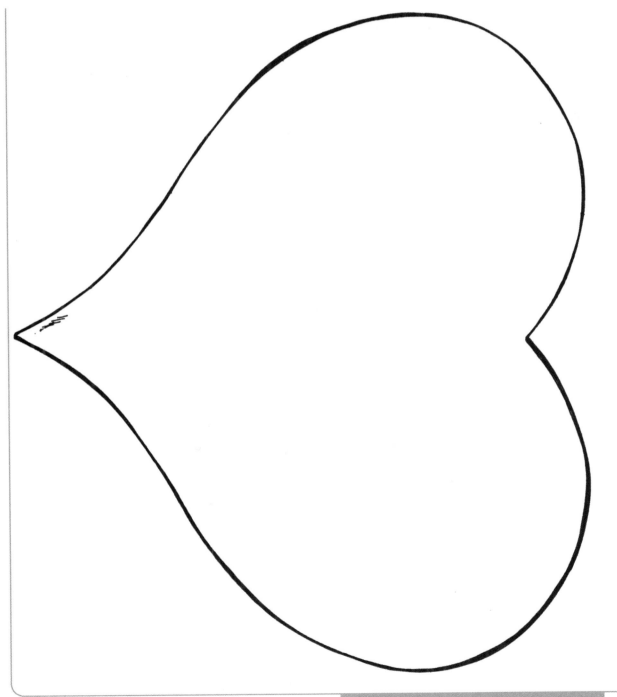

- CROWN PATTERN -

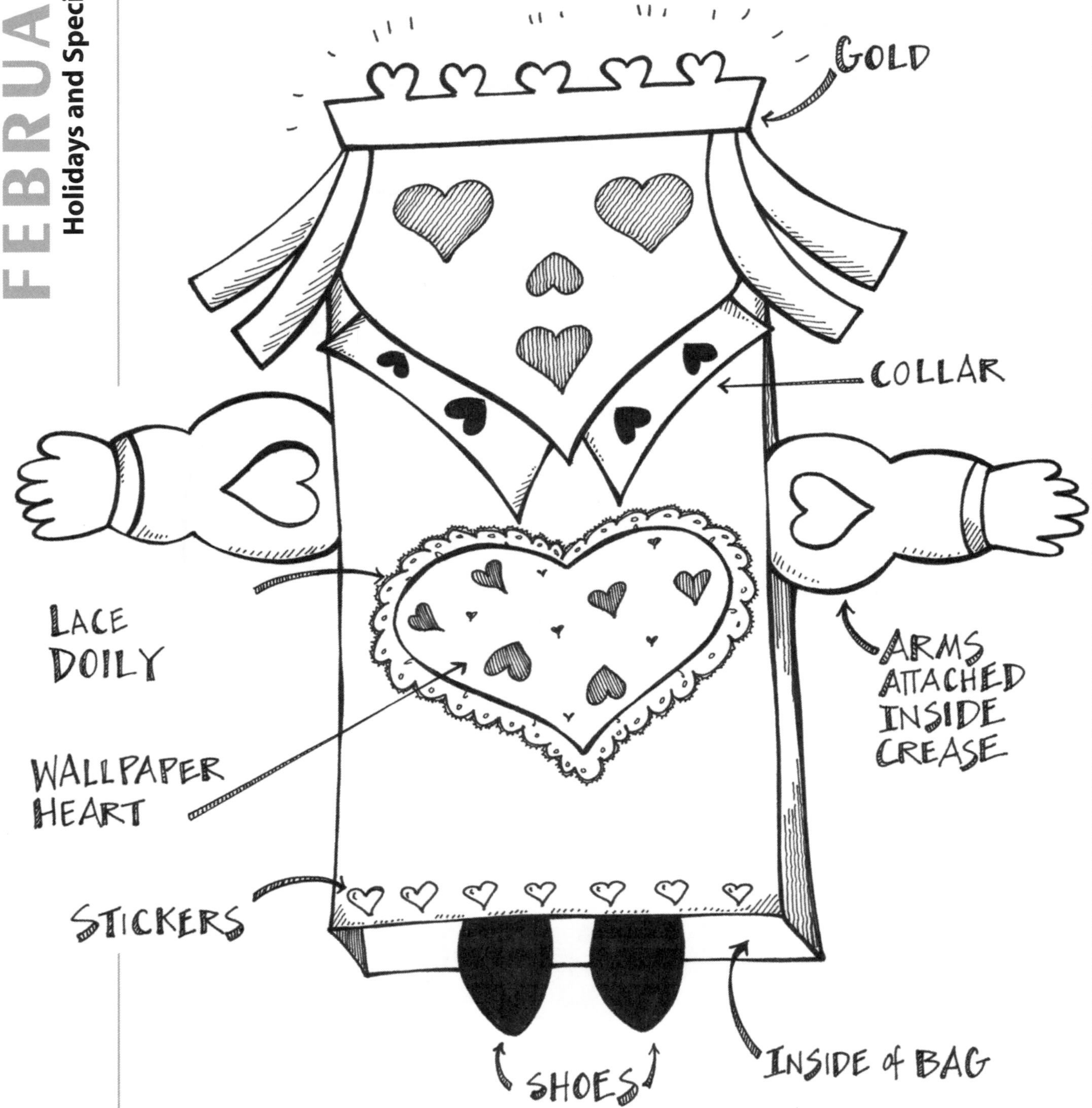

GOLD

COLLAR

LACE DOILY

WALLPAPER HEART

STICKERS

ARMS ATTACHED INSIDE CREASE

INSIDE of BAG

SHOES

*Mary Brehm, Aurora, OH*

# Stuffed Hearts

ART

**Materials**
pencil
red construction paper
scissors
stapler
paper towels
glue
red sparkles
hole punch
string

**What to do**
- Valentine's Day is February 14th.
1. Give each child two pieces of red construction paper. Show them how to put the pieces of paper together and fold in half.
2. Help the children draw half a heart shape on the folded paper.
3. Have the children cut out the heart shapes (there will be two identical shapes).
4. Help them place their two heart shapes together and staple the hearts together around the edges, leaving a 1" opening (to stuff).
5. Let the children stuff the hearts with paper towels until it is full, and then staple the hearts closed.
6. Encourage the children to drizzle glue on their hearts and sprinkle with red sparkles. Let dry.
7. Punch a hole at the top of the hearts. Place a string through each hole and tie. Hang them up from the ceiling or on a wall.
8. Let children give these hearts to their loved one for Valentine's Day, or place them in your classroom for a heart-filled room.

STRING

SPARKLES

STAPLES        STUFFED HEARTS

**Related books**
*Fluffy's Valentine's Day* by Kate McMullan
*Junie B. Jones and the Mushy Gushy Valentine* by Barbara Park
*The Night Before Valentine's Day* by Natasha Wing
*The Very Special Valentine* by Maggie Kneen

 *Lily Erlic, Victoria, British Columbia, Canada*

# Tissue Paper Valentines

ART

**Materials**     two colors of tissue paper (pink, purple, or red)
plastic container or bowl
clear contact paper, cut into pairs of same-size squares
scissors
hole punch and ribbon (optional)

**What to do**
● Valentine's Day is February 14th.
1. Ask the children to tear tissue paper into small pieces (approximately 1" to 3"). Place them in a plastic container.
2. Give each child two squares of clear contact paper. Let them peel the backing from one square of contact paper and place on a table, sticky-side up, saving the other square for later use. (Younger children might need help taking the backing off.)
3. Encourage them to place the small pieces of tissue paper flat on the contact paper.
4. When the squares are covered in tissue papers, have the children remove the backing from the reserved contact paper. Help them place it sticky-side down, on top of the tissue-covered square. Encourage them to smooth out any air bubbles.
5. Show them how to fold the square gently in half and cut half a heart, starting in the fold of the paper (to make an evenly shaped heart). Younger children may need extra help with this step.
6. Children unfold the heart to find a beautiful Valentine! Encourage them to give it to someone special on Valentine's Day.
7. If desired, let them punch a hole in the tops of their hearts and thread ribbon through. They can hang their hearts on doorknobs, windows, or anywhere for a pretty Valentine decoration.

**Related books**     *Arthur's Great Big Valentine* by Lillian Hoban
*Be My Valentine* by J.M. Carr
*Clifford's First Valentine's Day* by Norman Bridwell
*One Very Best Valentine's Day* by Joan W. Blos

★ *Dawnelle Breum, London, Ontario, Canada*

# VALENTINE BOXES

ART

**MATERIALS**     take-out cartons from a Chinese restaurant (or milk cartons)
Valentine-related stickers
construction paper (optional)

**WHAT TO DO**     • Valentine's Day is February 14th.
1. Give each child a take-out carton from a Chinese restaurant. If you do not have access to these containers, you can use milk cartons. (Take-out cartons are preferable because they don't need covering and children love the little handles.)
2. Help the children write their names on their containers and encourage them to decorate their containers with various Valentine-related stickers.
3. Children can cut out construction paper hearts to glue to their boxes, if desired.
4. Place any extra boxes in the play area.

 *Linda Ford, Sacramento, CA*

# VALENTINE DANCER

ART

**MATERIALS**     construction paper
scissors
1" x 6" strips of paper (4 for each child)
markers
glue
hole punch
12" pieces of yarn

**WHAT TO DO**     • Valentine's Day is February 14th.
1. Cut out large hearts from construction paper and give one to each child. Give each child 4 1" x 6" strips of paper.
2. Encourage the children to draw a face on their hearts.
3. Show them how to glue two strips for arms and two strips for legs.
4. Have them punch a hole in the top and tie yarn through it (see illustration on the next page).
5. Encourage them to watch their valentines dance by jiggling the string.

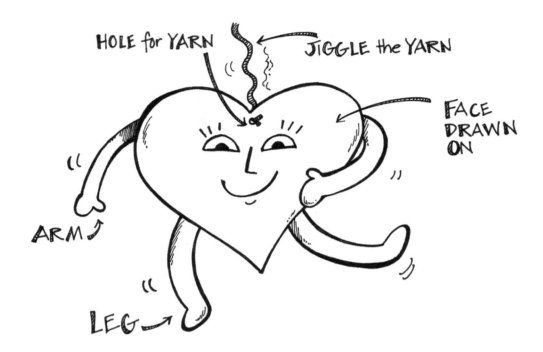

HOLE for YARN

JIGGLE the YARN

FACE DRAWN ON

ARM

LEG

**More to do**     **Movement:** Ask the children to pretend that they are a group of valentine dancers. Put them into groups of two, with one child acting as the puppet and the other as the puppeteer. Have the children switch after a few minutes.

**Related book**     *Arthur's Great Big Valentine* by Lillian Hoban

⭐ *Barbara Saul, Eureka, CA*

# Valentine Mice

ART

**Materials**     construction paper
scissors
6" of yarn
glue
pens

**What to do**     ● Valentine's Day is February 14th.
1. Cut out a large heart and two very small hearts from construction paper for each child.
2. Give each of the children a large heart. Show them how to fold the hearts in half to make the curved edges meet.

3. Help the children glue a piece of yarn along the inside crease of the valentine, allowing 5" to hang out past the narrow end (bottom) of the heart.
4. Have them glue the sides of their hearts together.
5. Give each child two small hearts, each folded in half.
6. Demonstrate how to glue the small heart to the pointed end of the large folded heart, matching folds. These will be the mouse's ears.
7. Encourage them to make a face for the mouse at the pointed end.
8. Glue the other small heart to the end of the yarn, for a tail.

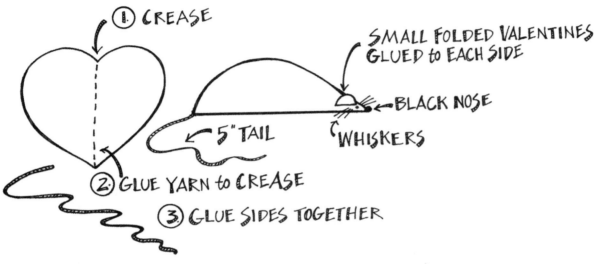

*Barbara Saul, Eureka, CA*

# Valentine Mobiles

ART

**Materials**    red, pink, and purple paper
scissors
red yarn
glue

**What to do**    ● Valentine's Day is February 14th.
1. Cut out hearts in a variety of sizes from red, pink, and purple paper.
2. Give each child an 18" length of yarn.
3. Let the children choose hearts to glue to the yarn, leaving 8" at the top.
4. Hang the mobiles from a hanger or the ceiling.

**Related book**    *How Spider Saved Valentine's Day* by Robert Kraus

*Barbara Saul, Eureka, CA*

# VALENTINE'S DAY "I LOVE YOU" CRAFT

ART

**MATERIALS**

construction paper in a variety of skin tone colors
red and pink construction paper
craft scissors
craft glue
narrow ribbon
self-stick craft magnets

**WHAT TO DO**

- Valentine's Day is February 14th.

1. Before beginning, show the children the sign for "I love you" (extend fingers and thumb, fold down middle and ring fingers while leaving thumb, index, and pinky fingers up). Tell them this is how to say, "I love you" without saying a word.

2. Ask the children to pick a piece of construction paper that they think matches their skin tone.

3. Help each child trace around one hand on the paper and cut out.

4. Ask the children to cut out two hearts: a large one from red construction paper and a slightly smaller one from pink construction paper.

5. Have them glue the pink heart on top of the red one. Let dry.

6. Ask the children to glue their hand cutouts on top of the hearts. Make sure they put glue on the palm part only. Let dry.

7. Help the children fold and glue down the middle and ring fingers on their hands. Let dry.

8. Have the children choose a ribbon. Tie each ribbon in a small bow. Let the children glue the bows to the bottom of their hand cutouts.

9. After everything has thoroughly dried, let the children attach a magnet to the back of their craft.

10. Encourage the children to give their craft to their parents for Valentine's Day.

**MORE TO DO**

**Games:** Play "I love you" bingo. Print the letters: I, L, O, V, E, Y, O, and U on a piece of card stock paper. Make one for each child. Make small cards that feature the same letters. Give the children some bingo chips. Show the letters one at a time and have the children cover them on their cards. When the last letter is shown, all of the children will have I LOVE YOU and everyone wins.

**Related song**    **The Love Song** (Tune: "The Barney Song")

*I love Mom,*
*I love Dad,*
*They're the best parents*
*A kid could ever have.*
*With a great big hug*
*And a little kiss or two*
*We always say, "I love you!"*

**Related books**    *Don't Be My Valentine* by Joan M. Lexau
*Happy Valentine's Day, Emma!* by James Stevenson
*A Sweetheart for Valentine* by Lorna Balian
*A Village Full of Valentines* by James Stevenson

★ *Virginia Jean Herrod, Columbia, SC*

# Five Little Valentines
FINGERPLAYS, SONGS, & POEMS

**Materials**    felt heart shapes and numbers (optional)
flannel board (optional)

**What to do**    ● Valentine's Day is February 14th.
1. Recite the following rhyme with the children. If desired, use the appropriate hand gestures (in parentheses).

*Five Valentines from the 10-cent store,*
*I sent one to my mommy and now there are four.* (use sign language for "mommy")
*Four Valentines, pretty ones to see,*
*I gave one to my brother, now there are three.* (sign "brother")
*Three Valentines pink, red, and white,*
*I gave one to my sister, now there are two.* (sign "sister")
*Two Valentines, my we're having fun,*
*I gave one to my Daddy, now there is one.* (sign "daddy")
*One Valentine, the story is almost done,*
*I gave it to the baby and now there are none.* (sign "baby")

2. If desired, use felt heart shapes and felt numbers on a flannel board so that the children can see the numbers and practice subtraction.

★ *Holly Dzierzanowski, Brenham, TX*

# FLOWERS ARE SWEET

FINGERPLAYS, SONGS, & POEMS

**Materials**   none

**What to do**   Sing the following song, using corresponding gestures when appropriate.

*Flowers are sweet* (nod "yes")
*That is true.* (nod head "yes")
*But for my Valentine*
*I'll choose you!* (point to a person)

★ *Kathy Kalmar, Macomb, MI*

# CAN YOU MEND MY BROKEN HEART?

GAMES

**Materials**   red construction paper
pencil
heart template or valentine candy box to trace
scissors
assorted stickers

**What to do**   ● Valentine's Day is February 14th.
1. Prepare by tracing and cutting out paper hearts (one for each child). Cut each heart in half horizontally, vertically, or diagonally, with different patterns to create two-piece puzzles. Make each puzzle different.
2. Put matching stickers on both pieces of each puzzle, using a different sticker pair for each puzzle. Laminate for durability.
3. Play a variety of games with the heart puzzles:
   ● Divide the children in half. Give one group the left halves of the puzzles and the other group the right halves. Encourage them to find their match. You can use this to create partners for other activities.
   ● Hide one half of each heart in the room and give each child one of the other halves. Encourage them to hunt for the piece with the matching sticker.
   ● During group or circle time, place one half of each heart on the floor and give each child one of the other halves. Let them find the match and assemble the hearts. To simplify the task, place the hearts with the

stickers showing; to make it more challenging, place the hearts with the stickers not showing.

- Sort the halves into two valentine candy boxes and leave on the table for individual matching play.

**Related book**    *Mouse's First Valentine* by Lauren Thompson

⭐ *Sandra Gratias, Dublin, PA*

# Valentine Spinner Board Game

GAMES

**Materials**    computer and color printer (optional)
computer-generated hearts or markers
tagboard
scissors
metal brad and paper clip, or spinner

**What to do**
- Valentine's Day is February 14th.
1. Prepare a spinner board by dividing an 8 ½″ x 8 ½″ square of tagboard into six pie sections.
2. Draw a heart in each pie section, each with a different design (stripes, dots, zigzag lines, checkerboard pattern, and so on).
3. Make two hearts of each heart design to make game pieces for two players.
4. Laminate the board and game pieces and cut out.
5. Use a metal brad and a paper clip to assemble the spinner or purchase a spinner at a teacher supply store.
6. Put the game in a center and encourage the children to visit the center in pairs.
7. To play the game, each child spins the spinner. The child can take the heart that matches the one on which the spinner lands. If he already has that heart, he skips a turn.
8. The partners alternate turns until one player accumulates all six hearts.

⭐ *Jackie Wright, Enid, OK*

# Galileo's Telescope

SCIENCE

**Materials**

black tissue paper
scissors
paper towel tubes
paint and paintbrushes
rubber bands
paperclips

**What to do**

• Galileo's birthday is February 15th. He was born in 1564.
1. Before the activity, cut two 6" x 6" tissue paper squares for each child.
2. Give each child a paper towel tube to paint. Let dry
3. Show the children how to put two pieces of tissue paper at the end of the tube and fasten it with a rubber band.
4. Help the children punch small holes in the tissue paper.
5. Encourage them to look through their "telescopes" towards a light and they will see "stars."

**Related books**

*Draw Me a Star* by Eric Carle
*Galileo's Treasure Box* by Catherine Brighton
*Little Rocket's Special Star* by Julie Sykes
*Twinkle, Twinkle, Little Star* by Iza Trapani

★ *Elizabeth Thomas, Hobart, IN*

# Happy Birthday, Clifford the Big Red Dog

SNACK AND COOKING

**Materials**

*Clifford's Birthday Party* by Norman Bridwell
several dog bone-shaped cookie cutters
sugar cookie mix or sugar cookie recipe
several child-sized rolling pins (clean and unused)
2 or 3 cookie sheets
4 or 5 large stuffed Clifford the Big Red Dogs
Clifford stickers
card stock paper in a variety of colors
variety of craft materials (buttons, sequins, fabric scraps)
craft glue
scissors

**What to do**
- February 15th is Clifford the Big Red Dog's birthday.
1. On February 15th, read *Clifford's Birthday Party* to the children. Explain that it is really Clifford's birthday. Ask if they would like to have a birthday party for Clifford.
2. Instead of a traditional cake, make dog bone-shaped cookies for the birthday party.
3. Use pre-packaged sugar cookie mix or any recipe you choose. Help the children follow the recipe or directions on the package to make the cookie dough.
4. Give each child his own portion of cookie dough. Help them use the rolling pins to roll out their cookie dough.
5. Let the children take turns using the dog bone-shaped cookie cutters to cut out at least two cookies.
6. Place the cookies on a prepared cookie sheet. Have an adult helper bake the cookies according to the directions on the package or in the recipe.
7. While the cookies are baking, get ready for the Clifford Birthday Party.
8. Place stuffed Clifford dogs in the dramatic play center along with empty boxes of dog food and small bowls. The children will enjoy pretending to have great adventures with Clifford.
9. Let the children make their own Clifford Birthday crowns. Let each child choose a piece of card stock paper. Help them cut the paper into a crown shape. Encourage them to use craft materials and bone cutouts to decorate their crowns. Fit the crowns to the children's heads and staple closed.

CROWN MADE OUT of CARDSTOCK

POM POMS
SEQUINS
DOG BONE CUT-OUT

10. Enjoy the cookies with a cold glass of milk. Everyone can wear their crowns and sing "Happy Birthday" to Clifford!
11. Give everybody a Clifford sticker at the end of the day.

**More to do**
**Art:** Let each child make his own little birthday cake for Clifford. Purchase small, round craft boxes from a craft store. Let the children paint and decorate them. Glue a single birthday candle to the top of each.

**Fine Motor:** Have children practice using their fine motor skills by wrapping packages. Provide colorful wrapping paper, children's scissors, and tape. Let the children wrap familiar items such as blocks in the block center or small toys. They can give the gifts to each other, unwrap them, and start again!

**Related books**   *Clifford and the Big Parade* by Norman Bridwell
*Clifford Celebrates the Year* by Norman Bridwell
*Clifford the Big Red Dog* by Norman Bridwelll
*Clifford's ABC* by Norman Bridwell
*Count on Clifford* by Norman Bridwell

 *Virginia Jean Herrod, Columbia, SC*

# Cherries on the Tree

ART

**Materials**
pastel construction paper
1" x 4" pieces of brown construction paper
5" circles of green construction paper
glue stick
plastic lid or small piece of aluminum foil
red fingerpaint or poster paint

**What to do**
• George Washington's birthday is February 22nd. President's Day is celebrated the third Monday of February.
1. Discuss the story of young George Washington chopping down his father's cherry tree.
2. Give each child a 1" x 4" rectangle of brown paper and a sheet of pastel construction paper.
3. Demonstrate how to hold both papers in a vertical position and glue the brown rectangle to the bottom half of the pastel paper.
4. Give each child a green paper circle. Show them how to glue the green circle to the top of the brown rectangle, forming the shape of a tree.
5. Put a small amount of red fingerpaint into a plastic lid or small piece of aluminum foil.
6. Encourage the children to dip their fingers into the red paint and make thumbprint "cherries" on their trees.

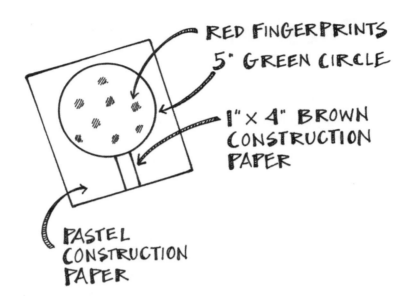

RED FINGERPRINTS

5" GREEN CIRCLE

1" × 4" BROWN CONSTRUCTION PAPER

PASTEL CONSTRUCTION PAPER

**More to do**   **Social Development**: Draw a large tree on tagboard and let the children add thumbprint cherries. Have each cherry symbolize an act of kindness by that child.

**Related poem**   *I'll pick some cherries from the tree,* (pretend to pick cherries)
*Five for you and five for me.* (show five fingers on each hand)
*We'll eat and eat—* (pretend to eat)
*5 — 4 — 3 — 2 — 1* (count down with fingers)
*Until the cherries are all gone!* (show empty hands and look surprised)

**Related books**   *Cherries and Cherry Pits* by Vera B. Williams
*Under the Cherry Blossom Tree* by Allen Say

⭐ *Christina R. Chilcote, New Freedom, PA*

# Presidential Birthdays

## LANGUAGE AND LITERACY

**Materials**
coins (penny, nickel, dime, quarter, dollar)
maps of your town, state, and United States
American flag
picture of George Washington and Abraham Lincoln

**What to do**
- President's Day is celebrated the third Monday of February.
1. With each child, recite the following information:
   - My name is _____.
   - I live in a _____(house, apartment, mobile home…).
   - I go to_____ (name of school).
   - I live in _____ (city). (Show the child a city map.)
   - (City) is in _____ (state). (Show a state map.)
   - (State) is in the United States. (Show a map of the U.S.)

2. Tell the children the following information:
   - George Washington was the first President of United States.
   - George Washington is called the "Father of our Country." His picture is on the quarter and dollar. (Show the children the coins).
   - Abraham Lincoln was the 16th president of the United States. He freed slaves during the Civil War. His picture is on the penny (show a penny).
   - This is our flag. It is red, white, and blue. It represents our country, the United States of America.

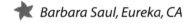 *Barbara Saul, Eureka, CA*

# MARCH

# Paper Daffodils

ART

**Materials**
yellow construction paper
scissors
yellow or orange tissue paper
tacky glue
green pipe cleaners

**What to do**

1. You can use this activity to talk about the arrival of spring. Daffodils are usually one of the first flowers to bloom in spring. You could also use this activity to talk about how things grow and the life cycle of a plant.
2. Cut out two flower shapes with five petals, about 4" wide, from yellow construction paper.
3. Cut out 3" squares of yellow or orange tissue paper.
4. Help children bunch up the tissue paper squares around their thumbs in a tube shape to make the middle of a daffodil. Let them glue the tissue paper to the middle of their flower shapes.
5. Provide green pipe cleaners. The children bend pipe cleaners in half to make stems.
6. Use another half of a pipe cleaner to bend a leaf around the stem.
7. Help children glue one flower shape underneath the stem and the flower shape with the daffodil middle on top of the stem. Let dry.

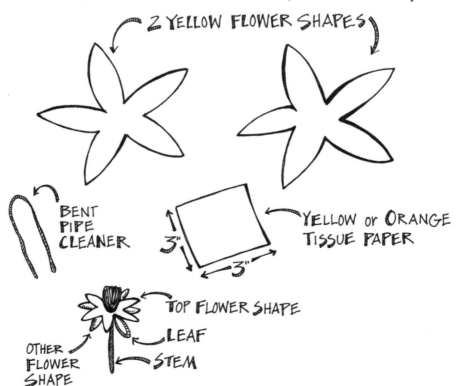

2 YELLOW FLOWER SHAPES

BENT PIPE CLEANER

3" 3" YELLOW or ORANGE TISSUE PAPER

TOP FLOWER SHAPE
LEAF
STEM
OTHER FLOWER SHAPE

 *Jennifer Galvin, Stafford, VA*

# Rainbows and Sunshine

ART

**Materials**
crepe paper streamers in several colors
empty rolls of paper towels (2 for each child)
glue or stapler

**What to do**
1. Provide each child with several strips of different colors of crepe paper.
2. For each child, cut the end of one of the paper towel rolls and slip it into the end of the other one far enough to make it sturdy. Glue or tape to secure rolls together.
3. Staple or glue the multicolored streamers close together onto the cardboard rolls.
4. Let the "rainbow flags" dry if using glue.
5. Encourage the children to run and play holding their rainbow flags! If desired, play children's songs about rainbows as the children run and dance.

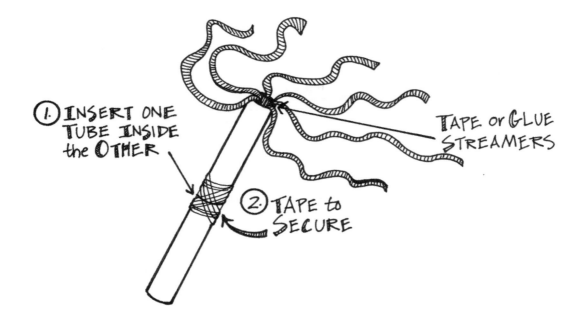

① INSERT ONE TUBE INSIDE the OTHER

TAPE or GLUE STREAMERS

② TAPE to SECURE

 *Renee Trudeau, Jamul, CA*

# Wind Painting

ART

**Materials**
fan or windy day
clothesline and clothespins
tempera paint (thinned and watery)
paper
paintbrushes, spoons, or eyedroppers

**What to do**
1. Tie a clothesline outside on a windy day. If doing the activity inside, hang the clothesline near a fan.
2. To illustrate the effect of the wind, have each child place some paint on a piece of paper. Take the papers outside or place in front of a fan set on high.
3. Clip the papers to the clothesline and watch what happens to the paint.
4. Let dry. Discuss what happened to the paint.

*Kristi Larson, Spirit Lake, IA*

# Windy Day

ART

**Materials**
thick, white fingerpaint
blue construction paper (one sheet per child)
clean combs

**What to do**
1. Place a blob of white fingerpaint in the center of each child's paper.
2. Encourage the children to use combs to swirl the paint on their papers, pretending the combs are the wind.
3. Lead a class discussion on wind. "How does it feel?" "Is it soft?" "Hard?" "Can it cool you?" "Can it hurt you?" "How does it sound?"

*Elaine Commins, Athens, GA*

# WEATHER WATCH MURAL

ART

**Materials**  clear contact paper
colorful tissue paper or other collage materials
scissors

**What to do**  1. Do this activity on a day with dramatic weather—windy, rainy, stormy, or snowy.
2. Explain to children that they will have fun watching the weather and creating an art project at the same time.
3. Tape a large sheet of clear contact paper across the largest window to which children have access. Make sure that the sticky side will face the children.
4. Provide collage materials. If desired, have the children cut out collage materials themselves.
5. Peel the backing from the contact paper. Invite the children to stick on the collage materials.
6. Admire the art and the weather simultaneously!
7. Let children take home sections of the mural at the end of the day.

TAPE

STICKY SIDE
of CLEAR CONTACT
PAPER

**More to do**  **Sensory:** Talk about which of their senses are involved in this activity.

**Related books**  *Lightning* by Seymour Simon
*The Snowy Day* by Ezra Jack Keats

 *Elisheva Leah Nadler, Har Nof, Jerusalem, Israel*

# I Feel the Wind

### FINGERPLAYS, SONGS, & POEMS

**Materials**     none

**What to do**     Sing the following song, making the suggested gestures when appropriate.

**I Feel the Wind**
*I can feel the wind* (wave hands back and forth)
*I can feel it blow,* (blow with mouth)
*I can feel the wind dance high and low,* (raise hands up and down)
*I can feel the wind blow fast and slow,* (move arms fast and slow)
*I can feel the wind from my head down to my toes.* (touch head and toes)

 *Susan Myhre, Bremerton, WA*

# Blow, Wind, Blow!

### FINGERPLAYS, SONGS, & POEMS

**Materials**     none

**What to do**     Recite the following poem with the children. Encourage them to act out the motions appropriate to the poem.

**Blow, Wind, Blow!**
*Blow, wind, blow!* (cup hands around mouth)
*You bring the clouds,* (outstretch arms, wiggle fingers up and down)
*The rain, the snow.*
*Blow, wind, blow!* (cup hands around mouth)
*You spread the seeds* (open hands, pretend to scatter seeds)
*From which plants grow.*
*Blow, wind, blow!* (cup hands around mouth)
*You fill the kites* (arms extended upward, pulling a kite string)
*And make things go.*
*Blow, wind, blow!* (cup hands around mouth)
*You stir the waves* (extend both arms, make large, circular motions)
*And waters flow.*
*Blow, wind, blow!* (cup hands around mouth)
*Sometimes friend* (cross arms in front of chest)
*And sometimes foe.* (extend arms as if to push away)
*Blow, wind, blow!* (cup hands around mouth)

 *Barbara Hershberger, Watertown, WI*

# It's Raining
FINGERPLAYS, SONGS, & POEMS

**Materials**　　none

**What to do**　　Sing the following song to the tune of "Mary Had a Little Lamb":

*It's cloudy and it's raining too,*
*Raining too,*
*Raining too.*
*It's cloudy and it's raining too,*
*I (We) cannot play outside.*

*I (We) hope that it stops raining soon,*
*Raining soon,*
*Raining soon,*
*I (We) hope that it stops raining soon,*
*I (We) want to play outside!*

 *Kristi Larson, Spirit Lake, IA*

# Thunder and Lightning
FINGERPLAYS, SONGS, & POEMS

**What to do**　　Sing the following to the tune of "Itsy, Bitsy Spider." Have the children make the appropriate gestures when prompted.

**Thunder and Lightning**
*Thunder and lightning are crashing all around* (clap hands together loudly)
*I'm a little frightened of all the loud sounds!* (cover ears)
*Down come the raindrops, drip, drip, drop.* (wiggle fingers)
*Boy, I hope this storm soon will stop!* (shake finger)

 *Kristi Larson, Spirit Lake, IA*

# MAKE IT RAIN AND SNOW!

GAMES

**MATERIALS**
newspapers, old telephone directories, and old magazines
music to suit rain or snowstorm
large plastic bags
small brooms
dustpans

**WHAT TO DO**
1. Explain to children that they will be making their own rain or snowstorm.
2. Show them how to tear and crumple newspapers and magazine pages into strips, small pieces, and balls.
3. Give each child a supply of paper to work with.
4. As the torn paper accumulates, add music.
5. Encourage the children to swim and dance through the "storm." Join them in the fun!
6. When the children tire of the activity, suggest cleaning up in a fun way. For example, "Let's be snowplows and clean this all away!"
7. Provide large plastic bags, small brooms, and dustpans for clean up.

**MORE TO DO**
**Language:** Discuss the differences between real precipitation and the paper play.

**RELATED book**
*Water* by Frank Asch

 *Elisheva Leah Nadler, Jerusalem, Israel*

# LION OR LAMB?

GROUP OR CIRCLE TIME

**MATERIALS**
tagboard
computer printer or marker
picture of a lion
picture of a lamb
name card for each child in your class
pocket chart

**WHAT TO DO**
1. Print the question: "Which would you rather be?" on a tagboard header card. Write "lion" and "lamb" on separate tagboard cards. Glue a picture of each animal next to the word.

2. Make a column for each answer choice underneath the question.
3. Place the header card in the top pocket of a pocket chart.
4. Tell the children the phrase, "March comes in like a lion, and goes out like a lamb." Explain what it means.
5. Give each child a name card. Ask them to place their name cards in the pocket chart in the column that represents their choice.
6. Count the responses and compare the results.

⭐ *Jackie Wright, Enid, OK*

# WEATHER SORT

GROUP OR CIRCLE TIME

**MATERIALS**
assorted clothing and accessories for rainy weather (rain boots, rain coat, umbrella, sweatshirt, thick socks)
assorted clothing and accessories for sunny summer weather (T-shirt, shorts, sun visor, sunscreen, sandals)
beach towel
blanket

**WHAT TO DO**
1. Spread the beach towel and the blanket next to each other on the floor.
2. Ask the children when they would use a beach towel and when they would use a blanket.
3. Hold up an umbrella. Ask whether it would go with the beach towel or blanket. Put the item on the blanket.
4. Continue to sort the rest of the rainy day and sunny day items on the towel or blanket.
5. If desired, add snow clothing and accessories as a third category. Put them on a thick comforter.

**MORE TO DO**
**Music:** Have a child select an item. The rest of the children sing the child's name, the item, and the weather condition.

(Tune: "Mary Wore Her Red Dress")
*Owen wears his rain boots, rain boots, rain boots.*
*Owen wears his rain boots*
*In the rain.*

*Clara wears her sandals, sandals, sandals,*
*Clara wears her sandals*
*In the sun.*

**Related books**  *Caps, Hats, Socks, and Mittens: A Book About the Four Seasons* by Louise Borden
*Four Stories for Four Seasons* by Tomie dePaola
*The Jacket I Wear in the Snow* by Shirley Neitzel
*Mud* by Mary Lyn Ray

★ *Cassandra Reigel Whetstone, San Jose, CA*

# Color Me a Rainbow
### GROUP OR CIRCLE TIME

**Materials**  white construction paper
red, blue, green, yellow, and orange markers
scissors

**What to do**
1. Draw a rainbow on a piece of white construction paper.
2. Cut out the rainbow and trace onto a second piece of construction paper. Color it to match the first rainbow.
3. Cut and separate each color of one of the rainbows, so there are individual arcs of blue, red, green, and so on.
4. At circle time, give each child one arc of the rainbow.
5. Place the intact rainbow on the floor in front of the children. Ask the children to come up individually and place their arc on the corresponding color of the rainbow.
6. Encourage the children to point out other things in the room that are similarly colored.

**Related book**  *What Makes a Rainbow* by Betty Ann Schwartz

 *Kimberly M. Hutmacher, Springfield, IL*

# Welcome Robin Red Breast
### OUTDOORS

**Materials**  yarn
string
dryer lint
hair

**What to do**
1. Gather scraps of yarn, string, dryer lint, and hair.
2. Scatter the scraps outside for birds to gather and make nests.
3. Watch the birds take away the materials.

**Related songs**
(From Mother Goose)
*I saw a little robin go hop, hop, hop,*
*And I said, "Little robin, won't you stop, stop, stop?"*
*I was going to the window to say, "How do you do?"*
*When he shook his little tail and away he flew.*

**The Robins Came Back** (Tune: "The Farmer in the Dell")
*The robins came back.*
*The robins came back.*
*Now it's spring and warming up*
*So the robins came back.*

*The robins came back.*
*The robins came back.*
*They didn't like the cold and snow,*
*So the robins came back.*

*Sandra Gratias, Dublin, PA*

# Bird Banquet

SCIENCE

**Materials**
clean, empty bleach and soda bottles
mesh produce bags
pinecones
peanut butter
large bag of wild birdseed
1 pound of softened lard
2 cups of oatmeal

**What to do**
1. Cut out four large squares from the sides of each bleach bottle, so they look like small gazebos. Leave the base and the top as they are. Attach a string around the top of each bottle for hanging.
2. Randomly cut "n" shapes around each soda bottle. Fold the "n" shapes down to form perches. Attach a string to the top of each bottle for hanging.

3. Fill the soda and bleach bottles with birdseed.

4. Tie strings to the tops of the pinecones. Spread peanut butter on the pinecones and roll each pinecone in wild birdseed.
**Note:** If any of the children have peanut allergies, skip this step.

5. Make Bird Pudding. Mix 1 pound of softened lard, 2 cups of oatmeal, and 4 cups of wild birdseed. Add a little hot water until the pudding is a doughy consistency.

6. Fill the mesh bags with Bird Pudding.

7. Take all the bird feeders outside and hang in the trees for a bird banquet. Make observations. What kind of bird visits most frequently? Which feeder do the birds prefer?

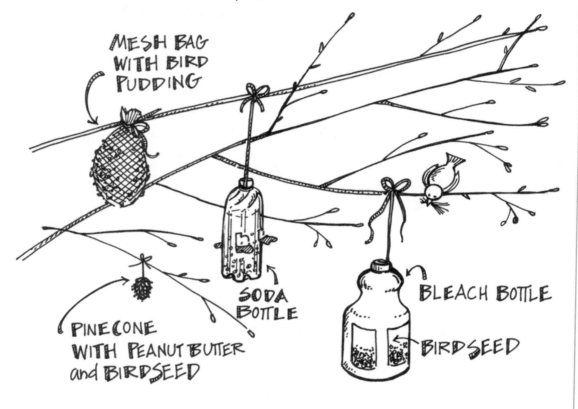

MESH BAG WITH BIRD PUDDING

PINECONE WITH PEANUT BUTTER and BIRDSEED

SODA BOTTLE

BLEACH BOTTLE

BIRDSEED

⭐ *Amelia Griffin, Pontypool, Ontario, Canada*

# CATCH A RAINBOW

SCIENCE

**MATERIALS**    jar
water
4' of white bulletin board sheet paper
crayons

**What to do**
1. Fill the jar to the top with water.
2. Put the jar on a windowsill in bright sunshine.
3. Place the white paper on the floor below the jar.
4. Let the children observe the rainbow reflected on the paper.
5. Draw lines on the paper to capture the rainbow. Have the children color the paper as the rainbow is reflected on it.

**Related books**
*All the Colors of the Rainbow* by Allan Fowler
*Let's Celebrate St. Patrick's Day* by Peter Roop
*Planting a Rainbow* by Lois Elhert
*A Rainbow of My Own* by Don Freeman

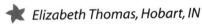 *Elizabeth Thomas, Hobart, IN*

# Rainbows

SCIENCE

**Materials**
paper
paint
hats and long scarves in every color of the rainbow

**What to do**
1. Draw a giant rainbow on a large sheet of paper.
2. Mix together all the hats and scarves on the floor.
3. Choose seven children for this activity. Each child grabs a hat and puts it on, then finds the matching scarf.
4. The children sit behind each other in a line on the floor in order to make a rainbow. (They may need help with this.)
5. Have the children put the scarves around their necks and hold one end in each hand to make long swaths of color, stretching their arms out to make the shape of the rainbow arch.
6. Then each child names his color, one after the other, starting with red. After violet they all say, "The colors of the rainbow."

**More to do**
**Art:** Let children color or paint their own rainbows.
**Books:** Read some folk tales about gold at the end of the rainbow.
**Science:** Talk about how, when, and why rainbows occur.

**Related books**   *Planting a Rainbow* by Lois Ehlert
*A Rainbow All Around Me* by Sandra L Pinkney
*Rainbow Bridge* by Audrey Wood
*Rainbow Fish* by Marcus Pfister
*Weaving the Rainbow* by George Ella Lyon

 *Anne Adeney, Plymouth, United Kingdom*

# The Water Cycle

SCIENCE

**Materials**   clear glass fish bowl large enough to fit over bowl
bowl or pie plate
water

**What to do**   1. Fill the bowl or pie plate with water and place in sunny warm location.
2. Place a fish bowl upside down over the bowl or pie plate.
3. Encourage the children to observe water condensation on the bowl as it warms.
4. Use simple words to explain evaporation. Tell that children that water evaporates when it warms, then condenses in the air, gets heavy, and falls as rain.

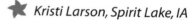 *Kristi Larson, Spirit Lake, IA*

# Endangered Animal Day

ART

**Materials**
balloons
newspaper
glue
paints
paintbrushes
mask decorations such as feathers, string, and fur

**What to do**
- March is Endangered Animals Month.
1. Discuss what it means to be "endangered."
2. Provide a list of endangered animals and let each child choose one (for example, elephant, panda, whale, rhino, turtle, and gorilla).
3. Blow up a small balloon for each child.
4. Demonstrate how to glue strips of newspaper (papier-mâché) to half of the balloon. Help each child build up the newspaper strips into the face of the chosen animal.
5. Make sure to leave two holes for the eyes before the papier-mâché dries.
6. When the masks are dry, remove the balloons and have the children paint their masks. Encourage them to add decorations, if appropriate.
7. Play music. Encourage the children to perform an "endangered animal dance" while wearing their masks.

**More to do**   **Science**: Research endangered animals and what is being done to save them.

 *Amelia Griffin, Ontario, Canada*

# THE PEANUT HOP

### FINGERPLAYS, SONGS, & POEMS

**MATERIALS**   brown construction paper or tagboard
scissors
markers
craft sticks
tape
wiggle eyes and tacky glue

**WHAT TO DO**   • March is National Peanut Month.
1. Cut out peanut shapes, 7" long, from brown construction paper or tagboard (one per child).
2. Let children draw two oval eyes and a simple smiling mouth at one end of the peanut shape.
3. Help the children tape the top third of a craft stick to the back of the peanut shape to form a peanut puppet.
4. Have children place dots of tacky glue on eye ovals and press wiggle eyes into the glue.
5. Use the peanut puppets with the following action rhyme:

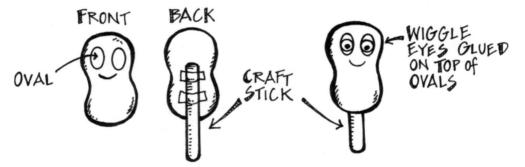

**The Peanut Hop** (tune: "Rockin' Robin" or "Rock Around the Clock")
*Out of the ground,* (jump up)
*Out of the shell,* (jump again)
*Into my tummy,* (rub tummy)
*You taste so swell.* (wave hands in the air)
*Do the peanut hop, hop, hop.* (hop three times)
*Do the peanut hop, hop, hop.* (hop three times)
*Do the peanut hop, hop, hop.* (hop three times)
*And turn around.* (turn around once)

**MORE TO DO**   **Science:** Lead a simple discussion of the difference between true nuts and legumes (peanuts) or about George Washington Carver and the many uses he discovered for peanuts.

**RELATED book**   *The Life and Times of the Peanut* by Charles Micucci

PEANUT

Christina R. Chilcote, New Freedom, PA

# Flying High

LANGUAGE AND LITERACY

**Materials**
construction paper
scissors
markers
tagboard
paper cutter
12" x 18" construction paper
color scanner
glue stick
laminating machine
scissors
pocket chart

**What to do**

- March is National Kite Month.
1. Cut out four kite shapes from construction paper. Label each with a different letter of your choice.
2. Form columns at the top of a pocket chart with a header card ("Flying High") at the top and the instructions: "Place the cards under the correct kites."
3. On tagboard, draw pictures representing the beginning sounds of each of the four letters on the kites.
5. Using a paper cutter, cut the pictures into cards of the desired size.
6. If desired, make a file jacket from 12" x 18" construction paper with the title and a kite picture on the front.
7. Using a color scanner, make a reduced-size color printout of the completed activity showing the header card with all the picture cards under the correct kites.
8. Glue the color printout to the back of the file jacket.
9. Laminate the header card, picture cards, and file jacket, and cut out.
10. To use this center, a child identifies a picture's beginning sound and adds it to the pocket chart under the appropriate letter kite.
11. When finished, he can look at the back of the file jacket and check his work.
12. This picture reference helps ensure that all pieces in the activity are accounted for when you put them away at the end of the month.

**Related book**
*Housekeeper of the Wind* by Christine Widman

⭐ *Jackie Wright, Enid, OK*

# Count the Claps

### LANGUAGE AND LITERACY

**Materials**
colored pictures of fruits and vegetables
scissors
tagboard
glue stick
laminating machine

**What to do**
- March is National Nutrition Month.
1. Use this idea to boost the children's phonological awareness.
2. Have the children practice saying each classmate's name and clapping the syllables ("Mi"-clap-"chael"-clap).
3. Explain that March is Nutrition Month.
4. Collect colored pictures of fruits and vegetables, cut them out, and glue them to tagboard.
5. Laminate them for durability, and cut out.
6. Hold up a picture and ask a child to name the food on the card and clap the word parts (syllables). For example, "ra"-clap-"dish"-clap.
7. Have the children identify the number of claps.

 *Jackie Wright, Enid, OK*

# Healthy Food/Unhealthy Food

### SCIENCE

**Materials**
old magazines
scissors
large easel paper
glue

**What to do**
- March is National Nutrition Month.
1. Talk to the children about healthy foods and unhealthy foods. Tell them about the food pyramid and the different food groups. Provide examples of healthy and unhealthy foods.
2. Divide the large paper into two columns with the headings: "Healthy Food" and "Unhealthy Food."
3. Invite the children to cut out pictures of food out from old magazines and glue them into the appropriate columns.

4. Discuss each food with the children.
5. If desired, make small copies of the chart and let the children put their pictures on their own charts.

**Related books**   *The Boy Who Ate Around* by Henrik Drescher
*Cloudy With a Chance of Meatballs* by Judith Barrett
*Green Eggs and Ham* by Dr. Seuss

★ *Barbara Saul, Eureka, CA*

# Fruit Explorers

SNACK AND COOKING

**Materials**   several varieties of fruit, especially less common types
serving platters
sharp knives (adult only)
small paper plates or cups
napkins

**What to do**   • March is National Nutrition Month.
1. Bring in several varieties of less common fruit, such as a star fruit, prickly pear, mango, coconut, passion fruit, and lychee.
2. Talk to the children about nutritious foods, especially fruit. Ask them what kinds of fruit they like to eat, and if they have heard of or tasted any less common fruit.
3. Show the children the fruit before cutting it up. Cut all the fruit into bite-size pieces and place each sample on platters or in small cups.
4. Encourage the children to sample all the fruit and tell about their favorites.
**Safety Note:** Be aware of any food allergies in the classroom and plan accordingly.

★ *Amelia Griffin, Ontario, Canada*

# Celebrate National Nutrition Month With Healthy Snacks

### SNACK AND COOKING

**Materials**
healthy foods (each beginning with a different letter of the alphabet)
bowls
plastic spoons and knives

**What to do**
1. Explain that March is National Nutrition Month, and that it is important to eat healthy foods every day.
2. Over the course of the month, eat various foods beginning with different letters of the alphabet.
3. On the last day of March, have a healthy food party. Explain how different foods can be mixed to make salads, and so on. Examples of healthy foods:

| | | | |
|---|---|---|---|
| Apples | Honeydew | Nuts | Ugli fruit |
| Bananas | melon | Oranges | Vanilla yogurt |
| Carrots | Ice cream | Potatoes | Watermelon |
| Dates | Juice | Quince | Extra virgin |
| Eggs | Kiwis | Rice | olive oil |
| Figs | Lettuce | Spaghetti | Yams |
| Grapes | Mangoes | Tangerine | Ziti |

⭐ *Lois McEwan, Levittown, NY*

# Celebrate Reading Month

### LANGUAGE AND LITERACY

**Material**
see below

**What to do**
- March is National Reading Month.
  Celebrate National Reading Month with a variety of activities, such as:
  - Invite the children to dress like characters from their favorite books or nursery rhymes.
  - Make paper hats and write "Hats Off to Reading" on them.
  - Talk like Dr. Seuss by rhyming.
  - Turn off the lights and let children read books using flashlights.
  - Have a pajama party. Have children wear pajamas to school and read bedtime stories.

 *Kathy Kalmar, Macomb, MI*

# CATS IN THE HATS/READ ACROSS AMERICA DAY

ART

**Materials**
*The Cat in the Hat* by Dr. Seuss
white easel paper
red tempera paint
1" paintbrushes
tape

**What to do**
- March 2nd is Dr. Seuss' birthday.
1. Celebrate Dr. Seuss' birthday on March 2nd by making "Cat in the Hat" hats.
2. Paint wide red stripes on easel paper, leaving white spaces in between each stripe.
3. When the paint has dried, help the children roll up the papers to fit their heads. Tape the paper to form a stove-pipe hat.
4. Have the children wear their hats while you read *The Cat in the Hat*.
5. If desired, make "Cat in the Hat" bowties by cutting a bow shape out of light blue paper. Tape the bow ties to a piece of elastic to fit over each child's head.

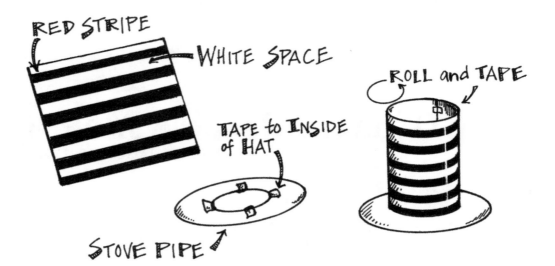

**More to do**
Use watercolors or face paint to paint cat whiskers on the children.

⭐ *Barbara Saul, Eureka, CA*

# OUR FAVORITE Dr. SEUSS BOOK

LANGUAGE AND LITERACY

**MATERIALS**
chart paper
markers
Dr. Seuss books

**WHAT TO DO**

● March 2nd is Dr. Seuss' birthday.

1. Tell the children it is Dr. Seuss' birthday and that he was an author. Let them know you are going to be reading some of the books he wrote.

2. After you read each story, write the name of the book across the top of the chart.

3. When you have finished reading your collection of Dr. Seuss books, ask the children which book was their favorite.

4. Write the children's names on the chart under their favorite book.

**MORE TO DO**

**Math:** Count how many children voted for each book. Encourage the children to compare the numbers, figuring out which book was their favorite and which one they liked the least.

★ *Monica Hay Cook, Tucson, AZ*

# HAPPY BIRTHdAY, DR. SEUSS!

PROJECTS

**MATERIALS**
list of Dr. Seuss titles
poster board
construction paper
markers
photographs of children and parents

**WHAT TO DO**

1. Prepare a list of Dr. Seuss titles and ask parents to sign up to read one of the stories during the week of Dr. Seuss's March 2nd birthday.

2. Write "Happy Birthday, Dr. Seuss!" at the top of a piece of poster board.

3. Decorate the poster board and add photographs of the children and parents reading the books.

4. Following are some suggested Dr. Seuss titles:
   - *Fox in Sox*
   - *Green Eggs and Ham*
   - *Hop on Pop*
   - *If I Ran the Circus*
   - *If I Ran the Zoo*
   - *Mr. Brown Can Moo! Can You?*
   - *One Fish, Two Fish, Red Fish, Blue Fish*

★ *Karyn F. Everham, Fort Myers, FL*

# Tissue Square Shamrocks

ART

**Materials**
newspaper
tagboard shamrock shapes about 10" wide
shallow containers
glue
paintbrushes
tissue squares in dark green, light green, yellow, and blue
scissors

**What to do**
- March 17th is St. Patrick's Day.
1. Ahead of time spread newspaper on the tables and pour glue into shallow containers.
2. Give each child a tagboard shamrock shape. Show them how to paint one third of the shamrock with glue and cover it with overlapping tissue squares. Encourage them to cover the area well, leaving some squares hanging off the edges.
3. Repeat, painting glue and placing tissue squares on the other sections of the shamrock.
4. Have them paint glue over the entire shamrock to seal the squares. Allow to dry.

COVER ⅓ AT A TIME
TAGBOARD SHAMROCK
GLUE
BRUSH
TISSUE PAPER

**MORE TO DO**   Have a Shamrock Day! Invite the children to wear green that day; serve grapes for a green snack.
**Math:** Collect pictures of items that come in threes or have three parts: tricycles, trios, triplets, triangles, and so on.

⭐ *Susan Oldham Hill, Lakeland, FL*

# LEPRECHAUN FOOTPRINTS

ART

**MATERIALS**   paper
green paint or green ink pad
small box
paint
chocolate gold coins

**WHAT TO DO**
- March 17th is St. Patrick's Day.
1. Help the children dip the side of one hand into green paint or a green ink pad and make a print on paper.
2. Invite the children to dip their index fingers into the green paint and make five dots above their prints (for toes), to look like miniature footprints. Some children may need you to guide their hands when making the dots.
3. Have them do the same thing with their other hand.
4. When dry, cut them out and tape them to the wall to look like footprints of someone climbing up the wall.
5. Invite the children to decorate a box to make a "leprechaun trap." Place the box near the footprints.
6. Before the children arrive on St. Patrick's Day, place some chocolate gold coins in the box for the children to discover!

DOTS (TOES)

SIDE OF HAND

TAPED FOOTPRINTS

WALL

GOLD COINS

DECORATED BOX

⭐ *Laura Durbrow, Lake Oswego, OR*

# SHAMROCK LACING

FINE MOTOR

**MATERIALS**
green paper
shamrock pattern
yellow yarn
hole punch

**WHAT TO DO**
- St. Patrick's Day is March 17th.
1. Draw a large shamrock on 8" x 11" sheets of green paper.
2. Have each child cut out a shamrock.
3. Use a hole punch to punch holes around the shamrock. The difficulty of this activity depends on how many holes you punch—you can tailor the activity to each child's level of ability.
4. Give each child a piece of yellow yarn with both ends taped (to make "needles"). Encourage the children to lace the yellow yarn through each hole.

**MORE TO DO**
**Art:** Let the children paint their shamrocks green. Let dry, decorate with glitter glue, and then punch holes.

 *Jill Martin and D'Arcy Simmons, Springfield, MO*

# HAPPY ST. PATRICK'S DAY TO YOU

FINGERPLAYS, SONGS, & POEMS

**MATERIALS**
none

**WHAT TO DO**
- St. Patrick's Day is March 17th.
1. Sing the following song, to the tune of "Happy Birthday":

*Happy St. Patrick's Day to you,*
*Happy St. Patrick' Day to you,*
*Happy St. Patrick's Day everybody,*
*Happy St. Patrick's Day to you.*

2. Substitute "Happy Irish Potato Day" or "Happy Shamrock Day" for St. Patrick's Day and repeat the song.

 *Kathy Kalmar, Macomb, MI*

# This Little Leprechaun

FINGERPLAYS, SONGS, & POEMS

**Materials**     none

**What to do**    • St. Patrick's Day is March 17th.
*This little leprechaun went to Ireland* (raise thumb)
*This little leprechaun stayed home* (raise index finger)
*This little leprechaun ate Irish stew* (raise middle finger)
*This little leprechaun ate none* (raise ring finger)
*And this little leprechaun cried, "Top of the morning to ye everyone!"* (raise
   pinkie)

 *Kathy Kalmar, Macomb, MI*

# Jack Jump

GAMES

**Materials**     small rope
empty toilet paper tubes
small paper plates
glue
small piece of tissue paper
paint and brushes

**What to do**    • St. Patrick's Day is March 17th.
1. Teach the children the following rhyme:

*Jack be nimble,*
*Jack be quick,*
*Jack jump over the candlestick.*

2. Have the children take turns jumping over a rope. Substitute the child's
   name each time ("Mary be quick").
3. Give each child an empty toilet paper tube to paint.
4. When the paper tubes are dry, show the children how to put glue around
   one end of the tube and glue it in the middle of a small painted paper
   plate. At the opposite end, let them glue a piece of tissue paper for the
   flame.
5. When the "candlesticks" are dry, encourage the children to practice their
   jumping as they say the rhyme in class.

6. Adapt this rhyme for St. Patrick's Day by substituting "leprechaun" for Jack ("Leprechaun be nimble…"). Paint the candlesticks green.
**Note:** Some children may need to work on jumping over smaller objects at first; the paper tube will not hurt them if it is kicked or jumped on.

TISSUE PAPER FLAME
PAPER PLATE
PAPER TUBE

**MORE TO DO**    At the beginning of the year, this can be a fun way to practice each child's name.
**Language:** This is good for language practice. Change words, for example, "Jack ran by the red chair" or "Jack crawled through the blue tunnel."

★ *Sandra Nagel, White Lake, MI*

# LEAPING LEPRECHAUNS
### LANGUAGE AND LITERACY

**MATERIALS**    two doll shoes
green tempera paint
small items such as a green doll hat or a chocolate coin

**WHAT TO DO**
● St. Patrick's Day is March 17th.
1. On the afternoon before St. Patrick's Day (March 17th), after the children have gone home, dip doll shoes into green paint and make green shoeprints all over the room—in children's desks, on the floor, up the wall, and out the window.

2. Hide the small items throughout the room so the children can find them.
3. When the children come in the next morning, they will see the "Leprechaun's path."
4. Encourage the children to dictate stories about how the leprechaun got into the room and what he did while he was there.

 *Barbara Saul, Eureka, CA*

# Shamrock Stories
### LANGUAGE AND LITERACY

**Materials**  green paper shamrocks

**What to do**
- March 17th is St. Patrick's Day.
1. Discuss what being lucky feels like.
2. Have the children dictate stories, "I'm lucky because...," while an adult writes the stories down.
3. Share the stories with the children.
4. Make a class shamrock book.

*Barbara Saul, Eureka, CA*

# Shamrock Shimmy
### MUSIC AND MOVEMENT

**Materials**  green paper
shamrock stencils
pencils
scissors
laminate or clear contact paper
Irish music

**What to do**
- March 17th is St. Patrick's Day.
1. Help each child make a shamrock using a stencil and scissors on green paper.
2. Laminate or cover the shamrocks with clear contact paper. Save them for gross motor/music time.
3. Spread the shamrocks around the floor for music time.
4. Play some Irish music and have the children dance.

5. When the music stops, ask them to find a shamrock to stand on until the music begins again.

6. If desired, add items such as shapes, numbers, letters, and so on to the shamrocks prior to laminating them for increased difficulty. Make cards to match the items (such as shapes) and give one to each child to hold. When the music stops, the children must find a shamrock that matches the card in their hands.

**RELATED BOOK**    *Lucky Leprechaun* by Dawn Bentley

★ *Ann Kelly, Johnstown, PA*

# PAPER CHAIN CALENDARS

MATH

**MATERIALS**    calendar
2" x 6" strips of colored paper
tape or glue

**WHAT TO DO**
- Easter is usually celebrated on the first Sunday after the first full moon following the vernal equinox (the first day of Spring). This can fall between March 22nd and April 25th.

1. Small children have difficulty assessing time, so this is one method of helping them judge its passing.

2. On a regular calendar count the number of days until Easter (or other appropriate holiday), a class concert, a child's birthday, or another upcoming event.

3. Show them the paper strips and explain that each strip stands for one day. Give each child enough strips for the amount of days until the event or holiday.

4. Help them make a paper chain by taping or gluing the paper strips together to form a "chain."

5. Every day, each child can cut or tear off one link from her chain. This provides the children with a visual image of how much time is left until the holiday.

6. If desired, use much larger strips of paper to make a group chain calendar, rather than individual ones. Have children take turns removing the links.

**More to do**   Talk about all the different ways we measure time.
**Math:** Children can use paper chains to learn the sequence of the days of the week. Designate a different color paper link for each day of the week. Write the sequence on a chart (for example, Monday is blue, Tuesday is green, and so on). Help the children make a monthly chain.
**More Math:** For older children, removing each link also provides good practice in counting backwards. After removing the day's link, count backwards to the end of the chain.

**Related books**   *Jumpstart K: Time and Measurement* by Maggie Groening
*My First Book of Time* by Claire Llewellyn
*Today Is Monday* by Eric Carle
*The Very Hungry Caterpillar* by Eric Carle

 *Anne Adeney, Plymouth, United Kingdom*

# Youth Day

PROJECTS

**Materials**   at least 10 rubber ducks
5 green and 5 red circle stickers
5 buckets or small boxes
small inexpensive prizes
at least 10 paper cutout fish
markers
commercial face painting kit
commercial child's bowling game
commercial child's basketball hoop and small basketball
cardboard
utility knife (adult only)
Polaroid camera and film

**What to do**   • March 29th is Youth Day in China.
1. About a month before you want to hold the festival, read a book about Chinese Youth Day. Explain that on Youth Day, families in China have parties to celebrate how happy they are to have their children. Ask the children if they would like to help plan a Youth Day Festival.
2. Brainstorm what games and activities to include in the Youth Day Festival. Ask leading questions such as, "What games do you like to play?" "What do you like to do to have fun?" and "What is your favorite thing to do?"

3. Following is a list of games and activities you might include:

- **Pluck the Duck:** Float rubber ducks with colored tags on the bottom in a low sensory table. Label buckets or boxes of small prizes with identical colors. The children pull a duck from the water, look at the colored tag on the bottom, and choose a small prize from a similarly colored bucket or box.

- **Fishing:** Make paper fish and draw shapes on their sides (circle, triangle, or square). Make pairs of fish (two squares, etc.). Label buckets or boxes of small prizes with identical shapes. Attach a paper clip to the fish's nose. Make a fishing pole by tying a length of string to a dowel rod and tying a magnet to the end of the string. The children use the pole to catch the shape fish. When a child catches two that match, she chooses a prize from a box with a similar label on it.

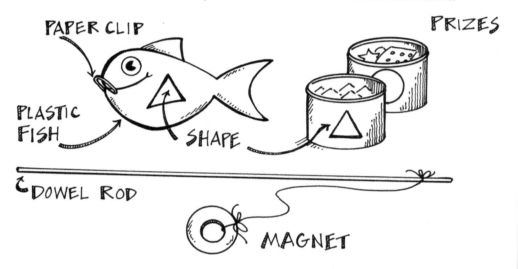

- **Face/Hand Painting:** Purchase face paints and have an adult paint simple designs or drawings on the children's cheeks or hands.

- **Bowling:** Purchase a child's bowling set and have an adult lead the children in taking turns as they bowl. Provide small prizes for everyone.

- **Basketball:** Purchase a child's basketball set and have an adult lead the children in attempting to score a goal. Provide small prizes for everyone.

- **Beanbag Toss:** Create an interesting shape or drawing on a large piece of cardboard. Cut holes in the cardboard (big enough for beanbags to fit through) and label each hole with a different number. Label buckets or boxes of prizes with matching numbers. Children toss beanbags through the holes and choose a prize from the bucket with the matching number.

- **Commemorative Photo:** Use a Polaroid camera to take photos of each family at the festival. Give these photos to the families as a memento of the day.

  **Note:** Assign a teacher, parent volunteer, or trusted adult to run each game or activity.

4. Let the children help create the chosen games. Encourage them to draw shapes on the fish, attach colored labels to the ducks, or draw designs for the bean bag toss. Get the children involved on every level.

5. Design flyers to advertise the celebration. Explain to the children that they need to work together to make a poster that lets people know when and where the festival is to be held and who is invited. Remember to set a certain time frame for the activities, such as from 10:00-11:30 a.m. for a half-day program or 4:00-5:30 p.m. for a full-day program. Create two or three posters to place around the school. Make sure everyone knows they are invited.

6. Ask some volunteers to provide simple healthy snacks for the party. Fruit, cheese, crackers, and pretzels are fun and easy to eat. Ask a volunteer to provide apple or grape juice to drink. If necessary, ask other volunteers to provide plates, cups, and napkins.

7. Ask volunteers to arrive early on the day of the party to help set up. At the designated time, get the party started and have fun!

**More to do**    **Art:** Let older children create a frame for the commemorative photo. Fold a piece of card stock paper in half lengthwise. Have an adult use a utility knife to cut a square slightly smaller then the size of a Polaroid photo on one half of the paper. Have the children decorate the frame with stickers and colored markers. On the day of the festival, tape the Polaroid photos of each family in a keepsake frame.

**Music:** If time permits, use this sing-and-respond song to end the festivities. As the festivities are winding down, gather the children to sing this song for their parents. The children sing the words and the parents respond by doing the motions. One week before the festival, teach the children the song:

**If You Love the Little Children** (Tune: "If You're Happy and You Know It")
*If you love the little children, clap your hands,* (clap, clap)
*If you love the little children, clap your hands,* (clap, clap)
*If you love the little children*
*And you want everyone to know it*
*If you love the little children, clap your hands.* (clap, clap)
(Continue with other verses: stomp your feet, shout "hurray," do all three)

**Related books**    *Chang's Paper Pony* by Eleanor Coerr
*Child of the Owl* by Laurence Yep
*In the Park* by Huy Voun Lee
*The Last Dragon* by Susan Miho Nune
*Shen of the Sea: Chinese Stories for Children* by Arthur Bowie Chrisman
*The Tiny Kite of Eddie Wing* by Maxine Trottier
*Yang the Third and Her Impossible Family* by Lensey Namioka

 *Virginia Jean Herrod, Columbia, SC*

April

# Class Big Book— Everything Grows

ART

**Materials**
photos of flowers, trees, animals, and children
large pieces of construction paper or oak tag
markers
glue
hole punch
yarn

**What to do**
1. Show the children a variety of pictures of things that grow: plants, flowers, animals, trees, and so on.
2. Let each child choose a different plant, flower, tree, or animal. Encourage the children to categorize the photos and then glue them onto large construction paper.
3. Encourage the children to draw pictures of their animals or flowers on the construction paper as well.
4. Bind all of the pages together using a hole punch and yarn. On the title page write, "Everything Grows."

⭐ *Deborah Hannes Litfin, Forest Hills, NY*

# Pussy Willow Thumbprints

ART

**Materials**
pussy willows (real or photos)
black and white fingerpaint
black tempera paint
straws
paper

**What to do**
1. If possible, show the children real pussy willows or photos of them.
2. Place some black tempera paint near the base of each child's paper. Ask the children to blow through their straws to spread the paint on the paper.
3. If needed, help the child spread the paint by holding the paper upside down and at angles to let the paint run.

4. Mix black and white fingerpaint together to make gray. Encourage the children to use their thumbs to make thumbprints for the soft gray part of the pussy willow. **Note:** Some children may find it easier to use their index fingers instead of their thumbs.

BLACK LINE

GRAY THUMBPRINTS

**RELATED POEM**     **The Pussy Willow Poem**
*I know a little pussy,*
*Its coat is silver-gray.*
*It lives down in the meadow*
*Not very far away.*

*It will always be a pussy,*
*It will never be a cat.*
*For it's a pussy willow*
*Now what do you think of that?*

*Meow, meow, meow, meow, meow,*
*Meow, meow, meow, meow,*
*Scat!*

 *Sandie Nagel, White Lake, MI*

# Raindrop Paintings

ART

**Materials**
easel
paper
tempera paints and brushes
spray bottle of water (with fine-mist setting)

**What to do**
1. If possible, place the easel near a window where the children can observe an outdoor view.
2. Invite each child to paint an outdoor scene showing the sky and earth. Encourage them to add trees, grass, flowers, and other natural features.
3. Allow the paintings to dry. Before doing the next step, explain to the children that they will be adding water droplets ("rain") to their pictures, which will dramatically change the way they look.
4. Elevate the children, one at a time, on a sturdy chair or stool. Direct the children to spray the top of their paintings gently with water and watch the droplets of water roll down the page.
5. Let the child continue as long as he enjoys the effect. He may wish to enjoy the process until all the paint has been rinsed away.

 *Susan A. Sharkey, La Mesa, CA*

# Raindrop Catchers

ART

**Materials**
white paper
blue paint
paintbrushes

**What to do**
1. Give each child an 8" x 10" piece of white paper. Ask the children to paint their papers dark blue. Set the paintings aside.
2. On the next rainy day, let the children run outside to "catch" raindrops on their papers. (This works best with a soft rain.)
3. Let dry on a flat surface.
4. Talk with the children about what happened. Notice how the drops changed the colors of the paint on their paper.

 *Jodi Sykes, Lake Worth, FL*

# Easy Basket Weaving

FINE MOTOR

**Materials**
plastic berry baskets (one per child)
pipe cleaners
assorted curling ribbons

**What to do**
1. Let the children choose a color of ribbon. Help them measure around the basket, leaving a little extra. Cut.
2. Demonstrate how to weave the ribbon in and out around one row of the holes all the way around the basket. When they reach the starting point, overlap the edges.
3. Let children continue choosing colors of ribbon and weaving each additional row of the basket.
4. To make a handle, twist two pipe cleaners together several times, leaving their ends free.
5. At each corner of the basket insert an end of a pipe cleaner. Secure it by twisting it around the edge of the basket.

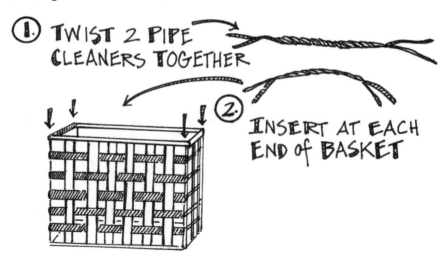

①. TWIST 2 PIPE CLEANERS TOGETHER

②. INSERT AT EACH END OF BASKET

**Related book**
*Lots and Lots of Zebra Stripes* by Stephen R. Swinburne

 *Sandra Gratias, Dublin, PA*

# I'm a Little Birdie

### FINGERPLAYS, SONGS, & POEMS

**Materials**     none

**What to do**     1. Sing the following song to the tune of "I'm a Little Teapot."

*I'm a little birdie* (point to self)
*Little and sweet,* (smile)
*Here are my wings.* (make wings with arms)
*Here is my beak.* (point to mouth)
*When I get all ready,*
*I will speak.* (open mouth)
*Hear me now,* (hand to ear)
*Tweet, tweet, tweet.*

2. Substitute "cardinal," "blue jay," "robin," and so on for "bird."

 *Kathy Kalmar, Macomb, MI*

# Mama Duck

### FINGERPLAYS, SONGS, & POEMS

**Materials**     none

**What to do**     1. Recite the following rhyme, making the appropriate gestures when prompted.

*Mama duck laid an egg* (make a fist for egg)
*And its insides grew,* (make fist larger)
*And grew,* (separate hands)
*And GREW!* (make a large space between hands)
*Then her duckling popped right through!* (raise hand, wiggle fingers)

2. If desired, substitute "chicken" and "chick" for "duck" and "duckling."

 *Kathy Kalmar, Macomb, MI*

# Mud Puddles

## FINGERPLAYS, SONGS, & POEMS

**Materials**  none

**What to do**  Sing the following song with the children, making gestures when appropriate.

*When the rain comes down* (use hands to motion raindrops)
*I am careful where I step.*
*You never know what's waiting* (shake head and finger)
*It's big and round and wet*
*And full of brown muddy water...*
*Can you guess what it is?*
*That's right! A mud puddle just for you!*

 *Susan Myhre, Bremerton, WA*

# Raindrops Falling

## FINGERPLAYS, SONGS, & POEMS

**Materials**  none

**What to do**  Sing the following song to the tune of "Frére Jacques."

*Raindrops falling,* (wiggle fingers, arms stretched high)
*Raindrops falling*
*From the sky,* (move fingers down like rain)
*From the sky.*
*Put up an umbrella,* (pretend to put up an umbrella)
*Put up an umbrella,*
*Nice and dry,* (fold arms around body and rub as though warm)
*Nice and dry.*

*Showers over,* (move arms out to the side)
*Showers over,*
*Sun aglow,* (arms form a circle overhead)
*Sun aglow.*
*See the pretty flowers,* (cup hands over eyes)
*See the pretty flowers,*
*In a row,* (point to each imaginary flower)
*In a row.*

 *Andrea Hungerford, Plymouth, CT*

# Springtime Bingo Game

GAMES

**Materials**
white oak tag
paper cutter
black marker
poster board
ruler
stickers with various springtime images

**What to do**

1. Cut oak tag into eight 8" x 8" squares to be used as bingo boards.
2. Make a square grid on the front of each bingo board, with sixteen 2" x 2" spaces.
3. Cut out 48 2" x 2" squares from oak tag.
4. Put one springtime sticker on each 2" oak tag square. Put the same image on each of the eight bingo boards, each in a different location.
5. Continue this process with each sticker until all the boards are covered randomly.
6. Cut ¾" square bingo markers out of colored poster board.
7. Shake up the picture squares in a plastic bag. Pick one out and show it to the children.
8. If a player has it, he puts a ¾" square piece on the picture.
9. Whenever a child gets a full row, she calls out "bingo."

**MORE TO DO** Use stickers with images from a different season or holiday, such as summer or Halloween, to play the game throughout the year.

 *Mary Brehm, Aurora, OH*

# SpRing Cleaning With Harry

GENERAL TIPS

**MATERIALS**
buckets
soap
washcloths
towels
*Harry, the Dirty Dog* by Gene Zion

**WHAT TO DO**
1. Have a spring cleaning day in the classroom. Encourage the children to wash dolls, paintbrushes, plastic toys, and so on.
2. Encourage the children to help straighten up different centers.
3. Read the book *Harry, the Dirty Dog* to the children.

**MORE TO DO** **Literacy:** Make bone-shaped cutouts from tagboard and label them with the letters of the alphabet for the children to put in order.

**RELATED books** *Harry and the Lady Next Door* by Gene Zion
*No Roses for Harry* by Gene Zion

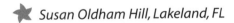 *Susan Oldham Hill, Lakeland, FL*

# Favorite Type of Weather

GROUP OR CIRCLE TIME

**MATERIALS**
tagboard
computer printer or marker
pictures of various types of weather
name card for each child in the class
pocket chart

**What to do**
1. Talk about different types of weather with the children.
2. Create a graph by printing a header card with pictures of four different types of weather under the heading: "What is your favorite type of weather?"
3. Display it in the top row of a pocket chart.
4. Have each child, in turn, come forward and vote to show her preference by placing her name card under her choice.
5. Discuss the graph with the children and determine which type of weather they like best (snowy, windy, rainy, or sunny).

⭐ *Jackie Wright, Enid, OK*

# Springtime Class Book

LANGUAGE AND LITERACY

**Materials**

children's books about spring
enlarged baby chick pattern or pencil
oak tag or poster board
glue stick
scissors
colored markers and crayons
laminating machine
11" x 17" paper
hole punch and yarn

**What to do**
1. Read several books about spring and talk about the signs of spring. Make your own class book about spring.
2. Draw or glue an enlarged baby chick pattern on two pieces of poster board or oak tag (about 11" x 17").
3. Cut around the shape to make the front and back covers.
4. Using markers, color the chick yellow and its beak and feet orange.
5. Laminate the covers for durability, and cut out.
6. Write the following sentence on small sentence strips: "My favorite thing about spring is _____."
7. Let each child dictate his response to fill in the blank, or let him write it himself.
8. Cut a class supply of 11" x 17" sheets of paper into the baby chick shape.
9. Glue each completed sentence frame to the bottom of a separate page.
10. Let each child use crayons to illustrate his sentence at the top of the page.

11. Assemble the finished pages and bind them between the covers using a binding machine or hole punch and yarn.

**Related book**    *Good Morning, Chick* by Mirra Ginsburg

★ *Jackie Wright, Enid, OK*

# CRAZY ABOUT CARROTS

LANGUAGE AND LITERACY

**Materials**    computer with color printer
computer-generated carrots
tagboard
paper cutter
pocket chart
12" x 18" construction paper
color scanner
glue stick
laminating machine
scissors

**What to do**
1. On tagboard, print computer-generated carrots programmed with sight words you want to reinforce.
2. Using a paper cutter, cut the cards to the desired size.
3. If desired, make a header card to go in the top row of a pocket chart. Print the title of the activity and instructions: "Place the carrots with words you can read on the word wall."
4. If desired, make a file jacket from 12" x 18" construction paper to hold the activity.
5. Using a color scanner, make a reduced-size printout of the activity showing the header card and all the carrot word cards. Glue color printout to the back of the file jacket.
6. Laminate the header card, carrot cards, and file jacket for durability, and cut out.
7. Hold up a word card. Ask the children to identify each word as you place it in the pocket chart.
8. Continue in this manner until all the carrots are in place.
9. Use the picture reference on the back of the file jacket to ensure that all cards are accounted for when you put them away at the end of the month.

★ *Jackie Wright, Enid, OK*

# Felt Eggs

LANGUAGE AND LITERACY

**Materials**  felt
scissors

**What to do**
1. Cut out an egg shape from felt. Cut it in half to look like a cracked egg.
2. Cut out shapes (triangle, square, circle, and so on) smaller than the egg shape from felt.
3. Put the egg shape on top of a shape.
4. Let the children "crack open" the egg and name the shape.
5. As a variation, use different colors of felt and have the children identify the colors.

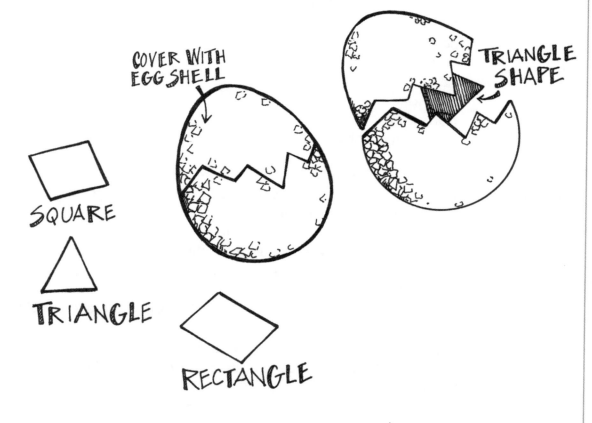

COVER WITH
EGG SHELL

TRIANGLE
SHAPE

SQUARE

TRIANGLE

RECTANGLE

*Kathy Kalmar, Macomb, MI*

# INSECT ABC's

## LANGUAGE AND LITERACY

**MATERIALS**
paper and markers or pictures of insects
manila file folder
markers
paper or card stock
self-adhesive Velcro
clear contact paper or laminate

**WHAT TO DO**
1. Draw or photocopy pictures (or cut from a magazine) of three different insects: one that starts with A, one that starts with B, and one that starts with C.
2. Place the pictures on a folder in different places and position a piece of Velcro next to each one.
3. On another piece of paper or card stock, write the names of each insect individually.
4. Cut out, laminate, and put Velcro on the back of each word.
5. The goal is for the children to match the written names with the pictures.
6. Consider other letters also, or using bugs that start with the same letter. For example:

| A | B | C |
|---|---|---|
| Ant | Bee | Caterpillar |
| Aphid | Beetle | Cricket |
| Arachnid | Butterfly | Cicada |

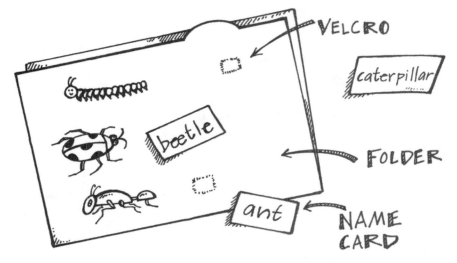

**MORE TO DO**
**Science:** Add a little science to this activity by putting one large bug on the page and writing body parts on the cards to match the corresponding parts of the picture (antennae, thorax, abdomen, and so on).

 *Kristi Larson, Spirit Lake, IA*

# HERE IS THE BEEHIVE FLANNEL BOARD

MATH

**MATERIALS**
dark gold felt (12" x 18")
yellow felt
yarn
tape
black fabric paint or fabric markers

**WHAT TO DO**

1. Cut out a beehive shape from dark gold felt. Outline with black paint or marker.
2. Cut out five bee shapes from yellow felt.
3. Draw or paint a black outline around each bee. Then paint one stripe on one bee, two stripes on another bee, three stripes on another bee, four stripes on another bee, and five stripes on the last bee.
4. Tape the bees in succession on a piece of yarn, with one at the top and five at the bottom.
5. Place the beehive on the flannel board. Tuck the string of bees behind and pull out one by one as you recite the following fingerplay.

*Here is the beehive,*
*Where are the bees?*
*Hidden away where nobody sees.*
*Here they come buzzing out of the hive*
*1...2...3...4...5!*

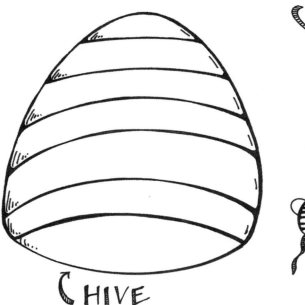

HIVE

BEES TAPED to YARN

1
2
3
4
5

⭐ *Kristi Larson, Spirit Lake, IA*

# Musical Weather

MUSIC AND MOVEMENT

**Materials**   variety of musical instruments

**What to do**   1. Discuss how different musical instruments can be used to sound like different weather conditions. For example, use rain sticks for the sound of rain and drums for thunder.
2. Ask the children to decide what instrument might represent snow, falling leaves, and so on.
3. Encourage the children to play different instruments to make sounds for each season.

**More to do**   **Movement:** Provide a variety of musical instruments and guide the children to move in a way that describes the instrument's sound; round rain sticks would likely inspire slow and quiet movement; bells would likely facilitate more active movement; drums would translate into marching, and so on.

 *Barb Lindsey, Madison City, IA*

# Read and Do Eggs

MUSIC AND MOVEMENT

**Materials**   plastic eggs
drawings of common activities (clapping hands, jumping, touching toes)

**What to do**   1. Draw or cut out pictures of people doing common activities, such as clapping hands, jumping, touching toes, and so on.
2. Insert pictures into plastic eggs.
3. Have each child take an egg, open it, and do the action depicted on the picture.

**More to do**   **Art:** Let children paint a large egg shape at the easel using pastel colors.

 *Kathy Kalmar, Macomb, MI*

# Our Springtime Walk

OUTDOOR PLAY

**Materials**
large rope for walking together
instant photo camera
magnifying glasses
binoculars
large paper bag
mini sack
large paper
pen

**What to do**
1. Before leaving the room, explain how to look for signs of spring. Provide magnifying glasses and binoculars as helpful tools. Tell them you will have a bag available if they want to collect objects on the walk.
2. Talk about all of their senses. Tell them to be aware of their senses on the walk, and that upon returning from the walk, they will make a group sensory story.
3. Take a nature walk with the children.
4. Upon returning from the walk, encourage the children to tell stories about what they saw, smelled, heard, and so on. Write down all the information as the children tell it.
5. Read the story back to the children. Ask if there is anything else they want to add.
6. Encourage the children to draw pictures to illustrate their stories.
7. Post the group story on the wall and surround it with children's springtime art and collected nature items.

⭐ *Jean F. Lortz, Sequin, WA*

# Rain Gauge

SCIENCE

**Materials**
clear plastic tumbler or container
permanent marker

**What to do**
1. During outside time, place a clear plastic tumbler or container outdoors to catch raindrops.
2. Ask the children to predict how many rainy days they think it will take to fill up the container.
3. After each rainy day, make a mark with a permanent marker.

 *Jodi Sykes, Lake Worth, FL*

# WHAT COMES FROM EGGS

### SCIENCE

**MATERIALS**

pictures of animals that hatch from eggs

different eggs or egg shells (emu, ostrich, duck, chicken)

plastic sandwich bags

magnifying glass

**WHAT TO DO**

1. Show children the different eggs. Put the eggs in sandwich bags so children do not handle the eggs directly (to avoid germs).
2. Talk about the sizes, shapes, and colors of the eggs.
3. Encourage the children to guess what animal came out of each egg.
4. Place the eggs on a table for children to view and examine with a magnifying glass.
5. Put pictures of animals next to the eggs and let the children match the animals to the eggs.

**MORE TO DO**

**Art:** Wash hard-boiled or eggs with the contents blown out. Let the children use tempera paint to decorate their eggs.

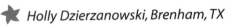 *Holly Dzierzanowski, Brenham, TX*

# HEDGIE'S SURPRISE SNACK

### SNACK AND COOKING

**MATERIALS**

*Hedgie's Surprise* by Jan Brett

hardboiled eggs

uncooked oatmeal

sesame seeds or raisins

maple syrup

apple butter

**WHAT TO DO**

1. Read *Hedgie's Surprise* to the children.
2. Let the children help cook oatmeal. Cook oats in water (supervise closely).
3. Add sprinkles (sesame seeds), maple syrup, apple butter, and raisins.
4. Serve hardboiled eggs and oatmeal for snack.
5. Make a picture graph entitled "Our Favorite Snack: Hardboiled Eggs or Oatmeal." Cut out bowl and egg shapes. Let children choose their favorite and add to the picture graph.

**MORE TO DO**

**Field Trip:** Visit a farm to see chickens and ducks.

**Science:** Hatch chicks or ducklings in an incubator.

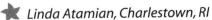 *Linda Atamian, Charlestown, RI*

# WATCH ME GROW

SCIENCE

**MATERIALS**

leaves
orange rinds
glass
plastic objects
pea pods
mustard seeds
beans
shovels
pots
soil

**WHAT TO DO**

- April is Keep America Beautiful Month; Earth Day is April 20th.
1. At the end of March, tell the children that April is Keep America Beautiful Month and April 20th is Earth Day. Talk about recycling and the importance of not littering.
2. Bury the various objects (leaves, orange rinds, glass, seeds, beans, and plastic objects) in separate pots.
3. Label each pot with the name of what it contains.
4. Water the pots daily.
5. After a month (on or near Earth Day), dig up the soil in the pots and remove the buried objects. Encourage the children to observe the objects.
6. Discuss the importance of recycling, decomposition, and proper garbage disposal.

 *Shyamala Shanmugasundaram, Nerul, Navi Mumbai, India*

# POETIC APRIL

LANGUAGE AND LITERACY

**MATERIALS**

**WHAT TO DO**

- April is National Poetry Month.
1. Throughout the month of April, set aside the last 10 minutes of class for parents to come in and recite their favorite children's poems.
2. Ask parents to teach simple refrains to the children.
3. At the end of the month, prepare and distribute a handmade book of favorite family poems.

4. A few of the many poets to choose from include:
   Arnold Adoff
   Jill Bennett
   Margaret Wise Brown
   Aileen Fisher
   Eloise Greenfield
   Nikki Grimes
   Lee Bennett Hopkins
   Myra Cohn Livingston
   Bill Martin
   A.A. Milne
   Eve Merriam
   Jack Prelutsky

★ *Karyn F. Everham, Fort Myers, FL*

# Drip, Drop Goes the Rain
## FINGERPLAYS, SONGS, & POEMS

**Materials**     none

**What to do**     • April is National Umbrella Month.
Sing the following song, making the appropriate gestures when indicated.

**Drip, Drop Goes the Rain**
*Drip, drop, goes the rain* (make rain motion with fingers)
*Drip, drop, down it comes* (raise arms up and down)
*One by one at first* (hold up one finger on each hand)
*And then I'm soaking wet!* (hold out hands palms up)

 *Susan Myhre, Bremerton, WA*

# Colorful Umbrellas
## LANGUAGE AND LITERACY

**Materials**     computer and color printer
computer-generated umbrellas (or construction paper umbrellas)
tagboard
paper cutter
laminating machine
scissors

**What to do**
- April is National Umbrella Month.
1. On tagboard, print computer-generated umbrellas in different colors or draw your own on different colors of construction paper. Cut into cards.
2. Make color word cards to match the umbrella colors. Write the words of each color used for the umbrellas on different cards.
3. Using a paper cutter, cut the cards to the desired size. Laminate.
4. Encourage the children to match the color word cards with the correct color umbrella card.

 *Jackie Wright, Enid, OK*

# Umbrella Graph

MATH

**Materials**
white paper
scissors
4 to 6 different colored crayons
masking tape

**What to do**
- April is National Umbrella Month.
1. Cut paper into umbrella shapes.
2. Provide each child with an umbrella shape. Offer a choice of four to six different colors of crayons and let the children choose one color to color their umbrellas.
3. Use a roll of ½" masking tape to make a graph on the floor or area rug. Make one column for each color, and place a color square for each color in the top grid.
4. Have the children join you on the floor around the graph with their umbrellas. One at a time, have them add their umbrellas under the proper columns and then tally up each column.
5. Discuss which colors had the most, least, same, and other observations.

 *Jodi Sykes, Lake Worth, FL*

# April Math

MATH

**Materials**
books about rain, such as:
- *Beneath a Blue Umbrella* by Jack Prelutsky
- *Bringing the Rain to Kapiti Plain: A Nandi Tale* by Verna Aardema
- *Come On, Rain!* by Karen Hesse
- *A Mushroom in the Rain* by Mirra Ginsburg
- *Rain* by Manya Stojic
- *Umbrella* by Taro Yashima
- *The Umbrella* by Jan Brett

paper clips or plastic chain links

**What to do**
- April is National Umbrella Month.
1. During the month of April, make books about rain available to the children.
2. Stand the books side by side on a table and tape a paper clip or plastic chain link on the edge of the table in front of each book.
3. Give each child a paper clip or plastic link and have them take turns hooking their clip to the clip that is under their favorite rain book, forming chains under each book.
4. When each child has had a turn, add up the totals. Leave the chains on display for the children to count and recount the results on their own throughout the day.

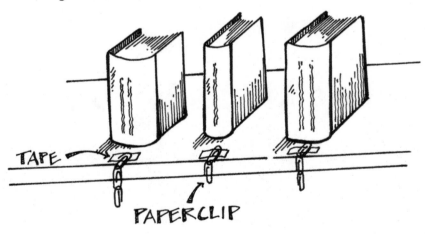

TAPE

PAPERCLIP

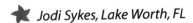

⭐ *Jodi Sykes, Lake Worth, FL*

# UMBRELLA REST AND RELAXATION

### REST OR NAPTIME

**MATERIALS**
several child-sized umbrellas
books
small cushions or pillows

**WHAT TO DO**
- April is National Umbrella Month.
1. Do this activity on a day when inclement weather prevents children from going outdoors.
2. Suggest an unusual type of relaxation activity and explain that children will be able to rest underneath their open umbrellas with a friend or alone.
3. Remind the children that umbrellas must remain on the floor and are not to be carried around indoors for safety reasons.
4. Let the children choose books, stuffed animals, pillows, and blankets to enhance their umbrella rest time.
5. Open umbrellas and encourage the children to get comfortable.
6. Consider singing lullabies together or reading a cozy book to the children such as *Goodnight, Moon*.

⭐ *Elisheva Leah Nadler, Har Nof, Jerusalem, Israel*

# FIVE LITTLE FLOWERS

### FINGERPLAYS, SONGS, & POEMS

**MATERIALS**
none

**WHAT TO DO**
- April is National Garden Month.
Sing the following song, using the appropriate gestures.

**Five Little Flowers**
*Five little flowers* (hold up hand)
*In the bright sunlight,* (make a sun over head)
*Watch them open in the light.* (put hand over eyes)
*Watch them close up* (close hand into a fist)
*When it is night.* (make sleeping motion, head on hands)

**MORE TO DO**    **Art:** Make a "flower garden." Cut out pictures of flowers from seed catalogs or greeting cards. Glue the flowers to Popsicle sticks and push the stick into an upside-down egg carton to complete the garden.

★ *Kathy Kalmar, Macomb, MI*

# This Is the Way We Plant Our Garden

FINGERPLAYS, SONGS, & POEMS

**MATERIALS**    none

**WHAT TO DO**

● April is National Garden Month.
Sing the following song to the tune of "This Is the Way We Wash Our Clothes."

*This is the way we rake the ground,*
*Rake the ground, rake the ground.*
*This is the way we rake the ground*
*To get the ground ready for the garden.*

*This is the way we dig the hole,*
*Dig the hole, dig the hole.*
*This is the way, we dig the hole*
*Before we plant the seeds.*

*This is the way we plant the seeds,*
*Plant the seeds, plant the seeds.*
*This is the way we plant the seeds*
*Before we water the garden.*

*This is the way rain waters the garden,*
*Waters the garden, waters the garden.*
*This is the way rain waters the garden*
*When we plant our seeds.*

**MORE TO DO**    **Science:** Have the children plant tomato seeds in an egg carton to take home to plant in a home garden.

★ *Kathy Kalmar, Macomb, MI*

# Budding Baskets

SCIENCE

**Materials**
strawberry baskets
markers
paper
glue
plastic sandwich bags
potting soil
grass seed
pipe cleaners

**What to do**
- April is National Garden Month.
1. Give each child a strawberry basket. Ask the children to decorate pieces of paper to fit the sides of their baskets and glue them to the outside of the baskets.
2. Put sandwich bags inside the baskets.
3. Let children put potting soil in the bags, and take a handful of grass seed and plant it in the soil.
4. Make a handle for the baskets by twisting two pipe cleaners together and attaching them to opposite sides of the baskets.
5. Put the baskets in a sunny place and water regularly.

*Barbara Saul, Eureka, CA*

# Starting Seedlings

SCIENCE

**Materials**
children's books about gardens
garden resource books
seed and gardening catalogs
potting soil
spoons
cups
markers or pens
vegetable seeds
sand and water table
spray bottles
craft sticks

**What to do**
- April is National Garden Month.
1. Read a variety of stories about gardens, and have resource books and seed and gardening catalogs throughout the classroom. Encourage the children to explore the materials.
2. Ask the children if they would like to plant a school garden. Explain that they will start the garden indoors and then transplant the seedlings outdoors after the danger of frost in your area has passed.
3. Add soil and spoons to the sand and water table. Use this area for a small group activity so that you can extend learning and provide support on an individual basis.
4. Let each child choose what types of seeds she would like to plant.
5. Write each child's name on at least one cup so that those who want to take a plant home may do so. The other cups will hold plants for the classroom garden.
6. Help the children write (assist those who are not writing yet) the name of the seeds they are planting on craft sticks. These will identify the seedlings as they grow.
7. Have the children spoon soil into their cups, place 2-3 seeds in the soil, cover with one or two spoonfuls of soil, and spray with water. Place all finished cups in a warm, sunny location.
8. Develop a watering schedule that is appropriate for the seeds/plants. It could be a job for the leader of the day. Make sure everyone has a turn.

**More to do**    **Math:** Chart the growth of the plants using a calendar and measuring once a week.

**Related books**    *The Carrot Seed* by Ruth Krauss
*From Seed to Plant* by Gail Gibbons
*How a Seed Grows* by Helene Jordan
*One Child, One Seed: A South African Counting Book* by Kathryn Cave
*Seeds Grow* by Angela Medearis

★ *Ann Kelly, Johnstown, PA*

# Papier-Mâché Frogs and Toads

ART

**Materials**

balloons
flour
water
paper strips (1" to 2" wide)
green and brown paint
paintbrushes
glossy sealer
glue
gravel
bowls

**What to do**

- April is National Frog Month.
1. Blow up balloons and tie them closed. Give one to each child.
2. Mix flour and water to make a watery paste (should have the consistency of runny white glue).
3. Demonstrate how to dip a paper strip into the mixture, squeeze off excess paste, and lay it across balloon.
4. Encourage the children to cover their balloons in this manner. Let dry. Pop balloons.
5. Ask the children if they would like to make a frog or a toad. Talk about the differences in these animals.
6. For those making frogs, have them paint their balloons green. Let dry and then apply glossy sealer (adult only).
7. For those making toads, have them paint their balloons brown. Let dry. Encourage them to paint over the brown paint with a mixture of glue and gravel.
8. This activity illustrates the difference between a frog's smooth skin and a toad's rough skin.

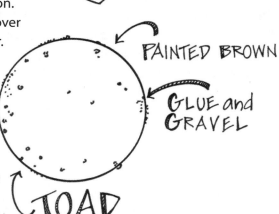

START LAYERING STRIPS

PAINTED BROWN

GLUE and GRAVEL

TOAD

 *Kristi Larson, Spirit Lake, IA*

# Frogs Hop

### FINGERPLAYS, SONGS, & POEMS

**Materials**     none

**What to do**
- April is National Frog Month.
Sing the following song, making the appropriate gestures when prompted.

*Frogs jump.* (jump like a frog)
*Caterpillars bump.* (creep like a caterpillar)
*Snakes slide.* (slide like a snake)
*Sea gulls glide.* (fly like a bird)
*Mice creep.* (creep like a mouse)
*Gazelles leap.* (leap)
*Lions stalk.* (stalk)
*Teachers talk.* (make talking motions with hands)
*But me,* (point to self)
*I walk.* (make fingers walk)

 *Kathy Kalmar, Macomb, MI*

# Three Frogs

### FINGERPLAYS, SONGS, & POEMS

**Materials**     none

**What to do**
- April is National Frog Month.
1. Do the following fingerplay with the children.

*Three little frogs* (hold up three fingers)
*Sleeping in the sun,* (raise arms in a circle over head)
*Here comes the heron* (make upside down "V" with fingers)
*See the frogs run!*

2. If desired, cut out frogs, a sun, and a heron from felt to use on a flannel
   board.

 *Kathy Kalmar, Macomb, MI*

# LEAP, FROGS, LEAP

GAMES

**Materials**    pictures of frogs, ponds, and lily pads
construction paper
pencils
scissors
tape

**What to do**    ● April is National Frog Month.
1. Show the children pictures of frogs, ponds, and lily pads. Talk about how frogs live near the water and how they leap on things in the water, such as rocks and lily pads.
2. Ask each child to draw a large rock or a lily pad on construction paper.
3. Cut out each rock and lily pad and tape to the floor about 1' apart from each other.
4. Encourage the children to pretend to be frogs and leap from rocks to lily pads.
5. If desired, sing "Five Little Speckled Frogs" as the children jump.

**Related books**    *Hop, Jump* by Ellen Stoll Walsh
*Jump, Frog, Jump* by Robert Kalan

★ *Monica Hay Cook, Tucson, AZ*

# COUNTING FROGS AND LILY PADS

MATH

**Materials**    green and blue paper
card stock
Velcro
laminating paper
black marker
glue

**What to do**    ● April is National Frog Month.
1. Cut five frogs out of green paper.
2. Draw one spot on one frog, two spots on the next frog, and so on until the fifth frog has five spots.

3. Laminate the frogs.
4. Cut 15 kidney-shaped lily pads out of green paper.
5. Cut out five ovals (for ponds) from blue paper.
6. Glue one lily pad on one pond, two lily pads on the next pond, three on the next, and so on.
7. Glue the ponds to card stock and laminate.
8. Put a piece of Velcro on the back of each frog and on the front of each pond.
9. Have the children match the frog with the same number of spots to the pond with that number of lily pads.

**MORE TO DO**   Use different items to match, such as:
- ducks or chicks and eggs
- frogs and tadpoles
- bees and flowers
- caterpillars and butterflies
- rockets and planets

⭐ *Kristi Larson, Spirit Lake, IA*

# FROG JUMP

## SCIENCE

**MATERIALS**

8 pieces of card stock for each child
pictures of stages in frog life cycle
hole punch
cord
large sheets of heavy green paper or card stock
scissors
giant foam or rubber dice or number cards

**WHAT TO DO**

- April is National Frog Month.
1. Use this game as part of a theme on growth, amphibians, pond life, or animals.
2. Make a large drawing or photocopy of the following life stages of a frog. Make a set of cards for each child.
   - clump of frogspawn (frog eggs)
   - tadpole with short tail
   - tadpole with long tail
   - tadpole with long tail and short legs
   - tadpole with four limbs and shorter tail
   - small frog
   - medium-sized frog
   - large frog
3. Punch a hole in two top corners of each card, reinforce the holes, and thread enough cord through each card so that it will hang comfortably around a child's neck.
4. Cut out huge lily pads from green card stock or paper and arrange these about four to six child-size jumps apart.
5. Put a pile of life stage cards beside each lily pad (the first lily pad will have the cards with the clump of frogspawn, the next lily pad will have the cards of the tadpole with short tail, and so on).
6. Have the children take turns throwing the dice and doing as many squatting frog jumps or hops towards the next lily pad as the dice allows.
7. When the child reaches a lily pad, she hangs a card around her neck, showing the frog's present stage of development.
8. Encourage the children as they play and give them additional pieces of life cycle information. "Wow, Ben, your tail has gone completely and you've got lungs instead of gills now!" or "Congratulations, Jenny! You're a three-year-old frog now—grown up at last!"
9. Adapt progression to suit age and ability of the children. For younger children, instead of rolling dice, you could use a single number card, which they have to recognize to move on.

**Grown up at last!**

LILY PADS

**More to do**    Discuss the differences between frogs and toads.
Collect frogspawn and watch frogs develop in an indoor aquarium.
**Math:** After the game, have the children mix up their cards and try to put
them in the correct order.

**Related books**    *Frog and Toad Are Friends* by Arnold Lobel
*Frog on His Own* by Mercer Mayer
*Frogs* by Gail Gibbons
*Jump, Frog, Jump* by Robert Kalan

⭐ *Anne Adeney, Plymouth, United Kingdom*

# The Wide-Mouthed Frog
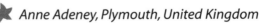
### SCIENCE

**Materials**    *The Wide-Mouthed Frog* by Jonathan Lambert
Velcro
construction paper
pipe cleaners
pencil
white paper
string

**What to do**

● April is National Frog Month.

1. Ask the children what they know about frogs. What do frogs like to eat? What makes a frog a good flycatcher?

2. Read the book *The Wide Mouthed Frog* to the children. Encourage them to say the repeated text and ask what the surprise was at the end of the story.

3. After reading the story, ask how a frog's tongue works.

4. Pair the children. Help each pair cut out a construction paper frog and glue a pipe cleaner "tongue" to the mouth. Help them attach a piece of Velcro at the end of the tongue.

5. Help each pair cut out a fly and attach a piece of Velcro and string to it.

6. Encourage the children to practice trying to catch a fly with their frog's tongue. One child will hold the string of the other's fly while the other uses his frog to catch the fly.

7. The child holding the fly may move it to make it more challenging.

8. Ask the children, "If you were a frog, how many flies could you catch in a minute?"

9. Record the children's predictions on a piece of paper.

10. Time each child for one minute as he tries to catch flies.

11. After the first child tries, let them switch roles and repeat the procedure.

12. Ask if (and why) they got better at fly catching with practice and if their predictions were correct.

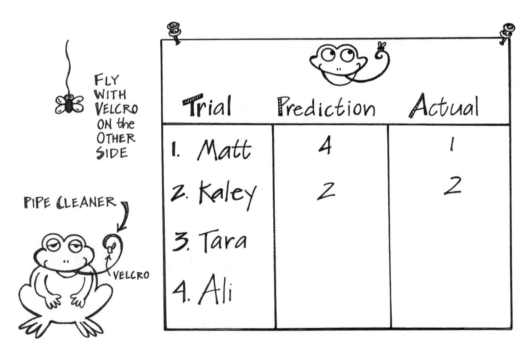

FLY WITH VELCRO ON the OTHER SIDE

PIPE CLEANER

VELCRO

| Trial | Prediction | Actual |
|-------|-----------|--------|
| 1. Matt | 4 | 1 |
| 2. Kaley | 2 | 2 |
| 3. Tara | | |
| 4. Ali | | |

 *Dr. Geraldine Jenny, Grove City, PA*

# Webbed Hands

SCIENCE

**Materials**
tub or water table
water
plastic sandwich bags

**What to do**
- April is National Frog Month.
1. Talk about how frogs can jump great distances, up to 20 times their body length. Their back feet are strong and webbed. Talk about what webbed feet look like and show the children pictures of frogs.
2. Ask the children if they want to find out what it is like to have webbed hands. Ask them to spread the fingers on one hand and swish it through the water in a tub or water table.
3. Talk about how easy it is to move their hands through the water when their fingers are spread out.
4. Now have the children put a plastic sandwich bag over one hand and move it through the water again.
5. Ask them if it feels different with the bag on their hands.

**More to do**
**Outdoors:** Take this activity outside and have the children do long jumps into the sand.

**Related books**
*If You Hopped Like a Frog* by David Schwartz
*Jump Like a Frog* by Kate Burns

 *Monica Hay Cook, Tucson, AZ*

# THE BACKWARDS MAN

### FINGERPLAYS, SONGS, & POEMS

**Materials**    none

**What to do**

- April Fool's Day is celebrated on April 1st. April is also National Humor Month.

1. Sing the following song to the tune of "The Muffin Man."

**The Backwards Man**

*Do you know the backwards man,*
*The backwards man, the backwards man?*
*Do you know the backwards man?*
*He's a very silly man.*

*He wears his hat down on his feet,*
*Down on his feet, down on his feet.*
*He wears his hat down on his feet.*
*He's a very silly man.*

*He wears his shoes up on his head,*
*Up on his head, up on his head.*
*He wears his shoes up on his head.*
*He's a very silly man.*

*His dog says meow, his cat says woof.*
*His dog says meow, his cat says woof.*
*His dog says meow, his cat says woof.*
*He's a very silly man.*

*Oh, do you know the backwards man,*
*The backwards man, the backwards man?*
*Do you know the backwards man?*
*He's a very silly man.*

2. Encourage the children to sing their own verses about the backwards man.

⭐ *Andrea Hungerford, Plymouth, CT*

# April Fool's

GAMES

**Material**     picture book about April Fool's Day

**What to do**

- April Fool's Day is celebrated on April 1st. April is also National Humor Month.
1. On April 1st, explain to the children about April Fool's Day.
2. Read the book *It's April Fool's Day* by Steven Kroll or another book about April Fool's Day.
3. Play the following game: Send one child out of the room. While that child is gone, the rest of the children alter their appearances. When the child comes back into the room, she guesses what each child is doing or wearing differently.
4. Repeat until each child has had a chance to leave the room.
5. A variation is to send a child out of the room. Have that child change his own appearance. When he returns to class, the children guess what the child has altered.

⭐ *Barbara Saul, Eureka, CA*

# Silly Day

GENERAL TIPS

**Materials**     none

**What to do**

- April Fool's Day is celebrated on April 1st. April is also National Humor Month.
  Have a silly day on April Fool's Day (April 1st).
  - Have children wear pajamas to school.
  - Make "mistakes" throughout the day such as singing the good-bye song at the beginning of the day.
  - Mix up the helper chart, for example, put a girl's name on the boy's leader spot, or have the name clips on the wrong side or upside down.
  - Tell a familiar story in a mixed-up way (great for teaching or reviewing opposites).
  - Use a mixed assortment of leftover paper products from previous holidays at snack and meals.
  - Eat dessert first, or breakfast at lunchtime.

**Related books**     *That's Good! That's Bad!* by Margery Cuyler
*Tops and Bottoms* by Janet Stevens

 *Sandra Gratias, Dublin, PA*

# April Foolishness

PROJECTS

**Materials**  *April Foolishness* by Teresa Bateman
paper and marker

**What to do**

- April Fool's Day is celebrated on April 1st. April is also National Humor Month.

1. During the last week of March, explain to the children that April Fool's Day is celebrated on April 1st.
2. Ask them if they know what it means to do foolish things. Record their responses and print them on a chart to display.
3. Read *April Foolishness* by Teresa Bateman. Talk about the foolish things the people in the story do.
4. Ask the children if they would like to do some foolish things to celebrate April Fool's Day. Make a list. For example:
   - Wear clothes backwards or inside out
   - Wear shoes on the wrong feet
   - Say goodbye instead of hello
   - Walk backwards
   - Sit on chairs backwards
5. Send the following letter home a couple of days before April 1st:

*Dear Parents,*
   *We will celebrate April Fool's Day by doing some foolish things in the classroom. On April 1st, please allow your child to wear his/her clothes backwards or inside out; wear his/her shoes on the wrong feet, and wear his/her coat backwards or inside out. When you and your child arrive at school, please say, "Goodbye" to the people you greet rather than saying, "Hello," and "Hello" instead of "Goodbye" when you leave.*

6. Encourage the children to follow the foolish plans they made. The children will have a great time! Make sure that you don't force anyone to participate.

**More to do**  **Art:** On April Fool's Day, make funny headbands. Simply tape two strips of colored construction paper together to fit each child's head. Have the children draw designs on their headband with markers or crayons. On the front of each band, print "Happy April Fool's Day."
**Snack:** Have a foolish snack by sitting on the floor and eating off a chair. For this activity, have a simple snack. Spread a large vinyl tablecloth on the floor for the children to sit on so they won't touch the floor while eating.

**Naptime:** Have a foolish nap by letting the children sleep on top of their blankets and cover up with their sheets. Do this only if you think the children will really sleep!

**Related books** *April Foolishness* by Teresa Bateman and Nadine Bernard Westcott
*April Wilson's Magpie Magic: A Tale of Colorful Mischief* by April Wilson
*Arthur's April Fool (Arthur Adventure Series)* by Marc Brown
*Michael Le Souffle and the April Fool* by Peter J. Welling

 *Virginia Jean Herrod, Columbia, SC*

# Tube Bunnies

ART

**Materials**
bunny ears pattern (cut from cardboard)
construction paper
markers
toilet paper tubes
white paper
scissors
glue
cotton balls

**What to do**
- Easter is usually celebrated on the first Sunday after the first full moon following the vernal equinox (first day of Spring). This can fall anywhere between March 22nd and April 25th.
1. Have the child trace the cardboard ears onto construction paper and cut out.
2. Help the children cut out a strip of paper to fit around their tubes.
3. Encourage the children to put glue on one side of the paper strip and wrap it around the toilet paper tube.
4. Let the children draw a bunny face near the top of the tube.
5. The children glue the ears onto the tube, above the face.
6. Encourage the children to glue a cotton ball on the back for a tail.

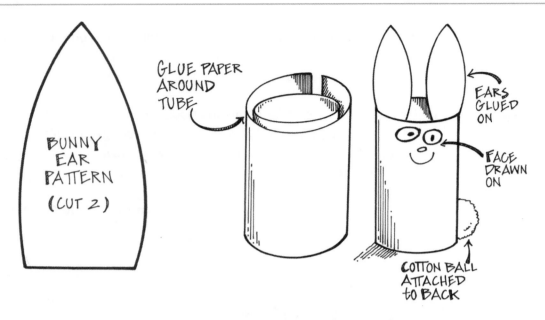

**More to do**     These can be made with playdough containers as well.

⭐ *Sandra Nagel, White Lake, MI*

# Easter Egg Extravaganza

ART

**Materials**     hard-boiled and plastic eggs
vinegar
food coloring in a variety of colors, including red
small baskets
crayons or small candles
ferns or small plants
stickers, sequins, and colored tissue paper

**What to do**     ● Easter is usually celebrated on the first Sunday after the first full moon following the vernal equinox (first day of Spring). This can fall anywhere between March 22nd and April 25th.
1. Explain that people from all over the world have different customs and traditions, especially for holidays. Tell the children that they will be decorating eggs and using some of them to play games from many different traditions.
   ● **Red Eggs From Greece:** Simmer washed eggs for 15 minutes in a large pan of water, vinegar, and red dye. Dry and polish with a little oil on cotton wool.
   ● **Egg Hunt From Germany:** Hide painted, chocolate, or plastic eggs around the room or playground. Have the children hunt for them.

- **Egg Rolling From Switzerland:** Use hard-boiled eggs or plastic ones and have an egg rolling race down a gentle slope.
- **Wax Egg Painting From Ukraine:** Ukraine Easter eggs are some of the most beautiful in the world. Let children draw patterns on their cooked eggs with wax (crayons or candles) and then put them into pots of food coloring. Place eggs into boiling water (adult only) to melt the wax. When dry, a white pattern will show up against the vibrant colors.
- **Egg Tapping From Bulgaria:** Have each child take a decorated, hard-boiled egg and take turns tapping it against other children's eggs. The child with the last unbroken egg is believed to have a year of good luck ahead.
- **Fern Eggs From Austria:** Austrians glue ferns or small plants onto the eggs before boiling in dyes. Then they peel off the ferns to reveal the beautiful white plant shape against the colored egg.
- **Egg Game From Slovakia:** Encourage the children to decorate their eggs and then play a game similar to marbles, called "Cokatisja." The children roll their eggs at each other and if one cracks another, the child who broke it wins the cracked egg.
- **Blown Eggs From Armenia:** In Armenia, as in many countries, eggs used for cooking are not broken; instead the contents are removed by piercing both ends of the egg with a large needle and blowing the contents into a bowl. Help the children with this step and then let them decorate the eggs carefully with sequins or stickers.

**MORE TO DO**  **Geography:** Put egg-shaped flags on a world map to show each country (above).
**Snack:** Make or bring in and eat Easter food from each country.
**Social Development:** Learn something about Easter traditions in each country.

**RELATED books**  *The Best Easter Egg Hunt Ever* by John Spiers
*Easter Bunny's Amazing Egg Machine* by Wendy Chevette Lewison
*Easter Egg Disaster: A Harry and Emily Adventure* by Karen Gray Ruelle
*Great Easter Egg Hunt* by Michael Garland
*Legend of the Easter Egg* by Lori Walburg

⭐ *Anne Adeney, Plymouth, United Kingdom*

# EASTER BUNNY

## FINGERPLAYS, SONGS, & POEMS

**MATERIALS**
none

**WHAT TO DO**

- Easter is usually celebrated on the first Sunday after the first full moon following the vernal equinox (first day of Spring). This can fall anywhere between March 22nd and April 25th.
1. Recite the following rhyme, performing the appropriate gestures.

**Easter Bunny**
*Easter bunny* (raise two fingers for bunny)
*Cute and fat,*
*Hops down the bunny trail* (make fingers hop, then clap)
*Just like that.*

2. Repeat, changing "'bunny" to "chick," "duck," or other animal.

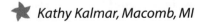 *Kathy Kalmar, Macomb, MI*

# Jellybean Sort

## MATH

**MATERIALS**
egg cartons
jellybeans of various colors

**WHAT TO DO**

- Easter is usually celebrated on the first Sunday after the first full moon following the vernal equinox (first day of Spring). This can fall anywhere between March 22nd and April 25th.
1. Give the children egg cartons and jellybeans to sort by color.
2. Encourage them to count the jellybeans and separate them by color into the egg carton cups.

*Kathy Kalmar, Macomb, MI*

# EASTER EGG SORT

MATH

**MATERIALS**
multi-colored jellybeans
plastic eggs

**WHAT TO DO**
- Easter is usually celebrated on the first Sunday after the first full moon following the vernal equinox (first day of Spring). This can fall anywhere between March 22nd and April 25th.
1. Depending on the age of the children, help them sort colored jellybeans into homogeneous piles or have them sort the jellybeans by themselves.
2. Show children how to open the plastic eggs.
3. Ask them to insert yellow jellybeans into yellow eggs, green jellybeans into green eggs, and so on.

**MORE TO DO**
**Math:** Encourage the children to count the jellybeans in each egg.

 *Jill Martin and D'Arcy Simmons, Springfield, MO*

# Go Global for Easter

OUTDOOR PLAY

**MATERIALS**
for Guyana: small kite or equipment to make one
for Finland: small pots and rye grass or other grass seed
for Russia: hand bells or bell music
fro Hungary: small plastic water bottle for each child
for Latvia: swings
for France: ball

**WHAT TO DO**
- Easter is usually celebrated on the first Sunday after the first full moon following the vernal equinox (first day of Spring). This can fall anywhere between March 22nd and April 25th.
1. Try out as many international Easter customs as possible with the children to introduce them to the variety of traditions celebrating the same festival.
2. Following are a few ideas from around the world.
    - **Make kites from Guyana:** Kite-flying is a very popular Easter activity in Guyana. People make them beforehand, then fly them on Easter Sunday and Monday. Help children make simple ones from tissue paper, cane, and string, or ask parents to send one in from home. Fly the kites together.

RYE GRASS

MAN from FINLAND

- **Grow Rye Grass as they do in Finland:** Well before Easter, have children plant rye grass seeds in little pots. Green grass is a sure sign of spring, even if it only grows on the windowsill. Encourage the children to decorate a pot to look like a face. When the grass grows, it will look like hair growing.

- **Hear bells from Russia:** At Easter in Russia, anyone is allowed in church belfries to ring the bells, and many people take advantage of the opportunity! Teach the children a very simple tune to play on handbells. Alternately play recordings of beautiful bells.

- **Do sprinkling from Hungary:** Hungarian sprinkling can take the form of anything from a dash of cologne to a bucket of cold water! A gentler outdoor alternative for a warm day would be to use small plastic water bottles with a few holes punched in the lid. Have the children give each other a little sprinkle.

- **Swing from Latvia:** For hundreds of years, children used to "Swing into Spring" by sitting on swings facing each other, while their friends pushed them as high as possible. Tell the children about this, but try swinging in a much safer way.

- **Play handball from France:** In France, playing handball was one of the earliest Easter amusements. The ball represents the sun, which is believed to take three leaps in rising on Easter morning. Incorporate this idea to make up simple ball games with the children.

**MORE TO DO**    **Group or Circle Time:** Use a world map to show children where activities come from. Talk about other countries in which the activities are also popular (such as kite flying in China).

**RELATED books**    *The Ball Book* by Margaret Hillert
*Curious George Flies a Kite* by H.A. Rey
*Fluffy Grows a Garden* by Kate McMullan
*Handbell for Hans* by Janet M. Wilson
*Kite Flying* by Grace Lin
*Swing!: Little Kippers* by Mick Inkpen

⭐ *Anne Adeney, Plymouth, United Kingdom*

# INTERNATIONAL EASTER Activities

PROJECTS

**Materials**    card stock, ribbon, glue, markers (Sweden)
paper plates, elastic, colored paper and tissue, paper cutouts (England)
wooden sticks and colored yarn (Mexico)
pussy willow branches, decorated blown eggs (Norway)
plain candles, pressed flowers and leaves (Poland)

**What to do**
- Easter is usually celebrated on the first Sunday after the first full moon following the vernal equinox (first day of Spring). This can fall anywhere between March 22nd and April 25th.

1. Tell the children they will be doing Easter crafts from different countries over a period of a week or so.

2. Make Easter cards from Sweden. Explain that on Maundy Thursday, Swedish boys and girls push letters or cards under their neighbors' doors. Have children make their own cards to give to friends and relatives. Ask them to try giving some anonymously, as they do in Western Sweden.

3. Make Easter bonnets from England. Tell the children that Easter was a popular day for getting married and women always wore newly decorated bonnets to church. Encourage the children to fold a paper plate in half, fasten with elastic, and decorate with colored streamers, cutout rabbits, chicks, lambs, eggs, and so on.

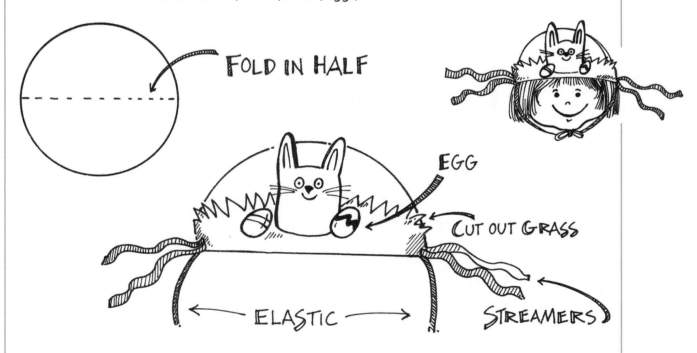

FOLD IN HALF

EGG

CUT OUT GRASS

← ELASTIC →

STREAMERS

4. Make Ojos de Dios ("Eyes of God") from Mexico. Explain that people asked God to look through designs to give the children health and long life. Show the children how to put two wooden sticks together in a cross shape and wind colored yarn around them in a diamond pattern.

5. Make Easter trees from Norway. Well before Easter, put a branch of pussy willow before the buds have burst open into a jug of water. The buds will blossom in the warm atmosphere and make a lovely tree for you to hang decorated eggs on.

6. Make flower candles from Poland. Let children stick pressed or paper flowers and leaves or stickers onto candles to make attractive decorations.

**More to do**    **Group or Circle Time:** Ask the children to find out about different Easter, Passover, and other springtime customs and family traditions and talk about them in circle time.

**Related books**    *175 Easy-to-Do Easter Crafts* by Sharon Dunn Umnik
*Crafts for Easter* by Kathy Ross
*Easter Around the World* by Shannon Knudsen
*Easter Bugs: A Springtime Pop-up* by David A Carter
*Five Little Chicks* by Lark Carrier
*The Golden Egg* by A.J. Wood
*Legend of the Easter Egg* by Lori Walburg
*The Night Before Easter* by Natasha Wing

⭐ *Anne Adeney, Plymouth, United Kingdom*

# Non-Sweet Easter Bunny Snack

SNACK AND COOKING

**Materials**    heavy whipping cream
salt
small plastic containers (one for each child)
bunny cookie cutters
bread slices
cheese slices
grape halves
cherry tomato halves
cream cheese
ketchup

**What to do**
- Easter is usually celebrated on the first Sunday after the first full moon following the vernal equinox (first day of Spring). This can fall anywhere between March 22nd and April 25th.
1. Make butter with the children by putting a small amount of whipping cream and a pinch of salt in plastic containers (one for each child). Encourage them to close the lids and shake for five minutes.
2. Use bunny cookie cutters to cut bread slices. Spread with butter.
3. Cut more bunnies from cheese slices and put them on top of the bread.
4. Encourage the children to decorate their snacks with grape and tomato halves, ketchup, and cream cheese.

**Related books**    *Read to Your Bunny* by Rosemary Wells
*Somebunny Loves Me* by Joan Holub

★ *Freya Zellerhoff, Towson, MD*

# Earth Day Wall Hanging

ART

**Materials**    small (6") blue paper plates
hole punch
green fingerpaint (or green poster paint and paintbrushes)
8" pieces of yarn
crepe paper streamers (blue, green, and white)
cellophane tape

**What to do**
- April 22nd is Earth Day.
1. Give each child a blue 6" paper plate.
2. Punch a hole in the top of each plate and double punch three holes spaced out at the bottom. (Double punch the holes to make them larger.)
3. Encourage the children to paint green "land" on the blue "ocean."
4. When the paint has dried, help the children loop and tie yarn through the top hole on their plates. This is the hanger.

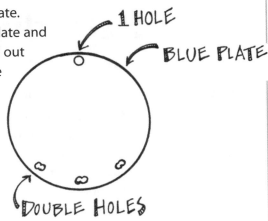

1 HOLE

BLUE PLATE

DOUBLE HOLES

5. Give each child one of each color of streamer (blue for water, green for earth, white for the clouds in the sky). Help them thread a different color streamer through each hole. It is best to pre-twist one end of each streamer to make it easier.

6. Gently pull about 2" of a streamer through a bottom hole and secure it to the back of the paper plate with cellophane tape.

7. Repeat with the other two streamers.

8. Hang the plates to have an Earth Day wall hanging.

YARN

GREEN PAINT

WHITE for CLOUDS

BLUE for WATER

GREEN for EARTH

**MORE TO DO**    Talk about recycling. If recycling is done at school, have each child bring in a clean, empty can to put in the recycling bin.

**RELATED BOOKS**    *Earth Day* by Amy Margaret
*Earth Day* by David F. Marx
*Earth Day Birthday* by Pattie L. Schnetzler

★ *Christina R. Chilcote, New Freedom, PA*

# HELP THE EARTH

GENERAL TIPS

**MATERIALS**    clean, empty soup cans
colored paper, buttons, stickers, and beads
newspaper and glue
old bleach bottles or soda bottles
glossy magazines
scissors
colored wool
pencils

**What to do**

- April 22nd is Earth Day.
1. Talk to the children about how they can help the environment by practicing the three R's: reuse, reduce, and recycle.
2. Following is a list of possible activities to do with the children. Choose a different one each day.
   - Start a compost pile for lunch leftovers and yard waste.
   - Reuse clean soup cans to make pencil holders. Have children cover a can with paper or fabric and decorate with buttons, stickers, or beads.
   - Plant a tree seedling, if possible. Give it lots of space.
   - Make bird feeders out of washed bleach bottles (cut out large squares in the sides and attach a string to the handle) or soda bottles (cut small "n" shapes around the bottle, pull the "n" shapes down to make perches, and attach string).
   - Use old newspaper and glue to make papier mâché gifts (vase, box or ornament).
   - Ask parents to reuse their plastic bags at the supermarket for the month.
   - Encourage parents to pack children a garbage-free lunch. Use washable plastic containers for sandwiches, snacks, and drinks.
   - Plant a garden or window box to attract helpful insects.
   - Use both sides of sheets of paper for a whole day.
   - Choose a day for the children to bring in old clothes and toys. Donate the items to a thrift shop (such as Goodwill or Salvation Army). Explain that the items are being recycled.
   - Make bead necklaces from old glossy magazines. Cut colorful pages into different-sized triangles. Roll the triangles tightly around a pencil one at a time, wide side first. Put glue on the last corner and hold it tight until dry. Pull the "bead" from the pencil. Make enough beads to make a necklace. Thread beads onto a piece of wool and tie the ends together.

DIFFERENT SIZE TRIANGLES

GLUE END DOWN

RUN YARN THROUGH

★ *Amelia Griffin, Ontario, Canada*

# Arbor Day Leafy Crown

ART

**Materials**

strips of brown tagboard (1' wide and 20" long)
pencil
green construction paper
tan construction paper
scissors
several rolls of cellophane tape
glue stick

**What to do**

● Arbor Day is usually celebrated the last Friday in April. Find out what day it is celebrated in your state (www.arborday.org).

1. Measure a strip of brown tagboard around each child's head and mark where the ends meet using a pencil.

2. Cut out 8 to 10 oak leaf shapes from green construction paper and 5 to 6 acorn shapes from tan construction paper for each child.

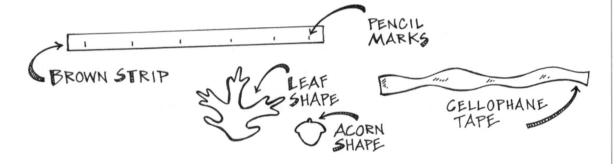

3. Have the children lay their strips of brown tagboard flat and arrange leaves and acorns between the two pencil marks on the brown strip.

4. Ask the children to use a glue stick to glue the leaves and acorns to the brown strip. Then have them secure the leaves and acorns with strips of cellophane tape.

5. Finally, with the ends of the brown strip touching the pencil marks, secure the ends with cellophane tape to finish the leafy crown.

6. Teach the children the following action rhyme with gestures:

**Little Acorn, Big Tree**
*Little acorn, tan and round,* (children squat, circling their arms to show "round")
*Spreads its roots beneath the ground.* (still squatting, children spread their hands along the floor)

*Soon it grows into a tree,* (children stand up)

*Green and tall, as you can see.* (children spread their arms and stand on toes)

**MORE TO DO**  Using money donated from parents or from a bake sale, buy a tree to plant on school property. Let the children help dig the hole, water the plant, and cover the roots with earth. Put a simple sign next to the tree, such as "Donated by Mrs. Smith's 4-year-old class—2006."

**Home-School Connection:** Contact your local state agricultural office or a local master gardener and ask if they have pine seedlings they would give to the class. Let each child plant a seedling in a 1-gallon coffee can and take it home to plant in his yard.

LEAFY CROWN

TIPTOES

**RELATED BOOKS**  *Acorn to Oak Tree* by Oliver S. Owen
*Arbor Day* by Mir Tamim Ansary
*Arbor Day* by Kelly Bennett
*A Tree Is a Plant* by Clyde Robert Bulla
*The Growing Up Tree* by Vera Rosenberry
*Jacob's Tree* by Holly Keller

 *Christina R. Chilcote, New Freedom, PA*

# Arbor Day Fingerplay
FINGERPLAYS, SONGS, & POEMS

**MATERIALS**  none

**WHAT DO TO**  ● Arbor Day is usually celebrated the last Friday in April. Find out what day it is celebrated in your state (www.arborday.org).
Sing the following song, making the appropriate gestures.

*Once I planted a seedling* (make a tiny space between fingers as if holding a seedling; pretend to plant it)

*And it grew* (raise hands up)

*And it grew* (raise hands up)

*Into an oak tree* (spread hands wide like a canopy above head)

*For you* (point to child)
*And you* (point to child)
*And you!* (point to child)

**MORE TO DO**   **Outdoors:** Plant a seedling.

⭐ *Kathy Kalmar, Macomb, MI*

# Arbor Day Appreciation
### SCIENCE

**MATERIALS**   several photos of different kinds of trees
samples of leaves that match the types of trees in the photos
nuts and fruit to match the photos (real or pictures)
books about trees

**WHAT TO DO**
- Arbor Day is usually celebrated the last Friday in April. Find out what day it is celebrated in your state (www.arborday.org).
1. Introduce the materials and talk about the names of the trees, their features, the colors of the leaves and fruit, and so on.
2. Ask the children if they think any of the trees match the other items you have shown them (leaves, nuts, and fruit).
3. Work with the group to match trees with leaves, nuts, and fruit.
4. Place the items in the manipulatives area for children to sort during free play.
5. As you join children in this task at free play, encourage them to sort in a variety of ways (all trees, leaves, fruit or nuts, leaves to trees, nut or fruit to trees, and so on).

**MORE TO DO**   **Science:** With a small group of children who are ready to explore where different trees grow around the United States, introduce a map and some sort of cards that represent a variety of trees. Help them place the cards on the map where they are likely to grow. Use reference books about trees to help the children learn.

**RELATED books**   *Acorn and the Oak Tree* by Lori Froeb
*Another Tree in the Yard* by Lucia Sera
*A Busy Year* by Leo Lionni
*Five Little Monkeys Sitting in a Tree* by Eileen Christelow

⭐ *Ann Kelly, Johnstown, PA*

# MAY

# WORM DANCE PICTURES

ART

**Materials**      pieces of string between 10" to 14"
paint
paint pans or pie tins
construction or drawing paper

**What to do**      1. Put a knot at one end of each string for the child to hold on to.
2. Encourage the children to make their "string worms" dance in the paint.
3. Show the children how to place their strings on a piece of paper with the knot off the edge of the paper. If desired, use brown paper to represent soil.
4. Ask them to fold their papers in half carefully.
5. Hold the paper down firmly as the child gently pulls the string. Ask the child to put the knot around the edge of the paper when pulling the string.
6. Open the paper to see the worm dance design.
7. Let the children repeat this with a couple of colors until there are lots of worm lines on the paper.

KNOT END

FOLDED PAPER

**More to do**      Remind the children to be gentle with real worms and explain that it would be inappropriate to use a real worm for this activity.
**Science:** Have real worms in a jar of soil for the children to observe.

**Related books**      *Inch by Inch* by Leo Lionni
*There's a Hair in My Dirt: A Worm Story* by Gary Larson
*Wonderful Worms* by Linda Glaser

★ *Sandie Nagel, White Lake, MI*

# BUTTERFLY BLOTS ART

ART

**MATERIALS**
manila paper
paint
markers

**WHAT TO DO**
1. Have the children put two dabs of paint on one side of their paper.
2. Help them fold their paper over in half. Show them how to smooth the paper, and rub gently.
3. Open to see a butterfly shape.
4. After the butterflies dry, encourage them to decorate their shapes using paint or markers.

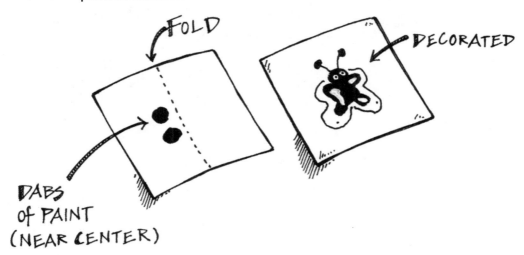

★ *Kathy Kalmar, Macomb, MI*

# Sock Caterpillars

ART

**MATERIALS**
colorful socks
wool stuffing
string
glue
pipe cleaners
wiggle eyes
felt scraps

**What to do**
1. Give each child a sock (or ask parents to send one in for their child).
2. Show them how to stuff one section of the sock at a time. Help the children tie each section with string.
3. Have them continue stuffing and tying until the sock is almost filled.
4. Sew the end closed (adult only).
5. Encourage the children to add pipe cleaner antennae, wiggle eyes, and felt scraps to make spots or stripes.

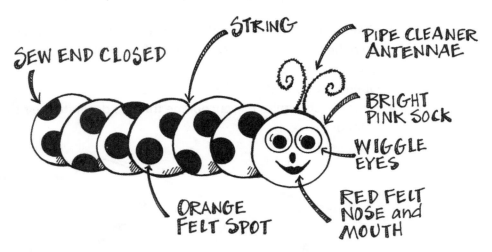

SEW END CLOSED
STRING
PIPE CLEANER ANTENNAE
BRIGHT PINK SOCK
WIGGLE EYES
RED FELT NOSE and MOUTH
ORANGE FELT SPOT

**Related book**    *The Very Hungry Caterpillar* by Eric Carle

 *Linda Atamian, Charlestown, RI*

# SUMMER VACATION

DRAMATIC PLAY

**Materials**    small suitcases or duffel bags
variety of summer dress-up clothes
snack food boxes
car keys (old or pretend)
maps
sunglasses

**What to do**
1. Encourage the children to bring in pictures of trips they have taken. Talk about how they traveled, who they went with, and what they saw on their trip.
2. Place a variety of vacation props in the dramatic play area. Encourage the children to role play packing for an imaginary trip.

 *Barb Lindsey, Madison City, IA*

# How Many Flowers Song

### FINGERPLAYS, SONGS, & POEMS

**Materials**     none

**What to do**     Sing the following song to the tune of "I'm a Little Teapot," making the appropriate gestures when prompted.

*I'm a little seed with great big dreams,* (put index finger and thumb close
     together, like measuring something small, then open arms wide)
*I'll begin to grow under warm sunbeams.* (move arms up body as if growing)
*With a little water I will grow,* (wiggle fingers like rain, repeat growing
     motion)
*And my flower will bloom before you know!* (open arms in arc like rainbow)

 *Kristi Larson, Spirit Lake, IA*

# Metamorphosis

### FINGERPLAYS, SONGS, & POEMS

**Materials**     none

**What to do:**     1. Read the following action rhyme and model the motions for the
     children.

*The caterpillar crawls around,*
*Munching tasty leaves of green.* (pretend to pick a leaf and eat it)
*Then he spins a soft cocoon* (spin around)
*Where inside he can't be seen.*
*When it's time, he "pops" right out* (jump one step forward)
*And stretches both left and right.* (stretch out arms)
*He feels the warm sunlight on his wings,*
*Flaps them and flies out of sight.* (flap arms and "fly" around)

2. Repeat the action rhyme as desired so the children can use the motions
     again.

**More to do**    **Music and Movement:** Have a Caterpillar Conga Line! Incorporate music and movement as children lightly hold each other at arm's length at the waist and become the segments of the caterpillar's body. Let them weave around the room following a leader as music plays.

**Related book**    *The Very Hungry Caterpillar* by Eric Carle

⭐ *Theresa Callahan, Easton, MD*

# The Fuzzy Caterpillar
### FINGERPLAYS, SONGS, & POEMS

**Materials**    none

**What to do**    Sing the following song to the tune of "Itsy Bitsy Spider."

*The little fuzzy caterpillar*
*Curled up on a leaf*
*Spun her little chrysalis,*
*And then fell fast asleep.*
*While she was sleeping,*
*She dreamed she could fly.*
*Later when she woke up,*
*She was a butterfly.*

**More to do**    **Art:** Make an egg carton caterpillar.

⭐ *Kathy Kalmar, Macomb, MI*

# If I Could Be a Flower

FINGERPLAYS, SONGS, & POEMS

**Materials**      none

**What to do**      Sing the following song to the tune of "Did You Ever See a Lassie?"

*If I could be a flower,*
*A flower,*
*A flower,*
*If I could be a flower,*
*What kind would I be?*
*A daisy, a pansy,*
*A tulip, a lilac,*
*If I could be a flower,*
*I'd be a _____.*

**More to do**      **Art:** Make egg carton flowers.

*Kathy Kalmar, Macomb, MI*

# Tap Goes the Woodpecker

FINGERPLAYS, SONGS, & POEMS

**Materials**      none

**What to do**      Sing the following song, making the appropriate gestures when necessary.

*Tap, tap, tap goes the woodpecker* (tap fingers on open palm)
*As he pecks a hole in the tree.* (make small circle for hole)
*He's looking for food* (hand to eyes)
*Not for you and me!* (shake head no, point to self and children)

**More to do**      **Science:** Discuss what woodpeckers eat. Ask how they can find out.

*Kathy Kalmar, Macomb, MI*

# Baa, Little Lamb, Baa!

GAMES

**Materials**     blindfold

**What to do**
1. Have the children form a close circle, with no gaps. They are the little lambs.
2. Blindfold a volunteer child (the "shepherd"). Spin the shepherd around three times, very gently.
3. The shepherd stretches out her arms and walks until she touches somebody. She then says, "Baa, little lamb, baa!"
4. The touched child must reply, "Baa, baa!" in a squeaky tone, disguising his voice as much as possible.
5. The shepherd must guess the little lamb's name. If she gets it wrong, she may say, "Baa, little lamb, baa!" one more time and guess again.
6. If she still cannot recognize the lamb's voice, she must turn around, walk across the circle, and try to identify another little lamb.
7. The first lamb the shepherd correctly identifies becomes the shepherd. If that child does not want to be blindfolded, find another volunteer.
8. Adapt the animal used to suit your theme.

**More to do**     **Group or Circle Time:** Talk about shepherds and how they look after their sheep. Show the children some untreated sheep's wool and talk about shearing sheep, making wool, and knitting garments.
**Holidays:** Use this game as part of an Easter theme.
**Music:** Sing "Baa, Baa, Black Sheep" and other sheep or lamb songs.

**Related books**     *Baa Baa Black Sheep* by Iza Trapani
*A Certain Small Shepherd* by Rebecca Caudill
*The Little Lamb* by Judy Dunn
*The Lost Lamb* by Melody Carlson

⭐ *Anne Adeney, Plymouth, United Kingdom*

# Parts of a Flower

LANGUAGE AND LITERACY

**Materials**     manila folder
laminating material
Velcro
markers

**What to do**
1. Draw a large picture of a plant on a manila folder.
2. Laminate the folder. Put pieces of Velcro on the different parts of the plant.
3. Make labels with the names of each part: roots, stem, leaf, petal, fruit, and so on.
4. Laminate and put Velcro on the back.
5. You can also do this with different parts of a flower: petal, pistil, stamen, and so on.

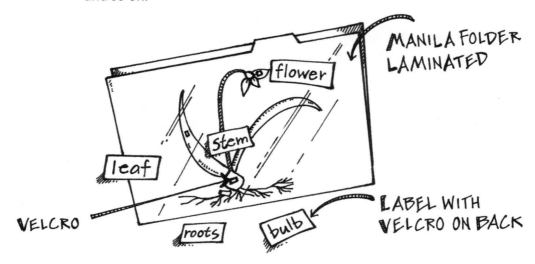

⭐ *Kristi Larson, Spirit Lake, IA*

# April Showers, May Flowers

MATH

**Materials**
construction paper (five different colors)
scissors
plastic water pail
chart paper
glue

**What to do**
1. Cut out five types of flowers, five of each type (for example, five daisies, five roses, five tulips, and so on). Place them in the pail.
2. Show the children the flower cutouts and talk about each type of flower.
3. Ask one of the children to pull out a flower from the pail and identify the flower.
4. Next, glue it on the chart paper.

5. Repeat, gluing each matching flower in a row and starting a new row for each different kind.

6. When everyone has chosen a flower to glue on the chart, count the number of flowers in each row. Compare the numbers and discuss *more, most, less, least,* and *equal.*

**More to do**  **Outdoors:** Go on a walk and look for flowers of various types.
**Science:** Plant flower seeds.

**Related books**  *The Carrot Seed* by Ruth Krauss
*Growing Vegetable Soup* by Lois Ehlert
*The Tiny Seed* by Eric Carle

 *Susan Oldham Hill, Lakeland, FL*

# Clouds

OUTDOORS

**Materials**  blue construction paper
white sheep's wool (or cotton balls)
glue sticks
crayons

**What to do**  1. Do this activity on a nice, partly cloudy day. Go outside with the children and have them lie down on their backs and look up at the sky.

2. Watch the clouds together.

3. Take turns playing "I Spy." Encourage the children to use their imaginations when looking at the clouds ("I spy a dragon").

4. Inside, ask the children to make one of the cloud shapes they saw using white sheep's wool or cotton balls. Encourage them to add details with crayons.

5. Hang the pictures on the wall.

**Related books**  *The Cloud Book* by Tomie DePaola
*It Looked Like Spilt Milk* by Charles Shaw

 *Linda Atamian, Charlestown, RI*

# SPRING NATURE Mobile

OUTDOORS

**Materials**
stick
string
scissors
collection of natural objects

**What to do**
1. Take the children on a walk outdoors.
2. Ask each child to select one natural object, such as a rock, pinecone, acorn, or feather.
3. Back in the classroom, look at the collection of objects as a group.
4. Turn the collection into a classroom mobile by connecting the objects together with string, and suspending them from a long stick.
5. Finish by hanging the mobile where everyone can enjoy it.

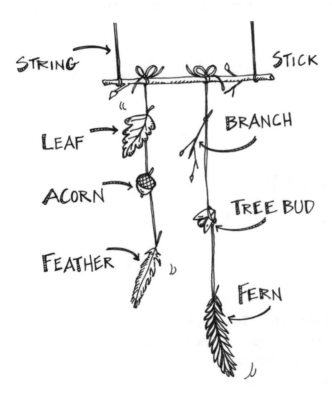

**Related book** *Spring Is Here* by Taro Gomi

⭐ *Erin Huffstetler, Maryville, TN*

# PRESSED FLOWERS

PROJECTS

**MATERIALS**
fresh flowers
flower press or several heavy books
wax paper

**WHAT TO DO**
1. Take a walk with the children and let them pick flowers, or have them bring flowers from home. (Be sure not to pick flowers from private property.)
2. Position the flowers in a flower press or place them in a piece of folded wax paper and put them inside or under large books.
3. After several weeks, remove the pressed flowers.
4. Make bookmarks by ironing the flowers inside the wax paper or placing them on colored paper and laminating them.
5. You can also use pressed flowers to make Mother's Day Cards.

**RELATED book** *The Tiny Seed* by Eric Carle

⭐ *Barbara Saul, Eureka, CA*

# POND WATER

SCIENCE

**MATERIALS**
jars
magnifying glasses
tap or distilled water

**WHAT TO DO**
1. Visit a pond with the children. Take jars to collect water.
2. After exploring the ponds, return to the classroom and compare the pond water to tap or distilled water.
3. Ask questions. "Do they look different?" "Do they smell different?"
   **Safety Note:** Do not let children taste the pond water! Many waterborne organisms can cause serious illness!
4. Encourage the children to use a magnifying glass to explore the water.

⭐ *Kristi Larson, Spirit Lake, IA*

# Flower Sorting

SCIENCE

**Materials**
fresh or artificial flowers
pencils
drawing paper
colored pencils
flower identification book (optional)

**What to do**
1. Take a walk outdoors to pick wildflowers, or use a variety of artificial flowers.
2. If desired, show the children a flower guide and explain how the flowers are sorted.
3. Have the children sort the flowers by color, leaf shape, and size. Discuss similarities and differences between the flowers.
4. Count the petals on each of the flower types and sort them. Tell the children that scientists use the color, leaf shape, and number of petals to identify different flowers.
5. Let the children use colored pencils to draw the flowers.

**More to do**
**Math:** Graph the flowers.

**Related books**
*The Legend of the Blue Bonnet* by Tomie de Paola
*Planting a Rainbow* by Lois Ehlert

⭐ *Barbara Saul, Eureka, CA*

# Edible Plant Parts

SCIENCE

**Materials**
sprouts
sunflower seeds
carrots (with stems, if possible)
lettuce
broccoli
grapes
poster showing different parts of a plant

**What to do**
1. Display a poster showing the different parts of a plant.
2. Show the children each food and explain what part of the plant it is.
   - A sunflower seed is a seed.
   - A carrot is a root.
   - Lettuce is a leaf.
   - Broccoli is a flower.
   - A grape is a fruit.
3. Invite the children to taste the foods.
   **Safety Note:** Be aware of any food allergies and do not serve any of those foods. Cut grapes in half so they do not pose a choking hazard.

⭐ *Kristi Larson, Spirit Lake, IA*

# Landscape Planning

SENSORY

**Materials**
cedar or cypress mulch
soil
pea gravel
sand
peat moss
vermiculite
glue
paper

**What to do**
1. Place samples of each planting material on a table.
2. Let each child examine it, feel it, smell it, and so on.
3. Encourage the children to "plan their landscapes" by gluing planting materials on their paper.

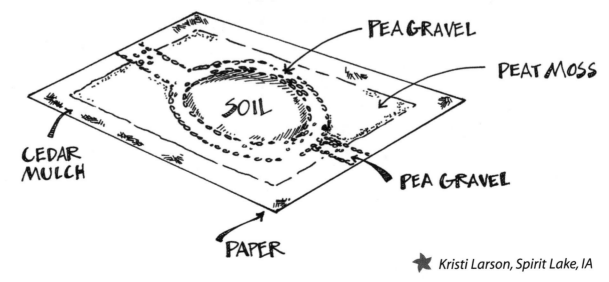

⭐ *Kristi Larson, Spirit Lake, IA*

# Birds' Nest Cookies

## SNACK AND COOKING

**MATERIALS**

½ cup butter
1 tablespoon honey
4 teaspoons molasses
2 eggs
2 teaspoons vanilla
⅛ teaspoon salt
1 ¼ cup rye flour
cookie sheet
mixing bowl and spoon
measuring cups and spoons
oven
marzipan (almond paste)
blue food coloring

**WHAT TO DO**

1. Let the children help with the following steps. Make sure each child is involved in some way.
2. Cream together butter, honey, and molasses.
3. Beat the eggs and add to the mixture. Add the vanilla. Add the salt and the flour.
4. Mix well.
5. Place by tablespoonful on an ungreased cookie sheet.
6. Push a thumbprint into each cookie.
7. Bake at 375° for 10 minutes. Let cool.
8. Color the marzipan blue.
9. Encourage the children to make marzipan robin eggs and fill their "nests" with the eggs. If desired, sculpt a marzipan robin for each child's "nest."

 *Linda Atamian, Charlestown, RI*

# Box Loads of Transportation Fun

### DRAMATIC PLAY

**Materials**
large box
paper grocery bags
clear book tape
tempera paint
ice cream bucket lids

**What to do**
- May is National Transportation Month.
1. Fold the flaps of the box in to support its sides.
2. Cover the box with large paper grocery bags. Use clear book tape to seal all edges.
3. Encourage the children to paint auto details on the box: white circles for headlights, red circles for tail lights, assorted colors for license plates, and so on.
4. For the steering wheel, use a 5-quart ice cream lid, cutting spaces to create a cross at the center of the wheel.

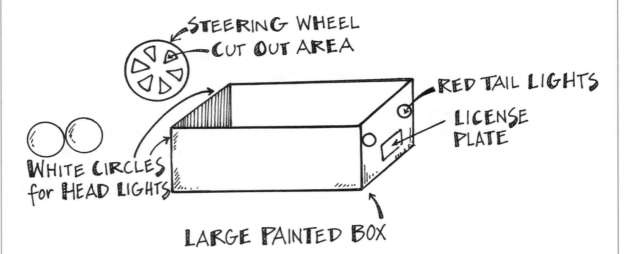

STEERING WHEEL
CUT OUT AREA
RED TAIL LIGHTS
LICENSE PLATE
WHITE CIRCLES for HEAD LIGHTS
LARGE PAINTED BOX

**More to do**
Cardboard wings can be attached to create an airplane; attach extra boxes to make a bus.

**Related books**
*Maisy Drives* by Lucy Cousins
*Wheels on the Bus* by Paul O. Zelinsky

⭐ *Linda Becker, Rochester, MN*

# OUR EGG BOOK

### LANGUAGE AND LITERACY

**MATERIALS**
paper
marker
crayons
scissors
construction paper
glue stick
tagboard
binding machine or yarn and hole punch

**WHAT TO DO**
- May is National Egg Month.
1. Draw an egg shape on a piece of paper. Make a copy for each child.
2. Encourage the children to decorate their egg shapes with crayons and cut out.
3. Give each child a piece of construction paper on which to glue her egg shape.
4. Have each child dictate a couple of sentences about eggs. Write their words underneath their egg shapes.
5. Make a front and back cover using tagboard. Write the title "Our Egg Book" on the front cover.
6. If desired, laminate the covers for durability, and cut out.
7. Bind the children's egg pages between the covers using a binding machine or a hole punch and yarn.

**RELATED book**
*Eggbert, the Slightly Cracked Egg* by Tom Ross

 *Jackie Wright, Enid, OK*

# Pet Shop Scramble

GAMES

**Materials**        none

**What to do**
- National Pet Week is the first full week in May.
1. Assign one pet to every two to four children in the group. For example, if there are 15 children in the group, assign three children "dog," three children "cat," three children "bird," and so on.
2. Have the children sit in a circle in any order. Make sure there is a space between each child.
3. Choose a child to be the leader, if desired. The leader (or you) calls out, "A customer wants to buy a...cat!"
4. When the animal's name is called out, the children with that pet must run round the outside of the circle and back to their place.
5. When the leader says, "Pet shop Scramble!" all the pets get up and race around the outside of the circle.
6. Continue playing the game, until all of the children have had a chance to be the leader or lose interest.

**More to do**    Use this game as part of a pet, animals, or shopping theme.
Adapt the game to suit your theme, using colors, numbers, shapes, and so on.
**Dramatic Play:** Use this pet shop scenario as a dramatic play activity. One child could be the shopkeeper, a few children can be a family of customers, and the other children can be the pets of their own choice. Encourage them to role play. For example, a child customer could pull on Dad's arm and say, "Please, Dad, we have to get a dog to take for walks!" Another could excitedly jump up and down saying, "No, I want a parrot, so I can teach it to talk!" A cat could purr and rub her head against the mother's leg, while a dog could sit up and beg. When each part has been practiced, encourage the children to act out the whole scene.
**Group or Circle Time:** Talk about pets and how to care for them.
**Music:** Sing "How Much Is That Doggie in the Window?"

**Related books**    *The Best Pet of All* by David LaRoch
*Buying a Pet From Ms. Chavez* by Alice Flanagan
*Dear Zoo* by Rod Campbell
*How Much Is That Doggie in the Window?* by Iza Trapani

 *Anne Adeney, Plymouth, United Kingdom*

# Favorite Pet Graph

GROUP OR CIRCLE TIME

**Materials**
tagboad for header card
marker
pictures of various pets
name card for each child in the class
pocket chart

**What to do**
* National Pet Week is the first full week in May.
1. Write "What is your favorite pet?" on a header card and put at the top of a pocket chart.
2. Display pictures of different pets at the top of each column.
3. Ask each child, in turn, to name her favorite.
4. Place her name card under the appropriate pet to indicate her choice.
5. Discuss the results of the graph.

**Related books**    *Angus and the Ducks* by Marjorie Flack
*Carl Goes Shopping* by Alexandra Day

 *Jackie Wright, Enid, OK*

# Stuffed Animal Parade and Show

GROUP OR CIRCLE TIME

**Materials**
several yards of colorful material (purchased or donated)
stuffed animals
CD or tape player
CD or tape of a march or the song "The Animal Fair"

**What to do**
* Celebrate Be Kind to Animals Week, the first week in May.
1. Prior to the day of the activity, ask a parent to donate several yards of colorful cotton material. Cut the material into 16" squares, and then cut each square diagonally to make a triangular scarf. Make enough so that each child gets at least one.
2. The day before the activity, remind children to bring in their favorite stuffed animals the next day.

3. On the day of the activity, have each child bring her stuffed animal to circle time. Make sure to have a few extra stuffed animals for children who forget to bring theirs.

4. Each child takes a turn standing up, showing her animal, telling the animal's name, and explaining what kind of animal it is.

5. Have the children line up. Turn on the music and lead them in a grand parade. If possible, have them move to another class or show their parents.

6. Return to circle time and give out the prize scarves to be tied around each animal's neck.

7. Make sure that each animal wins a prize in a different category (for example, the largest animal, the biggest ears, the furriest animal, and so on).

8. If desired, use stickers and ribbons too. Have an adult helper print the "winning category" on the sticker and present it to the child.

**MORE TO DO**    Invite a local animal shelter to bring in a puppy or a kitten and speak about the proper way to care for a pet.

Contact the American Kennel Club. They have free materials for children on taking care of a pet dog.

**RELATED books**    *Arthur's Pet Business* by Marc Brown
*The Best Pet of All* by David LaRochelle
*Emma's Pet* by David McPhail
*The Perfect Pet* by Margie Palatini

⭐ *Christina R. Chilcote, New Freedom, PA*

# May Baskets

ART

**Materials**
empty milk cartons
scissors
tissue paper
ribbon
flowers brought to school by the children to share: violets, tulips, daffodils, blueberry blossoms, pussy willows, forsythia

**What to do**
- May Day is May 1st.
1. Before doing this activity, send home a note asking children to bring in flowers to share (such as violets, tulips, daffodils, forsythia, pussy willows, and so on).
2. Wash empty milk cartons and cut off the tops to make vases.
3. Encourage the children to decorate their vases by wrapping them with tissue paper and adding ribbons.
4. Let the children choose flowers to arrange in their May Baskets.

**More to do**
Make May Baskets as gifts to other classrooms or for school helpers.
**Group or Circle Time:** Make a May Pole and have children dance around it at circle time.

**Related books**
*Complete Book of Flower Fairies* by Cicely M. Barker
*The Flower Alphabet Book* by Jerry Pallotta
*A Time to Keep* by Tasha Tudor

★ *Linda Atamian, Charlestown, RI*

# May Day/Mother's Day Flower Baskets

ART

**Materials**
books of discontinued floral wallpaper
brown construction paper
scissors
pastel construction paper
glue sticks or tacky glue

**What to do**

- May Day is May 1st, and Mother's Day is celebrated on the second Sunday of May.

1. In advance, cut out single flowers and small bunches of flowers from discarded wallpaper books. Also cut out basket shapes from brown construction paper (6" wide at top, 3" high, and 4" wide at bottom), one for each child.

2. Give each child a piece of pastel construction paper, a paper basket shape, and a glue stick.

3. Demonstrate how to place the pastel construction paper horizontally (landscape-sized) and glue the "basket" to the pastel paper (the bottom of the basket should be at the bottom of the paper).

4. Spread the cut "flowers" on a table and let each child choose two bunches and three or four single flowers.

5. Encourage the children to glue their flowers above the baskets. The flowers should look like they are growing in the basket.

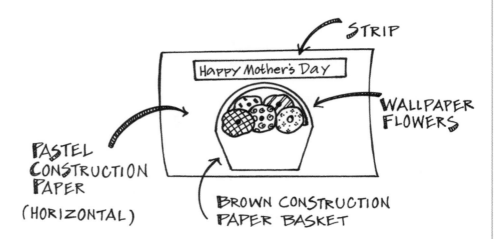

6. Optional: Write "For You" or "Happy Mother's Day!" on pieces of 1" x 4" paper. Help each child glue the message to the top of her picture.

**More to do**

**Group or Circle Time:** Briefly discuss the history of May Day or Mother's Day.

**Related books**

*Flower Alphabet Book* by Jerry Pallotta
*Flower Garden* by Eve Bunting
*Sunflower House* by Eve Bunting

★ *Christina R. Chilcote, New Freedom, PA*

# Celebrate Mother Goose

### GROUP OR CIRCLE TIME

**Materials**

white and black fleecy fabric
bonnets
pails
dresses
suspenders
rubber spiders
crowns
cardboard box boat and oars
rolling pin
candleholder
apron
mittens
umbrella

**What to do**

- Mother Goose Day is celebrated on May 1st.
1. During group or circle time, read various Mother Goose rhymes.
2. For each rhyme, choose a child or children to come up front and dress the part.
3. Since each rhyme is short, you will be able to do a number of them.
4. Following are some good rhymes to use:
   - Little Bo Peep
   - Baa, Baa Black Sheep
   - Jack and Jill
   - Eensy Weensy Spider
   - Little Miss Muffett
   - Old King Cole
   - Row, Row, Row Your Boat
   - Rub-a-Dub-Dub
   - Three Little Kittens
   - It's Raining, It's Pouring

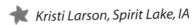 *Kristi Larson, Spirit Lake, IA*

# MOTHER GOOSE MATH

MATH

**Materials**     none

**What to do**
- Mother Goose Day is celebrated on May 1st.
  Use the following Mother Goose rhymes as a teacher resource for math.
  - Baa, Baa Black Sheep
  - Cobbler, Cobbler
  - One, Two, Buckle My Shoe
  - Simple Simon
  - Sing a Song of Sixpence
  - This Old Man
  - Three Little Kittens
  - Wynken, Blynken, and Nod

 *Kathy Kalmar, Macomb, MI*

# MOTHER GOOSE DAY

WORKING WITH FAMILIES

**Materials**     none

**What to do**
- Mother Goose Day is celebrated on May 1st.
1. Prepare for May 1st, Mother Goose Day, by asking parents to learn a Mother Goose rhyme. Invite parents to come in costume on Mother Goose Day and teach the rhyme to the children.
2. If desired, ask parents to make homemade hand puppets to dramatize the Mother Goose rhyme.

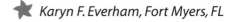 *Karyn F. Everham, Fort Myers, FL*

# Make Your Own Galaxies

SCIENCE

**Materials**
strong balloon for each child
markers

**What to do**
- Space Day is the first Thursday in May.
1. Talk to the children about galaxies in the universe and explain how they are made up of huge groups of stars clustered together. Tell them that scientists believe that the galaxies are moving farther apart all the time.
2. Give each child a deflated balloon and a marker. **Safety Note:** Make sure the children do not put the balloons near their mouths or try to blow them up.
3. Tell them that their balloons represent their own personal universe.
4. Invite the children to design their own galaxies, using a marker dot for each star.
5. Suggest that they draw many different-shaped galaxies all over their "universe" (for example, dots making a ring, oval, circle, or spiral shape).
6. Encourage them to watch as the balloons are blown up by you or other adult. The galaxies move apart as the balloon expands, just as they do in space.

**More to do**
**Language and Literacy:** Encourage the children to make up names for their galaxies.
**Math:** Use this activity to teach the differences between circles, ovals, and spirals.

**Related books**
*First Guide to the Universe* by Lynn Myring
*Looking Into Space* by Nigel Nelson
*There's No Place Like Space* by Tish Rabe

★ *Anne Adeney, Plymouth, United Kingdom*

# Cinco de Mayo Bracelet

ART

**Materials**

empty toilet paper tubes
scissors
glue
construction paper
markers and crayons

**What to do**

- Cinco de Mayo is celebrated on May 5th.
1. Before the activity, cut the cardboard tubes so that they are no longer tubes (cut one side open).
2. Cut each cardboard tube in half to make two bracelets.
3. Cut construction paper to fit each cut tube.
4. Give each child one half of a tube.
5. Have the children glue the construction paper to the cardboard bracelet.
6. Let dry.
7. Encourage the children to decorate their bracelets as desired.

**Related books**

*Cinco de Mayo* by Mary Dodson Wade
*Mud Soup* by Judith Head
*Saturday Market* by Patricia Grossman
*Uno, Dos, Tres: One, Two, Three* by Pat Mora

 *Elizabeth Thomas, Hobart, IN*

# Dragon Boats

PROJECTS

**Materials**

craft foam
craft sticks
craft glue
markers
stickers
pipe cleaners
scissors
tape
small basin of water

**What to do**

- May 5th is China's Dragon Boat Festival.
1. Read *Awakening the Dragon* by Arlene Chan. Tell the children that on May 5, people in China celebrate the Dragon Boat Festival. Explain that the people eat tzungtzu "zong zi" (rice dumplings filled with ham or bean paste and wrapped in bamboo leaves) and make fanciful boats that look like dragons.
2. Challenge the children to make their own boats using craft foam, craft sticks, pipe cleaners, craft glue, tape, scissors, stickers, and markers.
3. As the children work, offer help as needed. Provide a small basin of water so the children can test their designs frequently to see if they float.
4. If needed, show the children how a single square of craft foam will float if laid flat on the water. You can also show them how to bend up the ends of a rectangular piece of foam and tape it to form a rough boat shape.
5. Encourage the children to experiment with the pipe cleaners and small pieces of foam. They can even make sails by looping one end of a pipe cleaner and bending it at a 90° angle near the loop. This forms a stand for the pipe cleaner. Tape the loop to the foam piece to make a mast and tape a small piece of foam to the top of the pipe cleaner to form a sail. Make flags for the boats using the same technique.
6. After the children have finished their creations, fill the sensory table with water and let them float their boats in it.
7. Challenge the children to find different ways to make their boats move in the water. The can make ripples and waves with their fingers, gently shake the entire sensory table from side to side, or blow on their boats to try to get them from one end of the table to the other.

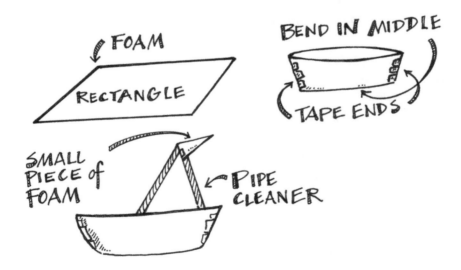

**MORE TO DO**

**Science:** Have boat races with several different types of boats (rafts vs. bow-shaped boats; square vs. rectangular boats). Which boats float better or faster? Graph the results.

**Sensory Table:** Add small plastic people to the sensory table. Challenge the children to put the people on their boats without causing the boats to sink. Ask how many people they get on their boats before they sink. Graph the results.

**Snack:** Make Tzungzu for the children. The cooking process is too involved for classroom use, but the children will enjoy tasting this unusual treat. The following recipe makes 10 dumplings:

50 sheets of bamboo or reed leaves

2 pounds glutinous rice

60 Chinese dates

Soak the rice and dates 12 hours or more until they are soaked. Wash the bamboo leaves and lay them out on a chopping board. Fold the leaves flat at the leafstalk to make a sheet. Hold the sheet, fold it round in the middle, and make a funnel until both ends are laid over each other in one direction. Use about 3 to 4 ounces of rice and 6 dates for each dumpling. Make sure to cover the dates with the rice so they won't lose too much syrup in cooking. Fold the leaves to seal the open side of the funnel and tie the bundle with a band made of twisted leaves. Make sure not to tie the bundle too tight or too loose so that the ingredients are well cooked. Put the dumplings in a pot of boiling water. Make sure they stay pressed and while being boiled. Cooking time: 40 minutes in a pressure cooker; 2 hours in an ordinary pot.

**RELATED POEMS**

**Dragon Boat**

*Dragon boat, dragon boat*
*The finest in the land.*
*I made this little dragon boat*
*With my two little hands.*

**If I Had a Dragon Boat**

*If I had a dragon boat*
*Of my very own,*
*I'd go and visit places*
*I have never known.*
*I'd sail the wide seas*
*And do just as I please,*
*If I had a dragon boat*
*Of my very own.*

**This Little Boat** (Tune: "This Old Man")
*This little boat,*
*It sailed away,*
*It sailed away on a very fine day,*
*With a knick-knack-paddy-whack*
*Happy Dragon Boat Day,*
*This little boat sailed away.*

**Related books**   *The Dragon's Pearl* by Julie Lawson
*A Time of Golden Dragons* by Song Nan and Hao Yu Zhang

⭐ *Virginia Jean Herrod, Columbia, SC*

# Mom's Day Surprise

ART

**Materials**   *Lots of Moms* by Shelley Rotner
sentence strips or 4" x 6" index cards
construction paper
crayons or markers
collage materials
yarn in black, brown, red, and yellow
glue
scissors
Sculpey (or other modeling clay) in a variety of colors
wooden skewers
ribbon
oven

**What to do**   ● Mother's Day is celebrated on the second Sunday of May.

1. Read *Lots of Moms* by Shelley Rotner. Ask the children to tell something about their own mothers (or grandmothers, stepmothers, and so on) and record what they say on sentence strips or index cards.

2. Ask the children to draw a picture of their mothers (or other special person) using crayons or markers. Provide yarn, buttons, small jewels, and other craft items along with scissors and glue for children to use to embellish their drawings. Encourage them to create hair, earrings, and other accessories. Set aside to dry.

3. Help each child make several small round beads with Sculpey (or other modeling clay). Show them how to roll and squish it between their fingers. Encourage them to mix colors if they wish, or make beads in different shapes. **Note:** Make sure the children wash their hands thoroughly after using the clay.

4. Push each child's beads onto separate wooden skewers. Make sure the skewer is through the center of the beads. This creates the hole which the children will later use to thread the beads. Make sure you keep track of which beads belong to which child.

5. Bake the beads according to the package instructions. You may want to ask a parent volunteer to do this step at home, as Sculpey does create a slight odor when baking.

6. After the beads have cooled, place each child's beads in a zipper-lock bag. Give each child her own bag and a length of yarn or ribbon. Help the children string their beads on the ribbon or yarn.

7. Poke a small hole on either side of the neck of the mother figure that each child created. Thread each child's necklace through the holes in her picture and tie in the back. The mother in the drawing "wears" the necklace.

8. Create a bulletin board entitled "All About Mom." Post the children's pictures on the board with their descriptive sentences posted under each picture.

9. Allow the mothers to take their picture and necklace surprise home on the Friday before Mother's Day.

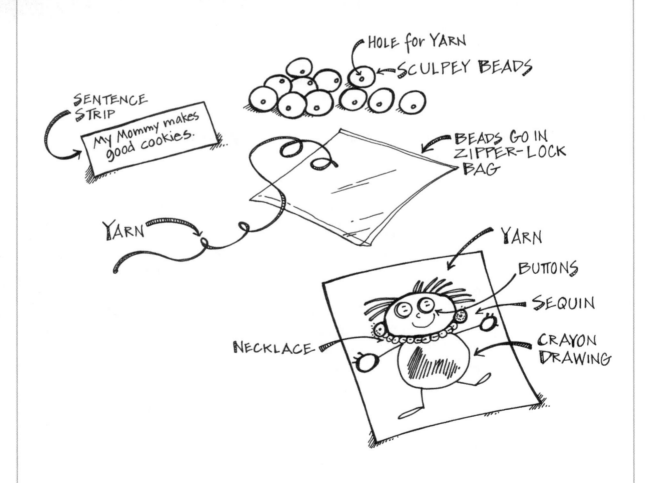

**MORE TO DO**   Have a simple Mother's Day Tea on the Friday before Mother's Day. If possible, let the children help bake and decorate simple sugar cookies and make iced tea and lemonade. Let the children help make a simple invitation for their mothers (or other special person) letting them know the time and day of the tea. Have the children use craft materials to decorate the room and tables for the tea. Remember to keep things simple and short, as parties often overwhelm young children.

**RELATED POEM**   **I Love My Mom** by Virginia Jean Herrod
*I love my Mom and she loves me,* (point outward, then point to self)
*I love her this much as you can see.* (spread arms wide)
*I love my Mom and I'll tell you why,* (shake finger at audience)
*She's like a diamond in the sky.* (make a diamond shape with forefingers and
     thumbs and hold above head)
*I love my Mom and she loves me,* (point outward then point to self)
*I love her this much as you can see.* (spread arms wide)

**RELATED books**   *In My Momma's Kitchen* by Jerdine Nolen
*Mommy and Me by Ourselves Again!* by Judith Vigna
*Mommy Far, Mommy Near: An Adoption Story* by Carol Antoinette Peacock
*Mommy's Office* by Barbara Shook Hazen

 *Virginia Jean Herrod, Columbia, SC*

# MOTHER'S DAY BOUQUET

ART

**MATERIALS**   12" x 18" construction paper in various colors
crayons
1" x 6" construction paper strips in assorted colors
jumbo crayons for curling
glue
2" paper circles in various colors
small balloons in assorted colors
adult scissors

**WHAT TO DO**   ● Mother's Day is celebrated on the second Sunday of May.
1. Give each child a piece of 12" x 18" construction paper positioned vertically. Ask them to color a big stem in the center of their paper, making it very tall and fat. Invite them to add leaves and ground as well.
2. Let each child choose about five strips of paper.

3. Demonstrate how to put a curl into the paper strip by rolling the paper tightly around a jumbo crayon, holding it for a moment, and then slipping the crayon out (keeping the curl intact). This curled strip becomes one curled "flower petal."

4. Show the children how to glue one end of the petal at the top of the stem so that the curl spirals up to make a three-dimensional flower. Repeat the curling process until there are about five petals arranged in a circle to form the flower.

5. Next, ask each child to choose a small circle and glue it on top of the ends of the strips, covering the ends to make the center of the flower.

6. Blow up the balloons until they are about 3" in diameter and tie them shut (adult only).

7. This step should be done by an adult. Use the sharp end of a pair of scissors to poke a hole in the center of the circle and ease the balloon through the hole so that the tied end is on the back of the picture and the balloon is sticking out as the flower's center. Glue another 2" circle on the back to secure the balloon.

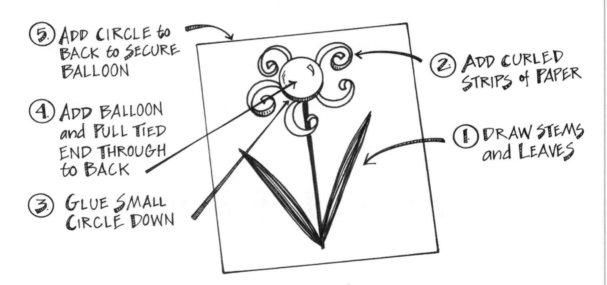

**More to do**    Have the children make the flowers into a card to take home before Mother's Day.

**Related books**    *Are You My Mother?* by P. D. Eastman
*Blueberries for Sal* by Robert McCloskey
*A Chair for My Mother* by Vera B. Williams

★ *Susan Oldham Hill, Lakeland, FL*

# THE KEY TO MY HEART

ART

**MATERIALS**
colorful paper
scissors
glue
photo of each child
pre-cut key shapes
key chains
hole punch
ribbons

**WHAT TO DO**

- Mother's Day is celebrated on the second Sunday of May.

1. Make a copy of the following original poem for each child:

**The Key to My Heart**
*You've loved me from the start,*
*I know you'll always care,*
*So here's the key to my heart*
*For the times I can't be there.*

2. Have the children cut out the poem and glue on colorful paper.
3. Place each child's photo on a piece of colorful paper and laminate for a key chain adornment.
4. Give each child pre-cut key shapes, a key ring, and her laminated photo. Help the children place the key shapes on one end of the key chain and the child's picture at the other end.
5. Punch a hole in the corner of the child's poem and tie the key chain to the card with a pretty ribbon.
6. Have the children give these key chains to their mothers for Mother's Day.

⭐ *Jill Martin and D'Arcy Simmons, Springfield, MO*

# GIVE A HUG CARD

ART

**MATERIALS**
3" x 30" paper strips
colored paper
pencils
glue
scissors

**WHAT TO DO**
- Mother's Day is celebrated on the second Sunday of May.
1. Help the children trace around their hands on colored paper.
2. Help them cut out their paper hands.
3. Have the children glue one hand to each end of a long strip of paper.
4. Give each child a sheet of paper that says, "Here's a big hug for you!" Ask the children to print their names under the sentence, offering help as needed.
5. Glue the paper in the center of the long strip of paper. Fold the paper to make a card.
6. Let children bring the cards home to give their mothers on Mother's Day.

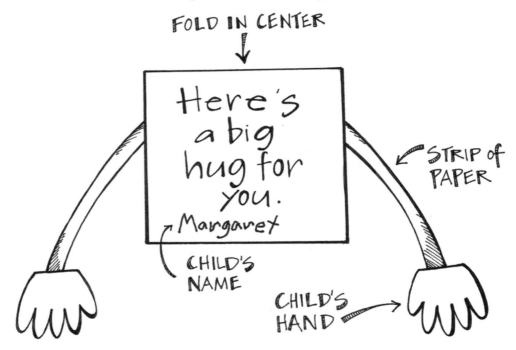

FOLD IN CENTER

Here's a big hug for you.
Margaret

CHILD'S NAME

STRIP OF PAPER

CHILD'S HAND

**MORE TO DO**
Have the children make a similar card for Father's Day.

**RELATED books**
*A Chair for My Mother* by Vera B. Williams
*Momma, Do You Love Me?* by Barbara M. Joosse
*Owly* by Mike Thaler

⭐ *Barbara Saul, Eureka, CA*

# Bath Salts for Mother's Day

ART

**Materials**

clean, empty baby food jars (2.5-ounce size)
gold spray paint
tacky glue
plastic gemstones and pearls
colorful cotton cloth circles
lace or silk ribbon
measuring spoons and cups
perfume
food coloring
Epsom salts
cereal bowls
spoons
tape
colored tissue paper
ribbon
gift tags
bubble wrap

**What to do**

- The second Sunday of May is Mother's Day.
1. Away from the children, spray paint the jar lids gold. Let dry.
2. Help each child follow this recipe. Supervise closely.
   - Measure 2 teaspoons of perfume and pour into a cup.
   - Add 1 drop of child's mother's favorite color (food coloring).
   - Measure ¼ cup of Epsom salts and pour into a bowl.
   - Add perfume and food coloring mixture to the bowl and stir well.
3. Encourage the children to enjoy the scent, color, and texture of this mixture before spooning it into their jars.
4. Provide tacky glue, an assortment of "jewels," 18" lengths of lace or silk ribbon, and 5" cloth circles (cut with pinking sheers).
5. Children can make jeweled lids or cloth lids. If they decide to make jeweled lids, have them glue the jewels on the lids and let dry before adding salts to their jars.
6. Help children spoon the salt mixture into their jars and secure the lids.
7. If a child is using a cloth lid, help her tie a 5" circle in place with a ribbon and make a bow.
8. Help the children wrap their jars in colored tissue paper.

9. Tape bubble wrap around each jar and wrap like a bundle. Add a gift tag designed by the child.

**RELATED BOOK**    *Five Minutes' Peace* by Jill Murphy

 *Susan A. Sharkey, La Mesa, CA*

# A Cookbook For My Mom

LANGUAGE AND LITERACY

**MATERIALS**    measuring cups and spoons
water tubs
paper
crayons

**WHAT TO DO**
- Mother's Day is celebrated on the second Sunday of May.
1. Let the children experiment and play with measuring cups and spoons in tubs of water to become familiar with them. As they are working, discuss the different measuring items, such as cups and teaspoons.
2. Before Mother's Day, discuss with the children all the ways their mothers (or other special person) help them. Mention that one of the things their moms might do for them is cook food. Explain that they will be making their own cookbooks to give to their moms for Mother's Day.
**Note**: Be sensitive to the fact that some children may not have a mother. Be sure to mention other special people in the children's lives, such as grandmothers.
3. Individually ask each child what her mom's favorite food is. Then encourage the child to tell you the recipe for that food, as best as she can. Write down exactly what each child says.
4. Assemble all of the recipes into a cookbook. Design the cover together as a class.
5. Make copies of the cookbook for each child to give his or her mom. Mothers will treasure this forever!

**MORE TO DO**    **Art:** Make a classroom "quilt" for the bulletin board. Ask each child to draw a picture of her favorite food on a 4" x 4" square of paper. Glue each of their pictures to a 5" x 5" square of construction paper. Attach the squares to a bulletin board or a wall in the shape of a quilt. Title it, "Our Favorite Foods!"

*Lori Dunlap, Amarillo, TX*

# Mother's Day Munch Book

## LANGUAGE AND LITERACY

**Materials**
recipe books
copy paper
colored pencils
thin black markers
stapler

**What to do**
- Mother's Day is celebrated on the second Sunday of May.
1. At circle time, ask the group if they know what special day is coming up. Lead them to Mother's Day and talk about the meaning of the holiday. Explain that it is nice to give mothers a gift on that day.
2. Show them a few recipe books. Talk about what they are for and how they are used.
3. Explain that they are going to make their own class recipe book to give to their mothers (or someone special) on Mother's Day.
4. Place the recipe books in the dramatic play area for future play.
5. One by one, ask each child what her mother's favorite food is. Have each child draw a picture of it using colored pencils.
6. Ask each child to dictate how the food is made.
7. Write down their recipes. You will be tickled by the creative ways that young children decide food can be made.
8. When all the children have dictated a recipe, make a cover for the book. It could be called "_____ Class's Mother's Day Munch Book."
9. Make enough copies for each child and staple them into a book.
10. Send the books home for the children to share with their mothers on Mother's Day.

**Related books**  *Let's Cook!* by Robert Crowther
*Let's Make a Cake* by Mary Hill

⭐ *Ann Kelly, Johnstown, PA*

# Mother's Day Chore Coupons

### LANGUAGE AND LITERACY

**Materials**
heart-shaped paper
glitter or stickers

**What to do**
- Mother's Day is celebrated on the second Sunday of May.
1. Give each child three or four pieces of heart-shaped paper.
2. Help them write chores they will do for their mothers on each heart shape. You might have to write for the children, depending on their writing skills.
3. Encourage the children to decorate the hearts with glitter and stickers.

**More to do**
Do the same activity for Father's Day.

*Kathy Kalmar, Macomb, MI*

# Mother's Night

### WORKING WITH FAMILIES

**Materials**
none

**What to do**
1. Have a "Mother's Night" or "Mother's Afternoon" at school. Invite each child to bring his or her mother (or other special person) to school.
2. Set up the classroom just like any other day, and let the children and mothers participate in the activities.
3. Do a circle time activity, an art activity, a sensory activity, and a music activity.
4. Take a lot of pictures throughout the night.
5. Before the event, encourage each child to dictate a story about her mother. For example:
   - My mother makes the best...
   - I love my mom when she...
   - My mom and I play together...
6. Have children draw a portrait of their mothers.
7. Post the stories and portraits all around the room for Mother's Night so the moms can read them.

*Holly Dzierzanowski, Brenham, TX*

# Japanese Fish Kite

ART

**Materials**

tagboard
scissors
pencils
butcher paper
paint
paintbrushes
glue
string

**What to do**

● Kite Day is May 12th. This is also a good activity to do in March (Kite Month) or on June 15th (Fly a Kite Day).

1. Before the activity, cut out fish patterns from tagboard for children to trace.
2. Give each child a piece of butcher paper folded in half. Demonstrate how to trace a fish pattern on the folded paper to make two identical fish.
3. Ask the children to cut out the matching fish.
4. Demonstrate how to glue the two fish together, leaving the mouth and tail unglued.
5. Have them paint one side of the fish and let it dry. Then have them paint the other side and let it dry.
6. Attach a string to the mouth of each fish.
7. Take the kites outside and have the children run, holding their kite's string.

FISH PATTERN (TRACE TWO)

GLUE AROUND EDGES

LEAVE OPEN

LEAVE OPEN

STRING

DECORATE

**More to do**

**Science:** Introduce the children to the wind by illustrating the movement of air when flying a kite.

**Related books**

*Can You See the Wind?* by Allan Fowler
*I Face the Wind* by Vicki Cobb
*The Kite* by Mary Packard
*Weather: Poems for All Seasons* by Lee Bennett Hopkins

 *Elizabeth Thomas, Hobart, IN*

# Armed Forces Drive

SOCIAL DEVELOPMENT

**Materials**

poster board
paper
markers
art supplies
copier

**What to do**

- Armed Forces Day is May 21st.
1. Invite a member of your local military or police personnel to come in and talk to the children.
2. Encourage questions, especially about what the military men and women who are around the world would like sent to them.
3. Make a list of the items mentioned.
4. Talk about a collecting the items on the list.
5. Encourage the children to design posters and flyers. Help them write the words necessary for advertising. Place the posters around the school and send copies of the flyers home to families.
6. Gather the donations, package them, and send them with notes from the children. Hopefully, you will get correspondence back to share with the children.

★ *Ann Kelly, Johnstown, PA*

# Repeat Week

PROJECT

**Materials**

**What to do**

1. At the end of May, show the children all of the photos that were taken of them throughout the year (in the classroom, outdoors, on field trips, and so on).
2. Talk about how they will be going to kindergarten (or pre-k or first grade) soon, and ask the children what activities they liked the best.
3. During the last week or two of June, re-do those activities with the children during "repeat week."
4. If the children want to repeat an activity from September, try to bump up the difficulty level a little bit. For example, if there is cutting involved, have the children do it themselves.

 *Linda Ford, Sacramento, CA*

# JUNE

# Fuzzy Little Caterpillar

ART

**MATERIALS**

flexible magnetic strip, ½" wide
scissors
¾" pompoms
plastic bowl
30-gauge cloth-covered florist wire (olive green, black, or white)
white glue
4 mm wiggle eyes

**WHAT TO DO**

1. Cut magnetic strip into 3" lengths and give one to each child. Have them remove the protective paper.
2. Put yellow, green, orange, white, black, tan, lime green, brown, and purple pompoms in a plastic bowl.
3. Cut cloth wire into 2" lengths and give one to each child.
4. Show the children how to bend the cloth wire in the middle and down on the ends to resemble drooping antennas.
5. Ask children to put five drops of white glue on the magnetic strip.
6. Let the children choose five pompoms, any color, and attach them to their strips.
7. When dry, have them glue antennas to the back of the fifth pompom. Add wiggle eyes as well.
8. When the caterpillars are dry, have the children attach them to a refrigerator, metal table, or metal magnet board.

SPOTS of WHITE GLUE

←— 3" MAGNETIC —→
STRIP

5 ¾" POMPOMS

**MORE TO DO**

**Art:** Encourage the children to paint a caterpillar on paper.
**Math:** Stick several caterpillars on a magnet board and ask the children to count them.
**Science:** Show pictures of various caterpillars and discuss.

**RELATED BOOK**

*The Very Hungry Caterpillar* by Eric Carle

⭐ *Mary Brehm, Aurora, OH*

# CRAYON RESIST OCEAN MURAL

ART

**MATERIALS**
white mural paper
crayons
watered-down watercolor or tempera paints
large paintbrushes

**WHAT TO DO**
1. Help the children draw seaweed, fish, coral, sharks, turtles, lobsters, and other ocean life on a large piece of mural paper. Encourage them to use bright colors and press firmly with wax crayons.
2. When completed, let the children paint over the entire mural with watered-down blue paint.

**MORE TO DO**
**Field Trip:** Visit an aquarium or a pet shop.
**Science:** Put a table, shelf, or indoor sandbox in front of the mural. Encourage the children to bring in shells, seaweed, sea glass, sea stars, and so on to make an ocean museum display.

**RELATED BOOKS**
*Fish Is Fish* by Leo Lionni
*Swimmy* by Leo Lionni

⭐ *Linda Atamian, Charlestown, RI*

# SHINING SEA STENCILS

ART

**MATERIALS**
crayons
paper
Styrofoam grocery trays
Exacto knife (adult only)
fingerpaint paper
water
paint smocks
blue and yellow fingerpaint
shallow trays
paintbrushes

**What to do**

1. Ask the children to draw simple fish outlines on paper. Use their outlines to create stencils by placing their drawings in Styrofoam trays and cutting out the fish using an Exacto knife (adult only).
2. Spray water on the tables and put fingerpaint paper shiny side up. Put a dollop of blue fingerpaint in the center of each dampened paper.
3. Help the children put on paint smocks.
4. Encourage them to cover their paper with the paint, using both hands and not just their fingertips. When they have spread the blue paint all the way to the edges, add a small amount of yellow in different places on different papers for variety. Explain to the children that since the ocean is many different shades of blue and green, their pictures will look more realistic if they spread the yellow around to look like a water current rather than covering the whole paper with the yellow paint. Allow to dry.
5. Return the dried paintings to the children. Ask them to color a dark area near the lower edge to resemble the ocean floor.
6. Pour bright colors of paint into shallow containers. Demonstrate how to position a fish stencil over the painting and brush on the paint to create a fish. Encourage the children to use different stencils and different colors of paint to create a "school" of fish.

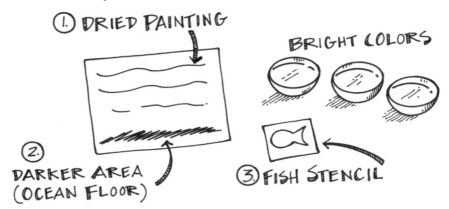

**More to do**

Put the fish stencils in the art area for children to use.
**More Art:** Repeat the fingerpainting experience another day, using a combination of red and blue to produce purple and yellow and red to produce orange.
**Math:** Cut out 11 fish from tagboard, write the numerals 0-10 on each one, and ask the children to put them in order.
**Music:** Sing "Down By the Bay."
**Sand Table:** Provide a variety of seashells for children to find and compare.
**Snack:** Give the children blue fruit drink and fish crackers.

**Related books**

*At the Beach* by Anne Rockwell
*Little Blue and Little Yellow* by Leo Lionni
*The Rainbow Fish* by Marcus Pfister

⭐ *Susan Oldham Hill, Lakeland, FL*

# Five Little Peas

FINGERPLAYS, SONGS, & POEMS

**Materials**      none

**What to do**     Do the following fingerplay with the children.

**Five Little Peas**
*Five little peas in a peapod pressed.* (make fist)
*One grew,* (raise one finger)
*Two grew,* (raise another finger)
*So did all the rest.* (nod)
*They grew and they grew,* (look surprised)
*They did not stop* (shake head no)
*Until one day when they all went POP!* (clap)

 *Kathy Kalmar, Macomb, MI*

# The Fish

FINGERPLAYS, SONGS, & POEMS

**Materials**      none

**What to do**     Sing the following song, making the appropriate gestures when prompted.

**The Fish**
*I hold my fingers like a fish,* (put hands together in prayer position sideways)
*I wave them as I go.* (wave hands back and forward in prayer position)
*See them swimming with a swish* (swish hands)
*So swiftly to and fro.*

 *Kathy Kalmar, Macomb, MI*

# I'm a Little Fish

FINGERPLAYS, SONGS, & POEMS

**Materials**  none

**What to do**  Sing the following song to the tune of "I'm a Little Teapot."

*I'm a little fish with great big fins,* (flap extended arms)
*I swish them around when I want to swim.*
*When I want to breathe I flap my gills,* (place hands on sides of mouth and
    move them back and forth)
*And I wave hello with a flip of my tail.* (wiggle your "tail")

 *Kristi Larson, Spirit Lake, IA*

# This Little Fox

FINGERPLAYS, SONGS, & POEMS

**Materials**  none

**What to do**  Sing the following song, making the appropriate gestures when prompted.

**This Little Fox**
*This little fox went through the forest* (raise thumb)
*This little fox stayed home* (raise index finger)
*This little fox ate berries* (raise next finger)
*This little fox had none* (raise next finger)
*This little fox ran far away from everyone!* (raise pinky finger)

**More to do**  **Science:** Cut out animals and their homes (nest, tree, log, pond, and so on) from felt. Have the children match each animal to its home.

 *Kathy Kalmar, Macomb, MI*

# Here's My Turtle

FINGERPLAYS, SONGS, & POEMS

**Materials**        none

**What to do**       Do the following fingerplay with the children.

*Here's my turtle* (point to fist)
*Here's his shell* (tap fist)
*He likes his home very well.* (nod yes)
*He pokes his head out* (poke thumb out of fist)
*When he wants to eat.*
*He pulls it back in* (bring thumb back to fist)
*When he wants to sleep.*

 *Kathy Kalmar, Macomb, MI*

# Insects All Around

FINGERPLAYS, SONGS, & POEMS

**Materials**        none

**What to do**       Sing the following song to the tune of "Twinkle, Twinkle, Little Star."

*Ladybugs and butterflies,*
*Buzzing bees up in the sky,*
*Teeny tiny little ants*
*Crawling up and down the plants.*
*Many insects can be found*
*In the sky and on the ground.*

**More to do**       Substitute caterpillars and beetles for ladybugs and ants.

 *Kathy Kalmar, Macomb, MI*

# The Caterpillar

FINGERPLAYS, SONGS, & POEMS

**Materials**       none

**What to do**      Do the following fingerplay with the children.

*"Let's go to sleep," the little caterpillar said.* (wiggle index finger)
*And she tucked herself into bed* (wrap other fingers around index finger)
*Soon she will awaken, by and by* (nod yes)
*And turn into a lovely butterfly.* (join hands at thumbs and flutter)

**More to do**      **Art:** Crumble tissue paper into a clothespin to look like a butterfly. Add pipe cleaner antennae.

⭐ *Kathy Kalmar, Macomb, MI*

# Two Little Rabbits

FINGERPLAYS, SONGS, & POEMS

**Materials**       none

**What to do**      1. Have the children hold both their hands up in front of them, extending their first two fingers, while holding down the other two with their thumbs. This makes the shape of a rabbit's head.

2. Encourage the children to recite the following rhyme, and make the appropriate corresponding hand movements.

*Two little rabbits sitting on a bank.* (hold up both hands, two fingers for ears)
*One named Sally* (left hand "rabbit" bows at its name)
*And one named Frank.* (right hand "rabbit" bows at its name)
*Jump down, Sally!* (put left hand behind back)
*Jump down, Frank!* (put right hand behind back)
*No little rabbits sitting on a bank.* (shake head sadly)
*Jump back, Sally!* (left hand comes out from behind back)
*Jump back, Frank!* (right hand comes out from behind back)
*Two little rabbits sitting on a bank.* (happy smile)

**More to do**    Draw a rabbit face on the backs of the children's hands with non-allergenic face paints, especially for parents to see.
**Literacy:** Explain to children that in this song, a bank isn't a place to get money, but a grassy mound where rabbits feed and play.
**Science:** Talk about rabbit burrows and warrens and how rabbits live. Explain the difference between rabbits and hares.

**Related books**    *Dinnertime!* by Sue Williams
*Guess How Much I Love You* by Sam McBratney
*Listen! Peter Rabbit* by Beatrix Potter

 *Anne Adeney, Plymouth, United Kingdom*

# Gone Fishing

MATH

**Materials**    colored construction paper
scissors
hole punch
play fishing rod
sand pail

**What to do**    1. Cut out nine fish from construction paper. Write a number on each fish (1 through 9).
2. Lay the fish on a table.
3. Read the following rhyming story:

*It did not take so very long*
*Before I caught number 1.*
*Then on my hook hung something blue,*
*What a surprise, 'twas number 2.*
*What a lucky day for me.*
*I also caught number 3.*
*I wondered now—could there be more?*
*Just then I caught number 4.*
*Sailing by was Captain Hive*
*When I reeled in number 5.*
*In the shade slept my dog, Sticks.*
*He never saw me catch number 6.*
*I took a rest, looked up to heaven,*
*Just waiting for number 7.*
*Then it got dark and very late.*
*By then I'd caught number 8.*

*And then...and then...this is real fine,*
*At last, I caught big number 9.*

4. Select a different child to put each number on the hook of a play fishing rod as you come to them in the story.
5. Remove each fish and put it in a pail so the next fish can be hung on the hook.

⭐ *Ingelore Mix, Gainesville, VA*

# MEASURE UP

MATH

**Materials**
growth chart
register receipt paper
3" paper circles

**What to do**
1. Hang a growth chart on a wall and measure each child. Using cash register paper, tear off a length equal to each child's height.
2. Give each child a pre-cut 3" paper circle.
3. Encourage them to draw faces on their circles and attach them to their register tape "bodies."
4. If desired, do this activity in the fall (beginning of school) and in late spring (end of school). Encourage the children to compare their fall "bodies" and their spring "bodies" or compare their heights with classmates.

3" PAPER CIRCLE

CASH REGISTER PAPER →

**More to do**
**Blocks:** Challenge the children to build a Lego or block tower as high as their heads.
**Math:** Let the children practice measuring things in the room.

**Related book**
*Inchworm and a Half* by Elinor J. Pinczes

**Related music**
"I Wonder If I'm Growing," *Singable Songs for the Very Young* by Raffi

⭐ *Linda Ford, Sacramento, CA*

# John Jacob Jingleheimer Swing!

OUTDOOR PLAY

**Materials**   none

**What to do**   Keep children occupied while waiting for a turn to swing by singing this version of "John Jacob Jingleheimer Schmidt."

*John Jacob Jingleheimer Schmidt*
*His name is _____ (child's name) too.*
*Whenever _____ (child's name) wants to swing,*
*The people always sing,*
*There goes John Jacob Jingleheimer Schmidt!*
*Tra la-la-la-la-la-la!*

 *Karyn F. Everham, Fort Myers, FL*

# Alphabet Party

PROJECTS

**Materials**
alphabet decorations
cutouts of letter shapes
magazines
glue
paper
scissors
foam letters
alphabet books
playdough
alphabet cookies and pretzels

**What to do**
1. This is a great activity to do at the end of the year after you have gone over the entire alphabet. Celebrate the alphabet with an alphabet party of centers!
2. About a week before the alphabet party, send home a note asking that children wear clothes with letters on them on the specific day.
3. Before the children arrive, decorate the classroom with all kinds of alphabet decorations.

4. In the art area, provide alphabet letter cutouts for children to make picture-sound collages.

5. In the literacy center, have children pick one letter and find pictures in magazines that begin with that sound (for example, couch, cat, and car).

6. Set up an alphabet reading center with alphabet books.

7. Play musical alphabet (like musical chairs) using foam alphabet letters for children to stand on. Play music and as you stop the music, call out a letter. See if the children can recognize the letter they are standing on. Play the game without removing any letters so that all the children can continue playing.

8. At the sensory table, encourage the children to form each of the alphabet letters with the playdough.

9. Provide alphabet pretzels and cookies for snack. Encourage the children to use the alphabet foods to spell out their names. Use the pretzel and cookie letters to distinguish the beginning sounds of words.

10. End the party by reading one of the alphabet books.

⭐ *Quazonia J. Quarles, Newark, DE*

# CREEPY CRAWLIES

SCIENCE

**MATERIALS**
several aquariums with tight-fitting screen lids
bugs (caterpillars, crickets, meal worms, and so on)

**WHAT TO DO**

1. Do some research about the bugs you intend to keep in the classroom.

2. Let children help decorate each aquarium to suit the bugs it will house. For example, earthworms need loose soil, some organic material for food, and an occasional light shower of "rain." They also need to be kept out of sunlight. A few small plants and stones could be used for decoration.

3. Introduce the bugs to the children. Explain what each bug eats and if it will turn into something else. For example, meal worms change into beetles and caterpillars turn into butterflies.

4. Encourage the children to make observations about the bugs each day.

5. Keep the bugs for the whole month or until metamorphosis is complete.

6. Release the bugs in a suitable environment.

⭐ *Amelia Griffin, Ontario, Canada*

# Vegetable Garden

SCIENCE

**Materials**   plot of land or bins of soil
shovels and rakes (size depends on if you are inside or outside)
hose or watering can
vegetable seedlings
plant markers
books or pictures about gardens
rulers

**What to do**
1. Introduce the concept of a vegetable garden to the children.
2. Talk about the children's experiences with home gardens, show pictures, and encourage questions.
3. Have seedlings (preferably grown by the children, but may be purchased) and other supplies ready at the plot.
4. Bring small groups of children to the garden whether it is indoors or outdoors.
5. Have each child choose a seedling to plant and give each child a marker that matches the plant.
6. Call the children by plant type and give them a ruler. Explain that all like plants should be planted in the same area of the garden and that their plants need to be 1' (ruler length) away from their classmate's plants.
7. Encourage the children to work out where their plants will go and claim their spots with a marker. (You may decide to put children's names on the markers as well or make this a community garden that everyone can be proud of.)
8. Provide the shovels and assist the children with the transplanting.
9. Don't forget to water the plants.
10. Have the children tend to the garden regularly—weeding, raking, watering, pruning, and finally picking. Eat the food as it is available or make vegetable soup with the children.

**Related books**   *Garden Animals* by Lucy Cousins
*Growing Vegetable Soup* by Lois Ehlert
*Inch by Inch: The Garden Song* by David Mallett
*Our Community Garden* by Barbara Pollack

⭐ *Ann Kelly, Johnstown, PA*

# Safety Rocks

ART

**Materials**
red poster board
scissors
marker
small rocks (one for each child)
red permanent marker
zipper-closure plastic bags

**What to do**

- June is National Safety Month.
1. Cut out a large red stop sign shape.
2. At the end of a unit on safety, invite the children to help make a list of rules to remember when they go out to play to stay safe. Write the rules on the stop sign shape.
3. Some rules could include:
   - Cross the street with a grown-up.
   - Do not talk to strangers.
   - Stay away from fire and matches.
   - Wear a helmet when riding a bike.
4. Draw a red heart on each rock. Tell the children that the heart represents the people who love them and want them to stay safe. The red means to stop and think before they do something, to make sure it is safe.
5. Put each rock in a zipper-closure bag for children to take home.
6. Put the following note inside each bag:
   *Put the rock inside your pocket*
   *When you go to play.*
   *The heart says to remember the rules*
   *And stay safe every day.*

**Related books**    *I Read Signs* by Tana Hoban
*Street Safety Hints* by Giovanni Caviezel

 *Sue Fleischmann, Sussex, WI*

# Red Light, Green Light

GAMES

**Materials**
black poster board
red, green, and yellow cellophane
scissors
tape
flashlight

**What to do**
- This activity is great to do during June, which is National Safety Month.
1. Cut a piece of black poster board in half lengthwise so that it is shaped like a traffic light.
2. Cut out three holes large enough to shine a flashlight through.
3. Cover the three holes with cellophane—red on top, yellow in the middle, and green on the bottom.
4. Hang from the ceiling, from a chart holder, or on an easel. Make sure nothing is behind it.
5. Clear the room for movement.
6. Gather the children, turn out the lights, and explain that they are going to play a game of Red Light, Green Light.
7. Encourage them to pretend to be cars driving around the room. Explain that when you shine a flashlight through the green cellophane, they should GO, the yellow cellophane means SLOW DOWN, and the red cellophane means STOP.
8. Play the game in this manner, shining the flashlight through the different cellophane circles. Once they get the hang of it, vary the speed and go from green to red to yellow to green, and so on.

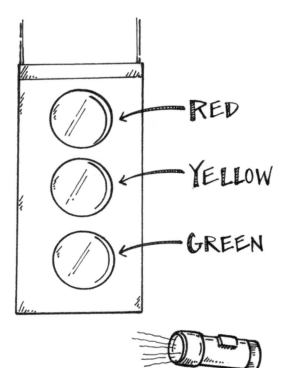

HANG FROM CEILING

→ RED

→ YELLOW

→ GREEN

**More to do**   **Art:** Place circle sponges and green, yellow, and red paint in the art area.
**Blocks:** Add traffic lights and cars to the block area.
**Dramatic Play:** Put safety vests and stop signs in the dramatic play area.
**Science:** Place colored cellophane and flashlights in the science area.

**Related book**   *Ready for Red* by Candace Whitman

⭐ *Shelley Hoster, Norcross, GA*

# Classroom Colors

ART

**Materials**
American flag
state flag
pictures of other flags
maps
construction paper
paint
glue
fabric scraps
glitter

**What to do**
- Flag Day is June 14th.
1. Show the children an American flag. Ask if they know what it is and what it is for.
2. Introduce the vocabulary word "symbol." Explain that the American flag is a symbol for the United States of America.
3. Continue a discussion about flags. Show pictures of different flags and maps showing the countries, states, and so on that the flags symbolize.
4. Provide art supplies and encourage the children to create a flag for their home or the classroom.
5. Display the flags proudly in the classroom.

**More to do**
Have the group vote on a flag to be a symbol for their classroom. Hang the chosen flag in a place of honor, such as at the entrance to the room or next to the American flag. Chart the votes so the children have a visual count of their votes. Help the children tally the votes by counting together. Write each total down so they can see written numbers, and use words such as "more" and "less" when discussing the results.

**Related book**   *Meet Our Flag, Old Glory* by April Prince

*Ann Kelly, Johnstown, PA*

# Flag Day Riddle

### FINGERPLAYS, SONGS, & POEMS

**Materials**   none

**What to do**   • Flag Day is June 14th.
Encourage the children to solve the following riddle:

*I'm red, blue, and white.*
*I have stars and stripes.*
*You wave me but not at night.*
*What am I?*

**More to do**   **Literacy:** Make a riddle book asking children to make up their own riddles. Put it in your classroom's book center.

⭐ *Kathy Kalmar, Macomb, MI*

# Wave the Flag

### FINGERPLAYS, SONGS, & POEMS

**Materials**   small American flag

**What to do**   • June 14th is Flag Day. The week in which Flag Day occurs is National Flag Week.
1. Recite the following rhymes, modeling each line's appropriate action.
2. Have the children practice the rhymes several times.

**Wave the Flag**
*Wave the flag high,* (wave a small flag or hands in the air)
*Up to the sky,* (point to the sky)
*Red, white and blue,* (show one finger for red, two for white, three for blue)
*We salute you.* (put right hand over the heart)

**See Our Flag** (Tune: "Farmer in the Dell")
*See our flag wave*
*In the land of the brave,*
*Red, white, and blue,*
*To our country we are true.*

**MORE TO DO**  **Art:** Have the children make copies of the original American flag. Give each child a 4" x 6" piece of white paper with a square in the upper left-hand corner and 13 uncolored stripes. Starting at the top, have the children color every other stripe red and the square blue. Give them 13 silver adhesive stars to place on the blue square. Help the children tape a craft stick to the backs of the flags for a flagpole.

**More Art:** Have children cut out pictures of red, white, and blue food from old magazines and use them to make collages.

**RELATED BOOKS**  *The American Flag* by Joseph Ferry
*F Is for Flag* by Wendy Cheyette Lewison
*Flag Day* by Kelly Bennett
*The Flag Maker* by Susan Campbell Bartoletti
*The Flag We Love* by Pam Munoz Ryan
*Red, White & Blue: The Story of the American Flag* by John Herman

⭐ *Christina R. Chilcote, New Freedom, PA*

# Flag Day

PROJECTS

**MATERIALS**  American flag
poster of international flags
8" x 11" white paper
crayons or markers
firmly rolled newspaper

**WHAT TO DO**
- Flag Day is June 14th.
1. Explain that Flag Day is the "birthday" of the American flag. Tell the story of Betsy Ross and the making of the American flag.
2. Examine the American flag with the children. Discuss its colors, number of stripes, number of stars, and what these things stand for.
3. Show the children pictures of flags from other countries, explaining that each country has a flag of its own.
4. Let each child make a flag similar to those on display. Sketch the design of each child's chosen flag on a piece of paper, and let the children copy the colors of the example flags.
5. Write the name of the country on the back of each child's flag and staple to a newspaper "flagpole."
6. On a map or globe, show each child the country whose flag he has chosen to draw. Ask questions about the countries. Is it big or small? Near water? Close to the United States?

7. When all the children have learned the names of their countries, have them introduce themselves to the children by saying, in turn, "I am a child from Ireland," or "I am a child from Greece."
8. Play the song "It's a Small World" and have a grand flag-waving parade around the room!

**RELATED books** *Everybody Cooks Rice* by Norah Dooley
*Lon Po-Po* by Ed Young

⭐ *Iris Rothstein, New Hyde Park, NY*

# MONA LISA SMILES

ART

**MATERIALS**

pictures of famous paintings
copy machine
glue
file cards
laminating machine (optional)
magnetic tape

**WHAT TO dO**

● Father's Day is the third Sunday in June.
1. Reduce pictures of famous paintings to about 2" x 3".
2. Glue the small pictures to file cards and trim. Laminate.
3. Give each child a picture and a piece of magnetic tape. Ask them to put the tape on the backs of their pictures.
4. Read stories about the painters of the works you've used.

5. Encourage the children to paint a picture using the same colors as the paintings.

6. Have the children give these refrigerator magnets and paintings as Father's Day gifts.

**More to do**    **Field Trip:** Take a trip to a local art museum, or ask a local painter to come in and talk about art.

**Related book**    *Leonardo and the Flying Boy* by Laurence Anholt

⭐ *Barbara Saul, Eureka, CA*

# Father's Day Bookmarks

ART

**Materials**
colorful poster board
scissors
variety of stickers
small pictures cut from greeting cards
glue sticks
markers and crayons
clear contact paper
yarn
hole punch

**What to do**
• Father's Day is the third Sunday of June.

1. Cut poster board into bookmark size. Place bookmarks, scissors, stickers, small pictures, glue sticks, and markers on a table for the children.

2. Let the children decorate bookmarks using the materials.

3. When they are finished, help them cover their bookmarks with clear contact paper to ensure that materials will stay.

4. Punch a hole in a corner of each bookmark so the children can tie tassels.

5. Help the children make tassels by gathering several pieces of yarn together and tying them together at one end. Knot to the hole in the bookmark.

6. Let the children bring the bookmarks home to give to their fathers (or other special adults) on Father's Day.

⭐ *Penni Smith, Riverside, CA*

# Dad's Night

WORKING WITH FAMILIES

**Materials**   none

**What to do**

- Father's Day is the third Sunday of June.
1. Invite the children to bring their father or other special male to school for a "Dad's Night."
2. Before the event, have the children dictate stories about their dads/special males. Help the children think of ideas, for example:
    - My father (uncle, grandpa, stepdad, etc.) makes the best...
    - I love it when my father...
    - My father and I play together...
3. Ask the children to draw a portrait of their dads or special males.
4. Post the stories and portraits around the room so the dads/special males can read them. This gives the parents a chance to see what their children do in the classroom and the children a chance to show their parents what they do at school.
5. Set up the classroom just like any other day. Encourage the children and their fathers/special males to participate in the activities together.
6. Do a circle time activity, an art activity (such as having the father and child paint at the easel together), a sensory activity, and a quick music activity.
7. Take a lot of pictures throughout the night.
8. Help the children make a book about the event and send the books home as a gift for the parents.

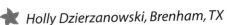 *Holly Dzierzanowski, Brenham, TX*

# July/August

# SAND BUCKET AND SHOVEL

ART

**MATERIALS**    white oak tag
crayons
scissors
yarn
small cup
clean sand
sturdy, shallow box
crayons
watercolor paint and paintbrush
white glue

**WHAT TO DO**
1. Draw a shovel and bucket on white oak tag and cut out. Make one for each child.
2. Cut a 10" length of yarn for each child.
3. Put sand in a small cup with a pouring spout. Have a shallow box nearby.
4. Encourage the children to draw decorations on their paper shovels and buckets with crayons.
5. Invite the children to paint their sand buckets and shovels with pastels and watercolors, going down the bucket in a rainbow fashion.
6. Ask them to cover the center of their sand bucket with white glue.
7. Help the children pour clean sand over the glue on their sand buckets (hold over the sturdy box).
8. Help each child tie the handle of her shovel to the handle of her sand bucket with yarn.

SAND WITH GLUE

DECORATE

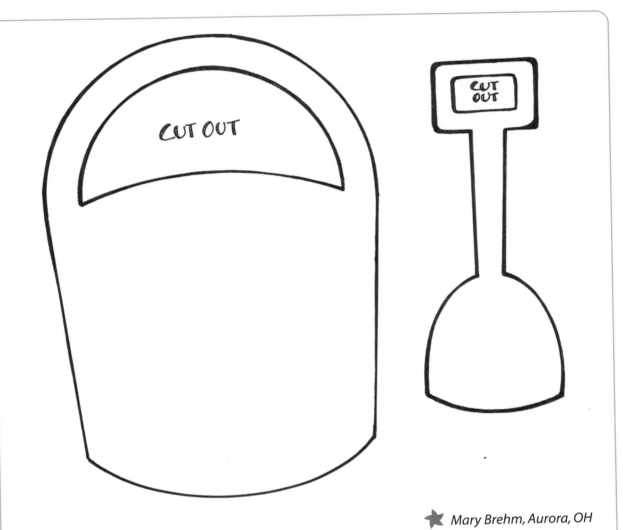

CUT OUT

CUT
OUT

CUT
OUT

⭐ *Mary Brehm, Aurora, OH*

# Stand-Up Sailboat

ART

**Materials**

oak tag for pattern
pencil
scissors
12" x 18" white paper
markers
white glue

**What to do**

1. Draw and cut out a basic sailboat pattern on oak tag.
2. Fold 12" x 18" paper in half.
3. Help the children trace the sailboat on a piece of folded paper, with the fold below the bottom of boat.
4. Have them cut out the double shape, making sure not to cut along the fold.

5. Encourage them to color and decorate their sailboats with markers.

6. Have them color the water blue. Ask them to color their boats and water the same on the reverse side.

7. Invite them to glue the two flags together and attach at the point of the sail.

8. Demonstrate how to fold up the white area below the water to form a base for the boat to stand on.

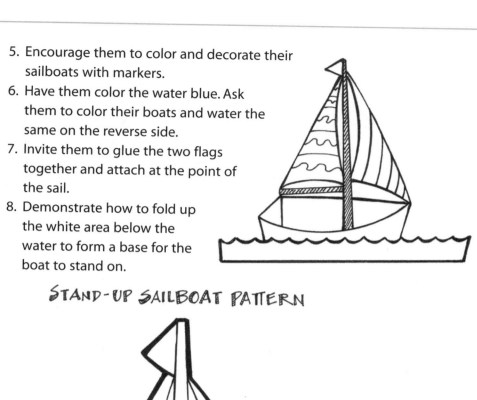

## STAND-UP SAILBOAT PATTERN

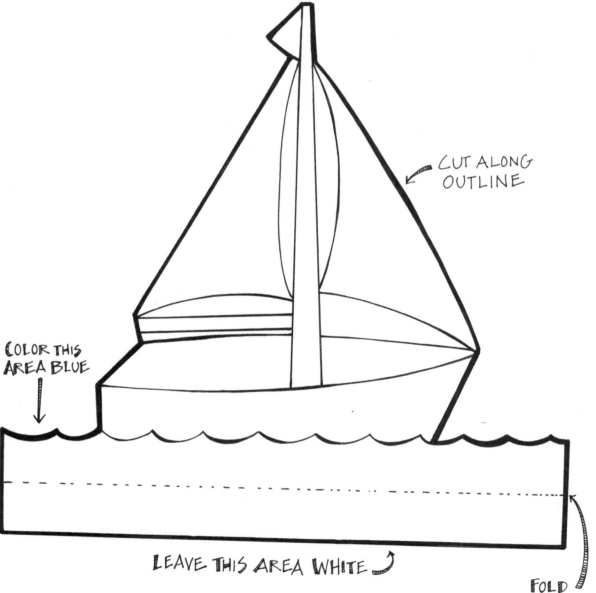

CUT ALONG OUTLINE

COLOR THIS AREA BLUE

LEAVE THIS AREA WHITE

FOLD

**More to do**   Invite the children to bring toy boats from home and have a boat show.
**Dramatic Play:** Put sailor hats in the dress-up area.
**Group or Circle Time:** Show the children examples of different boats, including rowboats, pirate ships, cruise boats, freighters, sailboats, and so on. Discuss what makes ships move.

 *Mary Brehm, Aurora, OH*

# "Stained Glass" Starfish
ART

**Materials**   newspaper
liquid starch
small containers
wax paper
tissue paper (red, brown, orange, yellow, and purple)
scissors
paintbrushes
9" x 12" black construction paper
tagboard starfish patterns (about 7")
glue
jumbo paper clips
crayons

**What to do**   1. Discuss starfish with the children. Show pictures, if available.
2. Spread newspaper over the tables and pour starch into small containers. Cut wax paper into 8" squares and colored tissue paper into 1" squares.
3. Give each child an 8" wax paper square. Demonstrate how to paint starch on half of the square and then cover the area with tissue squares.
4. Encourage the children to paint starch on their wax paper squares and then overlap tissue squares to cover all of the painted area.
5. Have them repeat with the other half of the wax paper.
6. When all the tissue squares have been added, encourage them to paint over the entire surface with starch to seal the tissue squares.
7. While the tissue is drying, give each child two pieces of black paper attached together with a paper clip.
8. Show the children how to trace the starfish pattern with a yellow crayon on the black paper.
9. With adult scissors, poke a small hole on the inside of the starfish outline and cut out the center portion of both sheets of paper, leaving an outline of the starfish (adult only).

10. Return the dry wax paper to the children. Show them how to slip it between the two sheets of black paper and position it so that all the tissue squares can be seen through the opening.

11. Help them glue or staple the three layers together, making sure the wax paper is securely attached.

12. Display the finished starfish on a window so the sunlight will filter through, making them glow.

STARFISH PATTERN

**MORE TO DO**    **Group or Circle Time:** Compare the starfish with stars such as the star of Bethlehem, the stars on the American flag, the Star of David, and so on.
**Snack:** Slice star fruit for a star-shaped treat.

**RELATED book**    *At the Beach* by Anne Rockwell

 *Susan Oldham Hill, Lakeland, FL*

# SEA SCENES

ART

**Materials**
A House for Hermit Crab by Eric Carle
fingerpaint
paper
tagboard outlines of fish
rubber cement or glue sticks
colored pens

**What to do**
1. Read A House for Hermit Crab to show the children how the author (Eric Carle) illustrated the book by using cutouts of fingerpaint drawings to make collages.
2. Give each child a piece of painting paper. Write their names on the back of their paper.
3. Invite the children to choose precut fish outlines for their paintings.
4. Help the children place their cutouts on their paper and glue them in place.
5. Give each child about ¼ cup of fingerpaint. Encourage them to paint all over their paper and fish cutout. After about five minutes, ask them to paint wavy lines on their papers.

WAVY LINES

CHILD'S NAME ON BACK

6. As soon as they are done, remove the fish from each child's paper. This should leave the paper white where the fish was.
7. When dry, have the children use pens to make fish eyes and scales.

FISH SHAPES

**Related book**    Swimmy by Leo Leoni

★ Barbara Saul, Eureka, CA

# UNDER THE SEA

ART

**Materials**
heavy duty art paper
watercolors
watercolor brushes
cups of water
paper towels and sponges
crayons

**What to do**
1. Encourage the children to draw an underwater scene with crayons. Make sure they press the colors firmly on their paper.
2. Have them dip the brushes into water and squeeze a drop of water into each watercolor they will use.
3. Encourage them to mix the water into the paint.
4. Show them how to wet their paper with sponges. While the paper is still wet, ask them to brush blue paint over the scene, using broad, sideways strokes.
5. When the watercolor dries, the picture will look like an underwater scene.

**Related books**
*Little Clam* by Lynn Reiser
*The Rainbow Fish* by Marcus Pfister

*Barbara Saul, Eureka, CA*

# Make Leis

ART

**Materials**
pictures of leis
green construction paper
Styrofoam packing peanuts
plastic embroidery needles
string
tree branch
empty coffee can
sand

**What to do**
1. Show the children pictures of people wearing leis. Explain that leis are a sign of love, welcome, honor, and joy.
2. Provide Styrofoam packing peanuts and strips of green construction paper.
3. Help children alternately string packing peanuts and strips of green paper to make leis.
4. Place a tree branch in a coffee can filled half way with sand. Store leis on the branches until your luau!

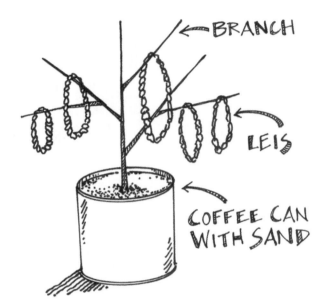

**More to do**  Provide cutout paper flowers instead of packing peanuts.

⭐ *Kathy Kalmar, Macomb, MI*

# Hula Skirts

ART

**Materials**  yarn
green bulletin board paper
scissors

**What to do**
1. Fold green paper over yarn to make a waistband.
2. Draw a line 6" from the waistband. This is a no-cut line.
3. Encourage the child to cut the paper in thin strips several times, stopping at the no-cut line.

4. Wrap the skirt on the child, and tie with yarn. Make sure the hula skirt is more like an apron than a skirt so it doesn't rip in the back when the child sits.
5. Encourage the children to move and dance to "hula" music.

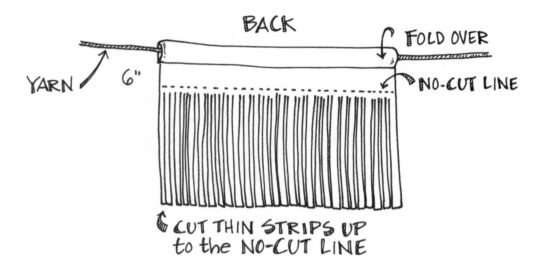

⭐ *Kathy Kalmar, Macomb, MI*

# Once I Had a Seagull

FINGERPLAYS, SONGS, & POEMS

**Materials**     none

**What to do**     Do the following rhyme with the children:

*Once I had a seagull,* (extend arms, flap slowly)
*And he flew and flew and flew* (flap arms gently)
*Until he found some driftwood,* (make hand go to eyes)
*Where he rested as long as he could.* (land "gull" on forearm; nod yes)

⭐ *Kathy Kalmar, Macomb, MI*

# The Hermit Crab
### FINGERPLAYS, SONGS, & POEMS

**Materials**    none

**What to do**

1. Read the following action rhyme and model the motions for the children.

   *A shy little fellow,*
   *In his shell tucked tight.* (wrap arms around self)
   *He's very, very careful*
   *When he comes out in the light.* (step very slowly forward a few steps)
   *Pick him up and hold him*
   *On your palm; keep it flat!* (mimic placing hermit crab on flat palm)
   *Slowly he'll stick his legs out* (stick out one finger of the opposite hand)
   *And tickle you—just like that!* (gently rub flat palm with extended finger)

2. Repeat the action rhyme as desired so the children can use the motions again.

**More to do**    **Art:** Give each child a seashell (or an outlined picture of one). Encourage the children to decorate their shells with crayons and glue on sequins, bits of colored paper, or other decorations. This activity goes well with the book *A House for Hermit Crab*.
**Science:** Bring in a real hermit crab, if possible. Many seaside shops and pet stores have these very easy-to-care for creatures.

**Related book**    *A House for Hermit Crab* by Eric Carle

 *Theresa Callahan, Easton, MD*

# Lightning Bugs
### FINGERPLAYS, SONGS, & POEMS

**Materials**    pictures of fireflies and beetles

**What to do**

1. Explain to the children that fireflies are not flies at all, but are actually beetles.
2. Compare fireflies to other types of beetles.

3. Sing the following song about fireflies to the tune of "Did You Ever See a Lassie?"

**Did You Ever See a Lightning Bug?**
*Did you ever see a lightning bug,*
*A lightning bug, a lightning bug?*
*Did you ever see a lightning bug flying in the night?*
*He goes blink, blink. He goes blink, blink.*
*Did you ever see a lightning bug flying in the night?*

*Did you ever catch a lightning bug,*
*A lightning bug, a lightning bug?*
*Did you ever catch a lightning bug and put him in a jar?*
*He goes blink, blink. He goes blink, blink.*
*Did you ever catch a lightning bug and put him in a jar?*

*Did you ever let the lightning bug go,*
*Let the lightning bug go, let the lightning bug go?*
*Did you ever let the lightning bug go flying in the night?*
*He goes blink, blink. That's his thanks, thanks.*
*Did you ever see a lightning bug flying in the night?*

*Mary Brehm, Aurora, OH*

# TAKE ME OUT TO THE BALLGAME

FINGERPLAYS, SONGS, & POEMS

**Materials**
magazine photographs of popcorn and peanuts
paper plates
scissors
craft sticks
glue

**What to do**
1. Teach the children the words to the following song ("Take Me Out to the Ballgame" written by Jack Norworth and Albert Von Tilzer):

*Take me out to the ballgame,*
*Take me out with the crowd.*
*Buy me some peanuts and Cracker Jack,*
*I don't care if I never get back.*

*Let me root, root, root for the home team,*
*If they don't win, it's a shame.*
*For it's one, two, three strikes,*
*You're out*
*At the old ball game!*

2. Ask parents to help their children find and cut out magazine photos of popcorn and peanuts. (This can be a school or home activity.)
3. Have the children glue the photos onto paper plates. Glue one craft stick onto each paper plate.
4. Sing "Take Me Out to the Ballgame" again. Demonstrate how to wave the paper plate when singing the words "buy me some peanuts and Cracker Jack."
5. Invite parents to sing along.

**MORE TO DO**   **Snack:** Invite parents to help prepare, serve, and eat a popcorn and peanut snack. **Safety Note:** Check for peanut allergies. If anyone is allergic, just serve popcorn.

★ *Karyn F. Everham, Fort Myers, FL*

# Ship Ahoy!

LANGUAGE AND LITERACY

**MATERIALS**   none

**WHAT TO DO**   1. Begin by teaching the children the actions that go with the following commands:

- Captain's coming aboard! (*Stand to attention and salute.*)
- Scrub the decks! (*Mime scrubbing on hands and knees.*)
- Dance a jig! (*Fold arms and kick alternate legs.*)
- Climb the rigging! (*Mime climbing with alternate arms.*)
- Look out for pirates! (*Hold hand flat above eyes and peer all around.*)
- Steer starboard! (*Mime turning large wheel to left.*)
- Steer port! (*Mime turning large wheel to right.*)
- Walk the plank! (*Mime walking forward with arms outstretched.*)

2. Reduce the number of commands and leave out *port* and *starboard* for younger children. Encourage older children to make up extra nautical commands.

3. Practice each movement a few times.

4. Call out the commands in quick succession. Encourage the children to try and do all the actions as you call them out faster and faster. This is a lot of fun!

**More to do**   Use this game as part of a ship/boat or pirate theme.
**Art:** Encourage the children to make up a name for a sailing ship and design a flag illustrating its name.
**Dramatic Play:** Make or bring in pirate costumes. Encourage the children to pretend they are on a tall sailing ship.
**Group or Circle Time:** Use pictures and books to show children about life on huge, old-fashioned sailing ships.

**Related books**   *Arabella* by Wendy Orr
*Everything I Know About Pirates* by Tom Lichtenheld
*Sailing Ships: A Lift-the-Flap Discovery* by Thomas Bayley
*Theodore and the Tall Ships* by Ivan Robertson

⭐ *Anne Adeney, Plymouth, United Kingdom*

# The Loud Lid Parade
### OUTDOOR PLAY

**Materials**   variety of noise makers (pan lids, spoons and cups)
chalk

**What to do**

1. Invite parents to participate in a loud outdoor parade. Ask them to help their children find and bring items that are not traditionally used to make music, such as pan lids, small boxes, plastic cups, spoons, and so on.

2. Prior to the parade, draw a parade route with chalk on the playground. If space permits, draw different types of routes, including a circle, straight line, and zig-zags.

3. After the parade, discuss the children's favorite "music."

**More to do**   **Art:** Ask children to draw the shapes of the parade routes on paper.

 *Karyn F. Everham, Fort Myers, FL*

# A Sizzling Summer Camp-Out

OUTDOOR PLAY

**Materials**
pup tent
2 flashlights
2 sleeping bags
backpack
children's cooking utensils
wood scraps

**What to do**
1. Pitch a pup tent outside the classroom.
2. Put two flashlights, two sleeping bags, and a backpack filled with cooking utensils. Place wood scraps nearby.
3. When the children play outside, invite them to pretend to camp out.
4. Encourage them to sit around the "campfire" and sing camp songs together.
5. If possible, do this activity in the winter and then repeat it in the summer (see "Camping in the Cold" on page xxx in the January chapter). After the children have done both, encourage them to compare and contrast experiences. Ask questions, such as "How are summer camping and winter camping the same? How are the different?" "What would you do while summer/winter camping?" "Which did you like best? Why?"
6. You also could have them pretend they are camping in the winter and then the summer.

 *Karyn F. Everham, Fort Myers, FL*

# Water Relays

OUTDOOR PLAY

**Materials**
swimwear or change of play clothes
2 identical buckets for each group of players
water
dry-erase marker
cups (one per child)
large sponge (one per group)

**What to do**

1. Dress children for wet play. Explain that they are going to play two water relay games (Water Brigade and Sponge Squeeze). Each relay can be played as a cooperative game, with as many as ten players standing in a row, or children can be divided into separate teams.

2. Play Water Brigade. Fill a bucket with water and mark the outside of it to show the top water line. Give each player an empty cup.

3. Place the filled bucket at one end of the row, and an empty bucket at the opposite end. The children stand in a row between the two buckets.

4. Shout "Ready, Set, Go!" to signal the first player to dip his cup in the water bucket and pour it into the cup of the player next to him. This player pours the water in her cup into the cup of the next player, and so on.

5. The last player pours the water in his cup into the empty bucket.

6. Shout "Hooray!" when the first bucket is empty.

7. Mark the top water line on the second bucket. Place the buckets together and compare the volume of each.

8. Now play Sponge Squeeze. Fill a bucket with water and mark the outside of it to show the top water line. Place this bucket at one end of the row, and an empty bucket at the opposite end.

9. Give the first child in the row a dry sponge and shout, "Ready, Set, Go!"

10. At the signal, this child saturates the sponge in the water bucket and begins passing it along the row.

11. When the sponge reaches the last player, he squeezes it into the empty bucket and runs to the front of the row. He dips the sponge in the water bucket and passes it along.

12. Play continues until the first bucket is empty. Conclude the game as above.

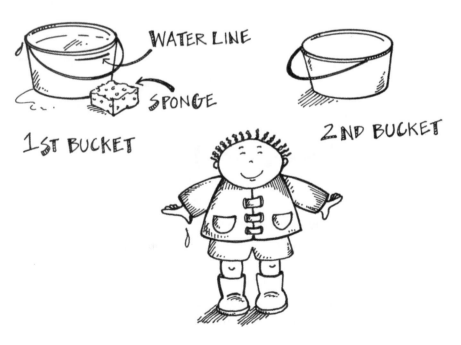

WATER LINE

SPONGE

1ST BUCKET

2ND BUCKET

⭐ *Susan A. Sharkey, La Mesa, CA*

# WATER TOSS

OUTDOOR PLAY

**MATERIALS**  zipper-seal sandwich bags
large bucket of water

**WHAT TO DO**
1. This is a great activity for a hot summer day when the children are dressed in swimwear and or have easy access to dry clothing at the end of playtime.
2. Fill the bags with water by dipping them in the water bucket and zipping them shut. (**Note:** This is a great alternative for games requiring water balloons because the bags are much easier to fill and close, and usually can be reused. Bags can be filled at a sink, but the bucket is handier for refilling them.)
3. Divide the children into groups of two. Partners should stand about 2' apart and face each other.
4. Each pair tosses a water bag back and forth. The object is to toss it gently and carefully so that the bag doesn't break open or drop. Children may count their successful tosses aloud as they play.
5. Refill or replace bags as often as needed. Partners who succeed at a short distance can gradually move further away from each other to increase their skill level.

**MORE TO DO**  This game may also be played with wet sponges.

 *Susan A. Sharkey, La Mesa, CA*

# FELT STAR MAPS

SCIENCE

**MATERIALS**  map of summer constellations or *Star Gazing, Comet Tracking and Sky Mapping* by Melvin Berger
black felt squares, 6" x 6"
star stickers (plain or glow-in-the-dark)

**WHAT TO DO**
1. Show children a star map of summer constellations (Hercules, Pegasus, Scorpius, Cygnus, Sagittarius, Cassiopea, and the Big and Little Dippers). These constellations can be found in *Star Gazing, Comet Tracking and Sky Mapping* by Melvin Berger.
2. Ask the children to look at each constellation and count the number of stars in that constellation.

3. Give each child a piece of 6" x 6" square of black felt. Provide sheets of star stickers.

4. Encourage each child to stick stars on her felt square to make three or four summer constellations.

5. If using glow-in-the-dark stickers, hang the constellations on a bulletin board or tape them to a wall, turn off the lights, and watch them light up.

**More to do**    **Science:** Show the children where they find the constellations in the evening sky. Encourage them to go outside at nighttime and find the constellations they made on their felt squares.

**Related books**    *Heavenly Zoo* by Alison Lurie and Monica Beisner
*How the Stars Fell Into the Sky* by Jerrie Oughton and Lisa Desimini
*The Sky Is Full of Stars* by Franklyn M. Branley
*The Usborne Complete Book of Astronomy and Space* by Lisa Miles and Alastair Smith

⭐ *Randi Lynn Mrvos, Lexington, KY*

# Frozen Color

SCIENCE

**Materials**    ice cube trays
food coloring
water
blue Kool-Aid®, pink lemonade, or another brightly colored drink (red or grape may be too dark for this activity)
small cups (clear plastic, if possible)

**What to do**    1. Add a few drops of food coloring to the water and pour into ice cube trays. Make sure the food coloring is different than the color of the drink.
2. Freeze the colored water.
3. Pour the brightly colored drink into small cups.
4. Let the children add the colored ice cubes to their drinks. Encourage them to observe how the drink changes color as the ice melts.

⭐ *Kristi Larson, Spirit Lake, IA*

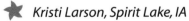

# Popsicles

SNACK AND COOKING

**MATERIALS**   strawberry juice (available in most health food stores) or lemonade
Popsicle sticks
paper cups

**WHAT TO DO**
1. Let children help put strawberry juice or lemonade in tiny paper cups.
2. Insert Popsicle sticks and freeze.
3. Serve later as a delicious summer snack.
**Safety Note:** Be aware of any food allergies and plan accordingly.

**MORE TO DO**   **More Snack:** Make Orange Yogurt Popsicles. Mix 2 cups of plain yogurt, a 16-ounce can of frozen orange juice concentrate, and 2 teaspoons of vanilla. Stir together and freeze in empty yogurt containers or paper cups.

 *Linda Atamian, Charlestown, RI*

# Rainbow Picnic

SNACK AND COOKING

**MATERIALS**   snacks in specified colors (see activity below)

**WHAT TO DO**
1. Ask each parent to sign up to bring in a food in a specified color. For example:
   - red: apples, strawberries, plums, pears
   - purple: grapes, pitted cherries, plums
   - blue: blueberries, blue iced cake or cookies
   - green: celery, grapes, pears, apples, kiwi fruit
   - yellow: apples, pears, bananas, lemons, pineapple, sandwiches on yellow potato bread
   - orange: mango slices, orange slices, apricots
2. Buy cups, plates, and napkins in solid colors.
3. Arrange the foods on a table by color.
4. Encourage the children to select at least one food from each color.
5. Eat your rainbow!
**Safety Note:** Be aware of any food allergies and plan accordingly.

**MORE TO DO**    **Art:** Make rainbow streamers by attaching colored crepe paper steamers or ribbons to rings cut from plastic lids or heavy paper plates. Encourage the children to run with them and watch the colors fly behind them.
**Outdoors:** Let children use colored chalk to draw a rainbow on the ground.
**More Outdoors:** Shoot a fine spray of water from a garden hose and show the children the rainbow held within it.
**Science:** Use a prism to create a rainbow on paper.

**RELATED books**    *A Rainbow All Around Me* by Sandra Pinkney
*What Makes a Rainbow?* by Betty Ann Schwartz

⭐ *Sandra Gratias, Dublin, PA*

# Cool Summer Smoothies

SNACK AND COOKING

**MATERIALS**    milk
vanilla ice cream or frozen yogurt
crushed ice
fresh fruit or fruit juice
food coloring (optional)
blender

**WHAT TO DO**    1. Blend 2 cups ice cream or yogurt, 1 cup crushed ice, 1 cup orange juice, and milk as needed to thin the drink out.
2. Add food coloring, if desired.
3. Enjoy a cool orange smoothie.
4. Substitute various fruits or fruit juices to make smoothies of different flavors.

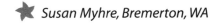 ⭐ *Susan Myhre, Bremerton, WA*

# Leaf Placemat—
# Canada Day

ART

**Materials**
tagboard
scissors
construction paper
crayons
contact paper

**What to do**
- Canada Day is July 1st.
1. Create maple leaf patterns using tagboard
2. Tape the leaf stencils to the tables.
3. Give each child a piece of white construction paper.
4. Show the children how to place the paper over the leaf patterns.
5. Ask them to rub crayons over the leaf patterns.
6. Cover the front and back of the paper with contact paper to make placemats.
7. Children can set the table with their placemats and pretend to celebrate Canada Day.

**More to do**
Hang a cut-out tree shape on a wall. Take the children outside to look for green leaves. Attach the leaves to the paper tree. In the autumn, remove a leaf each day, and place a colored leaf in its place. Observe the children to see whether they notice the changes in the leaves.

**Related books**
*Canada ABCs* by Brenda Haugen
*Fall Leaves Fall* by Zoe Hall
*Leaves, Leaves, Leaves* by Nancy Wallace
*Red Leaf, Yellow Leaf* by Lois Ehlert
*Why Do Leaves Change Color?* by Betsy Maestro

 *Elizabeth Thomas, Hobart, IN*

# Make Cool Fireworks Pictures and Shakers

ART

**Materials**

glue
blue construction paper
glitter
dowel rods
red, white, and blue curling ribbon
scissors

**What to do**

- Independence Day is on July 4th.
1. Invite the children to use glue to make fireworks shapes on their blue paper.
2. Have them shake glitter on the glue to make sparkly fireworks.
3. Cut two pieces of each color of ribbon for each child.
4. Help the children tie the ribbons on a dowel rod.
5. Have them put glue at the top of the dowel rod and slide the ribbon knot over the top to secure the ribbons. Let dry.
6. Use scissors to curl the ribbons loosely from the end (adult only).

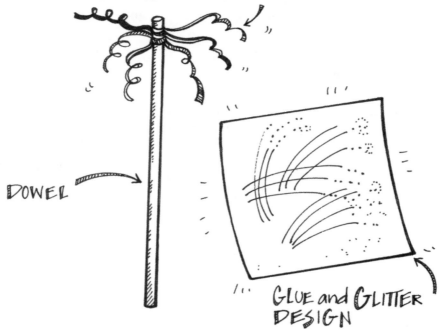

RED, WHITE and BLUE
RIBBON— CURLED

DOWEL

GLUE and GLITTER
DESIGN

**MORE TO DO**   **Group or Circle Time:** Talk about the Fourth of July and how it is also called Independence Day. Talk about how fireworks are used to celebrate our country's independence from England.

**RELATED POEM**   (This acrostic poem is by Jennifer Galvin.)
*Fly*
*Into the night sky,*
*Rocketing up,*
*Everywhere sparkling,*
*Whizzing around me and*
*Over the crowd who*
*Roars their approval, the sparks*
*Kissing the stars*
*Surrounding us in glorious light.*

⭐ *Jennifer Galvin, Stafford, VA*

# Roller Painting Red, White, and Blue

ART

**MATERIALS**   empty thread spools
wire coat hangers
wire cutters
red, white, and blue paint

**WHAT TO DO**   
- Independence Day is on July 4th.
1. Cut the bottom wire of each clothes hanger at the ends, in the middle of the curves.
2. Bend the center of the hanger in so the ends almost touch.
3. Attach thread spools to the ends of the wire hangers. This creates a handle on each empty spool and makes for easy rolling.
4. Pour red, white, and blue paint into shallow containers.
5. Let the children roller paint with their patriotic colors.

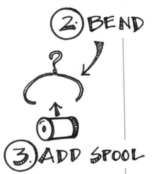

⭐ *Susan Myhre, Bremerton, WA*

# Star-Spangled Napkin Rings

ART

**MATERIALS**    blue, red, and white poster board
scissors
ruler
glue
tape

**WHAT TO DO**
- Independence Day is on July 4th.
1. Cut blue poster board into 5" x 1" strips and red poster board into 5" x ½" strips.
2. Give each child a blue strip and a red strip. Show them how to glue the red strip in the center of the blue strip. Let dry.
3. Have them bend their strips into a circle. Overlap the ends about ¼" and secure with tape.
4. Cut a star for each child out of white poster board.
5. Help children tape a star over the secured ends of their rings.
6. Have them fold or roll a napkin and slip it into their napkin rings.

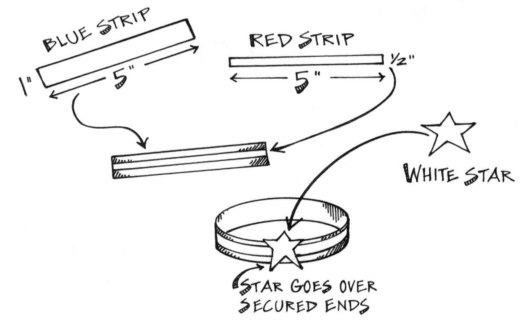

**MORE TO DO**    **Social Development:** Use this craft to teach children about table settings and manners.

*Rose Ross Zediker, Elk Point, SD*

# Tissue Paper Stars and Stripes

ART

**Materials**  newspaper
glue
small containers
paintbrushes
9" x 12" white construction paper
red and blue tissue paper
self-adhesive stars

**What to do**
- Independence Day is on July 4th.
1. Cover the work surface with newspaper and pour glue into small containers.
2. Let children help tear red and blue tissue paper into small pieces.
3. Give each child a piece of white paper. Demonstrate how to paint a design on their paper with glue.
4. Before the glue dries, show them how to glue crumpled bits of torn tissue paper over the surface of the paper. Allow to dry.
5. Once the glue dries, distribute self-adhesive stars for the children to add to their "patriotic papers."

**More to do**  Ask all the children to wear red, white, and blue one day.
**Music:** Sing "I'm a Yankee Doodle Dandy" or "This Land Is Your Land."
**Snack:** Serve strawberries, blueberries, and whipped cream for snack.

 *Susan Oldham Hill, Lakeland, FL*

# Fireworks of Art

ART

**Materials**  newspaper
black construction paper
neon or glow-in-the-dark poster paints (3 or more colors)
drinking straws
glitter glow

**What to do**
- Independence Day is celebrated on July 4th.

1. Cover the work surface with newspaper or plastic.
2. Test the paint in advance by gently blowing gently through a straw to see if it flows easily across the paper.
3. Add water to the paint, if necessary, to attain the right consistency.
4. Place a few drops of paint on each child's black paper. Invite the children to blow "explosive" bursts of color on the "night sky." Let dry.
5. If desired, encourage the children to trace interesting elements in their designs with glitter glue.

**More to do**    **Bulletin Board:** Frame the paintings with red, white, and blue borders for an attractive monthly bulletin board display.
**Music:** Play patriotic background music during this activity.

★ *Susan A. Sharkey, La Mesa, CA*

# Independence Day Sparkle Collage

ART

**Materials**    *Independence Day* by Willma Willis Gore and Michael P. French
black construction paper
glitter paint or glitter glue
tissue paper scraps in a variety of bright colors
white glue
glitter in a variety of colors

**What to do**    ● Independence Day is July 4th.
1. Read *Independence Day* by Willma Willis Gore and Micheal P. French. Ask the children what their families do to celebrate Independence Day. Ask them to describe how fireworks look and sound. Record their responses by writing them down.
2. Ask the children to draw pictures of firework displays they have seen in the past. If some of the children have never seen fireworks, ask them to imagine how they might look.
3. Give each child a piece of black construction paper. Provide bottles of brightly colored glitter paint or glitter glue, brightly colored scraps of tissue paper, white glue, and glitter.
4. Encourage the children to make a fireworks picture. Give them time to experiment with the materials. Encourage individuality and creativity. Make positive comments about what they are doing.

5. Create an Independence Day bulletin board display using the drawings. Title the display: "Sparkles in the Sky." Hang the pictures and post the children's comments (see step 1) on sentence strips underneath their drawings.

**More to do**   **Group or Circle Time:** After Independence Day, have a follow-up discussion. Ask the children if the fireworks were anything like what they thought they would be. Ask them to describe what they saw and heard at the fireworks displays. Compare their comments after seeing the fireworks with their comments from before.
**Literacy:** Post fireworks words (*boom, crack, rocket, sparkle, zoom*) in the writing center for the children to print.

**Related song**   **Sparkle, Sparkle In The Sky** (Tune: "Twinkle, Twinkle, Little Star")
*Sparkle, sparkle in the sky*
*See the fireworks way up high.*
*Red and blue, yellow and green,*
*The brightest colors you have ever seen.*
*Sparkle, sparkle in the sky*
*See the fireworks way up high.*

**Related books**   *Independence Day* by Robin Nelson
*Independence Day* by Nancy I. Sanders

★ *Virginia Jean Herrod, Columbia, SC*

# MOON FESTIVAL

PROJECTS

**MATERIALS**

large black paper
easel
large white paint paper
white and black paint
paper plates

hole punch
white string
scissors
tape
glue

**WHAT TO DO**

• August 15 is the traditional time for the August Moon Festival. The Festival is a holiday marked by family reunions, moon gazing, and the eating of moon cakes (round pastries stuffed with red bean paste and an egg yolk, or fruit and preserves).

1. Ask the children to describe the moon. Record what they say.

2. Explain that in China people have parties to celebrate the moon. Tell them this celebration is called the Moon Festival and that it takes place in the middle of August. Read a book about the Moon Festival. Ask the children if they would like to have their own Moon Festival in the classroom.

3. Cut large black paper to fit the easel. Encourage the children to paint a nighttime sky on the paper using white paint. After these have dried, display them around the room. Print what the children said about the moon on lined paper and post their statements under their paintings.

4. Place large white paint paper on an easel and encourage the children to paint another nighttime picture. Encourage them to leave a circle of white paper showing to represent the moon.

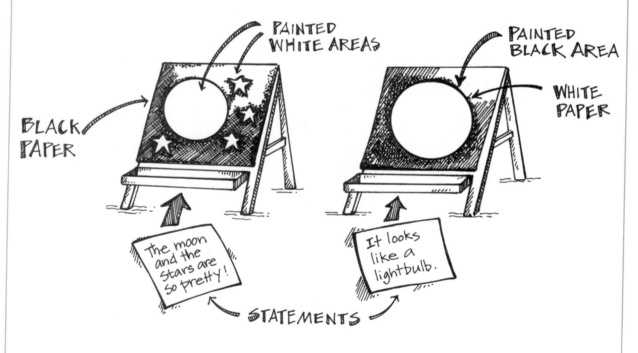

PAINTED WHITE AREAS

PAINTED BLACK AREA

WHITE PAPER

BLACK PAPER

The moon and the stars are so pretty!

It looks like a lightbulb.

STATEMENTS

5. Make a Moon Mobile. Help the children punch holes around the edge of a paper plate and tie white string through the holes. Tie moon and star shapes (created by the children) to the strings. Hang the moon mobiles around the room.

6. Encourage the children to look for the moon when they are out at night with their parents.

7. Place photos of the moon around the room.

8. Take a pretend trip to the moon. Tell the following story to the children and act it out together as you go along:

*We're going on a trip to the moon. Everyone get on your spacesuits* (pretend to put on space suits). *Don't forget your helmets* (pull helmet over head). *Now, everyone get in the spaceship.* (everyone sit in a chair). *Put on your seatbelt*s (make motion as if pulling seatbelt across your body). *Check your instruments* (reach over your head and pretend to turn dials and switches). *Are we ready to go? Then let's count down!*
*10, 9, 8, 7, 6, 5, 4, 3, 2, 1, blast off!* (bounce around in your chair and make engine noises).

*Okay, we are out of earth's gravity. Engine's off* (stop making engine sound). *Now, we are floating in space. Look out your window* (turn head slowly to one side). *See the earth down there?* (point with one index finger). *It looks blue and white from here. Can you see your Grandma's house? Wave to Grandma!* (wave one hand). *Oh, look* (turn head slowly to other side). *There's a shooting star! See how fast it goes.*

*Let's go on a space walk! Unfasten your seatbelts* (make motions as if unfastening a seat belt). *Everybody stand up* (move slowly as you stand). *Okay, let's go!* ("float" around the room together). *Wow, look at the earth from here. It's just a little tiny ball* (squint eyes and point off in the distance). *I wonder if we'll see any space aliens* (continue floating around the room together). *Oh, look at the stars; they are so bright out here in space.*
*Okay, everybody back in the spaceship* ("float" back to the chairs). *Everyone in their seats* (slowly sit down) *and fasten your seatbelts* (make motions as if fastening a seatbelt). *Now, we are ready to land on the moon.*
*Check your instruments* (reach over your head and pretend to turn dials and switches). *Ready? Reverse engines* (bounce in your seat and make engine noises). *Okay, we've landed. Engines off!* (stop making engine noises).

*Let's go look at the moon! Unfasten your seatbelts* (make motions as if unfastening a seatbelt). *Get your gravity boots on* (pretend to put on boots). *Let's go! Follow me!* (walk very slowly around the room). *Wow, the surface of the moon is soft* (squat down and touch the floor). *Let's go look at those moon rocks over there. What pretty rocks! Let's take some back with us. Get out your bags* (pretend to shake out a bag). *Let's get these pretty rocks here* (pretend to pick up rocks and put them in a bag).

*Oh, no* (look at watch on wrist). *Look at the time. We have to get back. Hurry back to the spaceship* (bounce and hop back to the chairs). *Have a seat and buckle up* (pretend to fasten a seatbelt). *Take off your gravity boots* (pretend to remove boots). *Check your instruments* (reach over head and pretend to turn dials and switches).

*Let's go! 10, 9, 8, 7, 6, 5, 4, 3, 2, 1, blast off!* (bounce around in the chair and make engine noises).

*I wonder how long it will take us to get home* (check watch). *Okay, reverse engines* (bounce in chair and make engine noises). *Here we go!* (pretend to steer the space ship) *Quick, hit the brakes* (push with feet and make a screeching noise like a loud brake, bounce in chair). *Okay, everybody unbuckle* (pretend to unfasten seatbelt). *Out we go* (walk normally around the room).

**MORE TO DO**

**Art:** Make pretend telescopes from paper towel tubes. Decorate the tubes with stickers, and color with markers or paint with tempera paints. Pretend to gaze at the moon.

**Snack:** Make your own moon cakes. Bake a flat rectangular cake according to the package instructions. Let the children use a round cookie cutter to cut the cake into "moon" pieces. Give each child two pieces. Let the children spread jelly or preserves on one moon shape. Cover with the other moon piece to make a moon cake. Enjoy with a glass of cold milk or apple juice.

**RELATED SONG**

**I See the Moon** (Tune: "I See the Moon")
*I see the moon and the moon sees me*
*Down through the leaves of the old oak tree.*
*Please let the light that shines on me*
*Shine on the one I love.*
*The moon shines brightly overhead*
*As Mommy and Daddy tuck me into bed.*
*The moon's bright light that shines on me*
*Shines on the ones I love.*

**RELATED BOOKS**

*Dragon Kite of the Autumn Moon* by Valerie Reddix
*Goodnight, Moon* by Margaret Wise Brown
*Grandpa Takes Me to the Moon* by Timothy R. Gaffney
*Moonbathing* by Liz Rosenberg
*Moon Bear* by Frank Asch
*The Moon Lady* by Amy Tan
*Moonlight* by Jan Ormerod
*No Moon, No Milk!* by Chris Babcock
*Papa, Please Get the Moon for Me* by Eric Carle

 *Virginia Jean Herrod, Columbia, SC*

# POSTCARDS FROM HAWAII

LANGUAGE AND LITERACY

**MATERIALS**  Hawaii travel brochures
scissors
index cards
glue

**WHAT TO DO**  • The third Friday in August is Admission Day in Hawaii. It celebrates Hawaii's admission to the Union on August 21st, 1959.

1. Talk about Hawaii and explain that it did not become a state until 1959.
2. Encourage the children to cut out a variety of scenes from Hawaii travel brochures.
3. Have each child choose a scene and glue it to one side of an index card.
4. Let each child dictate a postcard message and write it on the blank side of the index card.
5. Start a classroom post office to "mail" the postcards from Hawaii.

 *Kathy Kalmar, Macomb, MI*

# "THE KISSING HAND"

WORKING WITH FAMILIES

**MATERIALS**  *The Kissing Hand* by Audrey Penn
paper
pencils or markers
lipstick or lips stamp

**WHAT TO DO**  • The first day of a new school year falls sometime in August or early September.

1. Many schools have a classroom visitation day before school starts for children and parents to meet the teachers and see the classroom. If your school does not have this, send the following note home a week or two before school starts and ask parents to respond before the first day of school.
2. Attach a note to a blank piece of paper explaining that you will be reading *The Kissing Hand* on the first day of school. Explain that this book is about a young raccoon that worries about going to school and leaving his mommy. The mommy kisses his paw and tells him that the kiss will stay with him and keep him safe until they see each other after school.

3. Ask parents to write their child a short note about how proud they are of him or her and how they hope the first day of school goes well. Ask parents to either kiss the note (for moms with bright lipstick) or use a "lips" stamp to "pretend kiss" the note.

4. Save all of these notes for the first day of school.

5. Start the day by reading the book. Tell the children that there is a surprise for each of them after the book.

6. Pull out the letters and read each one aloud and show the kiss on the note.

7. Give the children their notes. Ask them to keep their notes with them until they see their mommy or daddy that afternoon.

8. This activity brightens the children's faces and makes them less wary of the day.

 *Wanda Guidroz, Santa Fe, TX*

# ANYTIME

# LEARNING COLORS BY THE MONTH

ART

**MATERIALS**
paints, crayons, and markers
construction paper in a variety of colors
tissue paper
glitter and sequins
glue
scissors
paper plates
sticks, yarn, and magnets

**WHAT TO DO**
Do the following art activities with the children each month to learn about colors.

- **September:** Cut brown basket shapes from construction paper. Ask children to color precut apple shapes green, yellow, and red. Have them glue the apples in the baskets.
- **October:** Have the children glue autumn leaves to a drawing of a tree on the wall.
- **November:** Make a Thanksgiving mural with the children. Encourage them to paint orange pumpkins, brown turkeys brown, yellow corn, and so on.
- **December:** Cut out stocking shapes from green, red, and white construction paper. Have children glue colored tissue paper to the stockings.
- **January:** Explore the colors of winter: white, gray, and silver. Provide large pieces of white construction paper. Encourage children to paint with gray and silver paint and add glitter to make winter pictures.
- **February:** Give each child a paper plate with the center cut out. Have them glue red and pink paper hearts around the rim of the plates to make Valentine's Day door wreaths.
- **March:** Cut out large shamrocks from light green construction paper. Invite the children to decorate their shamrocks with gold glitter. Cover with clear contact paper and use as St. Patrick's Day placemats.
- **April:** Help children cut out yellow and light blue flower shapes from construction paper. Have them glue pastel-colored bits of tissue paper in different designs on their flowers.
- **May:** Make a piñata by covering a grocery bag with red or turquoise papier-mâché. Fill the bag with similarly colored cotton balls and tissue paper.
- **June:** Help children make fishing poles from sticks. Help each child attach a small magnet to the end of the fishing string. Cut out fish

shapes and invite the children to draw rainbows on the fish ("rainbow trout"). Glue a small magnet to each to facilitate catching.

* **July:** Make red, white, and blue parade streamers and stars out of crepe paper. Lightly dust them with gold glitter.
* **August:** On white construction paper, have the children paint pictures of starry, midnight blue horizons. Provide silver glitter for stars.

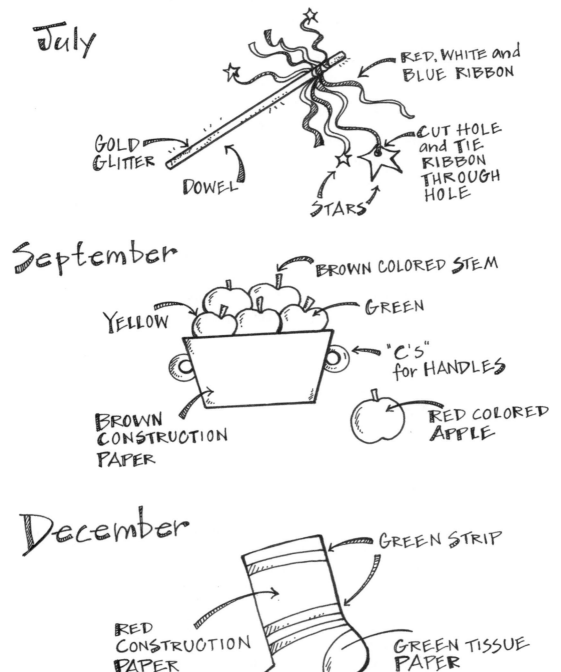

*Penni Smith, Riverside, CA*

# Monthly Cutting Portfolio

ART

**Materials**
blank paper
hole punch
string or yarn
scissors
construction paper
glue

**What to do**

1. Read the book *I.Q. Goes to School* by Mary Ann Fraser. Each month I.Q., the classroom pet mouse, learns and practices his skills.
2. Make a special cutting book for each child. Punch holes in each sheet of paper and tie the pages together with string or yarn. Make a page for each month of the school year.
3. Each month, ask the children to cut out a shape and decorate it. Provide the outline of the shapes for children to cut out. Glue the decorated shapes in each child's book.
4. These books document how the children's skills grow throughout the year.
5. Use the ideas below or use your own ideas:
   * **September:** Children cut an apple from red paper and glue on a yarn or pipe cleaner worm.
   * **October:** Children cut out a pumpkin from orange paper and draw or cut a face.
   * **November:** Children cut out a turkey shape and assorted colored feathers. Have them glue the feathers on the turkey.
   * **December:** Children cut out basic shapes (stars, candy canes) and decorate the shapes with white "frosting" (glue) and real sprinkles to make holiday cookies.
   * **January:** Fold a tissue paper circle into four pieces. Invite the children to hold the middle corner and cut pieces from the folded paper. Have them open the "snowflakes" and decorate with glue and white glitter or salt to make them sparkle.
   * **February:** Fold pink and red paper in half. Draw a half heart on the fold of each paper. The children cut on the line, open the paper, and a heart will appear.
   * **March:** Children cut a kite shape and add a ribbon tail, or they cut out a shamrock.
   * **April:** Children cut out a raindrop shape. Provide glue and blue glitter for decorating.
   * **May:** Children cut out assorted flower shapes. (Have younger children cut tulips while older children will be able to cut flowers with petals.)
   * **June:** Invite the children to cut out a yellow sun (using no template).

- **July:** Demonstrate how to cut a fish shape by cutting a triangle from a circle shape. Glue one point of the triangle to the back as the back fin. Decorate the fish with confetti.
- **August:** Each child cuts out a rectangle, and a red, yellow, and green circle. Show them how to glue the circles on the rectangle to make a stoplight.

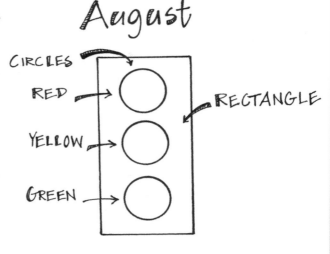

**More to do**     Talk about scissor safety.

**Related song**     (Tune: "Mary Had a Little Lamb")
*Fingers on the bottom, thumbs on top,*
*Thumbs on top, thumbs on top.*
*Fingers on the bottom, thumbs on top,*
*Cutting with a scissor.*
*Open and shut the scissor's mouth*
*Scissor's mouth, scissor's mouth.*
*Open and shut the scissor's mouth,*
*Cutting with a scissor.*

**Related books**     *A Busy Year* by Leo Lionni
*Chicken Soup With Rice* by Maurice Sendak

⭐ *Sue Fleischmann, Sussex, WI*

# Material of the Month

ART

**Materials**  different "surprise" materials for each month (see activity below)

**What to do**

1. Each month, bring in a different "surprise" material for the children to use creatively in the art center, such as fabric pieces, wood pieces, spools, plastic shapes, paper towel tubes, and so on. Look around your community for ideas (grocery stores, print shops, appliance stores, craft store discards, garage sales, flea markets, and so on). The materials should be varied, interesting, plentiful, and safe for the children to use.

2. Provide a variety of accessories for them to use in their creation or invention (glue, tape, twist-ties, yarn, string, rope, rubber bands, paper, cardboard, and so on).

3. When children are creating, stay nearby in case they want more items to complete their creations.

4. Display their completed projects and acknowledge their efforts. Do not give awards or rewards for the project itself.

*Judy Fujawa, The Villages, FL*

# Paper Quilts

ART

**Materials**  quilt
colored construction paper
scrapbook paper
white drawing paper
scissors
glue sticks
markers and crayons

**What to do**

1. Pre-cut squares of scrapbook paper and colored construction paper. Older children can cut their own squares.

2. Show the children a real quilt (or picture of a quilt) and have a discussion about quilts.

3. Have the children make their own quilts by gluing the paper squares on large drawing paper.

4. Encourage the children to decorate their quilts as desired.

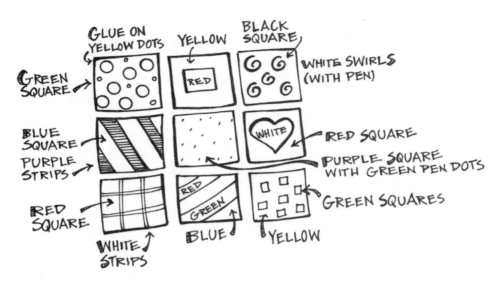

GLUE ON YELLOW DOTS
YELLOW
BLACK SQUARE
GREEN SQUARE
RED
WHITE SWIRLS (WITH PEN)
BLUE SQUARE
PURPLE STRIPS
WHITE
RED SQUARE
PURPLE SQUARE WITH GREEN PEN DOTS
RED SQUARE
RED GREEN
GREEN SQUARES
WHITE STRIPS
BLUE
YELLOW

**Related books**   *On Mother's Lap* by Ann Herbert Scott
*The Quilt Story* by Tomie de Paola

⭐ *Barbara Saul, Eureka, CA*

# Collage Game

ART

**Materials**   two large foam cubes
card stock paper or thin cardboard
glue
collage materials

1. Make your own dice to use with this game. On one large foam cube, print the numerals 1 through 6 and the dots to match. On the other cube, place pictures representing familiar collage materials, such as sequins, buttons, tissue squares, fabric scraps, paper scraps, and foam pieces. Put one type of material on each side of the cube.
2. Play this game with four to six children. Give each child a piece of card stock or thin cardboard and a bottle of glue.
3. Put the collage materials in the middle of table.
4. Explain to the children that they will roll the dice and add the number of collage materials shown on the dice. For example, if the number die lands with a four showing and the collage die lands with buttons showing, the child glues four buttons to her paper.

5. Let the children take turns rolling the dice. Continue taking turns until everyone has had a least four turns or the children grow tired of the game.

6. After they have dried, display the collages on a bulletin board. Title the display: Counting Collage. Include a paper with a short explanation of the game for parents to see.

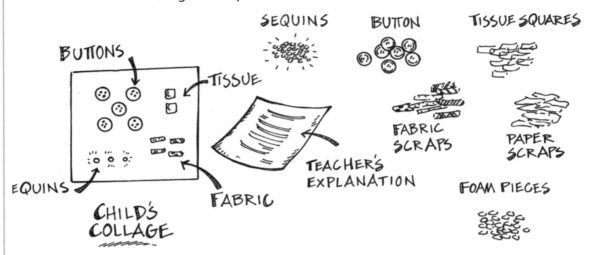

**MORE TO DO**   For older children, use real dice and have them add the numbers and put that number of items on their collages.

**RELATED BOOKS**   *Look What I Can Do* by Jose Aruego
*Lucy's Picture* by Nicola Moon
*Willy's Pictures* by Anthony Browne

⭐ *Virginia Jean Herrod, Columbia, SC*

# Friendly Wild Things

ART

**MATERIALS**   *Where the Wild Things Are* by Maurice Sendak
large black construction paper
colored chalk
tissues

**WHAT TO DO**   1. Read *Where the Wild Things Are* to the children.
2. Show the illustrations to the children again and ask them what they notice about the wild things. If they don't mention it, point out that the wild things have smiles and are happy and eager to play.
3. Encourage them to describe the wild things.
4. Invite the children to design their own wild things using colored chalk on black paper.

5. Encourage them to blend chalk colors, or leave the lines dark for a brighter look. They may want to use a tissue or their fingers to blend two colors together.

6. Share drawings of friendly wild things!

★ *Dr. Geraldine Jenny, Grove City, PA*

# MAKE YOUR OWN WILD THING

ART

**MATERIALS**

*Where the Wild Things* Are by Maurice Sendak
construction paper
scissors
hole punch
yarn
markers

**WHAT TO DO**

1. Before this activity, prepare booklets for the children by stapling two pieces of construction paper together. Cut two slits on the right side of the top sheet to form three horizontal flaps.

2. Read *Where the Wild Things Are* to the children.

3. Give each child a booklet and put the children into groups of three. Explain that they will work together in groups of three to create a "friendly wild thing."

4. Help the children write "My Wild Thing" on the front of their booklets (one word on each flap of paper). You may need to do this step for them.

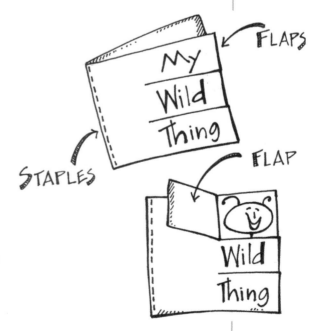

5. Ask the children to pull back the top flaps of their booklets and draw a head for their wild thing.
6. Have the children pass their booklets to another child in their group. This child pulls back the middle flap and draws a body for the wild thing.
7. The children then pass the booklets to the third child in the group, who draws the feet for the wild thing.
8. Tell the children not to open any flaps except the one they are working on.
9. Let each child reveal his wild thing at circle time and name it.

⭐ *Geraldine Jenny, Grove City, PA*

# Recycled Birthday Crowns

ART

**Materials**

leftover pieces of bulletin board borders
plastic gemstones (from a craft store)
glue
glitter

**What to do**

1. Measure and cut the bulletin board borders to fit around each child's head.
2. Help the children use glue to write their names on their crowns. Encourage them to sprinkle glitter on top of the glue and add gemstones.
3. When dry, staple the crowns to fit on the children's heads.

**MORE TO DO**  Have "un-birthday" celebrations for the summer birthday children. Assign days during the last month of school when they can celebrate birthdays as the other children do.

 *Barbara Saul, Eureka, CA*

# DECORATING A MEMORY BOX FOR YOU

**MATERIALS**                                                      ART

large, sturdy shoebox or gift box
glue
markers or crayons
paint and paintbrushes
variety of materials (lace; buttons; paper hearts and flowers; colorful
    pictures cut from magazines, greeting cards, or calendars; ribbon; pieces
    of fabric; glitter; and so on)

**WHAT TO DO**

1. Before doing this activity, decorate a shoebox. Fill it with your personal memorabilia, such as ticket stubs, greeting cards, photos, collectibles, drawings, pressed flowers, sports badges, jewels, and stickers.
2. Show the box and memorabilia to the children. Explain to them that many objects can hold precious memories for parents, relatives, and friends.
3. Ask the children to name some items that they would consider saving or sharing with others.
4. Provide a box and plenty of decorating supplies for each child. The children can present these memory boxes to someone special in their lives.

*Judy Fujawa, The Villages, FL*

# FEATHER DUSTER MURAL

ART

**MATERIALS**
feather dusters
bulletin board
paper
white paint
pie tins

**WHAT TO DO**
1. Hang a large piece of colored bulletin board paper on the wall.
2. Pour white paint into pie tins and provide feather dusters.
3. Encourage the children to paint the large paper using the dusters.

*Kathy Kalmar, Macomb, MI*

# Glitter Day

ART

**MATERIALS**
objects from home
glitter
glue
small containers
paper plates
plastic garbage bags
brushes
flashlight (optional)

**WHAT TO DO**
1. Send a note home to parents asking them to have their children bring in objects they want to cover in glitter (such as wood frames, small boxes, barettes, magnets, and so on).
2. Cut garbage bags open and line the water table with cut bags.
3. Put different colored glitter in small containers and pour glue onto paper plates. Place in the water table.
4. Invite the children to bring their objects to the water table to put glitter on them. Show them how to dip a brush into glue, paint glue on the object, then pour glitter on the glue.
5. When the children finish glittering the objects, turn off the lights and shine a flashlight on the objects so children can see them sparkle.

*Ann Scalley, Orleans, MA*

# FINGERPAINTING TIPS

ART

**Materials**
newspaper or plastic tablecloth
fingerpainting paper
easel paper
fingerpaint
tubs of water
paper towels

**What to do**
1. Cover a table with newspaper or a large plastic tablecloth.
2. Put fingerpainting paper (shiny side up) on top of a larger sheet of easel paper. When the child is finished, just lift the easel paper (with the painting on top) and move it to another place to dry.
3. Before the children begin painting, wet their papers with a sponge. Have a spray bottle handy to spritz the papers if the paint begins to dry
.4. Fingerpainting is a great way to teach color blending. Give each child a ¼ cup of yellow paint and a ¼ cup of red paint. Encourage them to spread it together to make orange. Repeat with other color combinations.
5. At another table, have colored paper ready for children to make handprints when they are done painting and are about to wash their hands.
6. At a nearby table, set up a clean-up site. Prepare one dish tub full of warm, soapy water, and another with warm clear water. Have a stack of paper towels next to the water. Each child washes her hands in the soapy water, rinses in the clear water, and wipes off with the towels.
7. Fingerpainting paper has a tendency to curl after drying. Staple the actual painting to a second piece of paper to make hanging easier.

 *Barbara Saul, Eureka, CA*

# EASEL PAINTING TIPS

ART

**Materials**
easels
newspaper
plastic dropcloths
paint shirts
paint
paintbrushes
2 nails
wooden clothespins
clothesline
liquid starch

**What to do**

1. Cover the front of each easel with newspaper. Put plastic dropcloths under the easels.
2. Have the children put on paint shirts (adult sized t-shirts).
3. Drive two nails into the front of the easel, one at each top corner. This makes it easy for the children to put easel paper on.
4. Use wooden clothespins and a clothesline to hang paintings to dry.
5. After drying, the paintings can be rolled up, taped, and labeled.
6. Make sure that each color of paint has its own brush. If desired, paint brush handles to match the paint colors.
7. Put a drop of liquid starch into each paint container. This makes the paint easier to wash out of clothes.

*★ Barbara Saul, Eureka, CA*

# Paper Plate Mobiles

ART

**Materials**

paper plates (one per child)
scissors or die-cut machine
clear contact paper
collage materials
hole punch
string

**What to do**

1. Cut out a large design from the center of each paper plate. Give a plate to each child.
2. For each child, cut two pieces of contact paper larger than the cutout design.
3. Help the children remove the adhesive back of one piece of contact paper and place on the plate over the cutout pattern.
4. Encourage the children to decorate the sticky side of the contact paper in the opening of the plate. Provide a variety of materials, such as colored sand, paper dots from hole punches, small pieces of paper, ribbon, yarn, glitter, confetti, and so on.
5. When children have completed their projects, help them place the other piece of contact paper over their creations to make a stained windowpane effect.
6. On the top of each plate, punch a hole and tie a string through to display.

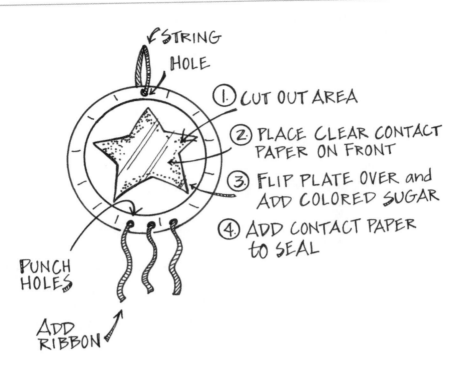

**MORE TO DO**  Use this concept to create letter mobiles. Make sure to select letters that look the same forward and reversed. Use cutout hearts for Valentines Day, flowers for Mother's Day, umbrellas for spring, and so on.

*Bev Schumacher, Racine, WI*

# Record Player Art

ART

**MATERIALS**  record player
thin paper plates
markers

**WHAT TO DO**
1. Place a paper plate on a record player. Turn on the record player.
2. Hold a marker firmly on the paper plate.
3. Turn the record player off to see your design.
4. Let the children take turns make designs.
5. Use different speeds on the record player and see what happens.
6. If desired, do the activity with crayons or watercolor paints.

*Kaethe Lewandowski, Centreville, VA*

# X-Rays

ART

**Materials**
tagboard
scissors
black and white tissue paper
glue
light box or window with bright light

**What to do**
1. Cut out a variety of bone shapes from tagboard for children to use as templates.
2. Talk to the children about the bones inside our bodies. Show pictures, if available.
3. Encourage the children to trace the bone templates on white tissue paper and cut them out. Have them glue the bones on black tissue paper.
4. Hold the pictures up to a light box or window. Talk about x-rays.

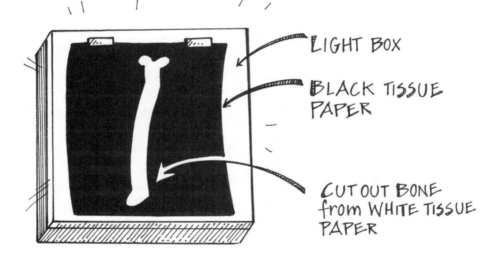

LIGHT BOX

BLACK TISSUE PAPER

CUT OUT BONE from WHITE TISSUE PAPER

⭐ *Kristi Larson, Spirit Lake, IA*

# Block Jackets

ART

**Materials**
photos of children in the class
pictures from magazines, old calendars, and greeting cards
scissors
clear contact paper
blocks

**WHAT TO DO**

1. Cut the photos and pictures into block-sized pieces.
2. Attach the pictures to blocks and cover with clear contact paper.
3. Mix and match the pictures or attach similar pictures (such as pictures of people, buildings, flowers, food, letters, or animals) to the blocks.
4. Change the pictures monthly.
5. These block jackets will add diversity, variety, and a new interest in the block center.
6. Children especially enjoy seeing their friend's pictures on the blocks.

★ *Judy Fujawa, The Villages, FL*

# Fabric Beads

FINE MOTOR

**MATERIALS**

muslin strips (1"-2" wide, 8"-10" long)
acrylic paints
damp sponges
paintbrushes
glue
straws
string or yarn

**WHAT TO DO**

1. Give each child a strip of muslin.
2. Have them dip sponges into the paints and paint their fabric.
3. Let dry.
4. Ask the children to paint their strips with glue, all but the last inch or less.
5. Give each child a straw. Show the children how to place their straws on the end of the fabric without glue.
6. Help the children start by wrapping the unglued end around their straws.

7. Help each child continue rolling her fabric strip around the same area of the straw, so that a "bead" is formed. Let dry.

8. You can have children make one bead or several.

9. After the beads are dry, slide them off the straw. (This will be simple to do if the children started rolling using the unglued side of the fabric).

10. Help children string their "beads" on yarn or string. Help each child tie the ends of the string together to make a necklace.

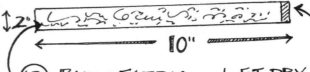

① CUT A STRIP of FABRIC

② PAINT FABRIC — LET DRY

③ PAINT WITH GLUE — ALL BUT ONE INCH or LESS

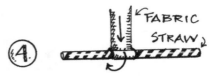

④ FABRIC STRAW

ROLL AROUND STRAW — START WITH END THAT IS NOT GLUED

⑤. LET DRY and SLIDE OFF STRAW

⑥.  "BEAD" STRING

★ *Kristi Larson, Spirit Lake, IA*

# ATTENTION EVERYBODY!

FINGERPLAYS, SONGS, & POEMS

**WHAT TO DO**   Do the following two fingerplays to get the children's attention.

Fingerplay #1
*1, 2, 3,* (hold up three fingers successively)
*Eyes on me,* (point to eyes)
*4, 5, 6,* (hold up four, five, and six fingers successively)
*Zip the lips,* ("zip" lips)
*7, 8, 9,* (hold up seven, eight, and nine fingers)
*It's quiet time.* (whisper)

Fingerplay #2
Teacher: *One, two, three…*
Children: *Four* (point to their ears), *five* (point at their eyes), *six* (zip their lips).

⭐ *Kathy Kalmar, Macomb, MI*

# Stoop and Stand

FINGERPLAYS, SONGS, & POEMS

**Materials**    none

**What to do**    Sing the following song, suiting the actions to the words.

*Stoop and stand*
*Hands in the air,*
*Wave your arms,*
*Touch your hair.*
*Bend your waist*
*And touch the floor,*
*Hold it while*
*We count to four,*
*1-2-3-4.*
*Slowly stand*
*And reach far out,*
*Grab a friend*
*Now swing about.*

⭐ *Kathy Kalmar, Macomb, MI*

# 1, 2, 3, There's a Bug on Me

### FINGERPLAYS, SONGS, & POEMS

**Materials**      none

**What to do**      1. Recite the following rhyme with the children.

*1-2-3, there's a bug on me.* (point to knee)
*Brush it away.* (brush away)
*Where did it go?* (look questioningly at children)
*I don't know.* (shrug shoulders)

2. Substitute other insects for "bug" (ant, fly, and so on).

⭐ *Kathy Kalmar, Macomb, MI*

# Insect Rap

### FINGERPLAYS, SONGS, & POEMS

**Materials**      none

**What to do**      Sing or rap the following song:

*A-B-C-D-E-*
*Insects have three parts, do we?*
*F-G-H-I-J-*
*How many eggs do they lay?*
*K-L-M-N-O-*
*They have six legs to help them go.*
*P-Q-R-S-T-*
*They don't have bones like you and me.*
*U-V-W-X-Y-Z-*
*Too many bugs just make me cry.*
*ZZZZZZZZ*
*Now there's a bug right on my knee.*

⭐ *Kathy Kalmar, Macomb, MI*

# Aloha, Everybody

FINGERPLAYS, SONGS, & POEMS

**MATERIALS**    none

**WHAT TO DO**    1. Sing the following song to the tune of "Happy Birthday."

*Aloha to you,*
*Aloha to you,*
*Aloha to you, Keike,*
*Aloha to you.* ("keike" means children)

2. Substitute other Hawaiian words, such as *makuahine* (mother), *makuakâne* (father), *ke tûtû* (grandma), *ke tûtû kâne* (grandpa). Pronounce every vowel.

 *Kathy Kalmar, Macomb, MI*

# Fe, Fi, Fo, Fum

FINGERPLAYS, SONGS, & POEMS

**MATERIALS**    none

**WHAT TO DO**    Recite the following rhyme, making the appropriate corresponding gestures.

*Fe, fi, fo, fum* (raise index finger and others one by one)
*Here are my fingers,* (show fingers)
*Here is my thumb,* (show thumb)
*Fe, fi, fo, fum* (raise index finger and others one by one)
*There goes my finger,* (put fingers behind back)
*There goes my thumb!* (make thumb disappear behind the back)

**MORE TO DO**    **Art:** Fingerpaint and make fingerprints.
**Language and Literacy:** Ask the children what their fingers do when they go home.

 *Kathy Kalmar, Macomb, MI*

# I'm A Little Button

### FINGERPLAYS, SONGS, & POEMS

**Materials**  none

**What to do**  Sing the following song to the tune of "I'm a Little Teapot."

*I'm a little button* (hands in a round shape)
*Smooth and round,* (hands make smoothing motion)
*I'm rolling down* (point fingers down)
*To touch the ground.* (bend knees and touch floor)
*When you pick me up* (straighten up and raise hands)
*I'll fit just right* (clap hands)
*Slip me in* (pointer finger slides into other hand, making a circle shape)
*And hold me tight!* (hug yourself!)

 *Jane Cline Rubicini, Kitchener, Ontario, Canada*

# Jumping on the Bed

### FINGERPLAYS, SONGS, & POEMS

**Materials**  five monkeys (stuffed animals, plastic figures, pictures, or cutouts)

**What to do**  1. Say the following rhyme with the children and encourage them to act it out.
2. Hold up five stuffed monkeys or pictures of monkeys. Take one away as each monkey bumps his head.

*Five little monkeys jumping on the bed.* (wave arms up and down)
*One fell off and bumped his head.* (put hand on head)
*Momma called the doctor and the doctor said,* (pretend to dial a phone, put extended thumb and finger to side of head)
*"No more monkeys jumping on the bed."* (shake finger as if scolding)

Repeat this poem until no monkeys are jumping on the bed.

**Related book**  *Caps for Sale* by Esphyr Slobodkina

 *Barbara Saul, Eureka, CA*

# Ten Little Deer

## FINGERPLAYS, SONGS, & POEMS

**Materials**   none

**What to do**   Invite the children to recite the following fingerplay, making the appropriate gestures when necessary.

*Ten little deer* (hold up ten fingers)
*Lived in a forest.* (nod yes)
*They listened to a bullfrog chorus,* (put hand to ears)
*They ran up the hill* (run up with fingers on arm)
*And down the hill.* (run fingers down other arm)
*They ran to the right,* (run fingers right)
*They ran to the left,* (run fingers to the left)
*They ran through the night*
*Until they all took a rest.* (rest head on hands, tilt head)

**More to do**   Substitute foxes for deer and repeat. Let children make suggestions and repeat until they no longer show interest.

★ *Kathy Kalmar, Macomb, MI*

# Old Man With a Beard

## FINGERPLAYS, SONGS, & POEMS

**Materials**   white furry material
scissors
elastic
card stock
markers
8 Velcro dots

**What to do**   1. Cut out a beard shape from a piece of white furry material, making it long enough to reach from a child's chin to her waist. Make a beard for each child.
2. Sew enough elastic at the top of the beard to fit around a child's head.
3. Draw or photocopy two owls, one hen, four larks, and one wren (for each child) onto card stock, making the scale of the birds accurate.

4. Cut out the bird shapes. Stick Velcro dots to the backs of the birds.
5. Arrange the birds on each beard so that they fit evenly, and then sew on white Velcro dots to match those on the birds.
6. Teach the children the following Edward Lear poem, "There Was an Old Man With a Beard." Choose nine children to act it out.

*There was an old man with a beard,* (old man with walking stick walks by)
*Who said,* (old man strokes his long beard)
*"It is just as I feared!"—* (old man looks stricken and shakes index finger)
*Two owls and a hen, four larks and a wren,* (eight children walk by, one after another, flapping their arms like birds)
*Have all made their nests in my beard.* (each sticks her card representation onto beard)

ELASTIC

BEARD

**More to do**    **Art:** Display a large reproduction of "The Old Man With a Beard" by Picasso.
**Language:** Read more delightful nonsense verses from Edward Lear.
**Literacy:** Show children that the same poem can be read in many different languages, using the book by Cheewan Wisasa (see below).

**Related books**    *Owl and the Pussycat* by Jan Brett
*Owl and the Pussycat & Other Nonsense Poems* by Edward Lear
*The Old Man With a Beard* by Cheewan Wisasa

★ *Anne Adeney, Plymouth, United Kingdom*

# Math Fingerplays

FINGERPLAYS, SONGS, & POEMS

**Materials**     none

**What to do**     Use the following familiar fingerplays to make math connections.

*The Ants Go Marching*
*Five Little Ducks*
*Five Little Monkeys*
*Five Little Pumpkins*
*Five Little Speckled Frogs*
*Here Is a Beehive*
*One Potato, Two Potatoes*
*Ten In The Bed*
*Two Little Blackbirds*
*Two Little Dogs*

★ *Kathy Kalmar, Macomb, MI*

# Who Stole the Cookie From the Cookie Jar?

GAMES

**Materials**     scissors
brown, tan, or cream paper
marker
laminate (optional)
plastic jar

**What to do**     1. Ahead of time, cut out one paper cookie for each child and at least five extra using a cookie pattern (circle shape).
2. On the back of each cookie, draw a smiley face or sad face. (Laminate, if desired, for durability.) Make at least four to eight cookies with sad faces.
3. Place all the cookies in the plastic jar.
4. Pick four to eight children (depending on class size) to choose who may have "stolen the cookie."
5. Pass the cookie jar around and instruct each child to remove one cookie.
6. Encourage the children to keep the cookie side up (smiley or sad face down) until you tell them to turn it over.
7. After all the children have removed cookie, ask them to peek at their cookies and not let anyone see whether their cookie has a smiley or sad face.

8. Instruct the children to turn the cookies back over.
9. The children who were picked earlier are the guessers. The guessers should say, "_____ stole a cookie from the cookie jar." The child whose name is called should reply, "Who me?" The guesser should answer, "Yes, you." The child should say, "Not me" if he has a smiley face or "Yes, me" if he has a sad face.
10. The child who guesses correctly exchanges places with the person who had the sad face cookie. Those who guess incorrectly also exchange places with those children left that have the cookies with the sad faces.

**RELATED book**    *Who Took the Cookie From the Cookie Jar?* by David Carter

★ *Quazonia Quarles, Newark, DE*

# DOUGHNUT COLOR RECOGNITION GAME

GAMES

**MATERIALS**    construction paper in a variety of colors
circle time rug

**WHAT TO DO**    1. Cut out doughnut shapes from construction paper in a variety of colors.
2. Have the children sit in a circle. Place the "doughnuts" in the center of the circle.
3. Sing the following song to the tune of "Little Bunny Foo Foo":

*Down around the corner*
*At the bakery shop,*
*There were* (number of doughnuts) *little doughnuts*
*With sugar on top.*
*Along came* (child's name*),*
*And he (or she) picked the* (color) *doughnut.*

The child picks up the specified color doughnut.

*And he* (action) *and he* (action) *and he* (action) *all the way home.*

Specify an action, such as run or hop. The child does the action around the circle and then returns to his place in the circle. For example, "And he ran and he ran and he ran all the way home."

**MORE TO DO**    Vary the game by using shapes, letters, or numbers instead of doughnuts.

★ *Andrea Hungerford, Plymouth, CT*

# A Tisket, A Tasket

GAMES

**Materials**   poster board
scissors
laminate

**What to do**
1. Cut out a large letter "T" from poster board and laminate it.
2. Sing the following song.
3. Have a child carry the T and drop it behind another child, who then carries on the game.

**A Tisket, A Tasket**

*A tisket, a tasket*
*A green and yellow basket,*
*I wrote a letter to my love*
*And on the way I lost it.*

*I lost it, I lost it,*
*And on the way I lost it.*
*A little boy (girl), he (she) picked it up,*
*And put it in his (her) pocket.*

*His (her) pocket, his (her) pocket,*
*He (she) put it in his (her) pocket.*
*A little boy (girl), he (she) picked it up,*
*And put it in his (her) pocket.*

 *Kathy Kalmar, Macomb, MI*

# Back Home From the Party

GAMES

**Materials**   household objects (plates, mugs, toothbrushes, shoes, eating utensils, shovel, jars, toys, books, pens, and so on)

**More to do**
1. Place all the household objects on a table.
2. Tell the children to pretend that you gathered the objects together for a party, but the party is now over and it's time to put the objects back.

3. Talk about where each object belongs (the shoes go in a closet, the toothpaste goes in the bathroom, and so on).
4. Recite the following rhyme with the children:

*Party's over,*
*Now go home.*
*Go, go,* (object name)
*Go into the* (place where it should be kept).

⭐ *Shyamala Shanmugasundaram, Nerul, Navi Mumbai, India*

# Sardines

GAMES

**Materials**      none

**What to do**
1. This fun version of hide and seek provides good practice in counting and keeping quiet. It can be played indoors or outdoors, as long as there are a number of good hiding places available. Outdoors, drape large play equipment with blankets to make hiding places. Indoors use a few rooms (if available). If you can, have children from several different classrooms play together and use all the different rooms.
2. Choose one child to go and hide. If you have a large group, divide the children into teams of six or eight and have one child from each group hide.
3. The rest of the children hide their eyes and count aloud to 20 (or whatever number is appropriate for the children in your class).
4. Tell the children that they are all silent "trackers" and must move very quietly (no talking or laughing) as they search for the hidden child and especially after they have found him.
5. When a child finds the hidden child, she must stay completely silent, creep into the hiding place with the hidden child, and wait for the other children to join them. Remind them not to speak or giggle so they won't give away their hiding place.
6. The game continues until all the children are squashed into the same hiding places, like sardines in a can.
7. If possible, show the children a can of sardines and demonstrate how tightly packed they are.

**MORE TO DO**  **Games:** Play other varieties of hide and seek.
**More Games:** Play other games that practice keeping quiet, such as Sleeping Lions.
**Group or Circle Time:** Invite the children to talk about times and places when silence is appropriate.
**Music:** Sing songs about fish and adapt one to make it a sardine song.

**RELATED BOOKS**  *Arlene Sardine* by Chris Raschka
*Everyone Hide From Wibbly Pig* by Mick Inkpen
*Five Little Monkeys Play Hide-and-Seek* by Eileen Christelow
*Little Quack's Hide and Seek* by Lauren Thompson
*Peek!: A Thai Hide-and-Seek* by Minfong Ho

 *Anne Adeney, Plymouth, United Kingdom*

# Body Shapes

GAMES

**MATERIALS**  masking tape
hula hoop

**WHAT TO DO**  1. In an open area on the floor, make a square and a triangle with 3' long strips of masking tape. Make a rectangle 3' long on two sides and 6' long on the other two sides.

TRIANGLE

2. Place a hula hoop on the floor for a circle, or use small pieces of masking tape to make the circle.
3. Ask two or three children to make a circle by lying along the borders of the hula hoop or masking tape circle.
4. Ask how many children are needed to make a triangle, and then have them do it by lying along the borders of the tape.
5. Repeat with the square and the rectangle.
6. Encourage discussion about what shapes they see, how the shapes are different from one another, and why different numbers of children are needed to make the different shapes.
7. The cooperative nature of working together to form a shape enhances cooperative play skills.

**MORE TO DO**  **Art:** Encourage the children to cut out shapes from playdough using cookie cutters or mold three-dimensional shapes.
**Blocks:** Ask each child to find a block or toy in the room that corresponds with each shape and place it inside the shape.
**Group or Circle Time:** Have the children form one giant shape—a circle, a square, a triangle, and a rectangle.
**Language:** Ask the children to identify large objects in the school that correspond to each shape (such as a table, door, window, and clock).

*Jeanne Moran, Tunkhannock, PA*

# Billy Brown Went to Town

GAMES

**Materials**  none

**What to do**  1. This game is good for memory, developing language, and learning colors.
2. The first child says, "Billy Brown went to town and bought some _____ " (child names a brown item, for example, chocolate).
3. The second child repeats the first child's item and adds another brown item: "Billy Brown went to town and bought some chocolate and a teddy bear."
4. Each following child repeats what has been said before and adds another brown item to the shopping list. It's okay if a child forgets some of the previous items.
5. When everyone has had a turn, change the color. For example, "Rosie Red went shopping and bought some strawberries."

**More to do**  Use this activity as part of a color or stores theme.
**Dramatic Play:** Encourage children to play games involving shopping.
**Group or Circle Time:** Talk about different types of stores.

**Related books**  *Carl Goes Shopping* by Alexandra Day
*Market!* by Ted Lewin
*On Market Street* by Arnold Lobel
*Sheep in a Shop* by Nancy E. Shaw
*To Market, To Market* by Anne Miranda

 *Anne Adeney, Plymouth, United Kingdom*

# Holiday/Season Hop

GAMES

**Materials**  colorful, simple holiday or seasonal pictures or clip art (two of each picture)
tape

**What to do**

1. Find matching pairs of colorful, simple holiday or seasonal pictures or clip art (same size, if possible). Laminate them, if desired.
2. Arrange the pictures on the floor in any arrangement that is suitable for the children's ages (hopscotch layout or circle). Place the pictures so that the matching pictures are not next to each other.
3. Tape the pictures to the floor.
4. If using a hopscotch layout, have the children stand in a line. Ask the first child to hop on both feet or one foot, depending on the child's skills, from one picture to its match. The child may keep hopping, or you may let the next child in line jump to two different pictures.
5. If using a circle layout, have one child stand in the middle and hop from one picture to its match, hopping back to the middle of the circle between hops.

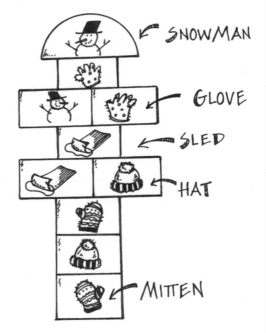

SNOWMAN

GLOVE

SLED

HAT

MITTEN

**More to do**  Picture ideas for different holidays include a black cat, pumpkin, scarecrow, trick-or-treater, ghost, witch, and bat for Halloween; a snowman, hat and gloves, and snowflake for winter, and so on.

**Math:** To incorporate math skills, use pictures of numbers and matching objects. For example, the child hops to the number 1, and then hops to the picture of one pumpkin. She then hops to the number 2, and then to a picture of two ghosts.

**Music:** Have the children hop while seasonal music plays. When the song ends, the child stops hopping and her turn is over

**Science:** Include pictures of seasons, such as trees with leaves, bare trees, and so on.

 *Jill Martin and D'Arcy Simmons, Springfield, MO*

# Collection Drive

**Materials**

computer and printer or paper and marker
large box

**What to do**

1. Prepare a colorful, eye-catching flyer entitled: "Collection Drive for Things to Use in Creative Learning."
2. Make a list of any items you might need in your classroom over the next few months. Think about upcoming themes, special celebrations, and holidays as well as your classroom centers (art, math, science, fine motor, housekeeping, and so on). For example, if you want to add some new items for counting and sorting, ask for keys, buttons, ceramic tiles, plastic bottle caps, discarded puzzle pieces, loose game pieces, shells, rocks, bag of rubber bands of various sizes and colors, beads, and so on.
3. Send the flyers home to parents.
4. Provide a child-decorated Collection Box and place it in a visible spot. This will also serve as a reminder to parents.
5. Be sure to acknowledge families and friends that respond to your collection drive.
6. Take pictures to show how the children utilized these contributions.

**More to do**

For items that are not typically found around the home, make a list of various businesses that have items available upon request by teachers and parents. For example, appliance stores have refrigerator boxes, framing stores have matte board, greeting card stores have envelopes, lumber stores have wood pieces, and so on.

 *Judy Fujawa, The Villages, FL*

# Alternatives to "Shhh"

**Materials**

Instead of telling the children "Shhhh" when you want them to quiet down, try using these alternatives:

- "Give me five": Stop, eyes on me, be quiet, listen, raise your hand.
- Count down: "5-4-3-2-1, listen."
- Say, "Freeze like a Popsicle!"
- Use snap or clap patterns (begins a snap-clap rhythm, children follow)
- Use a STOP hand signal.

- Say a nonsense word.
- Use the peace sign (V)
- Sing, "Are you listening?" Children respond, "Yes, I am."
- Use chimes
- Use a large hourglass or egg timer.
- Strike a piano key, pluck a string, use a tuning fork, use a xylophone.
- Use the American Sign Language sign for "quiet."
- Raise a finger to closed lips.

★ *Kathy Kalmar, Macomb MI*

# CHANGE-A-BOX

GENERAL TIPS

**MATERIALS**
large appliance box
knife (adult only)
paint
paintbrushes
aluminum foil
glue
bottle lids
thin cardboard
stuffed animals or hand puppets
packing tape

**WHAT TO DO**

1. Place box upright. Cut hinged doors and windows (leave one side uncut) large enough for children to crawl through. Leaving one side of each window and door uncut will enable you to tape the doors and windows down when you change the box.
2. Cut a postal slot in the door for children to receive mail.
3. Invite the children to paint the box like a house. Provide cushions and toys for children to arrange.
4. When the children get tired of the house, glue aluminum foil around the outside to make a spaceship. Glue bottle tops inside to make control buttons.
5. Make cone-shaped hats from cardboard and cover with foil for the "space people" to wear.
6. Invite the children to paint the inside of the spaceship.
7. When the children get tired of the spaceship, change the box into a "'puppet theater." Pull or cut the joints of the box apart and lay flat on the ground.

8. Tape windows and doors shut.

9. Create a corner to stand the box. The flaps of the box will help to keep it upright. Tape the flaps, if necessary, to strengthen the box.

10. Encourage the children to crouch behind the box and perform a puppet show. If needed, help them get started or provide a theme for them to work with. Let them take turns being the puppeteers and the audience.

**MORE TO DO**   Obtain a few boxes and make several houses to make a street.
Science: Talk to the children about recycling.

 *Sandra Saunders, Carrum Downs, Victoria, Australia*

# BE A WRITER/ARTIST ANYWHERE!

GENERAL TIPS

**MATERIALS**   firm cardboard or fiber board
binder clips
paper
writing tools
zipper-closure bags

**WHAT TO DO**

1. Cut cardboard or fiber board into a manageable size for the children in your class (younger writers need more space to write and draw, but keep the size manageable).

2. Use binder clips to attach a piece of paper to the cardboard.

3. Place writing tools inside a zipper-closure bag and clip to the back of the board.

4. Let the children take their writing/art boards outdoors.

5. Welcome open-ended work or make suggestions to get children started. For example, suggest that they draw the pattern they see on the bark of a tree or list things they see in the sky.

**MORE TO DO**   **Bulletin Board:** Make an art display of outdoor works.
**Group or Circle Time:** Do a story web in circle from the ideas they collected outside.
**Literacy:** Encourage the children to dictate a story about the drawings they made.

 *Bev Schumacher, Racine, WI*

# Stackable Storage Cubbies

### GENERAL TIPS

**Materials**    assorted cardboard boxes
scissors
old comics or rolls of decorative wrapping paper
double-sided sticky tape

**What to do**

1. Remove the cardboard box tops with scissors.
2. Wrap each box with old comics or decorative wrapping paper. Lay them on their sides.

   SCRAP PAPER and PENCILS

3. Stack boxes, using double-sided tape to make the boxes stick together.

   CRAYONS

4. Invite the children to fill the cubbies with coloring books, scrap paper, crayons, pencils, and so on.

WRAPPING PAPER

PUT DOUBLE-SIDED TAPE BETWEEN

COLORING BOOKS

⭐ *Penni Smith, Riverside, CA*

# Circle Song

### GROUP TIME

**Materials**    none

**What to do**

1. Sing the following song to the tune of "Bingo."
   *Sit right down and fold your hands,*
   *It's time to have our circle.*
   *C-I-R-CL-E, C-I-R-CL-E, C-I-R-CL-E,*
   *It's time to have our circle.*
2. Adapt the song to use throughout the day. For example:
   *Sit right down and fold your hands,*
   *It's time to read a story.*
   *S-T-O-R-Y, S-T-O-R-Y, S-T-O-R-Y,*
   *It's time to read a story.*

 *Phyllis Esch, Export, PA*

# I "Can" Can

GROUP OR CIRCLE TIME

**MATERIALS**

can or container
paper
glue
marker

**WHAT TO DO**

1. Cover a can or container with paper and write, "I can" on it.
2. Discuss how the children will use the can. Make it clear that all of the children will be a part of this positive experience and everyone will be able to make a contribution to the can.
3. Have strips of paper available for the children to write down what they have accomplished (something that they could not do before). What children write will range from simple to complex, depending on the child's ability, age, and developmental level. For example, "I tied my shoes today." "I prepared my own snack." "I read a book today."
4. At the end of each month, celebrate the children's accomplishments.

⭐ *Judy Fujawa, The Villages, FL*

# Eight Silly Monkeys

GROUP OR CIRCLE TIME

**MATERIALS**

*Eight Silly Monkeys* by Steve Haskamp (illustrator), or a similar book which counts backwards as part of the story

**WHAT TO DO**

1. Select eight children to stand in front of the circle.
2. As you read the story and each monkey disappears, have one child sit down until all are sitting.

**MORE TO DO**

**Math:** *The Monster Math* series by Anne Miranda has stories with different numerical combinations that all add up to the same number. Read one of these books and have the children rearrange themselves as you read.

⭐ *Kristi Larson, Spirit Lake, IA*

# Birthday Box

GROUP OR CIRCLE TIME

**Materials**
box
birthday wrapping paper
books about birthdays
playdough
real birthday candles
birthday decorations (plates, cups, napkins, banners, hats, blowers)
paper, folded (for making birthday cards)
crayons

**What to do**
1. Wrap a box with birthday wrapping paper and put books about birthdays, playdough, birthday candles, decorations, folded paper, and crayons inside the box.
2. Introduce the box to the children at the beginning of the year, or on the day of the first child's birthday celebration.
3. Put the box in a center and let the children celebrate the birthday child by reading books, making cards, decorating, baking and putting the candles on a pretend cake, and singing "Happy Birthday."
4. Use the birthday box whenever a child is celebrating her or his birthday.
5. Make sure each child has a special day.

★ *Gail Morris, Kemah, TX*

# Favorite Cookie Graph

GROUP OR CIRCLE TIME

**Materials**
tagboard for header card
computer printer or marker
colored pictures of various cookies
name card for each child in the class
pocket chart

**What to do**
1. Brainstorm various kinds of cookies with the children.
2. Create a graph by printing a header card with pictures of four different cookies under the heading, "What is your favorite cookie?"
3. Display it in the top row of a pocket chart.
4. Have each child, in turn, come forward and vote to show her preference by placing her name card under her choice.
5. Discuss the graph with the children and determine which cookie the children like best.

**More to do**     **Snack:** Bake a batch of cookies to match the class favorite.

**Related book**     *If You Give a Mouse a Cookie* by Laura Numeroff

★ *Jackie Wright, Enid, OK*

# A Book a Month

LANGUAGE AND LITERACY

**Materials**     chart paper
markers
paper
construction paper
laminate (optional)

**What to do**
1. When the children are studying something interesting or after a special event, encourage them to brainstorm ideas about the topic while you write them down on a piece of chart paper.
2. Talk to each child individually and have her dictate a story about what she saw at the event or what she thinks about the interesting theme.
3. Encourage the children to draw pictures to go with their stories. Put a picture of the child on her paper.
4. Glue the stories to larger pieces of colored construction paper and laminate them, if desired. Bind the pages into a book.
5. Make a different class book each month the same way.
6. Let the children take turns bringing the books home overnight. If desired, put a blank page at the back of each book for adults and children to write down what they thought of the book.
7. At the end of the year, take all the books apart. Reassemble the pages of each child into individual books. Children can bring their books home as a reminder of their year.

★ *Barbara Saul, Eureka, CA*

# My Name All Year

### LANGUAGE AND LITERACY

**Materials**   varies each month (see activity)

**What to do**   Help the children learn to recognize and write their own names by doing the following activities each month. Print each child's name on a separate sentence strip, glue her photo next to her name, and laminate. Children can use these name strips throughout the year to trace and if they need help writing their names. (Older children might want to practice writing their first and last names.)

- **September:** Print each child's name on a sentence strip. Cut the strips into three to four piece puzzles. Invite the children to take their puzzles home for practice.
- **October:** Use a yellow highlighter pen or marker to print each child's name on a piece of paper. Invite them to trace over their names with a pink highlighter pen. If they stay on the lines, their names will "magically" turn orange.
- **November:** Print each child's name on white paper using a white crayon. Press hard. Invite the children to paint over their names with watercolor. Their names will appear!
- **December:** Print each child's name using a blue marker. Have them trace over their names with a yellow marker to make a holiday green.
- **January:** Have each child trace her name in glue. Encourage them to sprinkle snowflake confetti or salt on their names for a snowy effect.
- **February:** Invite children to use rubber alphabet stamps to stamp their own names on heart-shaped red paper.
- **March:** Tape red, blue, and yellow crayons together with masking tape. Encourage the children to write their names with the crayons for a rainbow effect.
- **April:** Provide foam alphabet letters and ask the children to find the letters in their names. Give them sentence strips with their names written on them, if needed.
- **May:** Invite the children to practice writing their names using thick brown paint ("mud").
- **June:** Print each child's name in glue and let it dry. Invite them to make rubbings by putting a piece of paper over their name and rubbing with a crayon.
- **July:** Encourage the children to trave over the letters in their names with glue. Let them sprinkle star confetti or red, white, and blue glitter on the glue. For younger children, print their names on sentence strips and invite them to put star stickers on the letters.
- **August:** Have the children use chalk to write their names outside on the sidewalk.

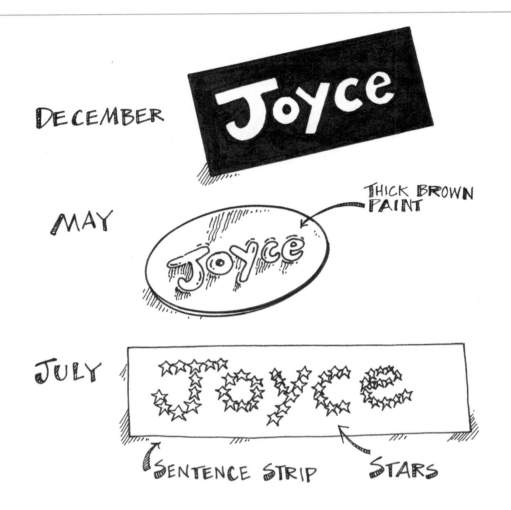

DECEMBER Joyce

MAY Joyce ← THICK BROWN PAINT

JULY Joyce ↗ STARS

↖ SENTENCE STRIP

**Related book** *Chrysanthemum* by Kevin Henkes

⭐ *Sue Fleischmann, Sussex, WI*

# Question of the Month

LANGUAGE AND LITERACY

**Materials** varies each month (see activity)

**What to do**
1. Following are some fun questions to ask the children each month of the year. This activity encourages expressive language and creativity, and it provides a good insight into what the children are thinking.
2. For each month, read the suggested book, write one or all of the suggested questions on a cutout shape for each child, and ask the children to dictate their answers as you write them on their shapes. In some cases, ask the questions before reading the story. Display the shapes and then put the shapes in the children's portfolios to keep.

3. Do the extension activities, if desired.

- **September:** Read *What Teacher's Can't Do* by Douglas Wood.
  - Print the following questions on an apple shape for each child. What do teachers do at night? Where do they live? What do they eat?
  - Extension Activity: Read other books about school, such as *David Goes to School* by David Shannon, *D.W.'s Guide to Preschool* by Marc Brown, and *Mouse's First Day of School* by Lauren Thompson.
- **October:** Read *We're Going on a Ghost Hunt* by Marcia Vaughan.
  - Print the questions on a ghost shape. How do ghosts celebrate Halloween? What does a ghost eat? What do ghosts do at ghost school?
  - Extension Activities: Make shaving cream ghosts on the table (use non-menthol shaving cream); paint the children's feet with white paint and help them make footprints on black paper. (The heel is the top.) Have them draw ghost faces.
- **November:** Read *A Plump and Perky Turkey* by Teresa Bateman.
  - Print the questions on a turkey shape. What do turkeys eat for Thanksgiving? What do you eat on Thanksgiving?
  - Extension Activities: Invite children to glue feathers on a construction paper turkey shape; ask them to dictate how to make mashed potatoes or other Thanksgiving food on a recipe card. Use the recipes to make a book.
- **December:** Read *Elton the Elf* by Lisa Mallen.
  - Print the following questions on a green Santa hat shape. How old are elves? What do elves learn at school? What are the elves names? What do elves eat?
  - Extension Activity: Make paper plate elves. Give each child a paper plate and provide several colors of skin-tone paint. Encourage them to make a face on the plate and add facial features and pointed ears. Have them glue on green Santa hats and jingle bells.
- **January:** Read *Snowmen at Night* by Caralyn Buehner.
  - Write the following questions on a tooth shape. What do snow friends eat? What do snow friends do at night?
  - Extension Activity: Give each child three different size circles, small fabric scarves, and a carrot shaped nose to make a snow friend.
- **February:** Read *Dear Tooth Fairy* by Alan Durant.
  - Write the following questions on a tooth shape. Where does the tooth fairy live? What does the tooth fairy do with all the teeth? What is his/her name?
  - Extension Activity: List all the children in the class who have lost a tooth on a giant tooth shape. Write a class letter to the tooth fairy. (Have the "tooth fairy" write back and tell children to brush, eat healthy foods, and visit the dentist.)
  - Extension Activity: Read *Alice the Fairy* by David Shannon. Make tooth fairy wands by gluing cutout stars on straws.

- **March:** Read *The Littlest Leprechaun* by Jane Fontes.
  - Write the following questions on a shamrock shape. What does a leprechaun look like? What do leprechauns eat? Why do leprechauns play tricks? How do you catch a leprechaun?
  - Extension Activity: Spray paint rocks with gold paint (away from children). Hide around the classroom and invite the children to find them. Count them together.
- **April:** Read *The Aunts Go Marching* by Maurie J. Manning.
  - Print the questions on a raindrop or lightning bolt shape. Where does rain come from? What does lightning look like? What does thunder sound like?
  - Extension Activity: Have children fingerpaint with black and white paint on a cloud shape and glue gold glitter on a lightning bolt shape. When dry, glue the bolt on the cloud.
- **May:** Read *What Mom's Can't Do* by Douglas Wood or *What Mommies Do Best/What Daddies Do Best* by Laura Numeroff.
  - Print the following sentences on a piece of paper: My mom's name is _____. My mom is _____ years old. My mom likes to _____. My mom is special because _____.
  - Extension Activity: Invite children to draw a picture of their moms (or caregivers). Display the pictures and questions together. Invite the mothers to guess which picture/description is them.
- **June:** Read *What Dad's Can't Do* by Douglas Wood or *What Daddies Do Best/What Mommies Do Best* by Laura Numeroff.
  - Print the following sentences on a piece of paper. My dad's name is _____. My dad is _____ years old. My dad likes to _____. My dad is special because _____.
  - Extension Activity: Invite children to draw a picture of their dads (or caregivers). Display the pictures and questions together. Invite the fathers to guess which picture/description is them.
- **July:** Read *Diary of a Worm* by Doreen Cronin.
  - Print the questions on a big worm shape. Where do worms live? What do worm eat? What do worms eat at school? What do worm mothers tell their children?
  - Extension Activities: Encourage the children to paint brown worms and add a pipe cleaner worm; look for worms after a rain; Have children pretend they are worms. Challenge them to move without using their arms or legs.
- **August:** Read *What the Sun Sees/What the Moon Sees* by Nancy Tafuri.
  - Print the questions on a sun shape. Where does the sun go at night? Where is the sun when it is raining? What is the sun made of?
  - Extension Activity: Have children paint a glue/water mixture on a sun shape and add yellow and orange tissue paper squares.

 *Sue Fleischmann, Sussex, WI*

# A Different Story Every Time

## LANGUAGE AND LITERACY

**Materials**   picture books with no words

**What to do**
1. Invite the children to take turns being the storyteller to the group.
2. Encourage the child to explain the story to the other children as it unfolds in the pictures of a wordless book.

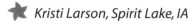 *Kristi Larson, Spirit Lake, IA*

# Birthday Books

## LANGUAGE AND LITERACY

**Materials**   paper
pencils
crayons
tagboard

**What to do**
1. On each child's birthday, ask the rest of the children to write or dictate something nice about the birthday child.
2. Invite the birthday child to create a cover for the book on tagboard.
3. Assemble the stories into a book. Read it aloud to the group.
4. Let the birthday child keep the book and bring it home or put it into the class library.

 *Barbara Saul, Eureka, CA*

# Talking Partners

## LANGUAGE AND LITERACY

**Materials**   red and blue markers or paint

**What to do**
1. Divide children into pairs.
2. Write a red "1" on one partner's hand, and a blue "2" on the other partner's hand.

3. During a story or presentation, when asking the group a question, instruct the "number ones" to give their answers to their partners (the "number twos") or vice versa.

4. In this way, each child will be able to express her own opinion.

5. Listen to what the partners say. Say, "I heard partners saying _____. That's a good answer!"

**More to do**
Cut out a stop sign from red paper and write "Stop" on it. On the other side, attach a green piece of paper (same size) and write "Go" on it. Tape or glue this to a craft stick. When it's time for children to talk to their partners, show the green side of the sign. When it's time to stop talking, flip the sign to the stop side.

*★ Barbara Saul, Eureka, CA*

# The Alphabet Grab Bag
LANGUAGE AND LITERACY

**Materials**
26 2" x 2" strips of paper
small cloth or paper bag
pen or marker

**What to do**
1. Write each letter of the alphabet (both upper- and lowercase) on a square of paper.
2. Fold each piece and place inside the bag.
3. Gather the children for circle time.
4. Ask the first child to pick a paper from the bag, open it, and say the letter and sound out loud. The child shows the letter to the class and the class repeats the letter and sound.
5. The child then says a word that begins with that letter sound. If the child cannot think of one, she can call on a classmate for help.
6. Have the child pass the bag to the child on her right, who repeats the process.
7. Continue until all the children have had a turn or all the letters have been used.

*★ Jane Annunziata, Sussex, NJ*

# Marking the Alphabet

## LANGUAGE AND LITERACY

**MATERIALS**
old newspapers
markers

**WHAT TO DO**

1. Distribute a sheet of newspaper to each child in the class along with a marker. Explain that they are going to mark every letter A they see in their newspapers.
2. Encourage them to scan the newspaper pages and circle as many A's as they can find. Help them, as needed.
3. Continue this game with other letters.

**MORE TO DO**
Have children find numbers, pictures of living things and non-living things, and so on.

 *Shyamala Shanmugasundaram, Nerul, Navi Mumbai, India*

# Big Beans On Blue

## LANGUAGE AND LITERACY

**MATERIALS**
blue paper
glue
woodchips

**WHAT TO DO**

1. Recite "Blue Bird, Blue Bird" with the children.

   *Blue bird, blue bird, in and out my window,*
   *Blue bird, blue bird, in and out my window.*
   *Blue bird, blue bird, in and out my window.*
   *Oh, blue bird, I'm so tired.* (hold hands in circle, move up and down; pretend to sleep)

2. Help each child trace a large letter B on blue paper.
3. Encourage them to put glue and brown woodchips over it.

**MORE TO DO**
**Science:** Use binoculars to watch for blue birds .

 *Kathy Kalmar, Macomb, MI*

# Ms. M

LANGUAGE AND LITERACY

**Materials**
chart paper
mauve construction paper
markers

**What to do**
1. Write the nursery rhyme "Little Miss Muffet" on chart paper. Say the rhyme with the children.
2. Encourage the children to find the M's on the chart paper
3. Draw an uppercase M on mauve construction paper, one for each child. Ask the children to trace it with markers.

**More to do**
Make P's on purple or pink construction paper after reciting "Peter, Peter Pumpkin Eater."

⭐ *Kathy Kalmar, Macomb, MI*

# Torn Tissue Paper T's

LANGUAGE AND LITERACY

**Materials**
*Tiny Tim* by Rose Impey
tissue paper
paper
glue

**What to do**
1. Read *Tiny Tim* to the children.
2. Write a large T on paper, one for each child.
3. Have children tear tissue paper into small pieces and glue the pieces on the T.

⭐ *Kathy Kalmar, Macomb, MI*

# "Goodnight Moon" Rhymes
### LANGUAGE AND LITERACY

**Materials**   *Goodnight Moon* by Margaret Wise Brown
pictures of or actual balloons, moon, bears, chairs, kittens, mittens, house, mouse, clocks, and socks

**What to do**
1. Read *Goodnight Moon* to the children. After reading the book, show them the illustrations again.
2. Show the objects or pictures from the book.
3. Have the children take turns choosing an object. Encourage them to name words that rhyme with their objects. For example: "Tia chose a balloon. What word rhymes with balloon?"

**Related book**   *A Fairy Went A-Marketing* by Rose Fyleman.

 *Linda Atamian, Charlestown, RI*

# Shopping Spree
### LANGUAGE AND LITERACY

**Materials**   pictures or replicas of different consumer goods and foods
store signs

**What to do**
1. This game is best played in a large room. Put up signs for four to six stores in different areas of the room (toy store, bakery, deli, shoe store, and so on).
2. Make up a shopping list (bread, sneakers, hamburger, cheese, and so on).
3. Ask the children to stand in the center of the room. Tell them they have to run to the correct store to get the item you call out. For example, if you call out, "doll," they would run to the toy store.
4. If desired, hold up objects and say, "Run to the store where you would buy this!" rather than using words.

**More to do**   **Math:** Encourage children to practice buying goods with real or artificial money.

**Related books**   *Aunt Lucy Went to Buy a Hat* by Alice Low
*Fairy Went A-Marketing* by Rose Fyleman
*You Can't Buy a Dinosaur With a Dime* by Harriet Ziefert

 *Anne Adeney, Plymouth, United Kingdom*

# Whisky, Frisky Fun

### LANGUAGE AND LITERACY

**MATERIALS**

4 die-cut squirrels
colored pictures representing beginning sounds
tagboard
glue stick
paper cutter
12" x 18" construction paper
color scanner (optional)
laminating machine (optional)
scissors
pocket chart

**WHAT TO DO**

1. Label each of the four die-cut squirrels with a different letter of your choice.
2. Use the squirrels to form four columns at the top of the pocket chart with a header card that has the title "Whisky, Frisky Fun" at the top and instructions to "Place the cards under the correct squirrels."
3. Glue or draw pictures representing the beginning sounds of each of the four letters on the squirrels.
4. Using a paper cutter, cut the pictures into cards of the desired size.
5. If desired, make a file jacket from 12" x 18" construction paper to hold the activity. Print the title and draw a squirrel on the front.
6. Using a color scanner, make a reduced-size printout of the completed activity showing the header card with all the picture cards under the correct squirrels.
7. Using a glue stick, glue the color printout to the back of the file jacket.
8. Laminate the header card, picture cards, and file jacket for durability, and cut out.
9. To use this center, a child identifies a picture's beginning sound and adds it to the pocket chart under the appropriate squirrel.
10. When finished, she can look at the back of the file jacket and check her work.
11. This picture reference helps ensure that all cards are accounted for when you put them away at the end of the month.

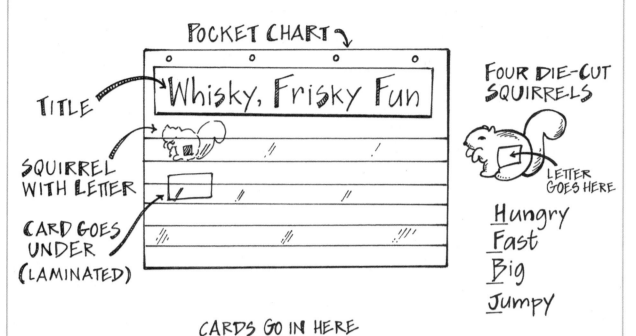

POCKET CHART

TITLE

Whisky, Frisky Fun

SQUIRREL WITH LETTER

CARD GOES UNDER (LAMINATED)

FOUR DIE-CUT SQUIRRELS

LETTER GOES HERE

Hungry
Fast
Big
Jumpy

CARDS GO IN HERE

Hungry

12"

18"

FILE JACKET

FEBRUARY

MARCH

DECEMBER

SHAPES to CUT OUT

SEPTEMBER

OCTOBER

**Related book** *Squirrels All Year Long* by Melvin Berger

*Jackie Wright, Enid, OK*

# Favorite Foods Cookbook

LANGUAGE AND LITERACY

**Materials**
chart paper
paper
markers and crayons
construction paper
hole punch
ribbon

**What to do**

1. Discuss favorite foods with the children.
2. Make a chart, listing everyone's favorite appetizers, vegetables, desserts, and so on.
3. Encourage the children to think about how their favorite foods are prepared. Ask them if they have ever prepared their own breakfast, lunch, or dinner, or watched someone prepare their meals.
4. Show them a few cookbooks so they can see how collections of recipes are presented. Explain that they are going to put together a class cookbook.
5. Individually ask each child to list the ingredients, the directions for preparation, and the time it will take to complete her favorite food.
6. Copy their recipe directions word for word. Don't put words in their mouth; simply encourage them to elaborate and clarify.
7. Encourage the children to illustrate their recipes.
8. Put all of the illustrated recipes together, make copies, and bind or tie them together. Invite the children to create their own covers for their books.
9. The children can give their cookbooks to a parent or other special person.

*Judy Fujawa, The Villages, FL*

# Question-and-Answer Book

LANGUAGE AND LITERACY

**Materials**
marker
paper
construction paper
hole punch
string

**What to do**

1. Make a list of questions to ask the children in one-on-one sessions. Examples of questions include:
   - What would you do if you were the president?
   - If you could drive, where would you go?
   - What are your favorite things to do?
   - What are your favorite books?
   - What are your three most special items?
   - What do you want to be when you grow up?
2. Sit in a quiet place with each child and ask her the questions.
3. Write or type each child's questions and answers on a separate piece of paper. Make copies and compile the pages into booklets, one for each child.
4. This makes for an amusing, interesting, and enlightening gift.
5. You can list each child's answers on one page, or list all of the answers to the same question on one page, and enjoy the variations.
6. Ask the parents to guess which list belongs to their child.

 *Judy Fujawa, The Villages, FL*

# Monthly Class Books

LANGUAGE AND LITERACY

**Materials**

examples of various types of books
crayons, markers, and pencils
variety of paper
hole punch
scissors
ruler
glue
tape
old magazines, calendars, catalogs, and greeting cards

**What to do**

1. Ask each child to contribute a drawing or decorated page to a class book every month. As a group, you might want to decide on a theme for each month. For example, Rain, Teardrops, and Wet Things; Holiday Fun; Bears, Beards, and Hairy Things; Having a Party; Razzle Dazzle, Glitter, and Things that Sparkle. Refurbish and rotate supplies on a monthly basis.
2. Provide a variety of new items such as stamps, stickers, silver contact paper each month to spur creativity.
3. Compile all of the pages and identify the month on the cover
4. Have all of the monthly class books available in the reading center.

**MORE TO DO**  Whenever possible, create a classroom big book after a special event or activity using large paper grocery bags. Cut the bottom from the bag. Cut up along the side of the bag and turn it inside out. Attach five bags together with wide, clear tape to form the binding. Encourage the children to add their drawings, art designs, and written words. You might want to divide each page into four sections.

★ *Judy Fujawa, The Villages, FL*

# Monthly Newsletter

LANGUAGE AND LITERACY

**MATERIALS**  paper
computer
printer

**WHAT TO DO**

1. Let the children help make a monthly newsletter to inform parents about what's new or has been happening in the classroom over the last month.
2. Talk about newspapers. Ask the children if their parents read newspapers. Explain that their newsletter will be like a newspaper from the classroom.
3. Each month, encourage the children to think of topics and ideas to include in the newsletter. Use the following format:
   - What's New?
   - New Songs
   - New Skills
   - New Books
4. Write the month at the top of the page. Invite the children to decorate the page with seasonal images.
5. Make a copy for each child to bring home to parents.

★ *Anne Lippincott, New Hartland, CT*

# Birthday Graph

MATH

**Materials**   large piece of graph paper
easel
felt-tip pen
yardstick

**What to do**
1. Use the yardstick and pen to make 12 columns on the graph paper. Label each one with the name of a month.
2. Let the children fill in a square in the month of their birthdays.
3. Use the graph to compare which month has the largest or smallest number of birthdays.

⭐ *Barbara Saul, Eureka, CA*

# Birthday Sequencing

MATH

**Materials**   12 1' long sentence strips
black pen
calendar

**What to do**
1. Label each sentence strip with the name of a month.
2. Encourage the children to put the months in the correct order, using the calendar as reference.

**More to do**   Lay the sentence strips on the floor. Have the children stand on those months that correspond to particular holidays (children's birthdays, Christmas, Halloween, Thanksgiving, and so on).

⭐ *Barbara Saul, Eureka, CA*

# Have You Ever Caught a Fish?

MATH

**Materials**
tagboard for header card
markers
die-cut fish (one for each child)
pocket chart

**What to do**
1. Prepare a header card for the pocket chart with the question "Have you ever caught a fish?" Draw a picture of a child fishing and put "Yes" on one side and "No" on the other to form two columns.
2. Print each child's name on a separate die-cut fish shape.
3. Place the header card in the pocket chart and ask each child, in turn, to respond.
4. Have them place their fish shapes in the appropriate column to indicate their answers.
5. Have the children count the total in each column and discuss the results.

**Related book**    *The Magic Fish* by Freya Littledale

 *Jackie Wright, Enid, OK*

# Holiday Sack Match

MATH

**Materials**
colorful, simple holiday pictures
holiday-themed gift bags
seasonal music (optional)

**What to do**
1. Purchase a variety of gift bags for different holidays, such as Christmas, Halloween, Valentine's Day, and birthdays.
2. Cut out a variety of seasonal and holiday pictures that match the gift bags.
3. Put the open gift bags on a table next to a pile of different holiday pictures.
4. Invite the children to take turns choosing a picture from the pile and putting it into the corresponding gift bag. For example, if the picture is of a heart it will go into a Valentine's Day bag. If the picture is of a Christmas tree, it will go into a Christmas bag.

More to do        **Fine Motor:** Have the children cut around pictures before placing them in the bags.

**Math:** Ask the children to count the pictures.

 *Jill Martin and D'Arcy Simmons, Springfield, MO*

# Join the Number Train

MATH

**Materials**        squares of paper
marker
tape

**What to do**    1. Write a number on each square of paper, depending on the number of children in your class. For example, if there are 20 children in the class, write the numbers 1-20 on separate pieces of paper (one number per square).
2. As each child enters the classroom, give her a number square. Help the children tape their numbers on their shirts.
3. Invite the children to find their place on the "number train" according to their numbers. For example, if a child has a number 9, she stands between number 8 and number 10.
4. The game continues until all the children have joined the train. The train keeps moving in a circle after every child joins the train.

**More to do**    Use letters instead of numbers. Children line up according to where their letter falls in the alphabet.

 *Shyamala Shanmugasundaram, Nerul, Navi Mumbai, India*

# Magnetic Graphing

MATH

**Materials**        roll of magnetic tape
photos of each child
magnetic board

**What to do**
1. Give the children their photos and strips of magnetic tape to attach to the backs of their pictures.
2. Divide the magnet board with lines for graphing. Label different categories, such as boy or girl; blonde, brown, black, or red hair; blue, brown, or green eyes; favorite sandwich; favorite ice cream flavor; and so on.
3. Have the children put their photos in the appropriate column.
4. After they have made their choices, discuss which column has the most pictures, which has the least, and so on.

⭐ *Barbara Saul, Eureka, CA*

# Sequencing of Numbers

MATH

**Materials**
old calendar with large font numbers
scissors
glue
chart paper

**What to do**
1. Cut out the numbers of each month into separate squares. Put the numbers of each month into separate bags.
2. Divide the children into several groups. Give each group a bag of numbers, glue, and a piece of chart paper.
3. Ask the groups to glue the numbers on the chart paper in ascending order.

⭐ *Shyamala Shanmugasundaram, Nerul, Navi Mumbai, India*

# All Together Now: Making Music Fun

MUSIC AND MOVEMENT

**Materials**
rhythm instruments
music CD
CD player
ribbons, scarves, and fabric pieces

**What to do**

1. Divide the children into small groups. Give the groups different instruments (the members of one group may have jingle bells, the members of another group may have shakers, and so on).
2. Encourage the children to become familiar with their instruments and practice playing them along with the music.
3. Have all of the groups come together for a classroom music-making experience. Play the music as children play their instruments. Children may also dance with ribbons and scarves to the music.

⭐ *Judy Fujawa, The Villages, FL*

# Seeing Sound

SCIENCE

**Materials**

bowl
aluminum foil
rubber band
uncooked rice
pan lid
spoon

**What to do**

1. Explain to the children that every noise they hear is made by something moving backwards and forwards very quickly and that it is called "vibration." Explain that sound travels in waves, which cannot be seen.
2. Tell the children that you are going to demonstrate how sound travels.
3. Make a drum by covering an empty bowl with foil and fastening a rubber band around it, so the foil is tight.
4. Put some uncooked grains of rice on the top of the "drum."
5. Tell the children to watch the rice carefully. Next to the drum, bang a pan lid with a spoon.
6. The sound waves from the pan lid will make the rice on the drum bounce into the air.
7. Another way to show sound waves is to ask the children to put an ear on the table, put a metal pan on the other end, and bang it. They will feel the vibration through the solid wood.

**More to do**

**Music:** Celebrate sound by singing noisy "sound songs," such as "Old MacDonald" and "Wheels on the Bus."
**Nature:** Play a tape of whales singing and explain that sound travels faster and further through water and that whales can hear each other from 50 miles away.

**Science:** Explain that thunder and lightning always happen at the same time, but we see the lightning before we hear the thunder because sound travels more slowly than light.

**More Science:** With older children who understand the concepts, tell them that sound waves travel through liquids, solids, and gases. Have them do experiments to hear sounds through all these.

**RELATED books**    *The Seals on the Bus* by Lenny Holt
*Too Much Noise* by Ann McGovern

 *Anne Adeney, Plymouth, United Kingdom*

# WATCH ME CHANGE

SCIENCE

**MATERIALS**

3 ice cube trays
water
spoons
food coloring (red, yellow, and blue)
freezer
12 large, transparent plastic bowls
newspapers

**WHAT TO do**

1. Fill three ice cube trays with water. Add red food coloring to the water in one tray, yellow to the water in another tray, and blue to the water in the third tray. Freeze to make colored ice cubes.
2. Remove the ice cube trays from the freezer. Fill the plastic bowls with water.
3. Add colored ice cubes to each plastic bowl and stir them until they dissolve.
4. Encourage the children to watch new colors emerge as the colored ice cubes melt. (Red and yellow ice cubes will melt together to form orange; yellow and blue ice cubes will melt and form green.)
5. Add different quantities of colored ice cubes to create different shades of colors.

*Shyamala Shanmugasundaram, Nerul, Navi Mumbai, India*

# Flower Power

SENSORY

**Materials**
several small- or medium-sized vases
various flowers or plants

**What to do**
1. Purchase one new flower or plant for the classroom each month. (Be sure to ask your florist if the flower or plant needs any special treatment.)
2. Introduce the flower or plant to the children
3. Ask the children to note the flower's name, color, and how long the flower or plant lasts.
4. Try to make the flower or plant fit with the month. For example:
   - January: orchids
   - February: miniature roses
   - March: shamrocks or daffodils
   - April: tulips
   - May: impatiens
   - June: daisies
   - July: lilies
   - August: sunflowers
   - September: tomato plant
   - October: mums
   - November: hydrangeas
   - December: amaryllis

 *Amelia Griffin, Ontario, Canada*

# Pot-Luck Super Soup

SNACK AND COOKING

**Materials**
big soup kettle
beef bouillon flavoring
water
ladle
plastic knives
cutting boards
salt and pepper
variety of vegetables

**What to do**
1. Discuss the concept of a pot-luck meal.

2. Ask the children to name some vegetables to add to a "pot-luck super soup." Make a list of the vegetables.
3. Send home a letter asking parents to send in a vegetable to add to the soup. Use the vegetables that children suggested.
4. Collect all of the vegetables from the children on the given day.
5. Let the children help wash the vegetables and cut them into bite-sized pieces.
6. Pour water into a large soup kettle. Add the vegetables and flavoring to the water and begin the cooking process. Cook the soup for about an hour or until the vegetables are tender. **Safety Note:** Keep children away from the stove while the soup is simmering.
7. Serve the soup to the children with crackers or bread for "dunking."
8. Make sure to acknowledge each child for his or her contribution to the super soup!

*Judy Fujawa, The Villages, FL*

# EAT YOUR SHAPES

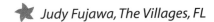

SNACK AND COOKING

**MATERIALS**    food in varied shapes (see activity below)

**WHAT TO DO**

1. Prepare different shapes of food. For example:
   - any shape—cut sandwiches, cheese slices, jello jigglers, brownies, or baked cookies as desired.
   - circles—crackers, banana slices, cucumber slices, pickle slices, circle-shaped cereal, pretzel rings
   - triangles—triangle-shaped thin crackers
   - squares—saltines, square crackers, cheese slices, square-shaped cereal
   - rectangles — graham crackers
2. Arrange the food by shapes on a table. Provide spreads for the crackers, if desired.
3. Encourage the children to choose at least one food of each shape.
4. Eat and enjoy.

**Safety Note:** Be aware of any food allergies and plan accordingly.

**MORE TO DO**

**Art:** Encourage the children to decorate an 18" x 12" piece of construction paper with different shapes. Staple the short ends together to form a cylinder. Have them staple yarn to the top and streamers along the bottom to make wind socks.

**Math:** Hide foam shapes outside and have a shapes hunt. After finding the shapes, encourage the children to sort and count them.

**RELATED books**   *Brown Rabbit's Shape Book* by Alan Baker
*The Shape of Things* by Dayle Ann Dodds
*The Wing on a Flea* by Ed Emberley

 *Sandra Gratias, Dublin, PA*

# Baking Bread and Sharing
SNACK AND COOKING

**MATERIALS**   *The Little Red Hen* by Paul Galdone
soft wheat berries
hand wheat grinder or coffee mill
empty jar
bowl
measuring cups and spoons
yeast packages
honey
warm water
white flour
oil
salt
baking pans
oven

**WHAT TO do**
1. Tell the story of *The Little Red Hen*. Tell it again but change the ending so that the little red hen shares the bread. Talk about sharing with the children.
2. Over a few days, let the children take turns grinding wheat berries into flour. Put the flour into a jar.
3. Make 12 small loaves (rolls, actually) for children to bring home to share with their families, and two small loaves for the children to share at snack time. Double the recipe, if needed, so that everyone can bring a small loaf home.
4. Add yeast and honey to warm water and let bubble.
6. Mix 4 ½ cups whole wheat flour (from the wheat berries), 4 cups white flour, 2 teaspoons salt, and 2 tablespoons oil. Add to the yeast mixture.
7. Mix. Divide into 12 rolls and two loaves. Sprinkle a mound of flour in front of each child. Encourage them to knead their rolls by pressing with the heels of their hands and folding the dough over.
8. Shape and let rise 15 minutes. Brush with milk and bake for 25 minutes.
9. Let children take home their own loaves to share with their families.

**MORE TO DO**   **More Snack and Cooking:** Make butter. Fill a jar half full with whipping cream. Demonstrate how to shake the jar safely. Let children take turns shaking it. Invite them to listen for a change in the sound and watch for a change in the color. When it turns to butter, paddle it to remove the liquid. Shape and refrigerate.

★ *Linda Atamian, Charlestown, RI*

# Potluck
## SNACK AND COOKING

**MATERIALS**   *Alligator Arrived With Apples* by Crescent Dragonwagon
food from home
camera and film

**WHAT TO DO**
1. Read *Alligator Arrived With Apples: A Potluck Alphabet Feast* by Crescent Dragonwagon (or other book about potlucks) to the children.
2. Tell the children they are going to have their own alphabet potluck meal!
3. Send home a letter to parents asking them to send in a food that starts with the first letter of their child's first or last name. For example, "Annie" could bring in apples, the Spitz family could bring spaghetti, and so on.
4. On the day of the potluck, take pictures of the children and their families as they arrive with their foods. Later, help the children organize these photos into an alphabet book.

**RELATED books**   *Eating the Alphabet* by Lois Ehlert
*Potluck* by Anne Shelby

★ *Linda Ford, Sacramento, CA*

# ANTS ON A LOG
## SNACK AND COOKING

**MATERIALS**   celery
cream cheese
raisins

**What to do**
1. When doing a unit on insects, talk about ants with the children.
2. Make this nutritious snack with the children's help.
3. Wash celery and cut them into 3" long pieces. Fill with cream cheese and top with raisins.
4. Sing the "The Ants Go Marching" while enjoying your snack!

 *Kathy Kalmar, Macomb, MI*

# Friendship Snack Mix
SNACK AND COOKING

**Materials**
large bowl
M&Ms
pretzels
Chex cereal
small round cereal (Cheerios)
teddy-shaped grahams
granola
raisins and dried fruit
goldfish crackers

**What to do**
1. Send home a letter asking families to send in an item to contribute to a "friendship snack" (provide suggestions using the list above).
2. When the snacks arrive, let each child pour her item into a large mixing bowl and give it a stir.
3. Explain to the children that they all contributed to this snack and that is what makes it so special.
4. Stir, serve, and enjoy for snack.

 *Susan Myhre, Bremerton, WA*

# Pit or Seed?
SNACK AND COOKING

**Materials**
fruits containing pits (apricot, cherry, peach, plum)
fruits containing seeds (grape, pear, apple, watermelon)
plastic knives
spoons and forks
bowls

**WHAT TO DO**
1. Explain to the children that some fruits have pits and some have seeds. Show the children the unopened fruits and ask them to guess whether the fruit has a pit or seeds.
2. Cut open the fruits one by one. Show the insides of the fruits to the children.
3. Remove the pits and seeds from the fruits.
4. Let children help cut up the fruits. Serve a fruit salad for snack.

★ *Shyamala Shanmugasundaram, Nerul, Navi Mumbai, India*

# SWEET HEALTHY FACES

SNACK AND COOKING

**MATERIALS**
small flour tortillas (one per child)
variety of healthy snack items (raisins, Cheerios, dried apricots, and so on)
cream cheese
honey
red or white grapes (halved)
red apples, thinly sliced
paper plates
plastic spoons

**WHAT TO DO**
1. In a medium bowl, mix cream cheese and honey until well blended. Use two parts cream cheese and one part honey. Set aside.
2. Give one tortilla to each child.
3. Help the children spread the cream cheese and honey mixture to the edge of the tortillas, thick enough for snack items to stick.
4. Invite them to use raisins for eyes, a grape half for a nose, an apple slice for a mouth, dried apricots for ears, and Cheerios for hair.
5. Fold and eat!

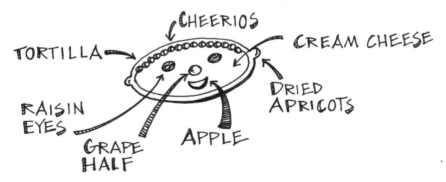

★ *Sally Phillips, Enfield, IL*

# Friendship Chain

SOCIAL DEVELOPMENT

**Materials**  photo of each child
strips of paper
glue
crayons

**What to do**
1. Take a photo of each child.
2. Let each child glue her photo to a strip of paper.
3. Ask the children what they like about school and to name a friend with whom they like to do that activity.
4. Encourage the children to draw pictures of their favorite activities and friends.
5. Staple the strips together to make a "friendship chain."

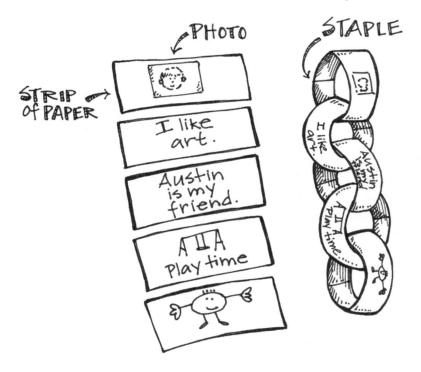

⭐ *Kaethe Lewandowski, Centreville, VA*

# POTATO PEOPLE

SOCIAL DEVELOPMENT

**Materials**
potatoes (one per child)
baskets

**What to do**

1. Make up a story about a potato. For example:

*This is my potato person named Farley. Farley fell off of his bike. Do you see the scratch on him? He also has a few bumps on his skin that I think will go away. Farley is a very kind person and is friends with everyone.*

2. Now, invite have each child to name and tell a short story about her own potato. After everyone has told a story, collect all the potatoes and put them in the basket.
3. Ask the children if they think they can find their very own potato person again.
4. Put all the potatoes on a table and encourage the children to locate their potatoes.
5. Discuss with the children how potatoes are like people—even though people are all human beings, each person is unique with his or her own story!

⭐ *Dr. Geraldine Jenny, Grove City, PA*

# PAJAMA PARTY

SOCIAL DEVELOPMENT

**Materials**
none

**What to do**

1. Send a note home announcing a Pajama Party Day, when all of the children and their teachers will wear pajamas and slippers to school. Encourage the children to bring special blankets, pillows, or stuffed animals.
2. On Pajama Party Day, encourage the children to take turns telling the class what kind of pajamas they are wearing and talking about what they do at night before they go to bed.
3. At story time or nap time, have them lie on their blankets to listen to stories or soothing music.
4. For math, use a floor graph to chart what kind of slippers the children are wearing. Help them sort the colors of the pajamas.
5. At the end of the day, have the children tell what they liked best about the day. Write down their thoughts to use for a morning message the next day.

⭐ *Barbara Saul, Eureka, CA*

# I HAVE MANNERS

## SOCIAL DEVELOPMENT

**Materials**        variety of books (see activity)

**What to do**       Read several of the following books to the children during a single month
to reinforce etiquette skills:

*Berenstain Bears Forget Their Manners* by Stan and Jan Berenstain
*Clifford's Manners* by Norman Bridwell
*Excuse Me! A Little Book of Manners* by Karen Katz
*It's a Spoon, Not a Shovel* by Caralyn and Mark Buehner
*Monster Manners* by Bethany Roberts
*Richard Scarry's Please and Thank You Book* by Richard Scarry
*Richard Scarry's Polite Elephant* by Richard Scarry
*What Do You Say, Dear?* by Sesyle Joslin

 *Diane Shatto, Kansas City, MO*

# COME ON BOARD, LITTLE CHILDREN

## TRANSITIONS

**Materials**        none

**What to do**       1. When transitioning from a center or clean-up to circle time, recite this
rhyme until every child meets in the circle.

*Come on board, little children,*
*Come on board, little children,*
*Come on board, little children*
*For there's room for many more!*

2. If there are particular children who are not coming to circle, substitute
their names for "children" in the song. ("Come on board, little Katy...")

**Related books**    *Freight Train* by Donald Crews
*The Little Engine That Could* by Watty Piper

 *Kaethe Lewandowski, Centreville, VA*

# The Alphabet Song

### TRANSITIONS

**Materials**  laminated copies of all the letters in the alphabet

**What to do**
1. Daily, pass out the laminated letter cards out so each child has one letter.
2. Have the children sing the alphabet song slowly as each child lines up with his or her letter.

**Related books**  *26 Letters and 99 Cents* by Tana Hoban
*Black and White Rabbit's ABC* by Alan Baker
*Chicka Chicka Boom Boom* by Bill Martin, Jr.
*Farm Alphabet Book* by Jane Miller

 *Kaethe Lewandowski, Centreville, VA*

# Hallway Simon Says

### TRANSITIONS

**Materials**  none

**What to do**
1. Play this version of Simon Says when children are waiting in line for the bathroom or changing rooms.
2. Do not give verbal instructions; instead give physical clues for the children to copy. For example, raise your right hand or wiggle your fingers.
3. Toss in a few silly things, such as making a funny face or mussing hair.
4. The children will be attentive, and this will help keep the hallway under control.

*Judy Contino, Ozone Park, NY*

# Monthly Calendar of Activities

WORKING WITH FAMILIES

**Materials**    a special decorated calendar page identifying the name of the class

**What to do**
1. Gather the children at the end of each month and schedule or plan the entries for the next month's activity calendar.
2. Be sure the calendar includes the following information:
   - contact information for teacher and staff
   - field trips
   - holidays/vacations
   - special days/celebrations
   - themes/focus ideas
   - volunteer schedules
   - reminders and requests
   - thank yous and acknowledgments
   - daily classroom schedule/routine
   - parent education articles
   - words of inspiration
3. Distribute this calendar to each family at the beginning of the month. It is an excellent was to keep up the parent/teacher communication.

⭐ *Judy Fujawa, The Villages, FL*

# Something Good Happened This Month

WORKING WITH FAMILIES

**Materials**    paper
computer and printer

**What to do**
1. Make a flyer with the title "Something Good Happened This Month" at the top.
2. On this flyer, list some of the good things that happened during the month. You might want to divide the flyer into sections, such as "In the Art Center…,""During Our Music and Movement Time…,""At the Snack Table…,""On Our Field Trip…," and so on).

3. Ask the children for their input on what to include on the flyer.
4. Make copies of the flyer and distribute to the families each.

★ *Judy Fujawa, The Villages, Florida*

# List of Holidays, Celebrations, and Special Days

Below is a list of different month-long celebrations, week-long celebrations, and special days, many of which have related activities included in this book. Use this list as a helpful guide for expanding your curriculum throughout the year.

## January

- It's Okay to Be Different Month
- National Bath Safety Month
- National Eye Care Month
- National Oatmeal Month
- New Year's Day (January 1st)
- Sir Isaac Newton's birthday (January 4th)
- National Bird Day (January 5th)
- National Milk Day (January 11th)
- Rubber Ducky's Birthday (January 13th)
- Thailand Games (2nd Saturday of January)
- Martin Luther King Birthday (January 15th, celebrated 3rd Monday of January)
- Ben Franklin's Birthday (January 17th)
- Birthday of A.A. Milne, author of "Winnie the Pooh" (January 18th)
- National Hugging Day (January 21st)
- National Pie Day (January 23)
- National Compliment Day (January 24)
- Mozart's Birthday (January 27th)
- National Kazoo Day (January 28th)
- National Puzzle Day (January 29th)
- Chinese New Year (starts with second full moon after winter solstice, ends with full moon; can start anytime between January 21 and February 19)

## February

- Black History Month
- National Heart Month
- International Friendship Month
- Library Lovers' Month
- National Dental Health Month
- National Cherry Month
- National Cherry Pie Month
- Groundhog Day (February 2nd)
- Lincoln's Birthday (February 12th)
- Valentine's Day (February 14th)
- National Child Passenger Safety Week (the week of Valentine's Day)
- Clifford the Big Red Dog's Birthday (February 15th)
- President's Day (3rd Monday in February)
- Washington's Birthday (February 22nd)

## March

- Music in Our Schools Month
- National Craft Month
- National Kite Month
- National Reading Month
- National Nutrition Month
- National Peanut Month
- Poison Prevention Month
- Endangered Animals Month
- Youth Art Month
- National Pig Day (March 1st)
- Dr. Seuss' Birthday (March 2nd)
- St. Patrick's Day (March 17th)
- Single Parents' Day (March 21st)
- Make Up Your Own Holiday Day (March 26th)
- Youth Day in China (March 29th)
- Easter (March/April)

## April

- Keep America Beautiful Month
- Mathematics Education Month
- National Frog Month
- National Garden Month
- National Humor Month
- National Poetry Month
- National Umbrella Month
- Zoo and Aquarium Month

National Library Week (April 1st–7th)
April Fool's Day (April 1st)
Hans Christian Anderson's Birthday (April 2nd)
World Health Day (April 7th)
Thomas Jefferson's Birthday (April 13th)
National Coin Week (third week of April)
Pet Owners' Day (April 18th)
Earth Day (April 20th)
Substitute Teacher Appreciation Week (last week of April)
Arbor Day (usually the last Friday in April)
National Puppetry Day (April 28th)
National Honesty Day (April 30th)

## MAY

Get Caught Reading Month
National Bike Month
National Egg Month
National Hamburger Month
National Salad Month
National Salsa Month
National Transportation Month
May Day (May 1st)
Mother Goose Day (May 1st)
Save the Rhino Day (May 1st)
Space Day (first Thursday in May)
Cinco de Mayo (May 5th)
China's Dragon Boat Festival (May 5th)
National Pet Week (first week of May)
Teacher's Appreciation Week (first week of May)
Be Kind to Animals Week (first week of May)
Mother's Day (second Sunday in May)
National Teacher Day (Tuesday of the first full week in May)
Child Care Provider Day (second Friday in May)
J.M. Barrie's Birthday (May 9th)
Kite Day (May 12th)
Brown vs. Board of Education Anniversary (May 17th)
Armed Forces Day (third Saturday in May)
Reading Is Fun Week (third week in May)
National Police Week (third week of May)
Memorial Day (last Monday in May)

## JUNE

Children's Awareness Month
Fireworks Safety Month
National Candy Month
National Rose Month
National Safety Month
Flag Day (June 14th)
Father's Day (third Sunday in June)

## JULY

National Baked Bean Month
National Hot Dog Month
National Ice Cream Month
Canada Day (July 1st)
Independence Day (July 4th)
Don't Step on a Bee Day (July 10th)
Parents' Day (July 29th)

## AUGUST

National Back to School Month
Watermelon Day (August 3rd)
National Mustard Day (first Saturday in August)
Clown Week (first week of August)
International Left-Handers Day (August 13th)
Moon Festival (August 15th)
National Aviation Day (August 19th)
Hawaii Admission Day Anniversary (August 21, 1959, celebrated third Friday in August)
Tooth Fairy Day (August 22nd)
Be Kind to Humankind Week (last week of August)

## SEPTEMBER

Library Card Sign-Up Month
National Chicken Month
National Food Education Safety Month
National Honey Month
National Piano Month
National Sewing Month
National Childhood Injury Prevention Week (first week of September)
Labor Day (first Monday in September)
National Grandparent's Day (first Sunday after Labor Day)

Teddy Bear Day (September 9th)

Patriot Day (September 11th)

National Play-Doh Day (September 16th)

National Farm Awareness Week (third week of September)

National Flower Week (third week of September)

National Student Day (September 20th)

International Day of Peace (September 21st)

Elephant Appreciation Day (September 22nd)

Johnny Appleseed's birthday (September 26th)

Deaf Awareness Week (last full week of September)

National Dog Week (last full week of September)

Rosh Hashanah (the first and second day of the seventh Hebrew month)

## October

Adopt-a-Shelter Animal Month

Child Health Month

Computer Learning Month

Diversity Awareness Month

End of Daylight Savings (currently last Sunday in October, but starting in 2007, it will be first Sunday in November)

Family Health Month

Family History Month

International Dinosaur Month

International Zoo Month

National Clock Month

National Crime Prevention Month

National Custodial Workers Day (October 2nd)

Fire Safety/Prevention Week (the week in which October 9th occurs)

National School Lunch Week (second week of October)

National Wildlife Refuge Week (second week of October)

Earth Science Week (second week of October)

Columbus Day (observed second Monday of October)

National Grouch Day (October 15th)

Dictionary Day/Birthday of Noah Webster (October 16th, 1758)

Shel Silverstein's Birthday (October 18th)

America's Safe Schools Week (third week of October)

National Health Education Week (third week of October)

National School Bus Safety Week (third week of October)

World Rainforest Week (last week of October)

Help Make a Difference Day (fourth Saturday in October)

Pablo Picasso's Birthday (October 25th)

Statue of Liberty's Birthday (October 28th)

Halloween (October 31st)

National Magic Day (October 31st)

## November

American Indian Heritage Month

International Drum Month

National Aviation Month

Peanut Butter Lovers' Month

National Family Literacy Day (November 1st)

Jewish Book Month (November 4th–December 4th)

Election Day (second Tuesday in November)

Veteran's Day (November 11th)

World Kindness Week (second week of November)

Children's Book Week (the week before Thanksgiving)

World Peace Day (November 17th)

Thanksgiving (fourth Thursday in November)

National Game and Puzzle Week (third full week of November)

National Family Week (Thanksgiving week)

World Hello Day (November 21st)

What Do You Love About America? Day (November 22nd)

## December

Human Rights Day (December 10th)

Pan American Aviation Day (December 17th)

First Day of Winter (December 21st or 22nd, depending on the winter solstice)

Humbug Day (December 21st)

Hannukah (25th day of Jewish Month Kislev)

Christmas (December 25th)

Kwanza (December 26th)

National Whiners' Day (December 26th)

## September

INDEX